Loaded Dice

Loaded Dice

The Foreign Office and Israel

Neill Lochery

continuum

Continuum International Publishing Group

The Tower Building, 11 York Road, London SE1 7NX
80 Maiden Lane, Suite 704, New York NY 10038

www.continuumbooks.com

First published 2007

British Library Cataloguing-in-Publication Data
A catalogue record for this book is available from the British Library.

ISBN 0-8264-9056-5
      978-08264-9056-8

Typeset by Kenneth Burnley, Wirral, Cheshire
Printed and bound by Cromwell Press, Trowbridge, Wiltshire

Contents

Preface

This book must start with a confession. I have always had a soft spot for those involved in diplomacy and have conversely been deeply suspicious of those attached to the use of force (both military and civilian leaders). In this respect, I have found conversations with British and Israeli diplomats a generally highly rewarding experience, but have found similar talks with the military, and politicians with close links to the military, much harder work indeed. Of all the Israeli military/political leaders that I have met over the years only Yitzhak Rabin struck me as having a political and diplomatic vision. The others treated politics as an extension of military politics, and this baggage has had generally negative consequences for the diplomatic process. A large part of me, as a consequence, believes that most diplomats start with good intentions even if, at times, their actions appear illogical and misguided. I suspect, if I am honest, that this positive, but not uncritical viewpoint of diplomats and diplomatic institutions can be traced back to my youth.

During my childhood we used to come to London a couple of times a year, usually on a school trip to visit one of the capital's museums or the Houses of Parliament and Whitehall. I can still recall the first time I walked along Downing Street, which was then occupied by arguably the last of the gentlemen Prime Ministers, Jim Callaghan. Downing Street, however, did not leave the greatest impression on me. My abiding memory of that day remains standing outside the Foreign Office having my photograph taken by one of my school friends. To me, there was always something rather exotic about the Foreign Office, something that hinted of Empire and faraway cultures and languages. Even its full name sounded full of worldly promise: the 'Foreign and Commonwealth Office'. My teacher informed me that the officials who worked inside its corridors were the brightest of the bright, drawn mainly from Oxbridge and selected through the most rigorous of fast-track civil service entrance exams. The phrase 'the best people for the best jobs' came to mind.

To an impressionable young boy, the Foreign Office was inspirational, and helped fuel a fascination with international affairs that went above and beyond any interest in British politics. To be honest, the latter always appeared to me to be a little grey and tribal. For this young schoolboy,

British politics was all about men in dark suits taking tea and eating sandwiches in smoke-filled rooms, making decisions that appeared to be of little interest to a youthful non-taxpayer. In my imagination the Foreign Office was quite the opposite. It was characterized by gin and tonics, its collection of beautiful works of art, and by officials making decisions that would influence events across the globe. Even at this early age I aspired to become an expert on far-off countries, which in my youth I had only read about. In retrospect, this was perhaps my own way of escaping the political and social greyness of Britain at the end of the 1970s.

Much later, in my professional life, the Foreign Office became an object of even greater curiosity to me. Being an expert on Israel and the Middle East led to several invitations to venture inside the building to attend meetings and social gatherings. On my first visit to an informal drinks evening with the Near East and North Africa Department I was somewhat surprised to discover that I was the only expert on Israel in the room. I wasn't sure if my invitation had been a mistake, or whether I was the only expert on the Jewish state who had agreed to attend. Though the splendour of the building was even better when viewed from the inside, I noted that the guests at the soirée reflected an often overlooked but striking reality: the 'Arab' Middle East is much larger and more economically and politically significant to Britain than Israel with its population of just over seven million.

The attention given to Israel by the Foreign Office, however, has consistently been much greater than its relative geographic size and population merits. To a certain extent, this can be put down to the continued centrality of the Arab–Israeli peace process (and especially the Palestinian–Israeli conflict) to British, and European, political and economic interests. It can also be explained by the fact that many in the Arab world continue to believe that British policy was the major cause of the creation of Israel: the Balfour Declaration, which promised the Jews a homeland, and the British decision to hand over the Mandate to the United Nations in 1947, are often cited by Arabs as reason enough for the British to stay engaged in the region. 'Sort out the mess you created' was a common shout until British power in the region declined to such a degree that this became impossible for Britain alone.

I recently returned with my children to the front entrance of the Foreign Office on a quiet Saturday morning, which in central London is unique to Whitehall. Watching my son, I noted his awe at the building. I couldn't help telling him that once upon a time this building was the centre of the world. In telling the story of the Foreign Office's relationship with Israel, it is worth remembering that despite Israeli attempts to bypass it, and the recent shift in power across the way to Downing Street, the Foreign Office has played a defining role in British policy towards Israel and the wider Middle East since 1948. In other words, the story of Britain's relationship with Israel can largely be told through charting the Foreign Office's often turbulent relations with the Jewish state.

Introduction

The story of the relationship between the Foreign Office and Israel has reached almost mythical proportions. When the *Jewish Chronicle* interviewed Margaret Thatcher on 12 June 1981 she was routinely accused by the newspaper of delegating foreign policy on the Arab–Israeli conflict to the 'old Arabists' in the Foreign Office.[1] The *Jewish Chronicle* had clearly taken its lead from David Ben-Gurion, Israel's first Prime Minister and chief author of the phrase 'those Arabists in the Foreign Office'. The presumption among Israel's political elite that the British Foreign Office has been institutionally anti-Israeli has survived the passing of the founding generation of leaders of Israel such as Ben-Gurion and can be seen even today among many of its political leadership.

The Arabists?

Look up the word 'Arabist' in any of the recognized dictionaries and you will find two definitions and uses. The first is the politically neutral 'a person who studies Arabic civilization or language'. It is, however, the second definition and use of the word 'Arabist' that goes to the very heart of this book. This definition is most certainly not politically neutral: 'a person who supports Arab nationalism or political interests'. To complicate matters further, in recent times the term 'Arabist' has taken on a new, more negative use, particularly by supporters of Israel; and let's presume for a moment that the *Jewish Chronicle* fits into this category, to mean pro-Arab and anti-Israeli.

So why does this really matter? Isn't an Arabist really just someone or a group of people who have signed up to the Arab cause? Well, the truth is that definitions do matter because it is from here that the central question and theme of this book devolves. Was the Foreign Office first and foremost an institution that was dominated by Arabist officials who collectively produced a string of Arabist policies that were, to use the dictionary definition, aimed at supporting Arab nationalism or political interests? If this was the case then the primary motivation for these officials would surely be the defence of Arab interests over the maintenance of British interests in the Middle East. You can say what you want about the Foreign Office, but the subordination of British interests to Arab interests would have almost been considered to be treasonable action among Foreign Office officials.

The central role of the Foreign Office has been, and will always be, to establish and define British interests overseas, where possible to expand and develop these interests further, but always to defend them when they come under perceived or real threat. So from all this we must presume that when people shout 'Arabist' at the Foreign Office they are referring to the more modern use of the word, which effectively means putting Arab interests over Israeli ones. Sometimes there is also an undertone to this definition that hints at anti-semitism at the Foreign Office. This charge, in truth, was more relevant to the period of office of Ernest Bevin that covered both the end of the period of the British Mandate in Palestine and the early years of the state of Israel.

Reasons for the bad blood

Those who argue that there is as a result of the Arabist nature of the Foreign Office hostility between it and Israel often disagree on the reasons for the alleged bad blood. The somewhat crude explanations can be divided into five major areas. Naturally, these explanations can be complementary rather than exclusive, and varying degrees of quantification can be attached to each one of them.

1. Colonial hangover

The British were very effectively forced out of Palestine by Zionist military and political resistance to their presence in the area. Eventually, when the cost of maintaining the size of a British garrison in Palestine, in both economic and human terms, outweighed the strategic value of the territory, the British handed over responsibility for the governance of Palestine to the United Nations. The subsequent decision of the UN to propose a two-state solution to the Zionist–Palestinian dispute angered the British, and in particular the Foreign Office led by Bevin. Since 1948, the Foreign Office has always conducted relations with Israel correctly but with a sense of the bitterness that was caused by the history of the creation of the state in 1948.

2. The strategic value of the Arabs to Britain

Throughout the British Mandate in Palestine (1922–48) and after, for whatever reasons the Foreign Office devised under the particular circumstances of the day, it was always argued that the Arabs were more important, strategically, to the British than the Zionists. During the 1930s there was genuine concern among key personnel in Whitehall that the Arabs might be tempted by Hitler to throw their lot in with Nazi Germany. During the period leading to the outbreak of the Second World War this resulted in considerable appeasement of the Arabs and their growing nationalist aspirations; nowhere more so than in Palestine, where British foreign policy was directed at checking Zionist nationalist aspirations. Since the establishment of the state, British policy has been guided by two related aims: protecting the supply of oil from the region and maintaining as much influence within the Arab political and economic elite as possible. In recent decades, the economic focus has shifted towards developing lucrative new markets for selling arms to the Arab states, ranging from Saddam Hussein's Iraq through to the oil-rich Persian Gulf states.

The idea that the Arabs have been more useful than the Zionists or Israelis to the attainment of self-serving British economic and political goals in the Middle East and therefore form the basis of foreign policy is politically rational rather than a result of any prejudice. The Foreign Office has naturally supported states that offer the greatest strategic value to Britain. Its atitude towards Israel is merely a reflection of the larger political and economic preference for the Arab states rather than a specific policy against the Zionist presence in the region.

3. The 'Lawrence of Arabia' old school

Among the political and intellectual classes in Israel, the so-called Foreign Office love affair with the image and work of Lawrence of Arabia is a popular explanation for British Foreign policy in the region. A further idea is that the romantic view of Arab culture is a residue of public schoolboy homosexual fantasy, because the Foreign Office was staffed almost exclusively by those educated at public schools. During the 1950s and 1960s it was often alleged in Israel that the Foreign Office was staffed by Arabists who saw themselves as modern-day Lawrences. And career development at the Foreign Office was often based on service in a British Embassy in the Arab world. To be posted to the British Embassy in Tel Aviv was often regarded as the end of a career. This somewhat crude mixture of ideas and influences upon advancement within the Foreign Office contributed to a framework for an alleged pro-Arab bias.

4. Israel as an occupying power – post-1967 reasons
When one talks to relatively recent Foreign Secretaries and officials at the Foreign Office it is clear that they almost all regard Israel's polices towards the Palestinians since 1967 as the main reason for the tensions in the relationship. Many cite Israel as an aggressor state that often flouts international law and conventions to maximize its control over the local Palestinian population in the West Bank and Gaza Strip. This group argues that if Israel does the right thing or is seen to do the right thing – allow the creation of a Palestinian state in 100 per cent of the West Bank and Gaza Strip – then relations between the Foreign Office and Israel will thaw and eventually warm to pre-1967 levels. Supporters of this explanation point to the fact that when Israel was making generous political concessions to the Palestinians between 1992 and 1996 the Foreign Office was extremely supportive of the Rabin/Peres governments.

5. Anti-semitism at the Foreign Office
This belief that there is actual anti-semitism at the Foreign Office is perhaps the least convincing and the most difficult influence to measure. It was raised during the tenure of Ernest Bevin as Foreign Secretary (July 1945 to March 1951), and more recently during the current difficulties in the Middle East peace process. The fact that a number of Jews have served in senior positions in the Foreign Office further complicates this issue. People who support this point of view downplay the rational options mentioned previously and argue that there are other regimes that the Foreign Office views as much more barbaric than Israel and yet is able to maintain at the very least cordial ties with.

The outline

Since the creation of Israel in May 1948, 22 British Foreign Secretaries have served in 12 distinct governments, and, with varying degrees and differing levels of success, all have had to deal with Israel. Five of those 22 Foreign Secretaries went on to serve as Prime Minister, including the pre-Suez Arabist Anthony Eden, the more pragmatic Sir Alec Douglas-Home and the diplomatically inexperienced John Major. Some of these figures are of greater significance than others to the Foreign Office's relationship with Israel. John Major, while going on to serve for nearly seven years as Prime Minister, only served as Foreign Secretary for a very short time and therefore had limited influence over its policies. Others such as Anthony Eden cut a very different figure as Prime Minister than as Foreign Secretary. Eden was correctly viewed as an 'Arabist' (in the loose sense of the word) during his time at the Foreign Office, but later while serving as Prime Minister he personally authorized the military collusion between Britain, Israel and France, which led to the Suez War of 1956.

The book is divided into the successive eras of post-Second World War British politics: the post-war Labour Government, the Tory years, the turnover period of Wilson, Heath and Callaghan, Thatcher's era, the Major years and the ten-year period of New Labour under Tony Blair. It intertwines this with a chronological approach to the major events in Israel and the Middle East to which the Foreign Office, and the wider British government of the day, had to respond. These events include the five major Arab–Israeli wars: the 1948 War of Independence, the Suez War of 1956, the June 1967 War, the October 1973 War and the Lebanon War of 1982. Amid all these wars there have been many diplomatic incidents and in recent decades a diplomatic process that is best known by its overused name label, the Middle East Peace Process.

Today, the Foreign Office is no longer the major instrument of British foreign policy, in either its formation or implementation. Since my schooldays much of the exoticness and glamour of the Foreign Office has declined. True, the building remains imposing and magnificent, especially when viewed from the inside. There is, however, a case to be made that the influence of the Foreign Office declined with the gradual decline and fall of the British Empire. The lowering of the Union Jack in Hong Kong marking the last major ceremonial act in the closing chapter of the Empire. The truth is, however, much more stark. The powers of the Foreign Office have been stripped away by successive prime ministers from both sides of the House of Commons who have developed a more presidential style of leadership. The days of *primus inter pares* for prime ministers have long vanished. In the current era the so-called New World Order foreign policy remains very much in the hands of the Prime Minister and his relevant advisers.

If somebody had undertaken a time and motion study of a week in the working life of Tony Blair the chances are that they would have found that he devoted considerably more time to foreign affairs than to domestic politics. Though the shift towards a more presidential style in the United Kingdom is far from complete (certainly when compared to the American executive) it has shifted policy focus away from the Foreign Office. This is largely true even when there is no pressing international crisis. The Foreign Office, as a result, has had to adjust to a new, slightly downgraded role. The Middle East fits into this new *modus operandi* of the Foreign Office with its officials trying to carve out new roles for it to increase its influence in a region that has long been regarded as holding perhaps the greatest interest to the high-flyers that have treaded its corridors.

To a certain extent, as I argue in the book, the decline of the Foreign Office can be traced back to the era of Margaret Thatcher. She succeeded Callaghan in 1979 and ruled for over a decade until late 1990. There are a number of complex reasons that brought Thatcher to power which have been given considerable attention in some excellent works on the subject.[2] Thatcher, in short, had little time for the Foreign Office, initially regarding it, along with the Treasury, as 'bastions of compliancy'.[3] Once Thatcher grew in confidence on foreign affairs she became determined to take on the Foreign Office and, at times, even her own Foreign Secretary, Lord Peter Carrington (the last of the genuine aristocrats to hold the position).[4] It was the Falklands War, however, that gave Thatcher the opportunity to finally move against the Foreign Office. In short, Thatcher blamed the department, a little unfairly, for the British diplomatic bungling of the period leading up to the Argentinean invasion.[5] In his memoirs, the former Defence Secretary John Nott points out that Lord Carrington had argued strongly for the retention of HMS *Endurance*, whose planned withdrawal from service played such an important role in the Argentinean invasion.[6] From this point onwards, however, a deeply distrustful Thatcher started to develop her own foreign policy unit at Number 10. The Thatcher revolution, in other words, reached the door of the Foreign Office, and the ground the latter lost to the expanded Prime Minister's office was never fully recovered.

In 2007, the Foreign Office represents one of the last bastions of 'Old England', this despite the best efforts of consecutive Labour Governments to modernize it. Although many of the mavericks and fierce intellects that once dominated the corridors of the Foreign Office have long disappeared, to be replaced by slightly greyer personalities, there still remains something of past glories, exoticness and hints of faraway places about it. The fact that its relationship with Israel is still much talked about is an indication of its enduring status as an important component of British foreign policy-making – even if it is, in reality, no longer the dominant force.

Part 1

The Post-War Attlee Labour Government: July 1945 to October 1951

1

The one that got away

It is young, intensely chauvinistic and highly-strung. Its people suffer from an acute inferiority complex and are preoccupied with themselves and their own affairs. They are incapable of seeing the other side's point of view or, on occasion, of admitting its existence. Thus opposition or even criticism by others must be due to anti-Israel or anti-Semitic feelings.[1]

British Diplomatic Report on the State of Israel, 1949

A painful birth

The first year of the state of Israel was dominated by armed conflict. Given the attitude of the Palestinian Arabs, the wider Arab world and even some Zionist groups to the partition plan adopted by the United Nations in 1947, this development could hardly be described as surprising. To complicate matters further, however, from the period leading up to the declaration of the state of Israel on 14 May 1948 there was a marked decline in the already strained relationship between the Zionists in Palestine and the British Government. Zionist leaders such as David Ben-Gurion argued that the British were doing everything possible in the twilight of the British Mandate in Palestine to help boost the Arabs and damage the Zionists. There was a widely held belief among the Zionists that the British, and especially the Foreign Office, remained sore at having been effectively forced to give up control over Palestine. Conversely, there was also marked lack of belief in British Government circles about the viability of the Jewish state, a point which was frequently articulated by the Foreign Office.

This view of the viability of a Jewish state was not unique to the Foreign Office, or indeed the majority of the British Government. In the United States there was a fierce debate between the largely pro-Israel President Truman and the more 'Arabist' dominated State Department led by Secretary of State George Marshall over this very issue. Marshall argued that the creation of a Jewish state would lead to increased bloodshed and a potential regional war, which would draw US troops directly into the conflict. After a lengthy debate and policy u-turns the

United States effectively said that it would recognize a Jewish state, if declared, but that such a state would stand alone in its armed struggle with the Arabs.

Events surrounding the 1948 war have been widely covered in works by a number of scholars. In essence, the war started even before the state of Israel was established, with an intensification of the battles between Zionist and Palestine Arab fighters since the vote in the United Nations General Assembly to support the partition of Palestine into two states. Almost as soon as the state was declared, the regular Arab armies invaded Palestine and the 1948 war officially started. In most accounts of the conflict the fighting is divided into two major stages: before and after the UN-brokered ceasefire. In simple terms, Israel was on the defensive during the first phase as the regular Arab armies made major progress within Israel's borders. With the acquisition of new weapons acquired during the ceasefire Israel went on the offensive during the second part of the war, pushing the Arab armies back and acquiring lands which were not designated by the UN Partition Plan to be part of the Jewish state.

Since the release of selected documents in Israeli archives, from the late 1980s onwards, the debate on events surrounding the war and the fighting itself has become extremely bitter, with historians dividing into three broad groups: Arab historians, new (revisionist) Israeli historians and the traditional Israeli historians. Sadly there are currently no documents available from the archives of the Arab states, so we can only go on what the Israelis have made public. The divisions between Israeli historians on the 1948 war are perhaps not surprising given the emotive nature of the subject material and the impact of the subject material on current events and future negotiations. The major areas of disagreement between the scholars are the causes of the Palestinian refugee crisis, the arms balance before and during the war, the question of how much the departing British authorities helped the Palestinian Arabs over the Zionists, and the question of the co-operation (or collusion as some term it) between the Zionists and King Abdullah.

Signs of paranoia

The annual report on Israel prepared by the British delegation to Tel Aviv in 1949 says much about the Foreign Office's attitude at the time to the state of Israel, which was only in its first year of existence.[2] Israelis were characterized by the report as having an inferiority complex and a sense of persecution.[3] What is more, this sense of persecution had made them aggressive and blind to the suffering of others.[4] The tone of the report became even more condescending to Israelis when it claimed that *de facto* British recognition of the state of Israel, and the establishment of diplomatic relations, had done much to flatter the pride of this abnormally sensitive people.[5] The report also claimed that the Israelis were paranoid about the British Government, and the Foreign Office in particular, whose Machiavellian hand it was claimed was seen by Israeli in every unwelcome development to the Jewish state.[6] This paranoia, however, appeared to be a double-edged sword, with the Foreign Office suspecting that behind Israeli action lay a plan to apply pressure to get something out of the British.[7]

The Foreign Office and Menachem Begin

It was not only the official Israeli Government that was experiencing frosty relations with the Foreign Office at this time. The Foreign Office could hardly hide its contempt for Menachem Begin, the head of the Zionist Revisionist movement and post-1948 the leader of the Israeli opposition in the Knesset. Begin was painted as an extremist and a rabble-rouser.[8] His alleged crimes against British soldiers, and specifically his alleged involvement in the killing of two British sergeants, Paice and Martin, in Natanya in July 1947, meant that he was subject of British efforts to, as they put it, bring him to justice.[9] One such scheme put forward by a relative of one of the dead men involved a plan to ask the United States to extradite Begin to Britain during one of his planned trips to Washington.[10] The Foreign Office took legal advice before vetoing the scheme (it thought there little chance that the US authorities would comply with a British request).[11] In a personal letter from the Foreign Secretary Ernest Bevin to the victim's relatives, the Foreign Office's frustration at the failure to bring Begin, whom they believed to be guilty, to justice, was clear.

British Intelligence speculated that Menachem Begin was an active Soviet Agent (though this was later dismissed in 1953, he continued to be viewed as merely strongly anti-British).[12] The original attempt to portray Begin as a Soviet agent could have been the result of either a reflection of the very lack of reliable intelligence the British had about the Revisionists, or less probably part of a wider attempted anti-Begin smear campaign. The accusations didn't stop there. Begin was also accused by the British Embassy in Brussels of taking part in so-called clandestine meetings held in Brussels in 1949 with shadowy figures and was considering what the British described as a new wave of terrorist attacks.[13] The Foreign Office, was, however, on this occasion quick to point out that even if this were true it was unlikely that such attacks would be directed against Britain as it had nothing more to do with Palestine.[14] Instead, it suggested that any attacks would be directed against either the Israeli Government or the international organizations in Israel.[15] In truth, the British had for some time great difficulty dealing with Begin and the Revisionist movement in Palestine (Israel post-1948). Begin enjoyed tormenting the British, claiming that it was the Revisionists that forced the British to leave Palestine.[16]

In October 1954 the Zionist Revisionist Organization contacted the Foreign Office through the offices of Clement Davies MP in order to ascertain whether Begin would be granted a visa to visit Britain.[17] Passport control had already responded in September on the advice of the Levant Department of the Foreign Office to refuse an entry visa for Begin.[18] This decision was in line with an earlier ruling given by the Passport Office in 1952 that somewhat bluntly read 'Every step should be taken to ensure that in *no* circumstances does this man arrive in the UK'.[19] At the end of October 1954 the question of Begin's visa application was causing a lot of anger among Foreign Office officials who held him personally accountable for some of the worst atrocities committed against the British in Palestine.[20] One short handwritten sentence on an internal document best summed up the Foreign Office's attitude to Begin's potential visit: 'I hope we will firmly repel this viper from our bosom.'[21] Consequently, it came as little surprise when on 3 November the Foreign Office stated that they didn't believe that the British public would welcome Begin's presence,[22] nor did they think that a visit by Begin would do anything to improve Britain's relations with the Israeli Government.[23]

Some 26 years later, in May 1979, Menachem Begin entered Number 10 Downing Street at the guest of the then British Prime Minister, Margaret Thatcher. Previously, Thatcher had sworn that she would never shake the hand of Begin because of his role in the bombing of the King David Hotel in Jerusalem on 22 July 1946, which killed 91 people.[24] Indeed, when Thatcher visited Israel in May 1986 she stayed at the King David, which she described as 'being full of associations for her and for all the British people'.[25]

In truth, the question of what to do with Israeli figures – many of whom the Foreign Office viewed as either shady figures, or in the case of the Revisionist leaders as terrorists, vexed many officials in Whitehall. One of the first decisions that Foreign Office officials had to take regarding Israel concerned issues of protocols for meetings with such Israeli officials. Orders were issued on 'social relations with the Jews' stating that there was no reason why British officials should not attend official lunches and dinners, provided that they were not of a political or contentious nature.[26] Celebrations of Jewish independence and events fêting so-called former terrorists remained off limit to British officials.[27] Decades later, the unease felt by even pro-Israel figures in London such as Thatcher about meeting Begin and later his successor Yitzhak Shamir illustrate the then emotive nature of the Anglo–Israeli relationship.

What about the Arabs?

It is worth noting that the wrath of the Foreign Office was not only directed towards Israel at the time. There was equal contempt for much of the Arab leadership among Foreign Office officials and diplomats. At a conference of Her Majesty's representatives in the Middle East in the summer of 1949, the British Government's attitude to existing regimes in the Middle East was defined in the following way:

> Most of the governments in the Middle East are traditionally corrupt, inefficient and to a large degree unrepresentative when compared with Governments such as our own . . . Corruption and inefficiency in the Middle East are not confined to governments but are endemic in the Arab world and are found at all levels and in all classes.[28]

The conference looked at ways of exporting and developing more democratic systems into the Arab Middle East, but concluded that working with so-called progressives within the existing Arab governments was the most prudent course of action.[29] No wide-eyed dreams of spreading democratic values here, as officials were afraid of causing violent changes that would lead to a political vacuum in the area.[30] The conference illustrated that at the very least the Foreign Office knew and understood the beast it was dealing with in the Arab Middle East. Whether or not it chose to turn a blind eye to its own assessment of the failings of the Arab world remains another question altogether.

Events and Issues in Anglo–Israeli relations

In terms of Anglo–Israeli events and issues the period following the creation of Israel was dominated by three core issues: the fall-out from the 1948 war, the question of British recognition of Israel, and the securing of British interests in the region (the preservation of oil supplies and military bases). Regarding the first of these there were two major incidents which damaged Anglo–Israeli relations: the assassination of the UN Mediator for Palestine, Count Bernadotte (allegedly by Jewish gunmen from a breakaway Revisionist group) and the direct military action on the Negev between the Israeli Air Force (IAF) and the Royal Air Force (RAF).

The assassination of Count Bernadotte in Jerusalem was an undisputed disaster for the Provisional Government in Israel. It reduced much of the goodwill that the new state had garnished from non-Aligned countries as a result of the Holocaust, and led to Ben-Gurion clamping down on the dissident groups. Or did the Israeli Government really clamp down? In the Foreign Office there was a degree of scepticism over whether the large-scale arrests and the passing of anti-terrorist legislation were inspired by a genuine attempt to 'root out the terrorists', or simply the authorities putting on a show.[31] As one official put it: '. . . I have seen little which leads me to suppose that any very drastic action has been taken against the terrorists concerned, and few signs that there is much chance of the Mediator's murderers being apprehended.'[32] In retrospect, it is fairly clear that the Israeli Provisional Government did instigate a clampdown on the dissident groups, and its actions were largely successful in both the short and long term. On this occasion, the suspicions of the Foreign Office were largely unfounded, but nevertheless they did reflect the deep-rooted tensions between it and the government in Israel.

Relations between Britain and Israel reached a low point during Israel's War of Independence when, in January 1949, Israel shot down five British planes that had been sent to protect Egyptian sovereign territory from a rapidly advancing Israeli army that had reached the border between the Negev and the Sinai Deserts.[33] At that stage there was a very real danger of this incident turning into something more dangerous. The decision by the Israeli Prime Minister David Ben-Gurion to withdraw Israeli forces from the area was taken in part to prevent a potential escalation of the conflict. The fighting in the Negev between Israel and Egypt constituted the last part of Israel's War of Independence and, with the war clearly won by Israel, it was a case of how much territory they would secure in the south. Israel wanted all of the Negev, but once this objective was secured Israel forces moved into the Sinai Desert and that appeared to put Egypt in mortal danger. As a result, the British made it clear that under its treaty obligations it would come to the aid of Egypt. Ben-Gurion's decision to withdraw Israeli forces back across the border was taken to both reveal an open clash with the British and also to prevent the potential fall of the Egyptian regime. Ben-Gurion believed that if the weak regime in Cairo collapsed it would be replaced by more hard-line elements that would prove to be even more hostile to Israel.

Back in London the Foreign Office was dealing with increased criticism of its Middle Eastern policy in the British press, with the *Daily Telegraph* characterizing the Secretary of State, Ernest Bevin's Middle East policy as having, at the very best, left the UK in the position of Oscar Wilde's character who had no enemies but was cordially disliked by his friends.[34] More significantly, given the political crisis over Israel's incursion into the Sinai there were calls for a more clearly defined articulation of its treaty obligations to Transjordan and Egypt.[35] Ernest Bevin, in response to a letter by Lyall Wilkes MP, defined British treaty obligations as under Articles and 3 and 4 of our Treaty of Alliance with Transjordan, stating that if one party becomes engaged in a war the other party is bound, unless it would prejudice the rights and obligations arising under the Charter of the United Nations, to come to the aid of the party attacked as a measure of collective defence.[36] Moreover, the effect of Article 7 of the treaty with Egypt is similar, and in addition, under Article 8 of that treaty the UK is obliged to co-operate with Egypt in defence of the Suez Canal.[37] In other words, the Foreign Office argued that there was a clear obligation on the part of the UK to aid Egypt or Transjordan if they were involved in a war and if their territory were attacked. In political terms, Britain's treaty commitments reflected its dual strategic British aim of protecting its interests in Transjordan and in the area of the Suez Canal.

A new man in Tel Aviv and *de facto* recognition

The British Government granted Israel *de facto* recognition on 29 January 1949, and on 17 May of the same year Her Majesty's Legation arrived in Israel.[38] The arrival of Sir Alexander Knox Helm, who was to eventually become the first British Ambassador to Israel, was cautiously welcomed in Israel.[39] The local English language newspaper, the *Palestine Post*, acclaimed Helm's arrival as a visible sign of British acceptance of a new relationship with Israel.[40] The paper, however, went on to warn that it would depend primarily on the British Foreign Office whether this relationship developed, as Israel wished, into a wiping out of recent memories and a renewal of fruitful Anglo–Jewish understanding, or into the continuation of the British Cold War against Israel.[41] The comments from the *Palestine Post* were of particular interest to the Foreign Office who regarded its editor, Gershon Agronsky, as strongly anti-British.[42] Agronsky appeared to nail his anti-British colours publicly to the mast in a speech in Cleveland in which he talked about a recent address he had given at Chatham House, a research think-tank with strong connections to the Foreign Office in London.[43] In his Cleveland speech Agronsky declared that his audience at Chatham House consisted almost exclusively of Jew-baiters and Zionist-haters.[44] He went on to suggest that they were Foreign Office pundits, War Office brass hats, Colonial Office stooges, Middle East architects of the Arab League (to which he added 'Rest in peace'), political writers who had guessed wrong, and ex-officers of the British Palestine Administration who, by their presence, were anxious to witness that they had been on the winning side all the time.[45] Agronsky concluded by stating that he had had to watch his commas and, as he put it, he inflicted a paper on them that took 50 minutes to read, and a good time was had by all.[46] In response to Agronsky's comments a Foreign Office official wrote two words on their memorandum of the event: 'What rot!'[47]

The major Hebrew paper, *Haaretz*, was as cautious as the *Palestine Post*, stating that the question in everyone's mind was whether the Minister's arrival denoted a change of political atmosphere.[48] It went on to argue that the past few months had witnessed events that suggested that the British Government was interested in correcting the terrible mistakes of the past. Sufficient proof was to be found in the British *de facto* recognition of Israel and the fact of Helm's arrival.[49] It was too early, however, to forget that until recently Britain had showed open enmity towards Israel.[50] The paper went on to make the somewhat grand claim that Britain had reconciled itself to Israel's existence and had realized that the tactics that it had previously employed had led to a serious political defeat for it.[51]

Conversely, Helm's first impressions of his Israeli hosts were equally insightful. To start with, Helm was not particularly taken with Tel Aviv and its somewhat regimental avenues and stark buildings. In his first major dispatch back to the Foreign Office, Helm speculated whether there could be a less attractive town in the world than Tel Aviv.[52] He added that it combined the worst features of the East and the West and had all the appearance of a prosperous new fifth-grade mid-west town on fair day.[53] The buildings, he claimed, were new and ugly, the narrow streets jammed with pedestrians and uncontrolled traffic, and there was noise everywhere.[54] The greatest trials, however, he argued, were the open-air café orchestras, gramophones and loudspeakers that blared out at the highest volume from 5pm until midnight, making conversation quite difficult and reading impossible.[55]

In terms of the Israeli people, Helm noted that he and his staff were cordially welcomed by Israeli officials who were keen to show him around. On his travels around Tel Aviv he was reminded of the dark recent history when he noted the rather faded notices in Hebrew and English worded 'British Invaders Out of Our Country'.[56] As any Foreign Office diplomat worth his salt would do, he made a mental note to bring this issue up at the earliest opportunity and suggest that they be removed as soon as possible.

In the good tradition of condescension towards Americans in the Middle East, which was something of a Foreign Office sport at the time, Helm could not resist passing comment on the US Ambassador to Israel, MacDonald.[57] Helm claimed that it would be easy to produce evidence (not least statements from MacDonald himself) to suggest that the American Ambassador was the most popular foreigner in Israel. Helm's initial contacts, however, told him that this tribute was more apparent than real, and that in fact, among respectable Israelis MacDonald was something of a laughing stock.[58]

If Helm had any premonitions about the difficulties that lay ahead for his mission in Tel Aviv they would have been soon confirmed after his arrival in Israel and before he had even presented his credentials to the Israeli President to officially assume his responsibilities. *Maariv*, the largest-circulation Hebrew newspaper, ran a story on 25 May 1949, the eve of the presentation of Helm's credentials, under the curious headline of 'The British Drop Balfour'.[59] In the article the paper claimed that the British were trying to improve relations with Israel, and to bring it back into the Sterling area and their sphere of influence. The obstacles, however, that they were putting in the path of the Israeli delegation in London did not help this matter. It went on to suggest that the British had dispensed with the services of Balfour in Israel. The reference was a clever play on surnames. It did not, of course, refer to Lord Balfour of Balfour Declaration fame but rather to an 'Oriental adviser' with the same name from what the paper somewhat sarcastically referred to as from the 'smart school', whom the British had originally asked to bring to Palestine.[60] Though anti-British pieces in the Hebrew press were not unusual at this time, Helm, given the timing of it, took great offence, protesting to local officials and promising to being it up in his first official meeting with the Israeli Foreign Minister, Moshe Sharett.[61] Back in London the Foreign Office was not as concerned or angry as Helm. Officials somewhat condescendingly stated that though *Maariv* was the largest-circulation paper, it was not particularly strong on politics and liable to indulge in personal anti-British remarks.[62] Officials suggested that it was best to keep British protests about this sort of piece on the level of informal condescension.[63] The *Maariv* piece, however, had clearly achieved its aim of causing friction at a highly symbolic time. Helm's tour of duty was not off to the best of starts.

Helm met with Sharett in the evening of 15 July 1949 and talked about Israel, the Middle East and the world situation for two hours. Given that this was the first official meeting between an Israeli Minister and the man in charge of the British diplomatic mission to Israel, Helm was naturally excited by the meeting and made much of the private comments that Sharett made during its course in his telegrams back to the Foreign Office.[64] During the meeting Sharett touched upon a number of important issues for Israel. He speculated whether the British Govern-ment wanted to develop its acceptance of Israel to its logical conclusion, or whether it was waiting to see if Israel would really last the distance.[65] The question of Israel neutrality was also touched upon, with Sharett stating that Israel did not want to choose between two major groups for fear that such a choice would involve a great disturbance, but was a democracy, so, if forced to choose, would know which way to go.[66] Sharett also warned of the dangers of dealing with the Middle East problem on the basis of Arab unity to be unreal.[67]

Back in London, Foreign Office officials were less enthusiastic than Helm about the meeting.[68] They argued that Sharett's outline of Israel's position regarding Anglo–Israeli relations, the Arabs and the rest of the world was in line with his past declarations, and with what moderate and intelligent Israelis would say in private conversations.[69] Several Foreign Office officials were overtly critical of Sharett's traditional Israeli perspective on Britain and the Middle East. Tellingly, they argued that Israel must accept Britain as a great power that has important interests in the Middle East. In a clear summary of British interests in the Middle East they accepted Israel's technical neutrality but stated that they could not tolerate Israeli opposition to British needs in matters that didn't directly concern Israel, such as questions relating to Anglo–Jordanian relations.[70] The officials then returned to the cornerstone of its Middle East policy, that British policy in the region must be primarily concerned with the Arabs who form the population and hold almost all the territory.[71] The officials predicted that it would be a long time before the Arabs forgot the disaster which befell them and for which they blamed Israel.[72] The tone of the response illustrated that there would be little change in the attitude of the Foreign Office towards Israel, which at the time, could be characterized as a willingness to work with the Israeli Government in areas of mutual benefit, but that the development of British interests in the Arab world was quite simply of greater importance to the UK.

When is a change not a change?

As events and meetings in the Anglo–Israeli relationship hadn't gone as smoothly as Helm had intended, it will come as little surprise that his opposite number, Dr Mordechai Eliash, the head of the Israeli delegation to the UK, was experiencing problems of his own with the Foreign Office. Dr Eliash held what he described as a largely successful meeting with Ernest Bevin on 19 July 1949, which he felt marked an important advance in Anglo–Israeli relations.[73] In the meeting he said that the Secretary of State had assured him that Britain did not want to turn Israel out of the Negev and also recognized Israel's need for an outlet at Aqaba in the south.[74] Twelve days later, however, on 1 September 1949, the Manchester *Guardian* ran a short piece entitled 'Reconciliation with Britain Aids Israeli Case at Lausanne', which caused a great deal of concern at the Foreign Office.[75] It was a case of double dread for the Foreign Office – a potential change in British policy which the Secretary of State could have privately made and which had not been disseminated across the Foreign Office, and the realization that the Israelis had leaked details of the private meeting between Bevin and Dr Eliash to the press.[76] Concern over the leak heightened in the Foreign Office when the French newspaper *Figaro* ran an article alleging a change in British policy towards Israel.[77] The article claimed that Anglo–Israeli relations had recently become more cordial, and that Britain had even supported Israel on some issues *vis-à-vis* the Americans.[78] To make matters worse for the usually highly efficient Foreign Office, Bevin had not kept a record of the conversation – it took place on the evening before he went on holiday.[79] Instead officials were left to check with another official who sat in the meeting as to whether Bevin's memory of the conversation confirmed Dr Eliash's version of the talks.[80] Following an investigation into the source of the story in *Figaro*, officials at the Foreign Office concluded that the leak had probably come from the Israeli delegation in Lausanne via the Ministry of Foreign Affairs in Jerusalem.[81] Dr Eliash, who had strongly protested his innocence in the affair when questioned by a Foreign Office official, was off the hook.[82] In terms of the content of the meeting, the Foreign Office stated that it was an informal private meeting with no record keeping and that Dr Eliash was obviously pleased with its outcome but had obviously put the construction most favourable to Israel on whatever Bevin might have said.[83] Whatever the truth about what Bevin might have said, and the various spins put on it by British and Israeli officials, the meeting, and the resulting leakage of it, created further tension in the diplomatic relationship between the two countries. Official Anglo–Israeli diplomatic relations were not off to a great start.

This, of course, was not the end of the story. The Foreign Office advised Sharett through Helm how much they would like to take Israel into British confidence more so than it had done in the past, but that every time it did there were leakages.[84] It suggested (some might say somewhat hypocritically given its own poor plumbing record) that the first essential for any discussions with Israel about broader matters of policy is that there would be no leakages, particularly in view of British difficulties in dealing with the Arab states.[85] The rest of the communication was aimed at showing Sharett that despite Israeli mischief-making there had been no significant change in British policy towards Israel.[86] When Helm returned to Tel Aviv after his summer vacation he met with Sharett on 22 September 1949.[87] In the meeting a rather defensive Sharett said that he was extremely gratified to learn that the British Government wished to take Israel more into its confidence than before.[88] He assured Helm that this trust would not be abused. He failed to offer any explanations as to how such 'scurrilous leaks' could have happened.[89] And so the diplomatic game went on.

In truth, the relationship between the Foreign Office and Israel was dogged by suspicions, misinterpretation, plumbing difficulties and mischief-making by both sides. It is also worth pointing out that career diplomats (particularly heads of ambassadors or heads of missions) are, in general, prone to talk up the significance of their local contacts and their official and semi-official meetings, when communicating back home to their respective governments. This is often done to illustrate the respective diplomats' so-called importance to the relevant diplomatic relationship. Foreign Office officials, as a result, often took any new policy or initiative that emerged from such a meeting with a large pinch of salt.

British internal instability, 1950–51

The British general election was held on 23 February 1950 following the first full term of a Labour Government.[90] At the election the ruling Labour Party saw its overall majority cut from 145 seats in 1945 to just five seats in 1950.[91] Accordingly there followed a period of great political instability in Britain, and the Labour Government was forced to go to the polls again in 1951. The elections had been followed with great interest in Israel. In Tel Aviv, Helm noted that in Israeli official circles there was no particular support for either the Labour Party or the Conservatives, though he sensed that there was a slight preference for a Labour victory simply on the grounds that a Conservative Government, even led by Winston Churchill, would have stronger pro-Arab sympathies.[92] There was a wider sense in Israel that this was the first British election that could be objectively followed and whose outcome would not, as Helm put it, be of vital concern for the Jews in Palestine.[93]

It was not long, however, before Bevin, who had been reappointed as Foreign Secretary in the second Attlee-led government, managed to anger the Israeli Government and cause Helm in Tel Aviv to undertake a much-needed repair job to the Anglo–Israeli relationship. During the Secretary of State's speech in the Foreign Affairs debate in the House of Commons on 28 March 1950, he mistakenly stated that Haifa had been allocated to the Arabs under UN resolution.[94] If that was not hard enough for Israel to swallow, he went on to suggest that it was difficult to deal with Israel because it never accepted UN resolutions.[95] It came as little surprise, not least to the Foreign Office, that the Israeli Chargé d'Affaires, Kidron, took Bevin's comments up with British officials at the earliest opportunity.[96] Israel charged that while the mis-statement of fact had been subsequently corrected and that the correction had shown that it was the Arabs who had refused to accept this UN resolution, no attempt had been made to modify the conclusion that Israel rather than the Arabs was careless of its international obligations.[97] The meeting was an important one, not because of the somewhat predictable nature of the Israeli response to the poor speech by Bevin, but rather because they revealed the major Israeli gripe against the British Government at the time – the thorny question of arms sales by HMG to Arab states.[98]

The question of British arms sales

At this time in Israel there was a growing feeling that the Arabs, and in particular Egypt, were preparing for a second round of confrontation with Israel.[99] From time to time, this belief was talked up in diplomatic circles in order to try to secure concessions on the key issue of the day, which was the question of arms sales. Much of the diplomatic games and bad feeling between Britain and Israel centred on this issue. While Sharett had brought it up previously in the general sense with Helm in Tel Aviv it came to dominate the diplomatic agenda from the first part of 1950 onwards.[100] From an Israeli perspective there was a lack of comprehension as to how the British Government could sell arms to the Arabs that went far beyond what they needed or internal security measures.[101] Israeli officials cited the sale of bomber aircraft, fighter aircraft and tanks by Britain and other countries primarily to Egypt and Iraq, but to other Arab states as well. They were of no use against potential attack by the Soviet Union or in dealing with the problem of internal disorder, therefore they might be wanted for a second round against Israel.[102] To make matters worse for the Israelis, a senior Foreign Office official, the Permanent Under-Secretary of State, Sir William Strang, had indicated that the British Government would not be prepared to supply Israel with arms until peace had been reached between Israel and its neighbours.[103] Israel charged the British Government with double standards, wondering why this condition was applied to Israel and not to the Arab states. They also argued that this amounted to an open invitation to the Arabs to refrain from making peace with Israel as they knew that until peace was made, Israel would be unable to obtain the arms from Britain.

In a move designed to increase the pressure on the British Government, the Israeli Air Force (IAF) announced that the British military attachés in Israel were to suffer discrimination in contrast to their American counterparts because of the policy of the British Government not to sell arms to Israel.[104] This decision came only a few days after a meeting between the Israeli Chief of Staff, General Yigal Yadin, and the British Air Attaché, Wing Commander J. A. O'Neill, at the Israeli Defence Force (IDF) headquarters in Ramat Gan (near Tel Aviv).[105] At the meeting, General Yadin made the linkage between the arms sales and the role of Air Attaché, declaring that the task of the Air Attaché was likely to be very difficult as long as the British arms policy continued. It would have come as little surprise therefore when Israel instigated its policy of discrimination against the British.

Helm blew a fuse when he heard the news of the proposed discrimination against members of his delegation, and requested a meeting with Moshe Sharett at the earliest opportunity. At the meeting an exasperated

Helm declared that he was going to talk personally and sincerely.[106] On a personal level, Helm expressed his belief that Israel, as he put it, was a fact and a factor of great importance, and it was important for Anglo–Israeli relations to be good.[107] He conceded, however, that despite a fairly good start things had gone wrong and were likely to get worse if not checked.[108] Helm explained that he understood Israeli disappointment over the arms issue, but did not welcome the threats made by General Yadin. Perhaps most revealing of all was Helm's attempts to cite a passage from Chaim Weizmann's book in which Dr Weizmann made the point that in his opinion not all British officials had been hostile when they first came to Palestine, and he had never been able to understand how it was that within a few months most of them became anti-Jewish.[109] Helm added that he was beginning to see one of the reasons for this change.[110] Back in the Foreign Office some officials already understood the stark truth that Anglo–Israeli relations would not be completely friendly until Britain could supply Israel with arms. The official confirmed that this was one of Israel's main aims, and until Britain agreed to this, Israel would be unable and unwilling to try to ignore the factor in its relations with Britain.

In the wake of the arms issue Helm brought up the charge made in the Israeli press that there were effectively two separate policies towards Israel originating from Whitehall: one led by Bevin and the Foreign Office which was hostile to Israel, and the more sympathetic one led by Sir Stafford Cripps and the Treasury (a financial agreement had just been signed by Britain and Israel).[111] Naturally, Helm denied that such a dualist policy existed, but nevertheless this Israeli accusation has been a constant theme in Anglo–Israeli relations and we will revisit it in the chapter on Anglo–Israeli relations during the era of the Tony Blair-led governments.

The arms issue gathered pace when at a meeting on 28 April 1950 to mark the previous British *de jure* recognition of Israel, Moshe Sharett once again raised the issue. With *de jure* recognition having been granted, Helm's job title was formally upgraded to that of Ambassador and this meeting marked the first one between the two following this change. As ever, Sharett was cautious in his choice of words but he indicated that the arms issue continued to cause Israel real concern.[112] In Israel, with the press giving a great deal of coverage to the arms story, the Minister of Foreign Affairs was coming under strong pressure to take a firmer line with Britain. Following reports in Israel that the British Government had intervened to prevent a jet deal with a Western European country, Sharett summoned the British Ambassador for a meeting on 2 May 1950.[113] During the course of the meeting Sharett talked in specific terms about British arms sales to the Arabs.[114] He cited the deliveries that had just been made to Egypt that included six Vampires bringing the total sold to 18, 20 Meteor aircraft, bringing the total to 30, with 12 further Vampires and ten Meteors ready for delivery.[115] On top of this, the UK supplied some six Furies, ten Halifax bombers and some navy craft. Sharett reminded the British Ambassador that Egypt was not the only Arab country to receive arms from Britain. Syria, with which Britain had no treaty agreement, had just signed a contract to buy 14 Meteor aircraft from Britain.[116] Eleven fighter aircraft were being supplied to Lebanon, which had previously had none.[117] As for Israel, Sharett reminded the Ambassador that there was still a blank refusal to let it have any weapons at all.[118]

In reality, while Sharett did have genuine concerns about the willingness of the British Government to sell arms to the Arabs, and its unwillingness to do the same for Israel, domestic Israeli factors were influencing the by now seemingly obsessive highlighting of the issue by the Israeli Government. Helm attempted to make the Foreign Office aware of this situation.[119] He argued that the real driving force in the arms question was the Israeli Chief of Staff of the IDF.[120] He cited the evidence of the language the Chief of Staff had used in his meeting with the Service Attachés.[121] The trail went higher up, as the Chief of Staff (as Helm put it) had the ear of David Ben-Gurion in his joint roles as Prime Minister and Minister of Defence.[122] The Ambassador concluded that Sharett was too weak to stand up to Ben-Gurion and General Yadin.[123]

The Ben-Gurion–Sharett rivalry dominated the early years of the state of Israel.[124] While much of the reason for the rivalry can be attributed to power politics – the desire to lead and dominate the ruling Mapai party – it could also be put down to seeming policy differences on relations between Israel and the Arabs. Though there was much common ground between the two of them, Sharett viewed the Arabs as less of a threat than Ben-Gurion and believed that Israel could in time secure diplomatic agreements with the Arab states. Ben-Gurion, on the other hand, was less optimistic, believing that Israel could not afford to make the kind of concessions that the Arabs would demand in exchange for formal peace agreements, and that the state of no war and no peace was the best policy option for Israel at the time. It hardly needs saying that the diplomatic core, including the British mission, much preferred dealing with Sharett, who they widely identified and referred to as a 'sensible Israeli'.

Israeli complaints about the injustice of the British arms policy were not falling on deaf ears at the Foreign Office. In a wide-ranging policy paper, originally circulated on 11 April 1950, Foreign Office officials warned of the danger of continuing to sell arms to the Arabs, but not to Israel. As they put it:

> There is growing discussion in the Arab press and among influential Arab circles that a second round [war] will soon be launched against Israel. The Israeli Government and people cannot be content with pacifying statements from Her Majesty's Government that the sale of arms to the Arab states is for their internal security purposes. Pictures of heavy tanks in military parades in Egypt, reports of record flights from London to Cairo by British planes destined for the Egyptian Air Force do not inspire confidence.[125]

The paper on went to remind officials that the United States was sticking to its policy of strict control of the sale of arms to the Middle East.[126] The Israelis therefore had to buy arms through 'devious channels' and at inflated prices.[127] As a result, they needed to spend a large proportion of their budget on defence and this was diverting resources from developing the country.[128] Pressure was building in the United States, however, for the President to lift the control over US arms sales to Israel, a fact that was widely expected to speed up the Middle East arms race.[129] The fundamental argument that some Foreign Office officials were starting to make was quite simply that if Britain's large-scale rearming of the Arab armed forces was one of the major reasons leading to a second Arab–Israeli war, then Britain's influence in the Middle East would suffer.[130]

A second report was submitted on 11 April 1950 which, in essence, contained similar arguments regarding the question of refusal to sell arms to Israel.[131] This report was more specific in outlining the number of weapons that Britain was selling to the Arab states as well as detailing the training that was taking place for Arab military personnel.[132] The pressure on the Foreign Office and the British Government to change their arms policy towards Israel was growing even from within Whitehall.

On 25 May 1950, the governments of Britain, France and the United States signed the Tripartite Statement on the Middle East. The agreement declared their deep interest in their desire to promote the establishment and maintenance of peace and stability in the area and their unalterable opposition to the use of force or threat of force between any of the states in that area.[133] The statement was well received in Israel, but largely on the basis that it heralded in the start of arms supplies to Israel from the UK.[134] The truth was, as Foreign Office officials later disclosed, that Britain was still in consultation with the United States regarding the issue.[135] Once again, Israel was to be disappointed with the outcome of this discussion.

Taking tea with the old man

The British Ambassador had been keen to have a meeting with Ben-Gurion for some time.[136] He believed that many of the Prime Minister's well-documented views on the Foreign Office and the Secretary of State, Bevin, were simply prejudices that could be addressed by some straight talking. During the meeting, which took place over tea on 29 June 1950, Ben-Gurion made it clear that while he recognized that there had been a real change in the British approach to Israel in the past year, some people still clung to the 'old ideas' and did not accept Israel.[137] The Prime Minister claimed that included in this group were the Secretary of State and 'some of his Middle East advisers'.[138] Naturally, Helm disagreed with the Prime Minister's assessment of the Secretary of State and the Foreign Office and spent the next 20 minutes attempting to convince him of the desire of Bevin and the Foreign Office to see peace and stability in the region.[139] During the course of the discussion, Ben-Gurion had hinted at the concept of there being two foreign policies in Downing Street (one led by the Office, the other by the Treasury and Downing Street).[140] Ben-Gurion's belief in this version of British foreign policy formation says much about his continuing suspicions about the workings and attitudes of the Foreign Office. For the Israeli Prime Minister, good news for Israel – such as financial agreements – came out of Downing Street or the Treasury, and bad news – such as the ban on arms sales to Israel – originated from the Foreign Office.

During the course of the meeting, Ben-Gurion once again identified the arms issue as being central to the Anglo–Israeli relationship.[141] As usual, the Prime Minister linked the arms questions to the issue of peace.[142] He argued that Israel needed peace in order to address the country's acute problems of immigration, foreign exchange and development, which could not be solved until Israel felt more secure.[143] Israel, in short, did not want to have to spend large amounts of money on arms, but had little choice. The Ambassador noted that Ben-Gurion was well informed about the state of Arab armaments.[144]

By the summer of 1950 Anglo–Israeli relations appeared to be on a relatively good course and Helm was given much of the credit for the improvement by the local Israeli press.[145] In an article in *Haaretz*, D. R. Elston summarized the changes and highlighted the fact that Israel and Great Britain were the only two non-Muslim countries that had important direct interests in the Middle East. The article also touched upon the question of arms sales, which in any case the British were now starting to reconsider. Helm left Tel Aviv for two months' leave in London over the summer of 1950, safe in the knowledge that his efforts in Israel appeared to be bearing fruit. In reality, much of this seeming improvement in relations stemmed from the Israeli perception that Britain was going to make significant changes to its arms policy towards Israel.

Eliahu Elath, the new Israeli Ambassador, arrived in London in the summer of 1950. Prior to taking up his appointment in London Elath had served as Israel's Ambassador to Washington where he had enjoyed a cordial relationship with the British Ambassador to Washington.[146] The British Embassy in Washington characterized Elath as a moderate Zionist and that he genuinely desired good Anglo–Israeli relations.[147]

By September 1950, the result of the consultation on arms was well known. The British Government, instead of selling arms to Israel, had chosen the path of banning all arms sales to countries outside the Commonwealth. Elath, was who now up to full speed in London, requested a meeting with the Parliamentary Under-Secretary, Ernest Davies, on 15 September 1950. The Ambassador, as was usual in such meetings, expressed the desire of Israel for peace, discussed various topical developments and Israel's domestic problems, particularly its attempts to absorb its newly arriving immigrants into the country.[148] The key part of the meeting, however, concerned the Ambassador's expression of Israeli disappointment over the fact that the Tripartite Agreement had not been followed up by the provision of arms to Israel.[149] Davies was quick to respond that the Foreign Secretary had informed him that there was now no discrimination as there was a ban on all arms exports outside the Commonwealth. The Ambassador retorted, however, that in the past Britain had built up Egypt's strength while refusing to sell arms to Israel.[150] Any hopes that the new British policy on arms would appease the Israelis had disappeared. In other words, the Israeli Government still wanted the British to supply it with the weapons that it believed it needed for its armed forces.

On 14 November 1950, the Israeli Ambassador returned to the Foreign

Office to meet with William Strang.[151] In the meeting, Elath outlined the Israeli positions in peace negotiations and called for the British Government to help bring about a deal between King Abdullah and Israel.[152] On the wider issues of the Arab–Israeli conflict he identified the key areas as being the return of the Palestinian refugees, territorial changes and compensation for the refugees.[153] Elath frankly spelt out Israel's positions on these issues: no Israeli government could continue to exist if it made territorial concessions and that the return of the refugees would be tantamount to economic suicide and a threat to Israeli security. In other words, there appeared to be little prospect of a peaceful resolution to the Arab–Israeli conflict at this time.[154]

Given the faint prospects of a diplomatic breakthrough, the Israelis were naturally concerned with developments on the strategic and military fronts. The Israelis now moved the arms issue on to a new tack. At the meeting with Strang, the Israeli Ambassador highlighted the need for Israel to move towards a closer *rapprochement* with the Western powers.[155] Elath now put his cards on the table, stating that in order for this to happen Israel needed to be nourished and that the Western powers needed to show confidence in Israel by not discriminating against it.[156] The objective of Elath's plea was to discover whether the British policy of a ban on arms exports to non-Commonwealth countries had changed. There had been a recent delivery of some 16 Centurion tanks to Egypt. Strang held out hope that soon Israel would be able to buy arms from Britain.[157] The Ambassador immediately indicated that Israel would require jets and tanks.[158] In respect of the tanks delivered to Egypt, the Foreign Office justified the shipment by stating that they were part of an earlier order and that the Egyptians had already paid 80 per cent of the price.[159] This issue of delivery of already placed orders was to become a difficult one during the subsequent years in the lead-up to the Suez Crisis.

In November 1950, Foreign Office officials admitted that virtually the only question outstanding between Britain and Israel was the question of the supply of arms.[160] Unfortunately for the Foreign Office, this issue had been identified by the Israeli Government as the most important sign of the nature and state of Anglo–Israeli relations. During a visit to London, Burstein, the Secretary-General of the Histadrut, called at the Foreign Office, in essence to expresses Israel's fears about the arms issue.[161] He met with Ernest Davies on 19 December 1950 and stated that the major fear in Israel was that Britain would make a deal with Egypt involving the supply of weapons to the Egyptian Army that would enable the

Egyptians to renew hostilities against Israel.[162] Davies informed the Secretary-General that the latest version of British policy was that in theory Israel was now free to buy arms from Britain, but that, as he pointed out, 'it would be mistake to suppose that we have a large surplus of arms for sale'.[163] Davies went on to remind the Secretary-General of the ban on the sale of equipment needed for the Atlantic Treaty countries and the Commonwealth, and he did not think therefore that Egypt would be receiving a great deal of heavy equipment in the near future.[164] The Soviet threat to Europe was now the main theatre in the arms race. This created a fear, which the Secretary-General articulated, that the Western powers had written off the Middle East and were concentrating on the defence of Europe.[165] For all the above reasons there appeared to be little prospect of the Foreign Office agreeing to the sale of the jets and tanks that Israel requested.

A farewell to Bevin

Initially, it was not electoral politics that led to a major change in British personnel dealing with Israel, but rather ill health. On 9 March 1951, Ernest Bevin moved from the Foreign Office to become Lord Privy Seal and was succeeded as Secretary of State by Herbert Morrison. Bevin died the following month. Much has been written about Bevin and his negative attitude towards Zionism.[166] It was Bevin who had returned Jewish survivors of the Holocaust who were trying to enter Palestine back to the displaced persons camps in Europe, a policy that was a public relations disaster for Britain. He opposed the creation of the state of Israel, and in Israel he is blamed for the British failure to peacefully implement the UN 1947 Partition Plan. Despite this, during his time as Foreign Secretary Britain and Israel developed diplomatic relations, albeit somewhat tense ties, and Britain recognized the permanent nature of Israel's existence in the region. On a personnel level, it is fair to say that the Israeli Government were not sad to see this polemic anti-Zionist figure depart from his dominant platform on the political stage.

Following the British General Election of 25 October 1951, the Conservatives under the leadership of Winston Churchill returned to power, this despite the fact that the Labour Party actually won more votes than the Conservatives. Following its victory the Conservative Party won subsequent elections held in 1955 and 1959, ensuring some 13 years of Tory dominance of UK politics. The first period of Anglo–Israeli relations had come to a natural end. Israel waited somewhat anxiously to see what the newly appointed Foreign Secretary, Anthony Eden, would try to do with the Middle East.

The start of a beautiful friendship?

Anglo–Israeli relations had come a long way in the relatively short time since the creation of Israel. On the whole, and given the fractious nature of Anglo–Zionist relations in the period up to 1948, the relationship was surprisingly cordial. Some officials in the Foreign Office might have characterized this cordiality in terms of as needs must. The key question regarded the role of the Foreign Office in setting the course and direction of this relationship. On a superficial level there appeared to be two sets of actors driving the relationship during this period. In one corner were the diplomats of the Foreign Office together with their Israeli counterparts in the Israeli Ministry of Foreign Affairs, and in the other corner Downing Street and the Israeli prime minister and his close advisers. In this argument the Foreign Office and Ben-Gurion's deep suspicions of it, and particularly of Bevin, would appear to make full normalization of relations impossible. As we have seen, however, it was the Foreign Office that took the lead in British policy towards Israel and the wider Middle East during this period. There was a general acceptance in Israel that the first British Ambassador, Helm, had handled his mission extremely competently and had enjoyed some successes in moving the relationship away from the darkness of its recent past and onto a new more positive footing.

It was clear, not least to the Israelis, that the Foreign Office continued to view the Arab world as much more important to British interests in the region than Israel. Foreign Office officials appeared quite open in expressing this belief. This fact, however, did not prevent the Foreign Office from coming to terms with Israel as a permanent feature in the Middle East, and with which it was in the British interest to develop strong relations – though not at the expense of its treaty obligations to Egypt and Transjordan and the wider Arab world. That said, there also remained a degree of dislike of Israel, and indeed aspects of the Jewish character as put forward by Helm in the annuals review for Israel for 1950. In the introduction to the review, Helm made the following remarks:

> Her [Israel's] greatest disability remains the more disagreeable features of the Jewish character, with an inability to realize that the obtaining of

the farthing does not necessarily mean the best bargain, that in an imperfect world unrelieved seriousness is not a virtue and, perhaps above all, that strength is not always best displayed through force.[167]

There was clearly much work to be done to develop a strengthening working relationship into a warmer one.

To suggest, as some did, that Ben-Gurion was not particularly well disposed to Britain is another simplistic and false argument. The Israeli Prime Minister remained openly suspicious of Bevin and his Middle East advisers, did not enjoy a close working relationship with British mission in Tel Aviv, but nevertheless viewed Britain as a natural friend and ally of Israel. As the British Ambassador pointed out, Ben-Gurion was not well connected with the international diplomatic circuit in Israel, preferring instead the company of men in uniform.[168]

There were two issues that remained unresolved and which came back to damage Anglo–Israeli relations in the period from 1951 to 1958. The first of these was the final borders of the state of Israel, and the call for it to make territorial compromise in order to secure peace agreements with the Arabs. The second concerned the issue that both parties openly admitted remained the most contentious between them, and that carried the greatest single threat to the continued improvement in Anglo–Israeli relations: the question of arms sales to Israel. With the likelihood of a second round of war between Israel and the Arabs hanging over the region, this issue become ever more important. As we shall see, the Israelis grew increasingly frustrated with the Foreign Office, who they believed were behind the reluctance of the British Government to allow the sale of top-of-the-range weapons to the Israeli armed forces.

Part 2

The Conservative Years:
July 1951 to September 1964

2

Growing pains

The Jews, said a statesman of the last century, are the cleverest people in the world and the least wise. Never has this dictum been truer in the last few years in Palestine.[1]

Sir John Glubb (Glubb Pasha), March 1953

The song remains the same

In truth, the relationship between the Foreign Office and Israel during the 1950s continued to be complicated by the experience of the British Mandate in Palestine, and by the conflict that led to the creation of the state of Israel in May 1948. This remained the case until 1958 despite the previously noted modest improvements in Anglo–Israeli relations at start of the decade and the collusion over the Suez War. A tersely worded confidential report produced by the Foreign Office at the time on changes in the Middle East provided a stark insight into the feelings of some Foreign Office officials towards Israel and its impact on British interests in the region. As they put it:

> The change in British policy in Palestine from the White Paper of 1939, which attempted to protect Arab rights, to the surrender to Jewish terrorists and U.S. politicians in 1948: this lost us an important base [Palestine] and the friendship of the Arab world.[2]

As the Cold War between the West and the Soviet Union deepened and the Middle East became an increasingly important theatre of the conflict, Israel looked increasingly to Britain in its quest for Western allies, and most importantly, despite its initial disappointments, still courted it as a major supplier of arms.[3] There were concerns in Israel about America.[4] Israel was said to distrust American policy and looked upon Britain as a safer and more reliable ally and wanted to restrain what Richard Crossman labelled 'the wild men of Washington'.[5] There was, as the British Ambassador in Tel Aviv put it, a whiff of anti-Americanism in the air, particularly in the Israeli press.[6] Opinion in Israel, the Ambassador went on, was resolutely anti-MacArthurism and was much concerned about the influence of the Republican Party there. Israel, as a result, had became more and more favourably disposed to Britain.[7]

British policy towards Israel, however, was naturally still shaped by national self-interest. In practical terms, this policy revolved around the regional defence system between Britain and the Arab states, which was under increasing threat with the start of Soviet penetration into the region.[8] With the rise of the Soviet threat to British interests, Israel was accredited a degree of strategic value to Britain but this value was deemed to be not as significant as that of the Arabs, whom many officials at the Foreign Office identified might, with the right inducement, cross into the Soviet camp.[9] The same officials argued that Israel, with its European democratic institutions and outlook, would not do so.[10] Israel, of course, did not have any oil, and the maintenance of the supply of oil from the Arabs to the British was never far from the minds of Foreign Office officials.[11] By the end of 1952, it was also clear to the Foreign Office that the Soviet Union had given up any hope of bringing Israel into the communist orbit.[12]

To make matters worse for Israel, many in the Foreign Office were increasingly concerned about what they termed Israeli expansion and the Arab fear of it as both a real and a potential threat to British strategic interests in the Middle East. In simple terms, any strategic co-operation with Israel risked damaging the UK's friendship with key Arab leaders and states with whom good relations continued to be much more important than Israel.[13] The Foreign Office, as a result, remained extremely reluctant to give Israel what it really wanted and authorize the sale of heavy weapons to it. This remained the case even in days before the Suez War and in the period immediately following it.

At the start of the 1950s, some attempts were made to deepen military relations between Israel and the UK.[14] This was undertaken primarily by the Foreign Office, and in spite of the grave concern of it over the Israeli policy of reprisal actions, particularly in Jordan. These raids were undertaken by Israeli forces and were intended to help stop the raids by Palestinian *fedayeen* groups into Israel which were resulting in an increasing number of Israeli civilian casualties.[15] The Foreign Office, and British diplomats in Tel Aviv, suspected that the raids were not simply retaliation ones and Israel's actions threatened the stability of Jordan and British interests.[16] The political fall-out from the raids, as a result, became a major factor in the deterioration in the Foreign Office's relationship with Israel during this period.

The British Army returns to Palestine?

In January 1951, the Permanent Under-Secretary at the Foreign Office, Sir William Strang, requested that the Israeli Ambassador in London get the permission of his government for a visit to Israel by the Commander-in-Chief of British Middle East Land Forces, General Sir Brian Robertson.[17] The original aim of the visit was to explore the potential of a pact or alliance with Israel, which would see the potential establishment of British bases in Gaza that might be connected to Jordan, by a corridor – or even the establishment of British bases in Israel itself. During the course of his meeting with Ben-Gurion on 21 February 1951, however, the Israeli Prime Minister dropped something of a bombshell on his unsuspecting British guests. Ben-Gurion suggested that Israel be allowed to join the Commonwealth. Both General Robertson and Knox (who also attended the meeting) were both initially impressed by the earnestness of Ben-Gurion's suggestion.[18] General Robertson came away from the meeting stating that this was meant to be a big event in Anglo–Israeli relations, and as not just a smokescreen devised to evade the General's detailed questions about potential strategic co-operation.[19]

Given the unexpected nature of Ben-Gurion's proposal, the Foreign Office was thrown into something of a state of confusion. Once Foreign Office officials had decided that Ben-Gurion was being serious, and his claim to be only speaking personally was dismissed, emphasis shifted on to the meaning of the phrase 'in times of emergency', which he had used with General Robertson.[20] In the meantime, as the ice had been broken in Anglo–Israeli relations, according to the Secretary of State, he suggested to Strang that the Israelis might be softened up, along with Britain's Arab allies (Egypt, Jordan and Iraq), by some goodwill gesture such as a visit by the Duke of Edinburgh.[21] The Secretary of State went on to suggest that Britain should consider some form of assistance for each of the four countries, which in the case of Israel he argued might be help over the citrus crop and potash.[22] There was still no sign of the sale of weapons to Israel, which was one of Ben-Gurion's major motivations in making his proposal.

Foreign Office officials were quick to check what exactly membership of the Commonwealth entailed and from this to check what Ben-Gurion meant by Israel should act in an emergency as if it were a member of the Commonwealth. Officials felt it clear at this stage that the Israeli Prime Minister had not suggested that Israel should become a permanent member of the Commonwealth.[23] To the probable relief of officials the summary of privileges and obligations revealed what they wanted to see on defence issues. It confirmed that there were no formal mutual defence obligations involved in membership of the Commonwealth, as there was in NATO, but membership of the Commonwealth did confer a special position in defence relations with Britain.[24] At this stage, the Foreign Office waited for further clarification from Israel. A formal Israeli request to join the Commonwealth in 1956 was rejected by the British on the grounds that it would confirm Arab thinking that Israel was a new outpost of European imperialism.[25]

Discussions on the original purpose of General Robertson's visit to Israel, namely Anglo–Israeli strategic co-operation, did not advance very far. In the end, the Israeli Prime Minister, David Ben-Gurion, who remained extremely suspicious of British intentions, and of the Foreign Office in particular, blocked the British initiative on strategic co-operation.[26] In truth, this initiative was the exception to the rule. The Foreign Office believed that in order to secure British interests in the region it was extremely important not to be seen to be appearing to have close relations with Israel. As a result, relations between the two countries remained formal in nature and without any real strategic co-operation until Suez.

Sharett comes to London

In the absence of any formal agreement on Anglo–Israeli strategic co-operation it was business as usual on the arms question when the Secretary of State, Anthony Eden, and his Israeli counterpart, Moshe Sharett, met in London in March of the following year.[27] Eden, who was suffering from flu and had cancelled all his other engagements for the week, left his sickbed to host the meeting.[28] Foreign Office officials, however, were extremely sensitive about the meeting. Fearing an Arab backlash, they drafted a statement that downplayed the significance of Sharett's visit to London that was to be used in any discussions with Arab states that asked for information.[29] Sharett, the Arabs were to be reminded, was not invited to Britain.[30] He had come to lecture and raise funds for the Anglo–Israeli appeal in aid of Jewish immigration to Israel.[31] In apologetic tones the memo went on to state that as Britain and Israel had diplomatic relations it was natural that Sharett should ask to see the Secretary of State and that Eden should agree to this.[32] Eden, however, did risk the further wrath of the Arab world by arranging a brief meeting between Sharett and the Prime Minister, Winston

Churchill.[33] Though, as Sharett commented in a thank-you note to Eden, his meeting with Churchill was so brief that he had no opportunity to mention the question of arms sales to Israel.[34]

At the meeting with Eden, Sharett employed different tactics from those used in previous meetings with his British counterpart when he brought up the issue of the supply of arms to Israel.[35] In referring to supplies that Israel had already ordered from Britain, Sharett argued that the guns and Mosquito aircraft for training were already obsolete and were no use to Britain, and therefore would the British Government not consider giving them to Israel for free or on some lease-lend basis or even long-term credit.[36] Not only did Israel want British weapons, it wanted some of them on them on the cheap. Israel was increasingly keen to sell equipment to the British Army. During the previous year a list of potential items for sale was drawn up, but as Sharett noted there had been little progress in developing this into orders.[37]

In truth, the Foreign Office was reluctant to authorize such orders.[38] The arguments put forward by it for 'this unhappy story' regarding the failure to buy from Israel were essentially economic in nature.[39] At the centre of this was the fact that a large number of goods offered by Israel consisted of textiles. In Britain, at the time, there was a severe recession in the British textile industries and resulting unemployment; Britain, as the Foreign Office put it, was far from being able to place new orders and was having to cancel old ones. In other words, Israel was not being discriminated against. A less ambitious scheme of allowing British Middle East Land Forces to make local purchases in Israel was also dropped when it transpired that this would amount to only around £50,000, and given the problems of inspection, customs and transit in Israel was deemed not to be worth pursuing.[40]

Though the British proved to be extremely reluctant to place orders with Israel, this did not stop the Middle Eastern rumour mill from circulating some extremely far-fetched gossip. One example of this was the meeting between A. D. Ross of the Foreign Office and the Syrian Ambassador to London on 16 May 1952.[41] The Syrian Ambassador claimed that an American firm was going to build a factory in Israel for the manufacturing of small parts for the British Army.[42] This was said to have been worked about in an agreement between Britain and Israel.[43] Ross was able to reassure the Syrian Ambassador that the British Government had found it impossible to discover any goods which Israel could supply and which Britain would want to order from it.[44]

In May 1952, the Foreign Office informed the Israelis that the British

Government would not be placing orders for any of the goods offered by them.[45] Any hope which the Israeli Government might have harboured about attempting to drive a wedge between the Foreign Office and the Ministry of Defence on the purchase of goods from Israel would have failed, as on this occasion at any rate the Ministry of Defence was in complete agreement with the Foreign Office decision. The Israelis, as a result, were officially informed of the decision on 25 June 1952.[46] Though Foreign Office officials were conscious of the fact that they were continually having to give negative answers to Israel, one official thought it not worthwhile bothering the Secretary of State with the wording of the Foreign Office's rejection of the Israeli request.[47] Given the length of time from the first proposal and the discussions of the idea of Israel selling to the British Army and the Foreign Office's reply, the Israeli Government was not surprised by the outcome of this decision.[48] Israel was naturally disappointed with the outcome but this was a sideshow to the pressing issue in Israel of tying to persuade the British Government to sell weapons to Israel and stop selling them to the Arabs, particularly Egypt.

Later that year, at the end of November and the start of December, A. D. Ross, the Head of the Eastern Department of the Foreign Office, extended a tour of the Arab capitals to include a couple of days in Israel.[49] In a testament to the open nature of Israeli political society, he commented that during his two days in Israel he met with more leading personalities in Israel than in any other country he visited during his trip. Though his meeting with Ben-Gurion was overshadowed by 'the Prague Trials', with which the Prime Minister was preoccupied, and speaking of little else, Ross held two important meetings with the Chief of Staff of the IDF and Sharett.[50]

Given Israel's increasing concern, in the wake of Egyptian revolution of July 1952, over the balance of arms in the Middle East, it would have come as little surprise to Ross when the Chief of Staff, General Yadin, launched into a long speech about the need for arms deliveries to Israel.[51] Echoing the theme put forward earlier in the year by Sharett, General Yadin called for Israel to be allowed to purchase war material on 'easy terms'.[52] If Britain was not willing to sell arms on the cheap to Israel it should, he argued, at the very least be willing to take part payment in the form of Israeli stores.[53] The Foreign Office's decision of 16 May on this issue had clearly not been taken as a final 'No' by the Chief of Staff. Furthermore, General Yadin warned Ross that he could expect more of the same on the arms issue from Sharett. Ross reported of his meeting with Sharett that the Foreign Minister had plunged straight into the question of British arms sales to the Arab states.[54] Sharett once more articulated the Israeli line that Britain should not sell fighter aircraft to the Arabs without insisting that the latter made peace with Israel.[55] Though Ross noted increased Israeli concerns on the arms issue when he returned to London, no change in British policy was introduced as the result of his visit.

An increasingly concerned Sharett, who was deeply irritated by what he saw as Britain's double standards in its policy of arms sales, released a detailed statement to the press that attempted to counter the arguments behind the British policy. Sharett argued that the present position was highly paradoxical.[56] The Arab states were being given arms by the Western powers for regional defence, but they still refused to shoulder the responsibilities for regional peace or agree to make peace with Israel.[57] The arms they received, as a result, were clearly for use against Israel, and not for the defence of the region. Moreover, Israel was being asked to ignore the resulting threat to its security.[58] Sharett went on to recommend that no arms be sold at all to the Arabs, but if it was considered necessary that arms must be given all round, then the fact that all the Arab countries were aligned together against Israel should be taken into account.[59] In other words, arms sales to all the Arab countries should be totalled together and a similar level of arms provided for Israel. In subsequent leader articles in Israeli newspapers, which British diplomats thought had the air of being officially inspired, Britain was reminded that the Arabs had given no assurances that they would co-operate in the defence of the Middle East, that Arab countries had no political coherence and that their regimes were for the most part irresponsible and undemocratic.[60] The articles went on to argue that Britain had for decades tried to build a defensive Middle East system on the basis of a special relationship with the Arab countries, but had received practically no return for the millions of pounds it had spent.[61]

The Foreign Office claimed to be surprised at Sharett's agitation on the subject.[62] By early January 1953, however, it was becoming increasingly frustrated with what it believed was an orchestrated campaign by the Israeli Government, and led by the Ministry of Affairs, against the supply of arms, particularly aircraft, to the Middle East.[63] In truth, since the middle of 1952 the British had been selling arms to all countries in the Middle East, in contrast to the United States who would only sell weapons within the framework of Western regional defence.[64] This fact naturally made British arms sales all the more important, along with the increasing level of export of arms from France. The Foreign Office continued to hold the key to British arms sales, all of which had to be approved by its offices, and was therefore the natural target of the Israeli campaign.

What lay behind the continued Israeli campaign, which was widely covered by the local media, were two major areas of concern. The first of these was that the British were fuelling an arms race in the Middle East for their own commercial purposes; in other words, they were endangering Middle East peace for their own selfish economic motives.[65] The second, and more important issue, was Israeli frustration that the British were only interested in selling to Israel obsolete military equipment that British forces no longer wanted, and indeed no other country wanted (the Israelis charged that the British had tried to first sell some of this equipment to countries in Latin America).[66] Central to this frustration was the question of the potential sale of Meteor jets to Israel, an aircraft that the Israeli considered to be nearly obsolete.[67] The Foreign Office responded in a typically robust manner, arguing that arms sales to the Middle East were to ensure that countries in the region would be able to defend themselves in the event of a major conflict, though they did accept that Britain was benefiting economically from the sale of arms to the region.[68] Facing an increasingly hostile Israeli Ambassador in London, officials at the Foreign Office suggested that, at a proposed meeting between the Ambassador and the Secretary of State, Eden should inform the Israelis that the deal to sell the jet aircraft to the Arabs was already finalized.[69] They also suggested reminding the Israelis of their belief that the sales of jet aircraft in no way constituted a risk to Israeli security.[70] That said, the Foreign Office admitted that relations between Israel and its neighbouring Arab states were deteriorating rather than improving, and that no progress had been made towards a peace settlement.[71]

Moving house to Jerusalem

During the course of 1952 another issue had arisen which caused great concern in the Foreign Office, largely because of its potential to destabilize Anglo–Arab relations. The proposed move of the Israeli Ministry of Foreign Affairs from Tel Aviv to Jerusalem raised questions as to whether the British, the Americans and other states, which still had their legations in Tel Aviv, should follow suit and move to Jerusalem. Sharett, naturally, defended the Israeli decision in purely logistical terms, arguing that the need for the move was caused by the difficulty that he and his senior staff had encountered in trying from Tel Aviv to keep in touch with the political developments in the Knesset and ministerial discussions in Jerusalem.[72] The decision, which was first put forward by the Israelis in the summer of 1952, was, of course, much more than a simple logistical one. Israelis were strongly committed to strengthening their hold on Jerusalem, which they believed was the external capital of the Jewish people. Britain, on the other hand, did not recognize Israeli sovereignty over the city. When it recognized the state of Israel *de jure* in 1950, the British Government clearly stated that it did not recognize Israeli sovereignty over any part of Jerusalem, though it would continue to recognize Israel's *de facto* authority in the part occupied by her unless or until the United Nations had established effective control there.[73]

For British diplomats and officials, anything to do with Jerusalem was a minefield in terms of appeasing Arab demands over Israeli actions in the city, and this proposed move to Jerusalem was a most unwelcome development. From a legal perspective the Foreign Office was informed that it would be perfectly possible to maintain Britain's refusal to recognize Israel's claim to sovereignty over the city even if the British Legation moved to Jerusalem.[74] In other words, there was no reason for the Foreign Office to oppose the move from the viewpoint of sovereignty or the United Nations (the internationalization of Jerusalem formed part of the original United Nations Partition Plan, which was passed by the General Assembly in November 1947). Officials concluded, however, that there might be an advantage in using the question of sovereignty as its rationale for opposing the Israeli move.[75] In reality, the issue of sovereignty provided a smokescreen for the real reason that the Foreign Office publicly opposed the move, the appeasement of the Arabs. As Ross concluded that if the British Government agreed to the move of the Israeli Ministry of Foreign Affairs to Jerusalem, and still more the move of HM Legation as well, it would be regarded in the Arab world as a sign of British partiality in favour of Israel and would be resented accordingly by them.[76] In private, Foreign Office officials, including the Permanent Under-Secretary, Sir William Strang, agreed with the policy put forward that Britain and the Western powers should make a joint effort to persuade the Israelis from making the move or, if that was not possible, to acquiesce.[77]

Much diplomatic gamesmanship followed during the summer of 1952. British officials in Tel Aviv grew increasingly concerned about the 'Wait-and-see' attitude of the Foreign Office, and wrote that they were extremely concerned that London was only going to make representations to the Israelis about the move after a very public series of approaches by the Arab Government to do so.[78] The Israeli Government responded to these approaches by announcing that it was speeding up the transfer of the Ministry to Jerusalem.[79] In the end, the Israelis moved to Jerusalem on 14 July 1953, but the American and the British retained their Legation in Tel Aviv.[80] The Arab missions in London all protested to the Foreign Office about the move, but officials there had the impression that much of the protest was 'for the record'.[81] The Foreign Office, which had kept the Arabs informed of its efforts to dissuade the Israelis, was largely not held to blame for Israel's actions by the Arab diplomats. At the time *The Economist* speculated as to whether the move was the last nail in the already sealed coffin of United Nations hopes for the creation of an international Jerusalem.[82] In retrospect, they were correct. The British initially adopted a 'wait-and-see' attitude to calculate the effect on its representations.[83] Over time this became permanent and both the British and Americans still have their embassies located in the Tel Aviv area, though the debate over the eventual moving of these missions to Jerusalem continues. The British Ambassador, Sir Francis Evans, commented at the time that Sharett appeared to be none too pleased that all the major foreign missions were located in a different city (Tel Aviv) from the Ministry of Foreign Affairs in Jerusalem.[84]

An increasingly sticky wicket

Border tensions between Israel and Jordan, as the Foreign Office termed them, dominated much of the attention of the Eastern Department of the Foreign Office in 1953. A series of Israeli raids into Jordanian territory had raised the diplomatic temperature, with the Foreign Office and Britain caught in the resulting crossfire. Sir John Glubb (Glubb Pasha), the British-born Commander of the Arab Legion, had been busy condemning the Israeli actions and looking for the most sinister explanations behind them.[85] Pasha had many friends and sympathizers in the Foreign Office and among British diplomats based in Arab countries, who were quick to defend his judgements and opinions against the charge of pro-Arab bias, as Furlonge suggested in a confidential communication from the British Embassy in Amman that Glubb was by no means blindly pro-Arab.[86] He understood the Arab mentality better than any European that Furlonge knew, and naturally he had much sympathy for the people among whom he had spent his life.[87] Furlonge went on to suggest that Pasha recognized their faults, and that his one desire was to do what he could for Jordan.[88] In reality, Glubb's polices on Israel differed from those of the Foreign Office. He did not favour direct negotiations with Israel to resolve the crisis.[89] Even on this issue there was much sympathy and understanding afforded to him as British diplomats argued that Glubb was of this opinion largely because he recognized the improbability of direct negotiations in view of the overwhelming strength of Jordanian public opinion against it.[90]

Glubb's comments in his report that 'the Jews, as a result of what they themselves have suffered, seem to find a psychological compensation in the arbitrary use of force against weaker people' illustrated his deep sense of suspicion of the Israelis.[91] He also cited the efficiency of the Israeli operations in Jordan, and claimed that Israel's influence in the press of the Western world was enough to keep the general public in ignorance of what was happening in Jordan.[92] The latter was a belief which, given the diverse nature of the Western press, was without much foundation, but was quite widely held among the Arab leadership at the time. The report concluded that Israel could have peace in a relatively short time if it made an attempt to reconcile with the Arabs, but that its ambition seemed to be rather to terrorize and dominate.[93] Strong words admittedly, but while it should be stressed that his opinions and policies were not those of the Foreign Office, he did enjoy influence in the Foreign Office and diplomatic circles. When this was taken together with his well-known prolific nature, he remained an important figure in framing British–Jordanian policy up to his sacking by King Hussein as Commander of the Arab League on 1 March 1956.[94]

Israeli frustrations about the border incidents did not go unnoticed in the Foreign Office. The British Ambassador, Sir Francis Evans, noted that conditions on Israel's frontiers had worsened despite the introduction of arrangements that were designed to improve them.[95] Infiltration for the motives of murder, robbery and smuggling had continued to harass Israeli border settlements and this had led the Israeli Government to adopt what he termed a policy of armed raids into Jordan, which also led to civilian death on the Jordanian side of the border.[96] The Ambassador speculated that the Israeli raids, which had culminated in a particularly bloody one in mid-October in the Jordanian village of Kibya (Quibya), and tried to resolve its deadlock with the Arabs by forcing the United Nations to intervene to apply pressure on Jordan to come to at least a partial agreement with Israel.[97] Given the strong international condemnation of Israel's actions, this tactic, if the Ambassador's analysis of Israeli thinking was correct, failed quite miserably.

To complicate matters further, Ben-Gurion, far from being on the defensive with the British over the raids, argued that British officers of the Arab Legion encouraged or incited the raids from Jordan into Israel.[98] The Prime Minister also wondered why the Arab Legion was always on training manoeuvres on Jordan's eastern border rather than policing its frontier with Israel.[99] Put simply, both the Foreign Office and the Israeli Government accepted for very different reasons that the situation on the Israeli–Jordanian border was harming Anglo–Israeli relationships.

Au revoir to the old man and hello to Mr Moderation

It was widely presumed in the Foreign Office that the Israeli Prime Minister and Defence Minister, Ben-Gurion, was the driving force behind its policy of retaliation. Officials had concluded for some time that little of importance happened in Israel without Ben-Gurion's knowledge and support. For this reason, and the fact that many officials viewed Ben-Gurion as an increasing obstacle to improved Anglo–Israeli relations and to a peaceful resolution of the wider Arab–Israeli conflict, few in the Foreign Office were sad to see the back of the Israeli Prime Minister; albeit, they suspected, on a sabbatical rather than full retirement.[100] The Israeli Prime Minister had submitted his resignation to the President on 7 December 1953. Before he departed, however, Ben-Gurion had left several of his own people in key positions. Perhaps the most important of these appointments was that of Moshe Dayan as Israeli's Chief of Staff, which was made the day before Ben-Gurion's resignation. General Dayan was one of Israel's bright young minds, but he owed his position to the patronage of Ben-Gurion.

Central to the Foreign Office's hope in the wake of Ben-Gurion's departure was that the new Prime Minister, Moshe Sharett, would pursue a more moderate foreign policy. They hoped, in short, that Sharett, with all his experience in foreign affairs, would make diplomacy rather than defence, as Evans put it, 'the favoured child in the family of national requirements'.[101]

It was quite natural that the Foreign Office should therefore view Ben-Gurion's departure as an opportune moment to attempt to improve Anglo–Israeli relations, and make renewed efforts to induce Israel and its neighbours to resolve their conflict. Sharett was widely seen in the Foreign Office as the most moderate Prime Minister that Israel was likely to choose.[102] Officials, however, were acutely aware that Sharett's position was much weaker than Ben-Gurion's and was likely to come under rapid threat if he was not able to deliver tangible results quickly.[103] Sharett, they noted, did not enjoy any degree of political loyalty from the

Kibbutzim, the Trade Unions Federation (Histadrut) or crucially from the armed services and defence establishment.[104] Consequently, senior Foreign Office officials concluded that it was in Britain's interests to do whatever it could to strengthen Sharett's hand against the extremists (who they believed would take over if Sharett fell).[105]

There was, however, the usual sting in the tail for Israel. The Foreign Office was worried about offering some form of economic inducement to the new Israeli Government in the form of direct capital transfers, for the usual two reasons.[106] The first was that, as they concluded, any improvement in the United Kingdom's relationship with Israel (economic or cultural) would seriously damage its standing in the Arab world.[107] The second concerned questions as to whether Britain had the money to strengthen Sharett's hand.[108] One political and one economic reason, but it is clear that the political fears of an Arab backlash were uppermost in the minds of Foreign Office officials.

There remained little doubt about what help Sharett wanted from the British. In addition to capital and help in securing cheaper oil, the major Israeli demand remained arms sales. The higher level of arms sales to Arab states than to Israel by Britain continued to be a bitter bone of contention in Anglo–Israeli relations.[109] It soon emerged, however, that the Foreign Office was thinking in terms of minor ways in which the British Government could support the new Sharett-led government rather than anything of a more substantial nature such as a major arms release to Israel. Once again, the reason behind this was the Foreign Office's belief that when they made gestures towards Israel they had to take into account Arab susceptibilities, which they admitted were unlikely to change in the near future.[110] The Foreign Office, as a result, would not be seen to help prop up Sharett, despite the widely held belief that he was good news for Anglo–Israeli relations and for the prospects of peace in the Middle East. In retrospect, this was a missed opportunity by the Foreign Office, but it remains questionable, given developments in the Middle East, whether Sharett would have had a long-term future even with a greater show of British support.

During the spring of 1954 the Israelis were becoming ever more concerned about the supply (or in its case the non-supply) of weapons to the Middle East. Israel's nervousness was not without good cause owing to the possibility of a British withdrawal from Egypt, the promise of military aid to Iraq by the United States and by the fact that the Americans had not responded to the Israeli request for military aid.[111] In a meeting on 12 May 1954 with Ian Kirkpatrick in the Foreign Office, the

Israeli Ambassador, Elath, inflicted an hour-long monologue on his unsuspecting official about Israel's deep concern about the deteriorating situation in the Middle East.[112] Kirkpatrick concluded afterwards that he had dared not say anything until the moment came to utter the word 'Goodbye'.[113] In the months that followed things went from bad to worse from an Israeli perspective. The agreement with Egypt over Britain's Suez was dominating the Israeli agenda. Britain had lifted an arms embargo on Egypt, though the Foreign Office somewhat defensively pointed out that there was no question of Egypt being treated as a privileged customer – it must pay for the arms it wanted.[114] On the other hand, sales to Israel were still assessed on a deal-by-deal basis.[115]

Given the Israeli belief that the strategic balance of the Middle East was turning against it, specifically in the arena of the arms race, it came as little surprise to the Foreign Office that Israeli officials were on a diplomatic offensive to secure more weapons from Britain. Gazit from the Israeli Embassy arrived at the Foreign Office for a meeting with Ivone Fitzpatrick on 16 September 1954 to talk about specific arms sales to Israel.[116] Gazit enquired whether the Foreign Office had come to a decision about the Israeli request to buy two frigates from Britain.[117] When the Foreign Office stalled, Gazit reminded it that Israel was also considering asking the French and the Italians about the possibility of buying similar types of ships from them.[118] Gazit went on remind Fitzpatrick that since the Egyptians already had the much sought-after Centurion tank then it appeared logical that in order to maintain the balance of power in the Middle East, the British should agree to the Israeli request to sell it ten tanks. A somewhat irate Fitzpatrick was quick to remind the Israelis that arms sales were regulated by the principles of the Tripartite Statement. Gazit was rather unconvinced, arguing that they appeared to be regulated in a much more arbitrary manner [anti-Israeli manner].[119] Though this was just one of many meetings between Foreign Office and Israeli officials, the frosty tone of it said much about the increasing tensions in Anglo–Israeli relations. Kirkpatrick had concluded the meeting on the issue of Israel's retaliation raid, the Foreign Office's major bone of contention with Israel. He told Gazit that he did not think that it was necessary for Israel to shoot Arab boys swimming in pools near the Israeli–Jordanian frontier in order to establish Israel's claim to its present frontiers.[120]

On the completion of his tour of his duty in Israel, the British Ambassador, Sir Francis Evans, noted to the Foreign Office how Anglo–Israeli relations during his three years in the post had remained static.[121] This assessment was, in retrospect, a fair and accurate one of the development of Anglo–Israeli relations.[122] Evans accepted that he had been unable to build on the foundations of his predecessor, Sir Know Helm, and develop Britain's restraining influence over Israel.[123] The tone of his report was generally sympathetic to Israel and he concluded with a warning that if more wasn't done to support Sharett, then those within the Israeli Cabinet who favoured the use of strong methods against the Arabs would defeat Sharett and his allies who were in favour of a policy of restraint.[124] He concluded by arguing that this static nature was dangerous and that some forward movement was necessary. As he put it, 'movement calculated to reassure, to demonstrate friendship and understanding, and to relax Israel's tension insofar as it is the product of a feeling of isolation'.[125]

In truth, as the Ambassador departed Tel Aviv, the relationship between the Foreign Office and Israel was in trouble. Israeli fears and suspicions about the sale of arms to the Arabs, and the reluctance of the Foreign Office to authorize similar sales to Israel, meant that this issue dominated much of the Israeli diplomatic agenda. For the British the Egyptian revolution and the arrival of President Nasser presented new challenges. When taken together with the increasing penetration of the Soviet Union into the region, this made the Arabs once again strategically extremely important to British and Western interests in the Middle East. The ongoing tension between Israel and Jordan over border infiltrations and retaliatory raids was of great concern for Foreign Office officials, many of whom were growing tired of their failure to restrain Israel from taking such actions. The minutes of diplomatic meetings during this period, as a result, were dominated by these three issues: arms, Egypt and Israeli–Jordanian tensions.

The Foreign Office was acutely aware that it was saying 'No' to Israel more often than not, but to its credit it did try to do whatever it could to ease relations with Israel with the proviso that such actions would not damage its relations with the Arab world. Could the Foreign Office have done more to help support Sharett at this stage? The answer is probably 'Yes', but they simply felt unable to offer any more than minor help for fear of upsetting the Arabs. By the time the Foreign Office, together with the State Department in the United States, did launch a major secret diplomatic initiative to resolve the Arab–Israeli conflict, starting in earnest at the beginning of 1955, it was probably already too late. Operation Alpha, the name given to this initiative, was in retrospect too late and, as we shall see, almost certainly doomed to failure from the start.

3

The road to Suez and beyond

> The centre of the infection in the region is Israel and I believe that we must treat the Israelis as a sick people. Their illness is psychological. Almost every individual Israeli bears some psychological trace of the past 2,500 years of Jewish history: unsureness, over-confidence, emotional instability, fierce intolerance, superiority complex, inferiority complex, guilt complex – one or more of these characterizes most Israelis, and there is invariably added a deep conviction that the world is in their debt. It is not reasonable to expect that a nation made up of individuals so psychologically unstable should be capable of a mature foreign policy.[1]
>
> Sir John Nicholls, British Ambassador to Tel Aviv, 8 March 1955

The period of Anglo–Israeli relations from 1955 until the end of 1958 remains one of the most fascinating in recent British diplomatic history. Within a relatively short period of time the Foreign Office's world was turned upside down by the anti-imperialist polices of President Abdul Gamal Nasser in Egypt, the resulting threat to British interests in the Suez Canal Zone which led to the Suez Crisis and eventually to the Suez War of 1956. Back in 1955, the very idea that British and Israeli national interests would align themselves, along with France, the other European power in the Middle East, to an extent that together they would collude to plan and launch a war together against Egypt would have appeared ridiculous. Certainly any Foreign Office official who predicted such a scenario would have been dismissed as mad and dispatched to faraway lands where they could recover their senses.

The Suez War remains an almost universally accepted disaster for Britain and its interests in the Middle East. Questions remain, however, as to what extent Suez was a turning point for British interests in the region. On balance, it is fair to say that the decline of Britain and its Empire had its origins in the Second World War. As a confidential internal Foreign Office report concluded: 'Mainly as a result of the [Second World] War, Britain no longer has military and economic resources to spare sufficient to guarantee, by themselves, that British interests in the Middle East are maintained and British policy is accepted there.'[2] The Suez War to some extent speeded up this decline, and perhaps more importantly served as a wake-up call to those remaining British officials, many of who staffed the Near Eastern and North Africa Department at the Foreign Office, that British power and influence was in a slow, but unalterable, decline. This decline, however, was not as spectacular or rapid as many people suggest. Though, following Suez, Britain and France were largely replaced by the United States and the Soviet Union as the two dominant outside powers in the Middle East, Britain still retained strong national interests in the region and was not completely without influence, though over time this influence became more related to Britain's close ties with the United States.

For the Foreign Office the Suez War was an even greater disaster. Not only did its outcome cause severe damage to the Foreign Office's defined British national interests in the Middle East, it was a war that was planned in great secrecy, and in which the Foreign Office was largely excluded from the decision-making process. The fact that the main driver for the war was the Prime Minister of the day, Anthony Eden, whom the Foreign Office regarded as one of their own, made matters all the more difficult to swallow.

The Foreign Office, as we shall see, initially struggled to come to terms with the changed post-Suez strategic world, and this was to a large degree reflected in its continued difficulties with Israel. These difficulties were compounded by the fact that the expectations of the Israeli Government and its people, in terms of Anglo–Israeli relations, were raised by Suez. When, during the post-Suez months, the Foreign Office resorted to attempting to pursue what amounted to pre-Suez polices towards Israel, particularly in the area of arms sales, there was a great deal of bitterness and resentment in Israel. This feeling was felt beyond Ben-Gurion and his circle of advisers and reached the Israeli Ministry of Foreign Affairs, the Foreign Office's main point of reference in Israel. It was not until 1958 that Anglo–Israeli relations settled down and became warmer and more productive.

Put simply, the 1956 Suez War had little strategic impact on Anglo–Israeli relations, and specifically on the attitude of the British Foreign Office towards Israel. This was the case even in the immediate aftermath of the collusion and the war. It is worth briefly outlining the defining characteristics of Anglo–Israeli relations, and the attitude of the Foreign Office towards Israel, in the period leading up to the 1956 war – making reference to the key area of arms sales by the British Government to the Middle East. Subsequently, it is important to also look at the period from the end of the war until 1958 in more detail, illustrating the various tensions and thaws in relations during this period. At the centre of these tensions in Anglo–Israeli relations was the Foreign Office, whose policies towards Israel and the Arab–Israeli conflict continued to be viewed with much suspicion in Israel – not least by the Israeli Prime Minister, David Ben-Gurion.

From alpha to omega

The idea of a joint American–British diplomatic initiative to resolve the Arab–Israeli conflict was first floated in the Foreign Office in early November 1954.[3] The Foreign Office argued that unless the British and the Americans developed and applied a joint policy aimed at easing tensions and bringing about a permanent settlement, the situation on the ground could only be expected to go from bad to worse.[4] The model for the initiative that the Foreign Office had in mind was Trieste. In that instance, the British and Americans had worked closely together with the aim of reconciling a complex dispute between countries with whom Britain and the US had a degree of influence.[5] American reaction to the British proposals was favourable so full-scale planning started.[6] The US Secretary of State, John Foster Dulles, was generally sympathetic and argued that as the exercise would in all likelihood be a long one it was all the more important to begin soon.[7]

From the outset of Operation Alpha, the name given to the initiative, secrecy was deemed to be of great importance. The main architect of the plan in London, Evelyn Shuckburgh, argued that the Arabs should be kept in the dark, at least until the British and Americans had agreed upon the outline of the plan.[8] Rather unsurprisingly given what was to follow, the Permanent Under-Secretary in the Foreign Office added that all efforts should be made to prevent a leakage to the Israelis as well.[9] The methodology for the plan was agreed in a meeting between Eden and Dulles in Paris on 16 December 1954. At the meeting, Eden and Dulles confirmed the importance of absolute secrecy (the French were also to be kept in the dark), and that once the details of the plan for a settlement had been devised they would be tried out first on Israel.[10] They also concluded that it would be essential to devise a cover story in case there was some speculation as to what they were doing together.[11] Later it was agreed that the initial contacts would take place in Washington as the arrival of US State Department experts in Israel and Arab affairs would no go unnoticed in London.[12]

Evelyn Shuckburgh outlined the first draft of the framework of the plan on 15 December 1954. The thinking behind the plan was that the time was ripe for a settlement between the Israelis and the Arabs for a number of reasons. Shuckburgh did not accept that the status quo between the parties in the region was maintainable.[13] Israel, as a result, would have to be asked to make territorial concessions in return for assurances and guarantees about its security from the major powers.[14] The framework document concluded that, in private, both the Israelis and the front-line Arab states, as well as the Palestinians, all accepted that there was a need for a negotiated solution. The problem, however, as Shuckburgh correctly identified, was that many of these leaders were extremely weak.[15] Sadly, those Arab states that bordered Israel (with the exception of Egypt) who had the most to gain for a settlement had leaders who, given Arab public hostility to Israel, might not survive (politically or even physically) reaching a settlement with Israel. The relative weakness of Sharett in Israel was again commented upon with the belief that Ben-Gurion was waiting in the background for an opportune time to return.[16] Interestingly, Shuckburgh noted a feeling of war-weariness among the Arabs, and particularly among the Palestinians, that could induce them to the table.[17]

Among the many actions that were required in the meantime was the need, according to Shuckburgh, to talk up the threat of communism to the region and strengthen British presence in the Middle East so as to make it appear a viable guarantor of agreements and to make no further concessions to pressure from either the Arabs or the Israelis. In terms of arms supplies it was suggested that there should be agreement not to supply the Arabs with any more weapons beyond what was already promised and to strictly limit supplies to Israel as well.[18] In terms of a proposed settlement the proposal made it clear that Israel would have to make some significant territorial concessions in exchange for peace.[19] The concept of land for peace was born, and has dominated the methodology of Middle Eastern peacemaking efforts to the present day.

Foreign Office officials did not universally welcome the plans for a diplomatic initiative. Sir John Sterndale-Bennett wrote to Shuckburgh outlining his fears that the time was not ripe for a genuine and lasting peace settlement.[20] He accepted that the parameters of a deal were clear to see, if the all the parties were reasonable, but concluded that there was little sign of either party being able to make the necessary concessions to make it work.[21] The issue of leaders being able to deliver the concessions needed to implement a deal and survive politically became a major factor in Middle East peacemaking, not least during the years of the Oslo Accords between the Israelis and the Palestinians.

The efforts of the Foreign Office and the State Department to bring about a settlement between Israel and Egypt (the cornerstone of Operation Alpha) eventually came to nothing.[22] The prognosis of Sterndale-Bennett proved to be the correct one. Neither Egyptian nor Israeli leaders could be enticed, or even coerced, into making the significant concessions required to make the plan work. Operation Alpha, as a result, never really went beyond the stage of talks about talks. The failure happened despite the efforts of Eden and Dulles, who both made public statements aimed at bringing the parties together. Even strong American pressure on Israel to make some territorial concessions in the Negev so as to create territorial continuity between Egypt and Jordan failed.[23]

After the initial failures Operation Alpha was given a last chance in 1956 when President Eisenhower dispatched a special emissary, Robert Anderson, to try to arrange a secret meeting between the Israeli Prime Minister and President Nasser. Anderson's mediation efforts involved close ties with the CIA and were known under the code name of Gamma.[24] Anderson's missions collapsed in March 1956 when the Egyptian leader refused to enter into direct negotiations with the Israeli representatives. The failure of the Anderson mission led to a hardening of attitude by both Great Britain and the United States against the Egyptian leader. From this point on, the State Department shifted its focus away from Alpha to a new plan that was given the name Omega. Central to this new plan was the aim to undermine and try to isolate the pro-Soviet Egyptian regime. This pursuit of this plan was one of the many reasons for the deteriorating Egyptian relationship with the Western powers that led to the Suez Crisis and subsequent war later that year.[25]

Putting the jigsaw together

Though Operation Alpha failed, it remains an important factor in understanding the relationship between the Foreign Office and Israel in 1955–56. The one aspect of the operation that could be deemed to have been successful was the question of secrecy. It was not until the 1980s, when Evelyn Shuckburgh published his diaries, that details of the operation started to emerge.[26] With the release of documents into the British Public Records archives and the State Department archives under the 30-year rule during the mid-1980s the full story of Operation Alpha became clear. In terms of the figures of the day in the Middle East, certain parts of the plan were revealed to them during the course of the doomed operation, but none of them held all the pieces of the jigsaw. Personalities such as the Israeli Ambassador to London, Eliahu Elath, suspected the existence of Operation Alpha but were kept in the dark about its actual existence. The issue of who also suspected what and when is extremely relevant to understanding the events of 1955–56. In terms of Foreign Office attitudes and policies towards Israel during this period, it is clear that it was largely governed by the framework of Operation Alpha, particularly in two key areas of Israeli's final borders and British arms sales to the region.

The thorny question of arms sales to the Arab world was brought into focus for the Foreign Office by the sale of Soviet military equipment to Egypt, known as the Czech arms deal, on 27 September 1955. Under the terms of the five-year agreement the Soviet Union agreed to supply weapons to Israel at bargain prices in return for Egyptian cotton and to also provide advisers and instructors to train the Egyptian armed forces in the use of the equipment. The arms deal shifted the strategic balance of the Middle East in favour of the Arabs, a fact that was not lost on the Israeli Government.

To a large degree, these arms sales removed any leverage that the Foreign Office had been able to exert over Egypt and given the Soviet willingness to sell to other Arab countries, as well as to the Arabs in general.[27] As Shuckburgh argued that the Russians had found a new way of breaking into the area.[28] The Russians, he suggested, had put their finger on the central weakness of the British position in the Middle East, the existence of Israel as a protégé of the West.[29] He went on to conclude that as Israel lay at the heart of the Middle East problem, efforts to reach a settlement between it and the Arabs were the only way out of Britain's growing problems with Egypt.[30] This served as a reminder to his colleagues of the importance of Operation Alpha. Worryingly for Israel, however, he argued that if such a settlement proved impossible then some form of abandonment of Israel would be the only alternative to the loss of Middle East oil.[31] The question of oil was, as ever, very much at the forefront of Foreign Office thinking. Fitzpatrick saw the Soviet move in terms of a deliberate attempt to open up a third front against British oil interests in the Middle East.[32]

Paying with Israeli currency: the Guildhall speech

In retrospect the Czech arms deal should have marked the admission of failure of Operation Alpha and the move towards a more hostile strategy towards Egypt. It did not. Evelyn Shuckburgh remained convinced that Operation Alpha did not offer any significant concessions to the Arabs and it would therefore be either dismissed or, if presented formally to the Egyptians, rejected by Nasser. Shuckburgh, as a result, recommended to Anthony Eden, who had succeeded Winston Churchill as Prime Minister on 7 April, that he mention the fact that the 1947 boundaries should be a factor in the settlement of the Arab–Israeli conflict.[33] In the Prime Minister's annual Foreign policy speech at the Lord Mayor's Banquet at the Guildhall on 9 November 1955, Eden subsequently called for a compromise to be reached between the Armistice agreements positions of 1949 and Arab demands that Israel resort back to the borders outlined by the United Nations in 1947. It came as little surprise that the majority of the Arab world welcomed the speech. The Israeli Government, on the other hand, was furious and the speech soured Anglo–Israeli relations for much of the following three years (with the exception of the period of the Suez War).

On the surface it appeared that the Foreign Office was bowing to the pressure of being willing to retain its influence in the Arab world at the expense of the Israelis. In the case of Egypt it was a hopeless case. Nasser's anti-imperialist rhetoric was popular with the Egyptian population and he showed no signs of either bowing to British pressure or being sucked in by British inducements. The Soviets had helped transform the Egyptian Army into the most powerful of the Arab armed forces and Egypt was very much in its sphere of influence. The Arabs, it appeared, had discovered their strong man and Nasser's popularity was not by this stage restricted to Egypt. Here was a leader who had stood up to the British and had an army that challenged Israel's military supremacy in the region.

In Israel, secret contacts authorized by Prime Minister Sharett and President Nasser had been quickly terminated by an allegedly rogue Israeli intelligence plot to bomb Egyptian cinemas.[34] The aim of the plotters in this murky affair had been to destabilize British–Egyptian relations. The subsequent trial and hanging of some of the perpetrators of the bombing in Egypt caused a public outcry in Israel whose population remained ignorant of the guilt of the operation. The conditions were ripe for the return of Ben-Gurion who, after a brief and bloody power struggle with Moshe Sharett, returned to lead Israel. Much of the thinking behind Operation Alpha had been based on dealing with the more moderate Sharett. Ben-Gurion, with his suspicions about the Foreign Office seemingly confirmed by the Guildhall speech, was in little mood for any British diplomatic initiatives. What Ben-Gurion wanted was British arms, both the release of those already promised but not yet delivered and the acceptance of new orders, particularly for aircraft and modern tanks. And on this issue the Foreign Office had not been particularly forthcoming, and even after the Czech arms deal became public still remained reluctant to commit arms to Israeli for fear of pushing other Arab countries into the Soviet camp.

In truth, the arms issue was always going to cause trouble. Israel continued at every opportunity to accuse the British of discriminating against Israel in this key area. To be fair, the Foreign Office did agree to the supply of some weapons to Israel, but not many. At the same time, Israel charged that Britain was supplying Jordan and Iraq with modern weapons (under the terms of its treaties with both countries). Moreover, in the previous year of 1954, the UK also supplied Nasser and Egypt with some 32 Centurion tanks and 45 aircraft and other weapons. Admittedly, in 1955 Britain did supply Israel with 20 Sherman tanks, but crucially the Foreign Office went back on an earlier promise to supply it with the heavy Centurion tanks, which were the tanks that Israel really wanted. Statistics would appear to confirm the imbalance in arms sales. For example, the arms shipment to Nasser in 1955 from the UK was more than the total arms sold to Israel by the UK for the previous seven years (1948–55).[35]

In simple terms, the policy of the Foreign Office was based on the logic that if the UK armed Israel then it would be surrounded by Arab states armed to the teeth. In other words, the British Government would be pressurized by the Arab states to sell more arms to them if they sold additional weapons to Israel. In reality, there was no policy of arming Israel to reach comparable standards with the Arabs. Despite this, the Foreign Office believed that Israel had enough weapons to defend itself against any Arab attack (either on single or multiple fronts). On a deeper level, it is impossible to separate the issue of arms sales to both the Arabs and the Israelis from Operation Alpha. Arms sales were one of the major carrots or inducements that the British believed they could employ. In Israel's case, however, promises of arms were sometimes made that were simply not kept. It was only after Nasser failed to co-operate with efforts to reach an accord with the UK did the Foreign Office argue for the limited release of arms to Israel which the Foreign Office decreed were necessary for Israel's defence. It also encouraged Israel, however, to buy arms from countries such as Canada, which had previously supplied it.

From disillusionment to hostility

The severe decline in the state of Anglo–Israeli relations that had taken place in 1955 was reflected in the Annual Review of Israel for 1955, which was prepared by the British Ambassador, Sir John Nicholls.[36] Overall, Nicholls concluded that all the positive signs of 1954 regarding Anglo–Israeli relations had been reversed in 1955.[37] Nicholls outlined the previously discussed stages of Operation Alpha that had been instigated over the year, but admitted that it was the arms issue that was causing the greatest damage to Anglo–Israeli relations. Though Operation Alpha retained its secrecy, the fallout from the co-ordinated Anglo–US action had the effect of bringing it home to the Israelis that its quest for defence pacts with either Britain or the United States that would guarantee its present boundaries had failed.[38] Equally worryingly for the Israelis, it was also becoming clear that its quest for Western arms in order to defend these boundaries was also about to fail.[39] Nicholls conceded that during the year the Israelis had made no significant addition to their armed strength except for the purchase of some 50 obsolete Sherman tanks (the Israelis, remember, wanted the Centurion tank), some light tanks, artillery and Outragen fighters supplied by France.[40] This was in contrast to the arms supplied to Egypt under the terms of the Czech arms agreement, the arms supplied by Britain and the United States to Iraq, and the British tanks and equipment sent to Egypt under existing contracts.[41]

Any sense of sympathy for the Israeli predicament, however, was lost on Nicholls. He argued that it was no flight of fancy to suggest that Israel, by its attack in Gaza on February 1955, was itself responsible for Egypt's decision in August to accept communist arms; and, by the same token, it was the irresponsible Israeli Kinneret raid in December which destroyed Israel's chances of acquiring counter-balancing arms from the West.[42] In other words, in the world according to Nicholls, the hot-heads in Israel were to blame for its weakened position. His comments, however, failed to take into account that the question of limited arms sales was part of Operation Alpha, a plan that Nicholls had full knowledge of and indeed refers to in his many dispatches to London (though not by its official name). In retrospect, Nicholls, in suggesting that Israeli actions had pushed both Nasser and the Western powers over the limit, was probably merely indulging in a bit of pure and simple Israeli-bashing.

Naturally, the Israelis did not blame themselves for the shift in the balance of arms in the Middle East. As Israeli leaders had no knowledge of Operation Alpha, they pointed the finger at the Foreign Office, not only for the failure of Britain to sell arms to Israel, but also for the unwillingness of the United States to meet Israel's requests for arms. Following the Guildhall speech, Nicholls conceded, things went from bad to worse, with the Israelis believing that British policy towards them was deliberately antagonistic. One of the strongest believers in this argument was Ben-Gurion, who, as Nicholls noted, like many Israelis, believed that Britain wanted either the whole or part of the Negev transferred to Jordan for British military purposes.[43] This suspicion further complicated Anglo–Israeli relations during the period of Operation Alpha.

It would be wholly unfair, and an exaggeration of his importance, to place the blame over the deterioration of Anglo–Israeli relations squarely on the shoulders of Nicholls. That said, Nicholls appeared not to be particularly sensitive, or indeed sympathetic, to the fears of the Israeli leadership, most of whom he appeared to regard with a degree of contempt, not least Ben-Gurion. Nicholls, two predecessors in the admittedly difficult role of the British Ambassador to Israel, the Scottish-born Sir Knox Helms and the Northern Irish-born Sir Francis Evans, appear to have at least brought some Celtic charm to the role.[44] Nicholls' comments, made in an official dispatch to London, that the Israelis were a sick people, remains totally out of order, as do some of his other observations. Nicholls, however, was given perhaps the most difficult of hands to play given the attempts of both the Foreign Office and State Department to pursue a diplomatic solution with Operation Alpha. A major part of Alpha was aimed at coercing Israel into making territorial concessions that its leaders were not only reluctant to undertake on grounds of Israeli national security, but also because they felt that the hand of the Foreign Office's attempts to strengthen Britain's position in Jordan were behind them. The best and fairest assessment of Nicholls' performance would be that he didn't help improve matters very much in terms of Britain's relationship with Israel, but neither was he a crucial factor in their seeming decline before the collusion over the Suez War in the autumn and early winter of 1956.

The road to the unexpected collusion

At the start of 1956 there were a number of concerns in the Foreign Office that the Middle East was not falling into shape quite as had been hoped. The Baghdad Pact had succeeded in creating a strong defence line from Turkey to Pakistan, but as Foreign Office officials noted, it lacked any depth.[45] Efforts were to be renewed to bring other Arab states into the pact.[46] There was a deep sense of frustration in the Foreign Office that previous efforts to broaden the pact had been, as they argued, checked by Egyptian and Saudi diplomacy and bribery, by veiled French opposition, by an American attitude that had seemed at times like equivocation.[47] The rift between Cairo and Baghdad was becoming wider, and the Foreign Office wanted one last throw of the dice to try to entice the Egyptians back from the brink of their increasingly anti-British and pro-Soviet orientation.[48]

Anglo–Israeli relations continued to be directly impacted by these attempts by the Foreign Office. Israeli officials tried a new tactic to prise weapons out of the British. Officials concluded that the major stumbling block for the British selling arms to Israel was not the Tripartite Declaration or any such diplomatic agreement, but rather fear of how to meet Arab complaints about anything that was delivered to Israel. In a meeting with Foreign Office officials, Gazit from the Israeli Embassy suggested a novel approach to the problem: sell the arms to Israel secretly.[49] If the Israelis had hoped to tempt the British out of their shelter of the Tripartite Agreement, their tactics failed as the British refused Israelis promises of getting total secrecy.[50] Even when Gazit argued that the British were selling arms to its friends in the Arab world (Jordan and Iraq), which the Foreign Office concluded that the Israelis did not appear to object to in principle, the British were also very anxious to supply Egypt.[51] Given Nasser's increasing anti-Britishness, this policy made no strategic sense to the Israelis other than being another example of the British appeasement of Nasser. Israeli frustrations, as a result, were running high.

If all this wasn't bad enough for Israel, the British Prime Minister, Anthony Eden, called for a Cabinet debate on the suspension of all arms deliveries to Israel following Israeli–Syrian border incidents and operations.[52] Even Nicholls in Tel Aviv concluded that a public decision to suspend the supply of weapons to Israel would not be a prudent course of action as it might have a serious effect on the willingness of the Israelis to negotiate a peace settlement.[53] In retrospect, this debate illustrated the simple fact at the start of 1956 that when Egypt under Nasser undertook actions that the Foreign Office regarded as anti-British, it provided it with more inducements. When Israel undertook military operations that threatened the British aim of bringing in more Arab countries into its defence framework, there were calls for it to be punished.

The Israeli Ambassador in London made the extent of the decline in

Anglo–Israeli relations clear to the British. The Ambassador, whom Foreign Office officials had noted was becoming 'ever more emotional', stated that Britain had thrown away all its sympathy by Anthony Eden's Guildhall speech and its refusal to sell arms to Israel.[54] Regarding the latter, Shuckburgh evaded answering the Ambassador's questions on the issue.[55]

At a meeting with Secretary of State Selwyn Lloyd, who on 20 December 1955 had replaced Harold Macmillan, on 6 April 1956 the Ambassador went straight to the point. He confirmed that what Israel really wanted from the British was the Centurion tanks.[56] The existing, unfulfilled Israeli order was for 30 tanks. The Israelis, however, now wanted to up the stakes and place an order for 50 Centurions.[57] Elath appealed to what he understood the Foreign Office knew and understood most, namely that it was in the British interests to give Israel the tanks. The Ambassador outlined the argument in detail; at its centre was the apparent Israeli belief that Egypt would not dare attack Israel if it was confronted by the same levels of armour that it had.[58] It was in the British interests to prevent a war as it would be drawn into the war and therefore every deterrent to Nasser should be provided.[59] The only winners if war were to break out would be the Soviet Union.[60] In Israel, the sale of the weapons would lead to a return of self-confidence and the Ambassador predicted that his renewed self-confidence would be accompanied by self-control. In other words, the Ambassador proudly proclaimed that for the first time British and Israeli interests marched together. Lloyd responded by arguing that if Centurions were sold to Israel it would not remain a secret for long. This, he conceded, might possibly have a good effect on Egypt, but it would have a disastrous effect in Iraq and Jordan.[61] In other words, despite the fact that the British now appeared quite willing to give up on Nasser, they were too worried about the rest of the Arab world to comply with Israel's request for the tanks it needed.

In Israel, the press were becoming increasingly hostile to Britain.[62] Not only were the British being blamed by Israeli editorial writers for the troubles in the Middle East, they were also seen as egging on the United States to adopt an anti-Israeli policy.[63] As the Israeli press did not have any knowledge of Operation Alpha, the British were blamed for preventing the Americans from becoming Israel's best friend. The arguments were usually taken a step further to suggest that the source of this anti-Israeli policy was the pro-Arab school in the Foreign Office and the Prime Minister.[64] Nicholls argued for a policy of sit tight, that there wasn't much that could be done to correct these trends in the Israeli press. As he put it: 'in the fullness of time, America would resume its position as the chief nigger in the wood pile'.[65] The Foreign Office did not appear unduly worried about the state of affairs in Israel. As an official argued, whether or not Britain is popular in Israel is purely incidental.[66] He went on to confirm that from the point of view of Britain's real interests, which lie in the Arab states rather than in Israel, there is a lot to be said for being unpopular.[67]

By April of the same year, however, Nicholls had changed his tune. Given that the Israelis had come to the conclusion that their long quest to acquire arms from the United States appeared at a dead end, the Ambassador suggested that the time was right for a small gesture towards Israel.[68] The French, Nicholls concluded, were trying to put themselves on the map in the Middle East, but they were not taken very seriously except as a minor source of arms supply.[69] At the end of the decade, the French would become a major supplier of arms to Israel and this was reflected in Franco–Israeli relations. In 1956, however, it was Britain that Israel looked towards for its salvation.[70]

By April 1956, the Foreign Office was internally discussing the possibility that Israel would launch a 'preventative war' against Egypt. During a routine visit by a Member of Parliament to Israel the MP had held a series of meetings with senior Israeli political and military leaders. Upon his return to Britain, Reginald Paget MP informed the Foreign Office of his impressions of the current thinking in Israel regarding a potential 'preventative' war with Egypt.[71] Paget thought that while Sharett was 'wholeheartedly' against a preventative war in any circumstances, Ben-Gurion did not altogether rule it out.[72] Paget spent some time with Israeli military leaders, among whom he found a much greater willingness to consider a preventative war and, given the right opportunity, Israel could launch an attack against Egypt.[73] Despite knowledge of the slow shift in opinion among the Israeli elite on confronting Egypt, the Foreign Office did little over the summer of 1956 to instal any sense of confidence in Israel that its polices might change in light of the growing Suez crisis. Paradoxically, with Nasser having gone overboard from the ship of British national interests in the region, keeping the other Arab states on board became all the more important.

The deal is struck at Sèvres

On 26 July 1956, Egypt seized the Suez Canal Company, in other words full control over the canal. Reactions to the Egyptian move among the

Western powers differed. In America, President Eisenhower wanted Nasser to be downgraded over time, but this should not be done in the full glare of the Suez crisis.[74] America, it should be noted, was not as reliant on Middle Eastern oil as were Britain and France. For once, the old imperial rivals Britain and France found themselves with shared interests in wishing to get rid of Nasser. Unlike the Americans, the British and French over time came to the conclusion that they would be willing to use force against Nasser as a last resort. The French appeared to hold an additional motive in that it was widely accepted at the time that Nasser was heavily supporting the rebels in Algeria in its fight for independence from France. To some degree, this turned out to be something of an exaggeration, with Nasser sending trainers to Algeria and pumping out propaganda through Radio Cairo.[75]

Intensive diplomatic activity took place over the summer and autumn of 1956 between Britain, France and America, aimed at finding a peaceful solution to the crisis.[76] It was not, however, until late October, when hopes of finding such a peaceful resolution were receding, that the Israelis became directly involved. At a secret conference at Sèvres on 22–24 October, the British, French and Israelis met to hammer out what was in effect a joint war plan for military action against Egypt.[77] While the French and Israelis were keen for some type of joint action, there remained deep suspicion between the Israelis and the British, which remained from the events of 1955 and the first part of 1956. Indeed, it was the French who acted as matchmaker between the British and the Israelis.[78] Ben-Gurion remained extremely sore about Eden's Guildhall speech. Moreover, the question of British arms sales to Israel had still not been settled to Israel's liking.

The Israeli delegation was personally led by the Prime Minister, David Ben-Gurion, and included two of his closest advisers and allies, the Chief of Staff, General Moshe Dayan, and Shimon Peres, the Director General of Ministry of Defence. A somewhat sceptical Secretary of State, Selwyn Lloyd attended the first day of the meeting and Guy Mollet led the French delegation. Given the degree of mutual suspicion between the British and Israeli delegations it was hardly surprising that things, at first, did not go very well. Indeed, when Lloyd returned home and briefed Eden, the Prime Minister announced in Cabinet the next day that following secret talks with the Israeli Government in Paris he was convinced that the Israelis were not about to launch an all-out attack on Egypt. A change of plan, however, by General Dayan, French pressure on the British and Eden's apparent willingness to be persuaded led to an eventually successful conclusion to the three-day meeting at Sèvres.[79]

The plan that was worked out called for Israel to launch a large-scale attack on Egypt during the evening of 29 October with the aim of reaching the area of the Suez Canal by the following day. After this there would be appeals to both Israel and Egypt to cease fire and accept the temporary occupation of key positions along and around the canal by British and French forces on 31 October. If Egypt rejected the ultimatum, British and French forces would launch military operations against Egypt during the early hours of the morning of 31 October. The ultimatum was kept deliberately short at the request of the Israelis, who were concerned that their cities would be vulnerable to attack by the Egyptian Air Force in the period between Israeli forces reaching the Canal Zone.

The secrecy of the collusion and the details of the operation were of great importance. Naturally, Eden was determined to achieve operational surprise, but he was equally determined that no one would be able to uncover the evidence of the collusion with Israel. In order to try to ensure this, almost nobody was given any advance warning of the operation. No Ambassadors were informed and only a handful of people within Downing Street and the Foreign Office were in the loop. The Foreign Office communications network was also not used.[80] Given the British policy that its true interests in the Middle East lay with the Arabs and not with Israel, the stakes were extremely high.

The war started on time at 5pm on 29 October with the dropping of Israeli paratroopers some 35 miles from the canal. The Israeli forces made their expected progress and the ultimatums were delivered as scheduled at 4.30pm in London and were due to expire at 4.30 British time on 31 October. From this point on, however, things started to go badly for Eden and the British. Almost immediately the Labour Party leader, Hugh Gaitskell, denounced Eden in the House of Commons. The next day Gaitskell returned to the floor of the office and accused Eden of a transparent attempt to seize the canal. Much worse was to follow for the Prime Minister. Gaitskell concluded his remarks by stating that there was a much worse story going round that the whole business was a matter of collusion between the British and French Governments and the Government of Israel.[81] And so the term 'collusion' was created about the Suez adventure.[82] Despite widespread press speculation and official denials from both Downing Street and the Foreign Office the story would not go away. Eden had tried to cover his tracks as much as possible; he ordered the British copy of the Protocol of Sèvres to be destroyed. Ben-Gurion, however, kept his copy and slowly the story of the collusion started to emerge, although the Israelis and the French only revealed the confirmation of it and the details of the meetings some 20 years later.

The military aspects of the campaign were in reality to be heavily dominated by the growing political pressure on Eden. The Americans had not been informed about the attack and President Eisenhower was angry that the attacks had come the week before the American presidential elections. Once the British and French bombing started on 31 October international protests, mainly conducted in the arena of the United States, grew rapidly, and worryingly for Britain much of it was led by the United States. In a twist of fate, the Suez Operation coincided with the Soviet Union's repression of the Hungarian uprising. The British and French landings did take place, but stiff Egyptian resistance often met them. With the diplomatic and economic pressure being applied by America, Eden was left with little choice but to call for a ceasefire at 2am local time on the morning of 7 November. The Prime Minister, as a result of the Suez Operation, left for Jamaica in order to rest and to try to regain his rapidly deteriorating health. He eventually resigned on 7 January 1957 on the grounds of ill health. Suez marked the last British effort to be a major power in the Middle East and to pursue a policy without American support. In military terms the British and French armed forces achieved much of what was asked of them, but from a political perspective Suez was a spectacular failure and the Foreign Office would have to rebuild British policy in the region that had been transformed by the ill-advised war.

Picking up the pieces, business as usual: the Foreign Office and Suez

Very few Foreign Office officials had any idea of the collusion with Israel agreed at Sèvres. For much of the Foreign Office therefore it was business as usual with Israel for both the duration of the war and the immediate period following it. Indeed, during the war Israel was still officially referred to as an enemy.[83] The Foreign Office report on the war was complied by Ross, the head of Levant Department, and it called for no major change in British policy towards Israel. During the course of the war there had been calls from Nicholls in Tel Aviv to use the war as a cover to move towards some kind of *rapprochement* with Israel. Donald Logan, who was one of the very select group of Foreign Office officials who knew about the collusion – he had been one of the British signatures of the Sèvres Agreement – rejected Nicholls, advising him not to become too understanding of Israel's problems (code for going native – the ultimate insult).[84] In retrospect, given that Nicholls could hardly be described as a lover of all things Israeli, his actions would appear, on the surface, difficult to fathom. It is more than likely that they were probably opportunist in nature, and from a British perspective poorly thought out. Given the fact that the collusion was still denied by official sources, it is clear that Logan and Downing Street hoped to get away without further inflaming the Arab world.[85] During the ensuing years, Israel was not given an easy ride by the Foreign Office, which was keen to try to rebuild its position in the Arab world.

One of the first tasks for the Foreign Office following the conclusion of the war was to deny the increasing number of stories that started to circulate about the collusion with Israel. At the time this was not too taxing for Foreign Office officials because many of the reports doing the rounds were actually rather wide of the mark. On 6 December, *Pravda* published a Tass report alleging that British and French Air Forces had arrived in the Israeli port city of Haifa.[86] The same report had appeared the previous day on President Nasser's propaganda mouthpiece Radio Cairo.[87] The Foreign Office was able to dismiss both reports, stating that no British troops were in any part of Israel.[88]

Dealing with the growing number of questions in the House of Commons was a trickier issue. On 22 November, the British Government in response to a parliamentary question had stated that there had not been any contacts either directly or in writing between Israel and Britain about the crisis in the Middle East.[89] The British Parliament had clearly been deceived. In December, the Labour MP and forces veteran, Dennis Healey, tabled a question in the House on 5 December to ask whether at any time after 27 October the Government had warned Israel unequivo-cally against an attack on Egypt.[90] The Secretary of State, Selwyn Lloyd, replied that the British Ambassador to Israel had warned the Israeli Gov-ernment to use restraint and of the danger of the result. Foreign Office officials were concerned about the Secretary of State's answer, arguing that they mustn't push this line too far as Nicholls' meetings with the Israeli Government had referred overwhelmingly to the possibility of an Israel attack on Jordan, and not Egypt.[91] In order to cover their backs, Laurence drafted a brief note to this effect for the Minister.

The previous day, Rab Butler, when asked a supplementary question seeking assurance that no member of the British Government had any prior knowledge of Israel's intention to attack Egypt, had been forced to feebly state that he had nothing to add to the statements by the Prime

Minister and the Foreign Secretary.[92] As a result of all the parliamentary activity, Rose issued instructions that as far as the Foreign Office was aware there was no prior indication of Israel's intention to invade Sinai, we should say so categorically and submit a draft reply.[93] In terms of prior information given to Israel about the Anglo–French ultimatum, Rose had to draft another carefully worded response to a parliamentary question.[94] Again Rose used the phrase, 'as far the department was aware there was no prior knowledge'.[95] The ultimatum, he argued, was delivered to the Israeli Chargé-d'Affaires in London at 4.15pm on 30 October.[96]

In Israel, the rumour mill was also in full swing. Israeli officials, however, continued to deny that either British or French forces had taken part in the operation in Sinai.[97] The Israeli press, which as Nicholls was prone to comment was not generally keen to write what the British wanted to see written, helped maintain the collusion, arguing that the British Ambassador had no idea about the timing of the Israeli operation in Sinai.[98] The story was printed in reply to a piece that *Time* magazine had run arguing that there had been a conspiracy and that it had taken.[99] The evidence that *Time* presented was bitty and fragmented and appeared to centre on the fact that the British and French military attachés had appeared to attempt to avoid their American counterparts at a party at the American Embassy in Israel on 27 October 1956.[100] It was a classic case of a correct verdict based on false evidence.

A return to arms

Given the deepening penetration of the Soviet Union into the Arab world, it came as little surprise that the issue that continued to dominate Anglo–Israeli relations following the Suez campaign was once more the role of the UK as an arms supplier to the region.[101] The Soviet penetration was illustrated not only by its efforts to rapidly rebuild the Egyptian armed forces but also in its actions elsewhere in region. The Middle East was now a major theatre of the Cold War between East and West. In this bipolar international system the imperial powers had been largely replaced by the superpowers of the United States and the Soviet Union. The United States at this stage, however, appeared reluctant to mirror the Soviet armament efforts in arming its allies in the region. The importance of British arms sales to Israel cannot be overestimated at this stage, particularly the heavy tanks that Britain made, and which France, Israel's other major source of arms, didn't.

The resulting tensions between Britain and Israel largely resulted from Israeli frustration on this issue as well as the wider realization that the Foreign Office continued to determine that British interests in the region lay with the Arab states and not Israel. It almost goes without saying that at the centre of this policy was the question of oil supplies to Britain and the securing of such supplies from an increasingly politically unstable region. In terms of Anglo–Israeli relations, there were three relatively distinct time periods in the post-Suez era. Following the end of the Suez campaign until the end of 1957, Anglo–Israeli relations were at a very low ebb. From January 1958 until the middle of 1958, however, there was a slow but steady improvement in the relationship. In mid-1958 Britain and Israel co-operated on a strategic level on the issue of RAF overflights in Israel with the intention of keeping King Hussein in power in Jordan. Israeli permission for these overflights was central to the happy ending for Israel of its long-standing quest to get what it most wanted from Britain, namely the Centurion tanks.

For once, the source of Israel's problem appeared not be to be the Foreign Office, but rather the United Nations. On 2 November 1956, in light of the Suez War, the United Nations General Assembly had passed a resolution calling for the suspension of arms deliveries to both Israel and Egypt. In the resulting months, however, Israel became very frustrated with Britain (mainly the Foreign Office) about the strict adherence of the British Government to the resolution. This frustration, and at times anger, was based on the usual Israeli arguments. With the British Government continuing to supply weapons to Jordan and Iraq, and with the Soviets supplying Syria, this shifted the Arab–Israeli arms balance once more in favour of the Arabs. To make matters worse for Israel, the Foreign Office, it claimed, had been up to its old tricks and had held up the delivery of military equipment that Israel had already paid for. This shipment included three Meteor jets. These were already obsolete as day fighters, but Israel desperately wanted them in order to complete a unit of night fighters.

The UK countered these Israeli arguments by claiming that Israel could perform well in the military sphere with fewer arms – as the Sinai conflict had just confirmed. Also that Israel had a great number of captured Egyptian/Soviet weapons from the Suez conflict which meant that it didn't need new purchases of arms. In reality, the Foreign Office argued that the UK could not afford to be seen to be in breach of a UN General Assembly resolution. As a result, Israeli suspicions of the UK at the time were very high. These were clearly articulated by the Israeli Ambassador to London, Eliahu Elath. In meetings with Foreign Office officials the Ambassador charged that British policy towards Israel was still based on the Guildhall speech – in other words, Israeli territorial withdrawal. Though there was clearly a degree of diplomatic brinksmanship in this accusation, the Foreign Office was worried that Israel kept returning to the Guildhall speech. As one official put it, there had been another outbreak of Guildhallitis among the Israelis.

These Israeli suspicions and frustrations were publicly articulated in a major series of articles on the state of Anglo–Israeli relations in the Israeli press at the end of 1956.[102] In *Al-Hamishmar* (21–24 December) its London-based reporter argued that British policy towards Israel was still guided by the Guildhall speech.[103] Put simply: the demand for Israeli territorial concessions towards the Arabs.[104] Furthermore, the paper claimed that the Conservatives in the UK were totally overlooking Israeli interests, and that appeasement and the romantic Arab policy had no roots in the British people and was shared only by the leading men at the Foreign Office, oil circles and the upper classes.[105]

This somewhat jaundiced view of British society was not welcomed by the Foreign Office, which wondered why Nicholls had bothered to comment upon it in his dispatch. The Ambassador had been given the brief to gather any material from the Israeli press or radio that was critical of the Baghdad Pact. As Rose commented, he was not asked to investigate the Israelis in this sense, but merely to report.[106] This was, in reality, another sign of the leftover baggage and growing tensions that had resulted from Nicholls' 'misguided' intervention during the Suez War that Britain should seek a *rapprochement* with Israel. Had the man who had described Israelis as sick people gone native? Clearly, within the Foreign Office there remained concerns that he was still making the case for closer Anglo–Israeli relations. It should of course be remembered that these were very sensitive times for the Foreign Office, particularly those few senior figures who understood the potential time-bomb of the collusion with Israel

Another Israeli daily, *Maariv*, carried an editorial with the same sentiment entitled 'The Arab Disease of the English'.[107] In a frontal assault on the Foreign Office and British policy in the Middle East, the paper made the following charge:

> The British are known for their conservatism. They are not prepared to learn from their past mistakes and, even now, after all their failures, after the card house which was based on treaties with Egypt and

Jordan has tumbled down, they are not ready to abandon their pro-Arab tradition. The British today do not have many friends among the Arabs. They drove them all away. However, the British cling to the few Arabs left to them . . . They refuse to recover from the Arab disease and support us . . .[108]

These strong words reflected the sense of betrayal which many Israelis felt over the unfinished military business during the Suez War. *Maariv* concluded that it had appeared for a moment as though Britain had recovered from its 'Arab disease' after its attempts at Suez; however, the burden of the heritage of British policy prevented the success of the military operation.[109] Put succinctly, Britain lost its nerve and didn't know how to face the new post-Suez Middle East.

The resignation on 9 January 1957 of Anthony Eden, long regarded by some in Israel, not least by Ben-Gurion, as one of the main architects of Britain's pro-Arab policy, had little immediate impact on Anglo–Israeli relations. Despite his relatively brief stint as Prime Minister, Eden was viewed by Israel as essentially a Foreign Office man.[110] The Israeli press, commenting on his departure, focused on the political rather than health reasons for his retirement, suggesting that as he had lost the support of some in his party he was bound to retire sooner or later.[111] Harold Macmillan's appointment as Prime Minister was generally well received in Israel – more in hope than with any real conviction that it would lead to a change in British policy towards it.[112]

In Israeli eyes this feeling of displeasure with the British Government, and especially with the Foreign Office, was compounded by the British decision not to join France in voting against a UN Resolution calling for Israel's unconditional withdrawal from the Sinai. The Israeli Ambassador and the Head of the Commonwealth Division of the Israeli Ministry of Foreign Affairs raised the issue with Ross in a meeting on 7 February 1957.[113] The Israeli officials claimed to be disappointed and bewildered at the British decision to vote against Israel.[114] This, they felt, was especially galling given the fact that Britain had used its veto in the Security Council of the United Nations in recognition that Israel was not acting as the aggressor in the 1956 war, but rather was acting in self-defence.[115] In response, Ross defended the Foreign Office's position, stating that the two resolutions in question had largely been unsatisfactory. In truth, the Israeli complaint to the Foreign Office would have been more routine and simply for the record, had its expectation of Anglo–Israeli co-operation not increased as a result of the war. Once more the Foreign Office appeared to be closing the door on strategic co-operation with Israel and help it clear up the post-war political situation in Gaza and Sinai. The fact that the Americans were applying pressure on Israel to be allowed to keep any of its war gains was not on the Foreign Office that was trying to rebuild relations with the Americans that had been badly strained by the war. At this stage, the Foreign Office was keen, wherever possible, to put as much distance between Britain and Israel as possible, for both ongoing strategic reasons *vis-à-vis* the Arabs, but also in case the great secret of the collusion were ever leaked by the Israelis.

But at this time the true Israeli test – as employed by David Ben-Gurion – of British policy towards Israel remained its willingness to sell arms to Israel. And much to Ben-Gurion's and Israel's dismay the UK delivered neither arms nor spare parts to Israel even after the final Israeli withdrawal from the lands it had captured during the 1956 war in March 1957. Shneerson had raised the issue of the delivery of spare parts, which Israel had not had delivered but had paid for, at the meeting with Ross. Despite some reassuring words from Ross, the Foreign Office, however, appeared reluctant at this time to authorize any shipments to Israel. Within one month, developments in the Middle East led to a partial change in Foreign Office policy regarding the sale of weapons to Israel.

The attitude of the Foreign Office on arms sales slowly evolved to recognize the need to balance the Soviet supply of arms to Syria and the supply of Soviet missiles to Egypt with a supply of arms to Israel. As a result, by the middle of March 1957 the Foreign Office was working behind the scenes in order to try to persuade the United States to agree to an end to the ban on the sale of weapons to Israel.[116] At this stage, though, the Foreign Office was still not willing to authorize the supply of either the Centurion tanks or the Hunter aircraft, which were the items that the Israelis were most keen on acquiring. The Foreign Office did, however, feel increasingly honour-bound to meet the existing obligations of arms sales to Israel which had been raised by Shneerson in February. This, however, did not become the official policy of the British Government until August 1957. In the meantime, an increasingly agitated Israeli Ambassador pushed Israel's case for arms at every opportunity.

During his meeting with the Secretary of State, Selwyn Lloyd, on 5 April 1957, Elath waited until the end of the meeting to introduce the question of arms; the bulk of the meeting had been spent repairing yet another apparent misunderstanding between the Secretary of State and Ben-Gurion.[117] Elath kept it simple this time, arguing that with the new Soviet arms sales to Egypt (which were later confirmed to be true by

British Intelligence) he hoped the British Government would soon agree to resume the delivery of arms to Israel.[118]

Perhaps because Foreign Office officials were already working behind the scenes to ease the arms situation with Israel via the United States, or simply because they were growing tired of Elath's constant request for arms and his persistent comments on the British arms sales policy, this appeared to strike a nerve with Foreign Office officials. Following a difficult meeting between the Ambassador and Sir William Hayter on 18 June, during which Elath denounced Britain's present attitude towards Israel and quoted its refusal to supply weapons to support his argument, Lawrence decided to do something.[119]

Tired of responding in the same old manner, Laurence prepared a list of grievances that the British Government held about the attitude of the Israeli Government.[120] The list was to be readied and used the next time that Elath complained about the arms issue.[121] Admittedly the issues seemed rather trivial in the greater scheme of events. Laurence listed that there were outstanding Mandatory Government balances in Israel that amounted to more than £100,000, which they had failed to persuade the Israeli Government to remit. There was also some £60,000-worth of British private bank accounts in Israel that remained blocked. He also brought up the fact that some British employees of the old Jerusalem Electric Corporation had not received any compensation for their apparent kidnap and eventual trial and acquittal on espionage charges made against them. He concluded with a gripe about the failure of Israel to give a satisfactory response to old BOAC earnings that remained blocked in Israel.[122] The somewhat bitchy nature of the minute reflected the growing tetchiness of the Foreign Office both towards Elath personally and towards the apparent attempt to seize the moral ground on the arms issue. It also reflected, in part, the thinking in the Foreign Office that given the increasing communist threat the arming of Israel in some small way might be a prudent policy. There was still a debate within the top echelon of the Foreign Office as to how to square this need without offending the Arabs.

A simple case of Guildhallitis and oil worries

The worsening state of Anglo–Israeli relations during 1957 was also sparked by Israeli fears that the Foreign Office was steering Israel back towards the Guildhall speech that called for major Israeli territorial concessions. The Israeli Ambassador had discussed the issue during his meeting with the Secretary of State earlier in the year, but he clearly sensed that all the Anglo–American co-operation that had defined the period prior to Suez was returning. In other words, he feared that Britain and the United States were preparing to make another attempt at essentially imposing a solution on the Arab–Israeli conflict. Elath raised his fears in a meeting with Sir William Hayter on 16 June.[123] In reality, the Ambassador was enquiring about the meeting between British and State Department personnel.[124] Although the Ambassador never knew about the existence of Operation Alpha he had suspected the existence of some kind of co-operation and co-ordination between the Foreign Office and the State Department.

At a time when both the Foreign Office and the Israeli Government were far from pleased with each other's respective attitude towards Anglo–Israeli relations, another issue erupted into a fully pledged diplomatic crisis. The decision of the Shell Oil Company to stop selling oil to Israel that originated from Iran or the Far East created a great deal of anger in the Israeli Government, which saw the decision as a political rather than an economic one, and placed the blame for it squarely on the shoulders of the British. The Foreign Office argued that the decision was taken on commercial grounds and that the British Government had not been consulted. This did not convince many people in Israel, or indeed in Britain, where the decision was widely viewed as being political. The British Labour Party was none too pleased either. When Selwyn Lloyd informed Aneurin Bevan of the decision, Bevan described the whole thing as monstrous and threatened to expose it publicly[125].

The question of oil was, naturally, extremely important to a small, modernized country such as Israel that was unable to purchase it from the Arabs. To make matters worse, following the 1956 war, the Soviet Union, without warning, had cut off oil supplies to Israel. As a result, this left Israel highly dependent on British oil supplies (two-thirds) and American oil (one-third).[126] The Shell Oil Company primarily supplied the British oil, but by mid-1957 the Israeli Government was faced with an imminent refusal of British oil companies to ship oil to Israel that was of either Iranian or Far Eastern origin. Israel urged the British Government to intervene on Israel's behalf, arguing that such moves would place the Israeli economy under severe stress.[127] Golda Meir, who had succeeded Moshe Sharett as Minister of Foreign Affairs the previous year, argued that if the British allowed the stoppage to go ahead, it would be adding the blockage of the Israeli Red Sea port of Eilat and helping the Arab boycott of Israel. Right from the start this issue was not a simple economic one of supply and demand, but one that had a huge political dimension to it as well.

On 14 July 1957, Meir informed the newly arrived British Ambassador to Israel, Sir Francis Rundall, of Shell Oil's decision to stop supplying Israel with crude oil from Iran and its decision to terminate its operations in Israel. This wasn't Israel's only fear at the time. There was real concern in Israel that Shell would also stop supplying Israel from other sources from South America. For his part, the Israeli Ambassador in London, Elath, made his usual rounds of the Foreign Office and accused the British Government of not doing enough to stop these developments. He also argued that the Foreign Office had known in advance the details of Shell's decision. Under orders from Jerusalem, Elath went on the offensive in meetings with Foreign Office staff, arguing that the British Government could influence the decision-making and cited the example of the British Government's shareholding in another oil company, British Petroleum, as evidence. Central to the Ambassador's argument was that the decision of Shell Oil to pull out of Israel was a political one – not an economic one – and moreover was part of an overall British policy towards Israel in the post-1956 war era which was characterized by appeasement of the Arabs and discrimination against Israel in all areas, but especially in arms sales. Although there appeared to be no direct linkage of the arms and oil issues by the Israeli Government, the latter certainly increased the pressure on the Foreign Office to do something positive for Israel on the arms issue.

From the British and Foreign Office perspective, perhaps the most telling meeting on the oil issue didn't involve any Israelis at all. The private meeting took place in the Prime Minister's Office in the House of Commons on 1 August 1957. The Prime Minister, the Secretary of State and the Paymaster General and their Labour Party shadow ministers attended the meeting. The agenda of the meeting contained only two items: arms for Israel and oil for Israel.[128] For some time the Labour Party hade been agitating that the Conservative Government's policy on both issues was unfair towards Israel. The Prime Minister argued on the oil question that there were really two questions at stake. Was Israel's supply of oil in jeopardy, and how far should the UK go in forcing British companies to sell oil to Israel? Regarding the former question, the Prime Minister felt that provided the Israeli Government did not kick up too much fuss then the resentment about under-the-counter arrangements it had in place for its oil from other countries could become permanent.[129] In terms of the second question, the Prime Minister refused to commit himself to applying any pressure.[130] Aneurin (Nye) Bevan disagreed with the Prime Minister, arguing that British companies should be made to get Iranian oil to Israel.[131] The Secretary of State, Selwyn Lloyd, however, cautioned against such moves, arguing that any public spat with the oil companies on this issue would only lead to the other countries supplying Israel pulling the plug.[132] In retrospect, the Secretary of State's motives for taking such a line were not altogether honest. The real fear in the Foreign Office was the need to appease the Arabs on this increasingly high-profile issue.

The one issue that had not been discussed at the meeting was the prohibitive cost to Israel of buying this oil under the counter. In the end, Israel was able to buy Iranian oil under the counter via Switzerland and the Standard Oil Company of Ohio, but at much higher prices than from Shell. In Israeli eyes the Shell affair was a major test of Anglo–Israeli relations, and the British Government, and in particular the Foreign Office, had failed to intervene on Israel's behalf. Anglo–Israeli relations, as a result, hit a new low point.

Israeli fears of a return to the Guildhall plan

In August 1957 Britain decided somewhat reluctantly to release the spare parts and maintenance equipment that had been previously earmarked for Israel. Foreign Office officials, however, reined, as ever, concerned about the impact of this very limited delivery of arms to Israel on its relations with the Arabs, particularly Iraq and Jordan. The British rationale at the time for the arms sales was that in light of the position of the reluctance of the British Government to sell arms to Israel and the Shell Oil affair, relations with Israel were extremely strained. In this instance, the aim of the Foreign Office was essentially political damage limitation. Foreign Office officials viewed this limited release, in other words, as a way of retaining some degree of influence in Israel. In return, the Foreign Office wanted to gain some assurances from Israel that it would cease its retaliatory raids into Jordan and consequently keep things quiet on the Jordanian border. The concern was that if this quiet did not prevail then either Egypt or Syria would use the situation as an excuse to send forces into Jordan. Israeli officials provided the British with the necessary assurances that Israel would indeed strive to keep the border quiet, and in return the Israelis received their spare parts.

Elath was extremely pleased and thankful for the Foreign Office concession on the spare parts, but still wanted the outstanding items delivered (three Meteor Night Fighters and Bofors naval guns).[133] This, the Ambassador promised, would put an end to Israel's obsession with arms.[134] To be fair, Elath did admit that he was speaking personally when he made his comments about ending Israel's obsession with arms.[135] In reality, his superiors in Jerusalem had little intention of letting the issue rest until Israel had received the Centurion tanks that it badly wanted to purchase from the British.

As ever, just as relations appeared to be improving, a new spanner was thrown in the works that resulted in a new chill. Israelis suspicions over Britain came to the surface again in early November 1957 when there was no still progress in other arms deliveries to Israel beyond the spare parts. The catalyst of this suspicion was a speech that the Secretary of State had given at the United Nations.[136] During his speech Lloyd had argued that when two sides to a dispute adopted widely divergent positions, there was no hope of any solution to the dispute unless both sides were prepared to make some compromise. The Israelis took this, publicly at any rate, as a renewal of British demands for Israeli territorial compromise. In a meeting between Elath and Foreign Secretary Selwyn Lloyd on 10 December 1957, the Israeli Ambassador returned, much to the indignation of Lloyd, once more to the Guildhall speech of November 1955.[137] The Israeli fear (genuine or not) was that the UK and the US were about to renew attempts to implement a joint plan. It soon became clear that the US was unwilling to pursue such a new initiative, if one had ever existed, and this led to a downgrading of Israeli fears by late December 1958.

In the complex art of diplomacy the Israelis were most likely attempting to create something of a crisis in Anglo–Israeli relations in the hope that in order to put out the fire the Foreign Office would authorize the delivery of the remaining military equipment to Israel and look favourably on other orders. The Israeli Government had noted that in the darkest hour of Anglo–Israeli relations earlier in the year, the Foreign Office had decided to offer an olive branch to Israel in order to prevent a potential total breakdown in relations. The Israeli Government was most probably hoping for a similar outcome on this occasion.

The Foreign Office's Annual Review for Israel starkly concluded that, as they put it, 'Anglo–Israeli relations have never been particularly cordial during the last year and have deteriorated appreciably during the last months.'[138] In the report, compiled by Sir Francis Rundall, the Embassy in Israel showed itself to be at least sensitive to the real core of the problem in Anglo–Israeli relations, which was perception versus reality. In short, most Israelis, as the Ambassador concluded, regarded the British Government with a great deal of suspicion. When things appeared to go badly for Israel, such as with the case of the decision of Shell Oil to stop supplying Israel, the Israelis immediately looked for the hand of the Foreign Office to be behind everything. The suspicion among Israelis at the time was quite correct in that the interests of helping Israel were subordinated to the necessity of improving relations with the Arab world, but it was a simple black-and-white argument.

Of course, the reality was much more complex. While it was certainly true that the Foreign Office appeared, in the period following the Suez War, to be totally committed to an attempt to rebuild British prestige and alliances among the Arabs, this did not mean that Israel was left out in the cold. During the course of 1958 the fruits of the Foreign Office's gestures towards Israel started to lead to changes in Anglo–Israeli relations, particularly when both countries found a common strategic interest in keeping King Hussein in power in Jordan.

The ice slowly starts to melt: British over-flights into Israel

On 1 January 1958, the British Government released the jets and artillery pieces that Israel had been demanding, and which the Israeli Ambassador had made reference to in his meeting with the Secretary of State. Despite the, by now, limited strategic value of the arms release to Israel, the sale led a further moderate improvement in Anglo–Israeli relations. This was almost immediately put to the test with the Arab Union between Jordan and Iraq on 14 February 1958. The relatively muted Israeli response to the Union was met with relief and even praise at the Foreign Office. The better state of relations was commented upon when the Israeli Ambassador met with the Secretary of State on 2 May 1958.[139] The Ambassador did, however, remind the Secretary of State that there was still some ill-will in Israel towards the Foreign Office and directed at the Secretary of State personally. During a meeting, Lloyd reported that the Ambassador had brought up the Guildhall policy (as Israelis called it) once more, but with much more restraint and less emotion this time than on previous occasions.[140]

By mid-June the Israelis noted that the Foreign Office now at least partially recognized Israel's positive role in checking and preventing Nasser's expansion in the region. Given the widely understood attempt of President Nasser to export his particular brand of pan-Arabism and destabilize other Arab regimes, particularly in Jordan, it would appear a little strange that the Foreign Office took so long to come to this conclusion. That said, the realization did not suddenly lead to an outbreak of strategic co-operation between the British and Israeli Governments aimed at checking the influence of Nasser.

The political background to the overflights request was rather complex and said much about the instability in the Arab world at the time. On 14 July 1958, the Prime Minister of Iraq, Nuri Said, was overthrown in a *coup d'état*. A day later, King Hussein of Jordan, who was faced with an uprising, naturally appealed to his allies in the West for help. That same day the British requested that Israel allow the Royal Air Force to over-fly Israel in order to help provide military assistance to the Jordanian regime. As events unfolded, Ben-Gurion came under increasing pressure in the Israeli Cabinet to intervene in Jordan in order to project Israel's eastern border. One of the parties in the ruling coalition in Israel, Achdut Ha'avoda, threatened to resign from the coalition if Ben-Gurion endangered Israeli security by missing a good opportunity to seize the West Bank. Throughout the crisis, though Ben-Gurion needed to carefully manage his ruling coalition, it was the British who were on the back foot and who needed Israeli help and co-operation. All of a sudden, following the effective collapse of British policy in the region, the Israelis had become strategically vital to British interests. Foreign Office officials, as a result, had to adapt to this new short-term reality very quickly indeed.

The Israeli Ambassador was summoned to a meeting with the Permanent Under- Secretary on 16 July 1958, at which he was briefed on the British response to the events in Iraq.[141] The Ambassador admitted that he fully understood the importance of over-flying rights and he felt reasonably confident that the Israeli Government would agree to the British request and that, as he admitted, it was very much in the Israeli interest to do so.[142]

Ben-Gurion appealed to the British that he understood that Britain had interests in the Middle East but, as he put it, 'at a pinch Britain could survive without them'.[143] It would have come as little surprise to Foreign Office officials that Ben-Gurion declared in dramatic terms that, at present, Anglo–Israeli relations did not exist, and if they did, why couldn't Israel get arms or tanks from the British?[144] In a carefully worded and astute assessment of his meeting with Ben-Gurion, the British Ambassador, Rundall, argued to the Foreign Office that the Israeli Prime Minister clearly considered the British position in the Middle East to be so radically worsened that, while Britain needed his immediate help in an operational matter, this was the psychological moment to extract a long-term price from the British.[145] Rundall speculated as to what this price would be. He sensed that it would include the integration of Israel into the Western defence system, at least a tacit agreement on Israel's present borders and the supply of the armaments that it needed.[146] The Ambassador, sensing that Ben-Gurion's requests would not fall on particularly sympathetic ears at the Foreign Office, warned that it would be a mistake to dismiss the Prime Minister's proposal as simply blackmail.[147] As Rundall put it: 'We must expect the [Israeli] Prime Minister to charge all he thinks the traffic will bear.'[148]

In the rapid wheeling and dealing that went on between the British and the Israelis, Ben-Gurion was eventually able to take advantage of the British request in order to secure arms orders and some guarantees of its border. There was talk at the time that Ben-Gurion wanted an alliance with Britain, but this was not the case. Ben-Gurion had informed the British Ambassador, Rundall, that he proposed a close working partnership with Britain along the lines of the one that already existed between Israel and France.[149] As always with his keen sense of history Ben-Gurion reminded Rundall of previous attempts at strategic co-operation between the two countries and the failure of anything of substance to merge from promising starts.[150] He quite naturally referred to the visit of General Robertson to Israel and his discussions with Herbert Morrison on the issue. The British Ambassador had warned the Foreign Office that it must expect the Israelis to be extremely distrustful of a short-term commitment from Britain that could be terminated when Britain no longer had any need for Israel's assistance.[151]

In reality, Ben-Gurion wanted arms. This was confirmed in a hastily arranged meeting between the Secretary of State and the Israeli Ambassador on 21 July.[152] The tone and content of this meeting were very different from those of past encounters. This time it was Selwyn Lloyd who shared his vision and fears about the Middle East with Elath. Such was the detail which Lloyd went into that Elath had to inform him that he had not expected the Secretary of State to speak to him about such matters, and so he was completely without instructions as to how to respond. Elath argued that the best sign of informal support for Israel by the British would be the resumption of the supply of arms. Although he was without formal instructions, the Ambassador managed to provide some ideas for what kind of arms Israel was looking for to help cement this 'beautiful new relationship'.

In reality, Ben-Gurion remained extremely distrustful of British long-term political commitments to Israel, which he suspected might not be honoured in light of the continued interests of Britain in the Arab world.[153] The Israeli Prime Minister understood better than most that the interests of Britain continued to lie with the Arabs and in particular the securing of its oil supplies from the region.[154] Following several conversations with Ben-Gurion, Rundall concluded that the Israelis wanted to be consulted and informed about future British moves in the Middle East in good time, much in the way that the Secretary of State had discussed with Elath earlier in the month. More to the point, Ben-Gurion was, given the collapse of the pro-British regime in Iraq and its replacement with a pro-communist one, looking for the admission of the total failure of past British policy in the region. For the Israeli Government the cornerstone of the Israeli dimension of this had been the 'British Guildhall policy'.[155] The Israelis, in short, were looking for some kind of public burial of this policy by the Foreign Office.[156] In other words, Ben-Gurion did not want the British to commit to a formal pact which it probably wouldn't be able to honour, but rather wanted specific commitments aimed at improving Anglo–Israeli relations.

The question of arms was another issue altogether. Although the French were supplying Israel, Ben-Gurion did not want to place too many eggs into one basket by becoming over-reliant on French supplies. Moreover, there was certain equipment that the French simply did not produce and which Israel desperately needed, such as the Centurion tank. The Israelis also talked about the purchase of heavy bombers, submarines and vessels for the Israeli Navy.[157] The presentation of a long Israeli arms shopping list to the Foreign Office, as a result, did not cause undue worry to the British.[158] The Foreign Office knew and understood that what Israel really wanted in the deal was the Centurion tanks.[159]

On 11 August 1958, the Israeli Minister of Foreign Affairs, Golda Meir, met with Selwyn Lloyd in London. Lloyd agreed to full co-operation with Israel and to establish relations of confidence with Israel. The groundwork for this improvement in Anglo–Israeli co-operation and understanding had been laid in Lloyd's meeting with the Israeli Ambassador in July. Ben-Gurion, as a result, had largely got what he wanted from the British, and the Foreign Office had not committed itself to any formal pact that would have placed severe strains on Anglo–Arab relations. Soon after the meeting, Britain agreed to sell Israel the Centurion tanks, which went a long way to satisfying the Israeli demand for Britain to sell it arms. The sale of the Centurion tanks (initially 55 in total) led to a warming up of Anglo–Israeli relations that led even the usually sceptical Ben-Gurion to note in his diary that there had been some shifts in the British attitude to Israel.[160] The Director-General of the

Israeli Defence Ministry, Shimon Peres, forever the dreamer (even at this early age), talked in terms of the beauties of some kind of commonwealth between the two countries.[161]

Coming full circle

In terms of Anglo–Israeli relations, the period both prior to and following the 1956 war was dominated by continued disputes over the sale of British-produced arms to Israel. For Israel, these arms sales on a general level were judged to be an extremely important part of its quest for security. On a specific level, arms sales from Britain were important to Israel because it feared that other sources of arms would either dry up or not be available. There was a fear that Israel's largest primary supplier of arms, France, would halt arms sales to it. Moreover, there was a consistent American unwillingness to sell arms at this stage to Israel. Finally, the British produced equipment that the Israelis badly needed. For instance, Israel desired a heavy tank such as the Centurion that the French didn't make and Britain did.

Overall, the Israeli view of Britain during this period can be characterized as believing it was a regional power whose influence was in terminal decline. Moreover, it was attempting to hold on to a degree of influence in the region by essentially appeasing the Arabs at the expense of developing ties with Israel. The Foreign Office was seen as being at the centre of these efforts and was widely viewed in Israel as the root cause of the 'Arab disease of the British'. This decline in British power was naturally speeded up by the events surrounding the Suez War in 1956 and by the loss of influence in Iraq in 1958.

Conversely, the Foreign Office viewed Israel as an increasingly important check on Soviet penetration into the region. Crucially, however, close relations with Israel were not seen as so important as the deepening of British ties with the Arab world as a means of preventing the spread of Soviet influence in the area. The Middle East had become increasingly viewed as a major theatre of the Cold War. The increased influence of the Soviets in the Arab world, which was starkly illustrated by the Czech arms deal of 1955 and later by events in Iraq in 1958, represented the single biggest threat to British influence in the region. The Foreign Office pursued a policy in the region that was based on attempting to retain as much influence as possible in the Arab world, but especially in Egypt, Jordan and Iraq. The tactics employed to achieve this aim varied from country to country, but they usually involved sizeable inducements. These inducements often continued well after their useful-ness had appeared to expire, as in the case of Egypt in 1955–56. Given Britain's declining economic wealth after the Second World War, the major inducement that could be offered to the Arab states was the sale of British-made arms.

These arms sales, while not on the scale of the Czech arms deal, and when taken in conjunction with Britain's reluctance to sell to Israel, impacted upon the arms balance in the Arab–Israeli conflict. This major source of Israeli irritation dominated much of the 1950s and it was not until the failure of British Middle East policy in 1958 that Israel was to start to take delivery of the weapons that it really wanted from Britain. The eventual co-operation between the UK and Israel grew out of a mutual desire to maintain the *status quo* in Jordan in 1958, and the demise of the Guildhall settlement that called for Israeli territorial withdrawal from some of the lands captured in 1948. For Britain the *coup* in Iraq was bad news not only on a political level but it removed one of the most lucrative arms markets for British firms. The Soviet Union was quick to supply the new regime in Iraq with arms. Britain, as a result, was left with the much smaller Jordanian and Kuwaiti arms markets. Israeli protests, as a result, against the UK arming the Arabs ceased to be a major bone of contention between the two countries. In other words, British arms sales were no longer a major factor in the Arab–Israeli arms race.

In light of all this we must question how important the 1956 war was to Anglo–Israeli relations. It appears that the collusion was an absolute one-off, a marriage of convenience for Britain in forming a common front against Nasser's threat to its interests in the Suez Canal area. After the war, normal service was resumed, with the Foreign Office once more at the centre of attempts to distance the UK from Israel. Indeed, it appeared, at times, that the Foreign Office was trying to put even more distance between Britain and Israel in order to try to impress the Arabs. In truth, it was not until King Hussein came under threat that Israel and Britain found themselves once more with a degree of mutual shared interest in helping the King remain in power. It was only at this stage that there was a degree of warming of relations between the two countries and of moving the relationship on to a new, more stable footing. Although, as we shall see, other crises occurred between the Foreign Office and Israel over the subsequent years, they were not on the same scale, or with the very real dangerous consequences that dominated this period. The seemingly ongoing crises from the end of 1956 and the start of 1958 were the darkest hours in Anglo–Israeli relations.

Finally, the British Ambassador saw the events of 1958 as leading to a maturing of Anglo–Israeli relations.[162] Gone, he argued, were the hysterical denunciation of Britain's weakness and its tendency to sacrifice Israel's interest in the appeasement of the Arabs to a point of confidence.[163] This change had been reflected in the attitude of the Israeli press, which had shifted somewhat from arguing that following the events in Iraq the British Government was frantically searching for friends in the Middle East, towards a more balanced line.[164] This line could roughly be summarized as having an understanding that Britain's general Middle Eastern interests would continue to guide its policy, but that didn't mean that Britain was hostile towards Israel, or wished to avoid having normal bi-lateral relations with it.[165]

In the ten years since its creation, this sense of maturity had been notable by its absence. Mistakes had been made on both sides. In the Foreign Office, while there was an understanding that Israel would be a permanent feature in the Middle East, this was laced with a sense of irritation about its existence and the complications that it brought to British Middle Eastern policy. On the Israeli side, the obsession with trying to obtain British arms, while understandable given its size and need for a qualitative edge in weaponry to make up for its deficiency in manpower, was largely ill advised. As perhaps the most favoured Israeli diplomat, Abba Eban, argued: never ask a friend for something to which you know he will have to say no. Israeli efforts at securing arms made the development of more normal bi-lateral relations all the more difficult. It also led to a degree of frustration at the Foreign Office, whose officials grew weary of trotting out the same old answers. As one official commented, 'Nobody likes to say no all the time.'

Even in 1957, the darkest hour of relations between the Foreign Office and Israel, there was no evidence of any institutionalized anti-semitism or love of all things Arab. Indeed, as we have seen, during this period many Foreign Office officials were equally dismissive about the Arabs, who were often portrayed as unreliable and indelibly corrupt, from the leadership down to the street-trader. The comments made by the third British Ambassador to Israel, Sir John Nicholls, that Israelis should be treated as a sick people, were unacceptable. Even here, however, it should be noted that Nicholls became the first British official to propose that it should throw its lot in with Israel rather than with the Arabs. The fierce reaction of the senior Foreign Office mandarin to Nicholls' suggestion was probably due to the pressure of his knowledge of the collusion at Suez rather than to any strong dislike of Israelis.

4

The times are a-changing: Israel goes nuclear

> Director Randers confirmed that the reactor, whose building has recently been reported in the press, is in fact the one for which the Norwegian Company has a contractual arrangement with Israel, and for which we sold a quantity of heavy water.
>
> *Letter from C. W. Hart-Jones to Croome,*
> *United Kingdom Atomic Energy Authority, 11 January 1961*[1]

Writing in 2007 there has been no official confirmation that Israel is a nuclear power. Its deliberate policy of ambiguity on the issue is designed for political reasons and avoidance of international treaties.[2] It was this issue that dominated much of the diplomatic agenda at the end of the 1950s and the start of the 1960s. The Israeli decision to build a nuclear reactor in Dimona was taken for a number of reasons, not least the willingness of the French to help and assist Israel in its quest to become a nuclear power. It recently emerged that the British Foreign Office might have unwittingly helped the Israelis as well by redirecting and selling on supplies of heavy water, which should have been returned to Norway, to Israel. Though this revelation of Britain's role gained a great deal of press attention and caused outrage among some groups, it was not the determining factor in terms of its impact on the ability of Israel to undertake a nuclear programme.

A new dawn, but old problems won't go away

The period following the over-flight deal between Britain and Israel was one of the most open, with Britain sharing information with Israel regarding its problems and ongoing issues on a much more regular basis. Confirmation of this new openness came on 10 February 1959 when the Secretary of State met with Elath.[3] During the course of the meeting, Lloyd was happy to brief the Ambassador on the state of the ongoing financial negotiations between Britain and Egypt, information that would most certainly not have been shared with the Israelis during the dark months of the immediate aftermath of the Suez campaign.[4] Lloyd conceded, however, that he was just as sceptical about Nasser as were the Israelis.[5] In completing his run-through of points of mutual agreement, the Secretary of State reminded Elath that Britain's policy towards Iraq was completely in line with the policy suggested by the Israeli Government.[6] The Israeli policy, at the time, centred upon giving the new Iraqi regime an opportunity, and calling for the West to do the same. The Israelis argued that if the Iraqi regime fell, then Nasser would be presented with a major opportunity to make mischief there.[7]

A degree of trust and of mutual confidence was also apparent in the dealings between the Foreign Office and the Israeli Embassy in London. This was useful when it came to the difficult issue of the shipment of British arms to Israel. The arrival of the Centurion tanks was not given any publicity by either the British or the Israelis, though, as Lloyd fully understood, their arrival couldn't remain a secret for ever. That said, Lloyd was keen that the imminent handing over of a second submarine to Israel would be kept on the same low-key level. With the Anglo–Egyptian negotiations ongoing the last thing Britain needed, Lloyd conceded, was a major Arab propaganda offensive. Elath confirmed that the Israelis were not planning any ceremony or press coverage and would agree to anything the British asked for regarding the delivery.[8]

A further sign of the growing normalization was the very low-key decision taken in the same month by the Foreign Office to lift the ban on contacts with the Israeli opposition party, Herut, which had its origins in the Revisionist Zionist movement, and was led, as far as the Foreign Office was concerned, by public enemy number one, Menachem Begin. The British Ambassador, Sir Francis Rundall, had been approached by a Herut Member of the Knesset (MK) and invited to Herut's exhibition in Tel Aviv celebrating the exploits of the underground fighters during the British Mandate.[9] Rundall's subsequent advice to the Foreign Office contained all the elements of classic British diplomacy: suspicion of the locals, Herut might try to make political capital out of his visit, fear of the Arab and Soviet reaction – they could view it as supporting Herut's ambition of expanding Israel's borders, and avoidance – in terms of not offending the official Israeli Government.[10]

Although the Foreign Office advised against contacts at the highest level, it did agree with the Ambassador's recommendation that low- to medium-level contacts should take place. As a Foreign Office official argued, Britain couldn't continue to ignore a party that one day might be the leading party in a governing coalition.[11] The Foreign Office did instruct the Ambassador to warn the Israeli Minister of Foreign Affairs,

Golda Meir, that the times were changing and that the Foreign Office no longer thought it necessary to avoid all contacts with Herut.[12] The decision to sanction contacts, albeit at a low level, represented a major u-turn in the thinking of the Foreign Office's attitude and the adoption of a more pragmatic stance towards the leading Israeli opposition party. The decision reflected a growing focus on the future rather than the past period of the British Mandate.

So on the surface everything appeared fine. Foreign Office officials probably no longer dreaded the requests of the Israeli Embassy in London for meetings, and the briefing papers prepared by officials for the Secretary of State's meetings with the Israeli Ambassador were not as defensive in tone or patronizing towards his guests. Beneath the surface, however, very real and growing problems remained between the Foreign Office and Israel. Israel's request to sell bonds in Britain, which was an important avenue for Israel to try to secure foreign credits, had been rejected on legal grounds by the Treasury.[13]

The rather weak foundations of Anglo–Israeli relations in 1959 admitted in the Annual Review for 1959 for Israel concluded that, given the political situation in the region (fragile peace and growing Soviet penetration), it was difficult to see how the Anglo–Israeli friendship could develop further, as the Western powers could not be expected to please Israel at the expense of Egypt.[14] This statement in effect amounted to a clear warning that there were to be rocky times ahead for Anglo–Israeli relations. In other words, the Foreign Office wanted to adopt a low-key approach of trying to rebuild relations with Egypt and gaining a degree of influence with President Nasser. At all costs it wanted to avoid another Arab–Israeli war that would make its continued attempts to rebuild its image in the Arab world following Suez, while also enjoying good relations with Israel, all the more difficult to maintain.

From tanks to missiles: Israel's new shopping list

Although the Israeli Government was naturally disappointed that there was to be little financial gain following its closer relations with Britain, it was once again the arms issue that was to be the determining factor in Anglo–Israeli relations from 1959 to 1962.[15] The issue, in part, continued to revolve around the sale of Centurion tanks to Israel, but the tanks were increasingly overtaken by Israel's quest for surface-to-air missiles from Britain (or defensive missiles, as Ben-Gurion constantly referred to them) that it believed it needed to counter the threat of the Air Force of the

United Arab Republic (Egypt and Syria). As Ben-Gurion was fond of reminding the British, the UAR had more planes than the Israelis and therefore the missiles were required to balance this state of affairs. In a replay of the earlier tale of the tanks, the missiles were sought from Britain because the Americans refused to sell them to the Israelis (during both the presidency of Eisenhower and the early days of the Kennedy administration).

The issue of the tanks simply would not go away despite the Foreign Office's more liberal line towards selling arms to Israel. In July 1959 it became clear to the Foreign Office that Israel was attempting to acquire some 100 tanks from South Africa.[16] Though the Foreign Office considered that it would be difficult to stop the South Africans shipping the 100 tanks to Israel (the sale would be conducted through agents) it wanted to take a tough line with Israel, arguing that it would subtract the number of South African tanks from the number that Britain had promised Meir the previous September to sell to Israel.[17] The affair of the South African tanks illustrated that the Foreign Office was still sensitive to charges of fuelling the arms race in the Middle East and to Arab and Soviet charges of arming Israel.

Waiting for Nasser: Britain's quest for influence and Israeli irritation

While not taking Israeli goodwill for granted, the Foreign Office was acutely aware that any move towards appeasing or developing ties with Nasser was viewed by the Israeli leadership as a loss to Israel. By early 1960 it was clear that the Foreign Office was finding it increasingly difficult to mange its policy of maintaining good ties with both Israelis and the Arabs.[18] At the heart of the dilemma for the Foreign Office lay the acute problem that it regarded the stock of Nasser as more important to British interests than that of Israel.[19] Tellingly, the Foreign Office noted Israel's relative weak position at the start of the 1960s. Israel was so short of friends that it could not easily risk damaging its ties with Britain.[20] There was a sense in the Foreign Office that the Israelis did not appear to be too disappointed with the British, despite that fact that the British were increasingly, as they put it, having to give Israel one or two knocks.[21]

The Israeli Foreign Minister Golda Meir was, however, becoming increasingly exasperated by the British policy of chasing Nasser. She did concede that she had no objection to Britain being represented in Egypt and trying to bring its influence to bear on Nasser. What irked her, and other Israeli leaders, most was the way that Britain (and the other Western powers) ran after Nasser.[22] She argued that all the Western powers appeared to be doing was hanging around Nasser cap in hand asking him from time to time whether there was any whim of his that he wished them to satisfy.[23] The efforts of the Foreign Office were naturally to attempt to dislodge Nasser from his communist connection and attempt to bring him back into the fold. But, as Meir commented, there was little evidence of such a change occurring.[24] In reality, Israel was once more becoming increasingly concerned about Nasser and his now heightened use of propaganda from Radio Cairo, which among other nasties called for the destruction of Israel. To make matters worse for Israel, there was an increasing belief within the Foreign Office that the Israelis were completely blind about Nasser. It was the belief of the Foreign Office that this was particularly true of Meir and Ben-Gurion, who were accused of being irrational in their paranoia about Nasser.

The Eichmann trial adds to growing tensions

The announcement by David Ben-Gurion to the Knesset on 23 May 1960 that Adolf Eichmann, one of the key architects of the Nazis' final solution for the Jews, had been arrested and was in Israel should have had little impact on Anglo–Israeli relations. It was after all an affair between Israel and Argentina – the country in which the Mossad agents had captured Eichmann. These, however, were no ordinary times, and with the growing bitterness felt by some Israelis over Britain's pursuit of Nasser despite his frequently articulated belief that he was going to destroy Israel, Britain was dragged into the Eichmann affair. Eichmann's capture, subsequent trial and eventual hanging dominated the political agenda in Israel and much of the world.

Though there was widespread pleasure in the Foreign Office that Eichmann was under lock and key there was also increasing concern over the various international laws that Israel had breached in its capture and transfer of Eichmann to Israel.[25] The Israeli Government did not welcome the various debates within the Foreign Office about the legality of the kidnapping of Eichmann and the decision by Britain not to send an official observer to the subsequent trial in Israel.[26] On this occasion, the Foreign Office's decision had more to do with its interpretation of law than with any political reasons.[27] The absence of an official British observer at the trial did not go down well with the Israeli press, but was not articulated as anything more than mild annoyance.[28] The fact that the British Ambassador chose to leave Israel during the Eichmann trial to go on holiday was also commented upon in some circles and in the Hebrew press. In reality, the Eichmann trial had little impact on Anglo–Israeli relations, with the Foreign Office keeping most of its doubts about the legality of the trial to itself: a clear case in the eyes of the Foreign Office of the product being more important than the process.

The old man comes to London

The visit of David Ben-Gurion to London in June 1961 marked an important point in Anglo–Israeli relations. June 1961 was an exciting time for diplomacy, with President Kennedy scheduled to arrive in London at the same time as the veteran Israeli leader. As ever, the Foreign Office was concerned about the signals that Ben-Gurion's visit would send to the Arab world, as a Foreign Office official confirmed that it could not justify a refusal to see Ben-Gurion. President Kennedy would have seen him in New York and the Arab governments must accept that Britain has normal contacts with the governments of countries with whom it has diplomatic relations.[29] Given the somewhat frosty nature of relations between the Israeli Prime Minister and the Foreign Office and the former's reputation for lecturing his hosts on difficult issues (arms sales), the Foreign Office and the Embassy in Tel Aviv did more than their fair share of preparation for the meeting. The key points that officials discussed bringing up with Ben-Gurion were the question of the Arab refugees, the issue of the Jordan waters and the question of Israel's nuclear reactor.[30] They argued, however, that Ben-Gurion's visit to Britain (along with his prior visits to Canada and the United States) had a lot to do with electioneering – elections were due to be held in Israel on 15 August.[31]

Ben-Gurion met with the Secretary of State on 2 June 1961 and shifted the debate on arms sales to Israel firmly onto the question of the selling of British surface-to-air missiles.[32] Foreign Office heads noted that this appeared to be the main object of his meeting with Alex Douglas-Home, who had succeeded Selwyn Lloyd the previous year.[33] Ben-Gurion put forward the classic Israeli case for the weapons that had been employed during the 1950s over the tanks and fighter aircraft. The argument was, in brief, that Israel needed the weapons in order to redress the arms balance in the region. On this occasion he pointed out that Israel had only three airfields against the United Arab Republic's 36 (Union of Egypt and Syria). The Israeli airbases were only some five minutes' flying time from the UAR bases, which made them extremely vulnerable to bombing. Ben-Gurion insisted that he did not mind the fact that the UAR had more planes than Israel, provided that Britain offered Israel the defensive missiles it was seeking.[34]

If the Israeli reasons for asking for arms were the same, so was the British response. Sir Alec Douglas-Home simply said that Britain did not want to be responsible for starting an arms race in the region, which might lead the Egyptians to ask the Soviets for all offensive and defensive missiles (heard that one before). Never one to give up, the Israeli Prime Minister responded that the Soviets understood the difference between defensive and offensive missiles, and anyway would give the Egyptians whatever missiles were in the Soviet interest, regardless of what Israel acquired.[35]

On the same day, Ben-Gurion met with the Prime Minister, Harold Macmillan. Despite Macmillan's attempts to primarily focus the meeting on Israel's nuclear programme, Ben-Gurion pressed his British counterpart on the missile issue.[36] Macmillan shared the concerns of his Secretary of State and did not hold out much hope for the Israelis. If the objective of Ben-Gurion's visit had been simply a photo opportunity for electoral purposes then his visit could be classified as a success. Both the Secretary of State and the Prime Minister warmly greeted him. If he had seriously held out hopes of getting the missiles then his visit was, in the short term, largely unsuccessful.

As Ben-Gurion departed, the Foreign Office was left to soothe the Arab world, which had become increasingly critical of the Israeli Prime Minister's tour. In Egypt all the Cairo papers gave prominence to Ben-Gurion's visit with headlines such as 'Ben-Gurion meets Churchill'[37] and 'Macmillan and asks for fresh arms for Israel'.[38] An editorial in *Guhuriya* highlighted the British problems in the Arab world at the time. The article claimed that after losing all its [military] bases in the Middle East Britain had no ally in the Middle East except Israel.[39] Moreover, by arming Israel, Britain intended to encourage instability and tension in the Middle East and to secure a permanent and dependable base. The article was also laced with a fair degree of references to Britain's imperial past and to the fact that in its eyes Israel was simply a tool of Western imperialism.[40] The reaction in the Iraqi press was similar, if a little more low-key. *Al Thawra* ran an editorial calling for the imposition of sanctions against countries that helped Israel, such as Britain.[41]

In truth, the notion of conspiracy between Israel and the Western powers was never far from the Arab mind. The official press in Morocco jumped from a simple factual reporting of the meetings between the Israeli Prime Minister and Alec Douglas-Hume and Harold Macmillan to the point that there was little doubt that the meetings were aimed at starting yet another conspiracy against the Arab countries.[42] This article, like the others from Egypt and Iraq, bore the stamp of 'the official line' and was aimed for domestic consumption. That said, the three articles demonstrate the difficulties that the Foreign Office encountered in dealing with the Arab world over Britain's relations with Israel. The Moroccan article serves as the best example, as the authors had printed (almost word for word) the Foreign Office release about how Ben-Gurion had not been invited by the British and that the meetings had only lasted about 30 minutes, during which time only general issues relating to the Middle East were discussed. From this narrative, however, the Moroccans had switched with ease into full-scale conspiracy theory. Little wonder that Foreign Office officials spent so much time preparing statements that appeared to appease the Arab world.

The reaction of the Israeli press to Ben-Gurion's London visit was very downbeat and presented the Foreign Office with the sense that the Israeli Prime Minister felt that his visit to London had been a failure, in contrast to his meetings in Washington and Paris. When questioned by the Israeli press, the Prime Minister had merely responded by stating that his talks in London had been more or less satisfactory.[43] The Israeli press subsequently deduced from these comments that Ben-Gurion had been coolly received in London and contrasted this with his reception in Paris.[44] With typical Israeli understated irony, the Director-General of the Israeli Ministry of Foreign Affairs, Dr Yahil, argued that the Israeli press had got it wrong. Ben-Gurion had not expected anything that he had not received. After all, Dr Yahil went on, he had invited himself, and at rather short notice.[45] In reality, the Foreign Office was not overtly concerned about the press headlines in Israel so long as they didn't argue that Ben-Gurion had been snubbed. What worried officials much more was how the Israeli and Arab presses put their respective spins on Ben-Gurion's visit to London. If the Israeli press appeared to adopt a downbeat tone over the visit, then this made the Foreign Office's job of managing Arab anger over Ben-Gurion all the easier.

One fact had emerged from Ben-Gurion's visit to London: Israel wanted the missiles, and the Prime Minister's plea to British leaders was merely the start of a concerted Israeli diplomatic initiative to pressurize the Foreign Office into agreeing to sanction the sale of the missiles to Israel. On 8 June the Israeli Ambassador in London, Arthur Lourie, had requested a meeting with Foreign Office officials (no doubt on instructions from his prime minister, as one official sarcastically commented).[46] Despite the Israeli cover story of this being a meeting about the general situation in the Middle East, Foreign Office officials knew what to expect. After the usual exchange of pleasantries the Ambassador launched into the real purpose of the meeting, which was to follow up Ben-Gurion's request for the missiles. The Israeli argument centred on reminding the British of the very real nature of the Arab threat from Egypt and Syria (UAR) – a threat that was being given considerable coverage in the state-controlled Arab news-papers and radio stations. The Ambassador pointed to an article by the Egyptian scholar and journalist Mohamed Heikal, who was close to Nasser, which stated that there would have to be a war with Israel that the Egyptians looked forward to it, and it would be the end of Israel.[47]

In a classic diplomatic move, Lourie said he understood the British counter-argument to Israel's request (he clearly understood the bottom line of diplomacy that you never ask your friends for something you know they can't give you). He went on, however, to suggest that perhaps Britain could share the missile technology with Israel, or exchanges of information as he put it.[48] He concluded by asking if it would be possible to enquire how much the missiles cost just in case, if one day Britain were able to sell them to Israel, they would know if they could afford them.[49] The Israelis had clearly learned the lessons from their head-on approach to the request for Centurion tanks during the 1950s. Crucially, Israeli officials also understood that Britain's position in the region was much weaker than during the 1950s and that the arms markets in the Middle East for British exports had significantly shrunk.

The Israelis were acutely aware of the Foreign Office's position on the missiles and, given its central role in sanctioning arms sales, there was little point in trying to appeal to other ministries which might have proved more sympathetic to the sale of the weapons.[50] The British were not the only door the Israelis were attempting to push open. Ben-Gurion had raised the issue of the missiles in his meeting with President Kennedy but with little luck. In truth, he did not push the Americans as hard as the British, believing that the American position was more immovable than that of the British.[51] He had also raised the issue with the French.[52] Part of the Foreign Office thinking on the issue was based on the belief that the French might sell the Israelis similar-type missiles. With export opportunities limited, there was a growing sense of frustration in the Foreign Office at the French arms policy, which appeared to be dictated by economic rather than political motives.

Israel's road to nuclear weapons

Much of the Israeli decision-making regarding the production of nuclear weapons was quite naturally shrouded in top secrecy at the time. Israeli leaders, including Ben-Gurion, and officials claimed that the Israeli nuclear programme was simply for peaceful purposes – in order to produce cheap electricity to help take the salt out of the sea water to irrigate the Negev Desert.[53] When questioned in detail, as Ben-Gurion had been during his visit to Canada in 1961, the Prime Minister simply made up figures or claimed that he had little grasp of the details.[54] Given the willingness of the French in selling nuclear technologies to Israel, the British were largely powerless to prevent the creation of Israel's nuclear programme and its eventual production of nuclear weapons. Foreign Office officials were acutely aware of this fact, and for them the most basic goal was attempting to reassure the Arab world that Israel's nuclear programme was for peaceful purposes only. Not an easy task at the best of times, but made all the more difficult by the suspicion that this wasn't completely true.

This task took the form of trying to arrange inspection visits to the site of Israel's nuclear reactors. The US State Department also adopted the same response, and one such visit took place in June 1961 when two US atomic scientists visited the Israel atomic installation at Dimona and reported that they were entirely for peaceful purposes.[55] At various times the Foreign Office worked in conjunction with the US State Department at trying to reassure the Arabs, but in other cases such as the reporting of the visit of the nuclear scientists to Dimona, the Foreign Office was left in the cold by the Americans, much to the irritation of its officials.[56]

In truth, and despite the public reassurances, by the spring of 1961 the Foreign Office knew and understood that Israel had the potential to produce enough plutonium to support a very limited military programme.[57] Moreover, the Foreign Office had known for some time before it was made public in December 1960 that the Israelis had a large secret industrial complex under construction near Beersheba and that this plant contained nuclear installations.[58] The Foreign Office's responses operated within the framework of its wider Middle East policy of trying to reduce tension in the Middle East and the threat of war. It thought that the best way of dealing with Israel was not to attack it in a public forum but rather to work behind the scenes with the Americans to limit the damage of Israel's nuclear reactor and to make sure that it did not lead to the production of a nuclear weapons programme.[59] One of the major problems facing the Foreign Office was the fact that the French were assisting the Israelis to build the installation, though the extent of French involvement at the time was not fully understood.[60]

If events were not already complicated enough for the Foreign Office, appeasing the Arabs over the Israeli nuclear programme and quietly criticizing the French for the sale of the nuclear technology that allowed Israel to commence its nuclear programme, another issue arose that was potentially highly damaging to British interests in the region. The Foreign Office had, in effect, sanctioned the sale of heavy water to Israel – a vital ingredient in Israel's nuclear programme. In other words, Britain had secretly helped build Israel's nuclear programme. The story of the sale is complex. Writing in March 1961, the Foreign Office argued that two lots of ten tonnes each of heavy water were consigned to a Norwegian company in June 1959 and June 1960, and not to Israel as was claimed. The two loads, however, were put on Israeli ships at a British port.[61] The sale was therefore not strictly a direct one, but the evidence available from Foreign Office minutes clearly points to the fact that officials knew that the heavy water was bound for Israel for, as they put it, 'peaceful use by Israel in a reactor connected with desert irrigation'.[62] Rather unsurprisingly, given the sensitive nature of this issue, a Foreign Office official marked the file that the above information was not to be used in response to enquiries about the heavy water.

When approached by the Israelis for more hard water, the UK Atomic Energy Authority referred the issue of the sale of the irradiated fuel to the Foreign Office for further discussion on 13 January 1961.[63] Even at this point there was still a debate about the sale of surplus heavy water to Israel, with the Office of the Minister of Science arguing that from a financial point of view there would be some profit in it.[64] This time the Foreign Office declined the Israeli request. The documentation serves as confirmation of the knowledge of the Foreign Office. This primarily lay in a letter that had been sent by Croome from the United Kingdom Atomic Energy Authority to Hainworth at the Foreign Office on 13 January 1961.[65] The main purpose of the letter was to provide the Foreign Office with some information about Israel's nuclear reactor that had been obtained by a visit to a Norwegian company who were providing the Israelis with heavy water. Croome enclosed a copy of a letter he had received from C. Hart-Jones, who had recently visited the Norwegian company. In the letter Hart-Jones confirms that Britain had provided 'a quantity of heavy water' for the nuclear reactor.[66]

On the surface this would appear to be a shocking discovery. The

British Government, which for so long during the 1950s had been reluctant to sell arms to Israel, helping it along the road to becoming a nuclear power? Could this be the same Foreign Office that was privately so critical of the French involvement in the Israeli nuclear project? Had this information been leaked by either the Norwegians or the Israelis it would have done untold harm to Britain's relations with the Arab states. Today the reality appears a little less shocking, though it does make for good newspaper headlines and television programmes. It remains quite clear that, despite its official denials, it was the French sale of nuclear technology that allowed Israel to move so rapidly to construct a nuclear reactor and subsequently nuclear weapons.[67] The supply of some heavy water by Britain was extremely helpful to the Israeli programme but was not the decisive issue. The sensitivities over the issue when it was made public in 2005–6, however, were clearly illustrated by questions in the House of Commons and an internal Foreign Office investigation over the issue.

It is worth pointing out that the sale of heavy water did not mean that the Foreign Office was in effect sanctioning two very different policies towards the Israeli nuclear programme: quietly opposing the project, while in secret helping the Israelis. There is little evidence to back this charge. Indeed, it would appear that the sale of the heavy water could be seen as one-offs and did not alter British policy one iota. In retrospect, the Foreign Office made a mistake, but the affair was successfully kept under wraps for 45 years. Clearly the impact of the release of the information in 2005–6 was much less damaging to British interests than had it leaked out during the 1960s.

In 1961 the major fear of the Foreign Office remained how the Arab world would react to Israel's ability to produce nuclear weapons. There was talk in the Arab press that the UAR should ask the Soviets for atomic weapons.[68] In the Foreign Office there was deep concern that such a development would lead the Soviets to increase their supply of conventional weapons to Nasser, particularly aircraft.[69] For once, Arab press reaction was more muted. A Foreign Office official thought that this might be because they were concerned about frightening their readers.[70] Clearly, the last thing the Foreign Office wanted was a non-conventional arms race in the Middle East. The assessment that it was unlikely that the Soviets would provide Nasser with an independent deterrent was largely based on the distrust between the Egyptian leader and his Soviet masters. Egyptian attempts at developing its nuclear programme using overseas scientists proved to be unsuccessful.

Implementing abstension and disengagement

British policy towards the Middle East at the start of the 1960s was characterized by withdrawal or, as the Foreign Office referred to it, as abstaining and disengaging.[71] The problem the Foreign Office was encountering in attempting to implement this policy was that the Arabs were not convinced that this was what was actually taking place. The hand of the British was seen as being behind much of the continuing skulduggery in the region. The Israelis argued that given the recent history of the Middle East it would be a long time before people absorbed and were convinced by this new British policy.[72] Israeli Ministry of Foreign Affairs officials argued that this was compounded by the fact that in the Middle East people looked for causes, plots and conspiracies often when none existed. More often than not the real cause of events was self-interest or simply stupidity. In other words, the hidden hand of foreign intelligence agencies was seen as being behind much of the instability in the region. The Israelis claimed that President Nasser based much of his political opinions on military intelligence and secret reports.[73] In the Foreign Office there was growing concern over Nasser's 'persecution mania' and its implication for relations with the British. Foreign Office officials rejected an Israeli suggestion that the British should try to use humour to defuse the conspiracy theories as being heavy-handed (as most Israeli humour tends to be, they added).[74] For its part, Israel appeared to accept the intent of the British policy of withdrawal and disengagement from the region, but remained concerned about what they viewed as continued British attempts to appease Nasser.

The Foreign Office and Diplomatic Service were increasingly pleased to report that Israel was quiet – meaning not giving us cause for concern.[75] The Annual Review for 1961 for Israel warned, correctly, that the period of seeming calm in the region was giving way to a period of movement and uncertainty.[76] Put simply, this period was to prove the calm before the storm of increasing tension in the region that centred on Nasser, his increasingly unsuccessful attempt to intervene in Yemen, and the rise in tension between the Arabs and the Israelis over the issue of water. The tone of the report prepared in January 1962 by Ambassador Hancock casts Israel in a generally favourable light. Taken in comparison with the report for 1948, which we quoted from at the start of the book, it is clear just how far diplomatic relations with Israeli had developed in the 13 years since the creation of the state. Hancock describes Israel as follows:

Surrounded by enemies, teeming with unassimilated settlers, not economically viable, Israel is nevertheless the internal state in the Middle
East and the only democratic one. Her strength resides mainly in the
character of the population and in the agreement prevailing among
Israeli Jews about the nature and aim of the state . . . In spite of
bickering and complaining most Israelis are ready to work and, if
necessary, to die for Israel. It is this unity, single-mindedness and concentration which makes Israel so much more formidable than her
neighbours. In these circumstances the survival of the state appears
increasingly probable.[77]

Hancock's comments reflect the wider, seemingly contradictory views
that a number of Foreign Office officials and diplomats held about Israel.
On the one hand, there appeared to be a grudging sense of admiration for
the Israelis as individuals and for the democratic institutions of the
country's state (many of which were based on British democracy). On the
other hand, there was, at times, a realization that Israel's existence not
only complicated British interests in the Middle East but provided the
Arabs with excuses to sign up to the Soviet camp.

Later in the year, Hancock made the mistake of uttering in public the
phrase about Israel being the only democracy in the region. Bad move.
The Jerusalem Arabic newspaper, *Al Jihad*, ran a piece under the banner 'A
First-Class Zionist Propagandist'.[78] The ensuing article claimed that the
British Ambassador had become a first-class Zionist propagandist and
was being exploited by the Jews who had invited him to give a lecture at
a Jewish Bond Drive in London.[79] In reality, the Ambassador had given a
talk to the Younger Jewish National Fund showing slides of forests in
Israel; forestry was a subject that he was very much interested in.[80] Given
the fact that he was talking about the work of the Jewish National Fund
(JNF) in Israel he later admitted that it might have been better had he not
given the talk.[81] Apparently he had made the comments about democracy
during the subsequent question and answer session.[82] The British
Embassy in Amman – East Jerusalem was then part of Jordan – reported
back to an increasingly anxious Hancock that he shouldn't worry about it.
Morris went on in vintage Foreign Office-speak to rubbish the local Arabic
press, arguing that: 'One of the less unfortunate consequences of the Arab
press being what it is, is that its attacks are regarded by its writers and
readers alike as a routine ritual; and even when there is a grain of fact in
a heap of chaff, few notice it, or even care if they do.'[83] Though Hancock
had clearly leaned the lesson of the sensitiveness of his posting, the issue

illustrated the deep paranoia that the Arabs still retained about the British. Hancock's casual remarks were taken to be part of a British plot to damage Arab interests. It was indeed clearly going to be a long haul for the Foreign Office to fully convince people that Britain was in effect disengaging from the Middle East.

The waters run deep

In 1962 the most pressing issue for the Foreign Office to deal with in regard to the Middle East was the issue that Israel was preparing to pump water from Lake Tiberias in order to help irrigate the land in the south of the country and help the acceleration of industrialization there.[84] In a region where water was scarce, and water resources were often interconnected and continually disputed, this was a major development, and one that led Syria to promise war if the Israelis went ahead with the project. Though the Syrian threat was largely hyperbole it was true that the water issue, if not managed and mediated properly, was as likely as the development of Israel's nuclear weapons to lead to conflict in the Middle East during the early 1960s. Before looking at the political dialogue between the Foreign Office and Israel on the issue, it is worth looking at the origins and development of the dispute.

In simple terms, the water dispute between the Israelis and the Arabs centred upon the issue of who could best exploit the waters of the River Jordan. The river itself is fed by three other rivers that run through Lebanon, Syria and Israel (the Hasbani in Lebanon, the Banias in Syria and the Dan, which runs through both Syrian and Israel). The River Jordan ran along the line between the West Bank (which was under Jordanian control from 1948 to 1967) and Jordan.[85] Today it forms a 16-mile stretch along Israel's self-declared eastern boundary with Jordan. In the north of the country it flows through the old demilitarized zone and flows into Lake Tiberias. From this point it heads south, where, to further complicate affairs, two other rivers, the Yarmuk, which originates from Syria, and the Al-Zarqa from Jordan, join it. It subsequently crosses into Jordan and runs into the Dead Sea.[86]

In political terms water is vital for the development of countries. Ben-Gurion feared that if water could not be diverted to the Negev the area could be lost for ever. The water issue was also linked to Israel's national security. The Arabs predicted that if Israel was able to divert the levels of water that it wanted to do in the 1960s then Israel's population could double. The issue of maintaining a growing population was vital to both the demographic and security needs of the Israeli state. To be more specific, the Arabian fears of the proposed diversion in 1962 were that it would help Israel become stronger economically and help settle another wave of immigrants. Conversely, it would make the Arabs weaker by rendering the lands in the Lower Jordan too saline for use by the Arab farmers in the area.[87]

A plan put forward by the American Special Water Ambassador for Water in the Middle East, Erik Johnson, back in 1955 that called for Israel to get 38 per cent of the river's water and for the rest to be distributed among the Arabs was accepted by the Israeli Cabinet but was rejected by the Arab League in November 1955 on largely political grounds.[88] Though the Johnson Plan was not formally adapted it did set the informal basis for the divisions of the river's water.

Given the importance of the issue and political tension that characterized the Middle East it will come as small surprise that this water issue became linked to other political issues. True, both the Arab and the Israelis desperately needed as much as they could extract, but often this served as a prisoner of issues such as the Palestinian refugees and the ongoing border disputes.[89]

The Foreign Office appeared to accept the Israeli plans to pump water from Lake Tiberias for irrigation purposes in the south. The official position was that the Foreign Office regretted that it had not been possible for the Israelis and the Arabs to agree upon a unified plan for the River Jordan.[90] As a result, there was little alternative but to implement the unilateral schemes by the various countries involved.[91] These schemes, however, should take into account the needs of the other countries. In terms of Israel this meant attempting to minimize the damage that the potential diversion from the Upper Jordan would do to farming on the Lower Jordan.[92] While the British position appeared to be clear cut there was a constant fear in Israel that the Foreign Office would cave in to Arab pressure and alter the policy. For once the Foreign Office was able to report that there was a degree of flexibility in the Israeli approach to the diversion in terms of the timing of it and methods that could be employed to minimize the danger to the Arab farms in the Lower Jordan.

Good news for the economy – or is it?

By 1962, Britain was clearly established as Israel's largest export market.[93] With the German War Reparations Agreement with Israel drawing to its end, Britain had replaced Germany as Israel's largest supplier of goods after America.[94] The Foreign Office also noted that Israel's agricultural exports to Europe were damaged by the effects of the Common Market; and with negotiations between Israel and Europe only just starting at the end of the year, Britain was expecting even higher levels of trade with Israel in the subsequent years. So what did all this do for the relationship between the Foreign Office and Israel? It, in short, helped cement an additional level of mutual dependency to the relationship. The Israelis, in the short term anyway, were becoming increasingly dependent on Britain for export markets, and Britain was realizing the importance of Israel as one of its most important export markets in the Middle East.

As in other aspects of the Anglo–Israeli relationship, everything was not quite as rosy underneath as it appeared to be on the surface. Israeli officials felt slighted that Israel had not been invited to join COMET, an organization set up for improving British trade links with the Middle East.[95] The Israelis argued that while they understood that Britain wanted to improve trade ties with the Arab countries, COMET claimed to be for the whole Middle East and included the non-Arab countries of Turkey and Ethiopia.[96] In truth, the Israelis suspected that the British were using the Israeli discomfort to buy favour with the Arab world, which would result in increased contracts for British companies in the Arab Middle East.[97] Although this issue originally fell within the remit of the British Board of Trade, the Foreign Office and the Embassy in Tel Aviv were left to deal with the political fall-out. In a meeting with the Assistant Director-General of Israel's Ministry of Foreign Affairs, British officials attempted to reassure the Israelis by putting forward an interesting argument. They suggested to the Israelis that such organizations as COMET were set up to foster trade when it was sluggish and such a thing could not be said about Anglo–Israeli trade relations, and it was therefore a credit to all that COMET had no application to them.[98] Put simply, the Israelis were a victim of their own trade success. Did they accept the argument? No, but neither did Israeli officials push the issue any further.

All this illustrated that despite the impressive bi-lateral trade figures between Britain and Israel, there were tensions caused by the Arab–Israeli conflict. At the root of this lay the suspicion on the Israeli side that the Foreign Office would sacrifice some economic goodwill to Israel in order to attract a potentially larger share of Arab markets. In the Foreign Office there was a sense that they must not let another country influence the trade policies of Britain, mixed with an irritation that the Israelis were wingeing on about what it viewed as a relatively minor issue.[99] Privately the Foreign Office concurred with the Israeli complaint on one level, the manner in which they had been informed by the Board of Trade of the decision not to include it in COMET. A shoddy piece of writing, admitted an official – the ultimate criticism from the Foreign Office.

A farewell to the old man again

Though he did know it at the time, the meeting that John Beith, the newly arrived British Ambassador, had with Ben-Gurion on 22 May 1963 was the last meeting between a British official and Ben-Gurion while the latter was in office. Ben-Gurion resigned the following month, on 16 June 1963 and was succeeded by Levi Eshkol, who formed a new Cabinet the following day. To be blunt, Ben-Gurion had been a shadow of his former self for some time before his resignation. His political judgement, which Israel had relied upon for so long, appeared to have deserted him as he became obsessed with resolving the Lavon affair of 1954. He stood in subsequent elections in a new party he never retuned to power. It was a sad end to a political career that included some 43 years of leadership (pre-state Jewish organizations in Palestine and in the state of Israel).[100]

As ever, in his meeting with Beith, the Israeli Prime Minister was in combative form, indulging himself in one of the last political pleasures open to him, namely taking liberties with the newly arrived British Ambassador.[101] Perhaps it was the fact that Beith was the new boy in town keen to impress his masters back in London or simply boyish enthusiasm for the job getting the better of him, but Beith made a crucial mistake. At the start of his meeting he provoked a long historical survey from the Israeli Prime Minister, who was keen to deal with the British use of the word 'contemplate' in Israeli action against Jordan. Foreign Office officials had been afraid of Israeli pre-emptive action in Jordan during the previous months.[102]

In truth, Ben-Gurion's pseudo-intellectualism had irritated the Foreign Office for as long as it had had dealings with him. Officials noted a sense of both moral and intellectual superiority in the manner in which Ben-Gurion addressed Foreign Office officials. Given the almost uniformly Oxbridge background of the senior Foreign Office officials of the day it is not difficult to see how much this apparent intellectual arrogance must have got under their skins. Apparently this feeling was not unique to Foreign Office officials; in his autobiography the Israeli novelist Amos Oz argued that Ben-Gurion saw himself as not only a statesman, but also maybe primarily as an intellectual.[103] As Oz put it, despite the rigours of office the Prime Minister still found time to pen lengthy philosophical pieces that from time to time filled the weekend supplements of the Hebrew press. Oz recounted a story that Isaiah Berlin once told him that Ben-Gurion's belief that he was an intellectual was based on two mistakes; the first was he believed wrongly that Chaim Weizmann was an intellectual, and the second was that he wrongly believed that Vladimir Jabotinsky was an intellectual.[104] As Oz wryly commented, in this way Isaiah Berlin had ruthlessly killed three prominent birds with one stone.[105]

In the meeting with Beith, Ben-Gurion's monologue went over ground very familiar to British officials.[106] The points included the prime minister's admiration for British resistance against all the odds against the Nazis and his comparisons between this and the same odds that Israel faced in dealing with Nasser. Ben-Gurion suggested that Nasser was a man that 'one could normally do business with, but not even Nasser could control the fury of Arab nationalism directed against Israel'.[107] The Prime Minister went on to reveal that he had once sent a message to Nasser through an intermediary suggesting that they settle their dispute by holding a meeting in Jerusalem. Nasser was said to have replied that he could indeed settle the dispute in Jerusalem in a couple of hours but that he would never afterwards be able to return to Cairo.[108]

By this time, Beith was able to focus the mind of Ben-Gurion on the issue at hand, which was to try to persuade Israel to give some assurance that it wasn't planning to intervene in an increasingly unstable Jordan.[109] The Israeli Prime Minister merely replied that anything might happen in Jordan and so gave no firm commitment to Beith. At the conclusion of their meeting Beith asked the Prime Minister if he did not value the support of the Western powers for the status quo in the region. The Prime Minister's reply said much about the underlying tensions and suspicions in Ben-Gurion's relations with Britain. While welcoming the strong support of President de Gaulle of France, he reminded the Ambassador that his request for the Bloodhound surface-to-air missiles had been turned down and that the British Prime Minister's promise to consider the matter further had come to nothing.[110] In this respect, Ben-Gurion's final meeting with a British official mirrored his first meeting, and indeed all his dealings with the Foreign Office: namely, Ben-Gurion asking for the supply of British arms to Israel.[111]

A new dawn but the same old issues

Both the Foreign Office and the new Israeli Government were keen to emphasize that it was 'business as usual' when the Secretary of State, Sir Alec Douglas-Home, met the Israeli Ambassador, Lourie, for the first time since the transition of power in Israel from Ben-Gurion to Eshkol.[112] Given the fact that the stakes in Anglo–Israeli relations remained high, both sides were keen to move on, making as little comment as possible about Ben-Gurion's departure. In reality, however, there appeared a palpable sense of relief on both sides that the transition appeared to have been so orderly.[113] For its part, the Foreign Office appeared to understand that this time Ben-Gurion was gone for good, and not just taking a sabbatical as had been the case during the early 1950s. There was also a realization that the prospects of Ben-Gurion and his lieutenants being back-seat drivers for the Israeli Government, as had been the case during his first sabbatical, were very remote indeed. Ben-Gurion was gone, but not by any means forgotten as a political force (this happened really only after his party's electoral defeat in 1965). There was a sense in the Foreign Office that the Eshkol Government, while following the same policy guidelines as set out by Ben-Gurion, would prove easier to deal with than the previous government's.[114]

The meeting between the Secretary of State and the Israeli Ambassador confirmed that little had changed on the political agenda of Anglo–Israeli relations in the immediate aftermath of Ben-Gurion's departure.[115] The main feature of the meeting was once again the question of the supply of British weapons to Israel. The Israelis were growing increasingly nervous about the increased supply of Soviet arms to Egypt. Though the Israelis no longer needed the surface-to-air miles that Ben-Gurion had pleaded for during his visit to Britain in 1961, the Americans had agreed to supply Israel with Hawk missiles, but it would be a year before those weapons were available, and Lourie was still concerned that there was a gap in Israeli's defences.[116]

Israeli concern over the growing military strength of Nasser existed despite the fact that the Egyptian military was losing sizeable amounts of equipment and money. In October 1963, Meir estimated that the Yemen operation had cost Egypt around £80 million but crucially she believed that the military equipment that was being lost was being replaced by the Soviet Union.[117] She went on to argue that the cost of this rearmament to Egypt had been small and that the military experience in Yemen might prove useful for Nasser's troops.[118] In simple terms, the Israelis wanted to convey the message to the Foreign Office that the war in Yemen was not necessary weakening Nasser's military capabilities in the medium term. Egypt remained a very real threat to Israel and wherever possible Israel was looking for arms and guarantees on all Israel's frontiers. On the latter point she suggested that all parties, including the Soviet Union, guarantee all frontiers in the region.[119] Given the very active state of the Cold War, this suggestion of some kind of agreement with the Soviet Union did not go down well in the Foreign Office.[120] As one official noted, Meir's insistence on a published guarantee with the Soviet Union was worth nothing.[121]

The real reason, however, for the Foreign Office's opposition to the idea of published guarantees for Israel's borders was that it believed that if Britain was forced to go beyond general statements of support it would enable the Arabs to identify Britain with the Israelis.[122] Consequently the Foreign Office argued that Britain would lose its influence with the Arabs, and that the Soviets would be able to strengthen theirs accordingly.[123] True, the Foreign Office was keen to help reassure Israel and to attempt to check the influence of Nasser, but in no way was it willing to abandon what it regarded as Britain's interests in the Arab world in order to do so. Given the continued importance of Britain securing oil supplies from the region, this reluctance to formally sign up with Israel could hardly be described as a shocking development.

At the very core of the Foreign Office's thinking at the time was the deeply held belief that in spite of all threatening noises and propaganda, the Arabs had too much respect for Israel's military strength to take any action against Israel over any of the issues of the day.[124] This simple assessment was thought to be correct even on the previously mentioned Israeli scheme for taking water from Lake Tiberias. In essence, the Foreign Office belief was that the Arabs would not provoke a war with Israel until they believed they stood a reasonable chance of emerging victorious from such a conflict, and given the events in Yemen, where the Egyptian Army was not performing well, this appeared to be a long way off. This feeling appeared to contradict Israeli thinking, which felt (correctly, as it later transpired) that a weakened Nasser might be tempted to use the populist anti-Israeli card in order to deflect from growing difficulties at home. In this instance questions over the rational fear of Israel's armed forces might not be as meaningful as trying to secure the political survival of the Egyptian regime.

Crisis in the Western leadership

The months of October and November 1963 were tumultuous times for the Western powers. In Britain, the Prime Minister, Harold Macmillan, resigned on 19 October 1963. Macmillan's resignation led to the appointment of the Foreign Secretary, Sir Alec Douglas-Home, as Prime Minister, with Rab Butler succeeding Sir Alec at the Foreign Office. Butler had been the self-appointed heir apparent to Macmillan, who appeared to have attempted to do all in his power to ensure that Butler did not succeed him. The reason for the personal and political differences between Macmillan and Butler go beyond the scope of this book, but the result was that the Foreign Office got a Secretary of State who, as they themselves put it, was not particularly pleased to get the job, but to whom they gave high marks for his sense of duty.[125] Butler's impact at the Foreign Office was limited anyway by electoral politics. Within a year the Conservatives were out of power, having lost the general election in 1964 to the Labour Party under Harold Wilson.

The assassination of President Kennedy on 22 November 1963 meant that only General de Gaulle of France was left from the leadership of three powers. Although there was a degree of continuity of succession in both Britain and America, it remained a time of great uncertainty (Vice-President Lyndon B. Johnson had succeeded Kennedy, with little immediate impact on American policy towards the Middle East).

Butler gets the job he didn't want

In Britain, Butler held his first official meeting with the Israeli Ambassador, Lourie, on 3 December 1963. In order to help bring its new boy, with his limited diplomatic experience, up to speed, Foreign Office officials excelled themselves, producing some of the most detailed briefing papers seen for such a meeting for a long time.[126] At the time of Butler's arrival in office three major issues continued to dominate the political agenda with Israel: the Israeli request for guarantees over its border, the extraction of water from Lake Tiberias and the continuing development of Israel's nuclear programme.[127] All this took place against a backdrop of continued uncertainty in the Arab world where there had been an army-led *coup d'état* in Iraq the previous month. The Foreign Office was keen to put out any fires on all the above issues that concerned Israel. Indeed, the Foreign Office in basic terms accepted Israel's position on all the issues. It could not, for reasons previously discussed, offer

Israel anything more than general statements of support for maintaining its frontiers.[128]

In simple terms, Anglo–Israeli relations remained in extremely good shape in 1963, with the Foreign Office relieved that there appeared to be no difficult decisions about the supply of arms to Israel on the horizon.[129] The Israelis had enough British tanks, the Americans had agreed to supply the Hawk missile system, and the French were supplying virtually all Israel's military aircraft.[130] Despite the Arab economic boycott of Israel, Anglo–Israeli trade was rapidly expanding and there was no sign of a reversal of this long-term trend.[131]

Water under the bridge: Mrs Meir comes to town

On 3 March 1964, the Prime Minister, Sir Alec Douglas-Home, met with the Israeli Minister of Foreign Affairs, Mrs Meir. The meeting took place in the shadow of the Arab Summit Conference, which had discussed the Arab response to Israel's move to divert water. The Foreign Office was to a large extent relieved that the Arabs had come out at the conference against adopting a military solution.[132] This was seen as confirmation that the Arabs, despite all their bluster, when the crunch came would not go to war with Israel as the Syrians had earlier threatened to do.

The Foreign Office continued to be generally supportive of Israel's position of not being drawn into the polemics on the subject and trying to avoid raising the political temperature by publishing the timing of its pumping operations.[133] Regarding the latter of these issues, Foreign Office officials suggested in a brief for the Prime Minister's meeting with Golda Meir that as a means of reducing tension further, the Israelis should address the most sensitive point. This point centred on the Arab fear that the Israelis were going to use huge amounts of water in the Negev and that this would lead to a large rise in the rate of immigration to Israel. As in the eyes of the Foreign Office these fears were based on false information, Israel should find a way of allaying the Arab fear on this point.[134] When the Prime Minister raised this point in his meeting with Meir, she replied in a somewhat prickly fashion, 'Who needed convincing?'[135] She went on to argue that there was nothing that Israel could say that would convince the Arabs, and the rest of the world was not particularly worried.[136]

During the course of the accompanying meeting between Meir and Foreign Secretary Butler on 3 March, the water issue was touched upon once more, with the Foreign Secretary suggesting that in light of

President Nasser's violent speeches on the subject, Britain and Israel should keep in touch on the issue through diplomatic channels.[137] Meir, however (though, as Butler noted, she was more relaxed and less excited about the Jordan waters), did make it clear that Israel was deeply concerned about Jordanian plans for a large dam on the River Yarmuk. This dam was to be a much larger one than the Johnson Plan had originally permitted and which the Jordanians were undertaking with the aid of Yugoslav consultants (Soviet bloc). Meir argued that this appeared to be an attempt to divert water from the River Banias into the Yarmuk. The Israeli fear was that the Soviets might lend the money for such a project. She warned that Israel would not be able to stand by and allow such a project to happen. Nasser, she informed Butler, must be made aware of this fact. The water issue, while never escalating into area conflict, simmered beneath the surface for much of this period. As we have seen, the Foreign Office appeared at this stage quite relaxed about the issue, hoping that quiet diplomacy would succeed in keeping the potential fallout from the Israeli moves from developing into a full-scale crisis. Despite Meir's warning, Foreign Office officials were relatively reassured that Israel was going to continue with its low-key softly-softly approach to the issue.

The end of the love affair

Just when everything appeared to be going so well, Meir dropped a political clanger of quite gigantic proportions for the Foreign Office's relations with Israel, something that she was prone to do from time to time during her entire period in office. At a press conference in London on 5 March 1964, she said that Arab action to cut off the headwaters of the River Jordan would be as much aggression against Israel as cutting off a part of its territory.[138] Foreign Office officials were furious that Meir had issued a threat to a third country while on British soil. The result was that officials became increasingly concerned that Meir's threats, when taken together with a number of high-profile visits by Israeli leaders, gave the impression that Britain was leaning too heavily to the Israeli side.[139] There was a sense among senior officials that something had to be done to redress this balance in the near future, and British ambassadors in the region were informed of this fact. In truth, Meir had not only managed to offend the Foreign Office on an issue on which there was broad agreement between Britain and Israel, but she had not served Israel particularly well either. Her coarseness and threatening language had given those in the Foreign Office who were uncomfortable at the cozening up to Israel the opportunity to strike back. It was a very poor case of diplomacy from a highly experienced Minister of Foreign Affairs who should have known better.

The process of diplomatic damage limitation for Meir's remarks was completed in a meeting between Israeli Ambassador Lourie and Secretary of State Butler on 2 July 1964. The meeting had been requested by Lourie to survey developments in the Middle East. At the centre of this lay the Israeli confirmation that water was now flowing from Lake Tiberias and that so far everything had gone off without incident.[140] Lourie speculated that with Nasser preoccupied in Yemen there had been no Arab military response or attempts made to sabotage the diversion.[141] Regarding the Arab plans to divert the head-waters of the River Jordan, technical preparations were under way but no work was taking place on the ground. Butler's response illustrated that although the Foreign Office was still angry with Meir's threats made during her visit to Britain, the general remit of British policy remained unchanged towards the Israeli diversion scheme.[142] He argued that he had been left in no doubt about the level of Arab feeling about the Jordan waters but had decided not to do anything about it yet.[143] Furthermore, the Secretary of State had informed Arab ministers visiting Britain that any Arab diversion plan would be regarded as an unfriendly act.[144]

Anglo–Israeli trade at the end of the Tory years

As the period of 13 years of unbroken rule by the Conservative Party in Britain came to a close in October 1964, the British Embassy in Tel Aviv published some very striking economic data. During the course of 1964, British sales to Israel had shot up by almost 25 per cent. Moreover, the performance of British exports to Israel during the first part of the 1960s was almost unprecedented. From this data the British Ambassador made the following assessment of its significance:

> If it were not for the fact that this performance is somewhat blanketed by our very large stake in the Arab countries that produce oil, I think that Israel would be more generally recognized in London for what it is, namely, per capita, about the fastest growing market in the world for United Kingdom exports and the most valuable.[145]

All this amounted to a clear case of loaded dice. For as long as Britain was dependent on Arab oil then there would no place for Israel at the high table of British friends. This despite the fact that in economic trade, at least, the Israelis merited such a place. To some extent this phase represented the period from 1958 to the end of the Tory years in October 1964. Much of the ideological baggage that had originated from the period of the British Mandate had been shed. Israeli officials rarely mentioned the pre-state period in any of their dealings with the Foreign Office, which were characterized very much by a focus on the present and future threats against Israel's security. True, the political demise of Ben-Gurion and his historical and intellectual baggage had helped this process no end. His successor, Eshkol, appeared not to retain the same level of suspicion as Ben-Gurion throughout his political career about the motives and darks deeds of the Foreign Office.

The one major issue that could have placed a long-standing strain on Anglo–Israel relations, the British refusal to sell Israeli surface-to-air missile systems (despite the best efforts of Ben-Gurion to push for this), was luckily solved when the Kennedy administration in America agreed to start supplying the Israelis with similar missiles. With the British keen to withdraw from the Middle East and keep it relatively quiet, Foreign Office officials were keen to maintain influence in Israel in order to make sure that Israel did not escalate any of the issues of the day. The management of the thorny issue of the division of the waters of the River Jordan and its surrounding waters was perhaps the most difficult to achieve. Though it is merely speculation to suggest that had Nasser not been so bogged down in Yemen then the Arab response to Israeli efforts to divert waters would have been stronger at a much earlier stage, there is certainly an element of truth in this argument.

With the exception of the water issue and increasingly aggressive Egypt, the one ticking bomb, so to speak, remained the question of Israel's nuclear development programme. Given the realization in the Foreign Office that there was little that Britain could do to stop Israel's nuclear programme, which was being built, despite the official denials for Paris, with the full support of the French, the Foreign Office did as best it could to limit the damage to the region's stability and to British interests in the Middle East. Of course, the so-called neutral inspections of Israel's facilities were shockingly superficial, but this error was down to the State Department in Washington, and not the Foreign office, which oversaw many of the visits. The sale of two shipments of heavy water to Israel was, from a British perspective, a mistake: a simple case of economic gains outscoring political downsides. Not so. Such arguments, the Foreign Office would be quick to point out, were more reflective of the French nuclear policy at the time rather than British policy. Nevertheless the sale of the heavy water remains difficult to explain in rational terms. Stories continue to circulate that Britain's contribution to the Israel nuclear programme did not stop here. Rumours continue to circulate that Britain provided Israel with some quantities of platinum in 1965, although the documentary evidence supporting this is not as clear-cut as some claim. The question of whether there was a British conspiracy to Israel's nuclear programme, even in the knowledge that it might not be for peaceful means, will remain unproven. The evidence available to date regarding the sale of the heavy water points to that very British of explanations, the cock-up theory. When the Israelis came knocking again in 1961 for more, the Foreign Office and other agencies of government firmly rejected the advances.

Given the poor relationship between the Foreign Office and Israel between 1956 and 1958, the period between 1958 and 1964 can be seen in a very positive light. In many ways, however, given the restraining factor of the British need to maintain its interests in the Arab world, Anglo–Israeli relations had gone as far as they politically could. The dark clouds of war were starting to gather in the Middle East and these were to lead to a conflict that would once more transform the Foreign Office's relationship with Israel.

Part 3

The Turnover Years:
October 1964 to May 1979

5

The road to war and beyond

We suffer from the disadvantage of being the nation nearest to being regarded as family by the Israelis. This means that we always have a delicate path to tread, even though we need not take too seriously the usual vicious tone of the press, which can be too easily worked up against us. This is usually reserved only for us and for polemics between Israelis themselves. It is indeed remarkable how often the Israelis can behave in a manner more Arab than the Arabs.[1]

Michael Hadow, British Ambassador to Tel Aviv, 22 January 1968

Soon after the 1964 British general election, which led to the return of the Labour Party to power, Israeli officials from the Embassy in London approached the Foreign Office and asked whether it expected that there would be any big changes in British Middle East policy. Morris from the Foreign Office gave a guarded reply that he expected that there would be changes, but not big ones, as he argued that the main lines of British policy towards the region were largely dictated by interests and circumstances that had not changed.[2] This was the answer that Evron from the Israeli Embassy expected to hear, but it was not the one he wanted. His masters back in Jerusalem appeared to expect more from the new government in London. In truth, the Israeli Government hoped that there would be a shift away from the British policy of balance and even-handedness towards Israel and the Arab states towards a new policy of a close relationship with Israel.[3] The Israeli Government had been making a concerted effort in order to try to bring this about. There had been an Israeli proposal for its Prime Minister to visit London, a suggestion that the British Prime Minister, Harold Wilson, should be the guest of honour at the annual dinner of the Friends of the Hebrew University, and the proposal that the Secretary of State should be the speaker at a dinner organized by the Zionist Federation of Great Britain.[4]

The Israeli ideas did not stop here. In the military sector it proposed that ships of the Israeli Navy should make a first visit to London, a public handover ceremony at Portsmouth for the submarines, which were being sold to Israel, joint dumps for Centurion ammunition in Israel, and more air intelligence sharing between the Royal Air Force and the Israeli Air Force.[5] The Foreign Office was acutely aware that many of these political and military suggestions, if taken in isolation, were unexceptional requests by Israel. In other words, it could find ways of counterbalancing them with similar gestures in the Arab world such as Ministerial visits to Arab capitals. Foreign Office officials were concerned, however, as they put it, that 'if we thicken up Anglo–Israeli contacts at the pace suggested by all these suggestions collectively, our policy of balance will have gone'.[6] This would lead to a severe reduction in British influence in the Arab world and as a result put British interests in the region at jeopardy, which was a risk that the Foreign Office was not about to take. True, with the Labour Party in power Israel believed it had friends in high places. Many of the Labour Party leaders were very similar to the Israelis and had either visited Israel personally or had at least ongoing contacts with Israeli leaders through international organizations, but, as the Foreign Office confirmed, little had changed in British policy towards the Middle East.

In reality, British interests, as defined by the Foreign Office at the start of 1965, continued to be the maintenance of peace, the preservation of the East–West balance and resistance to Soviet penetration, and finally the promotion and protection of British material interests in the region.[7] Naturally, the Arab–Israeli conflict was deemed to be the most serious threat to peace and, by this point, Britain and the other Western powers believed they had a moral obligation to stand by Israel if it were ever threatened with being overrun and destroyed.[8] Oil continued to be a central feature of British policy and the protection of the routes of supply were of optimum importance to the British. With regard to the Arabs, the realization that in the eyes of the Foreign Office they were both volatile and undependable had struck home long before, but was increasingly seen as complicating Anglo–Arab relations.[9] That said, either was also a very clear realization that British interests lay in maintaining the best possible links with the Arab world. Nasser was seen as a troublemaker whose policies were adverse to Britain and whose efforts at developing influence in the Arab world were seen as extremely threatening to British interests. The most effective weapon that Nasser retained was to show that the Western powers were supporting Israel against the Arabs. The Foreign Office, as a result, was keen not to place this weapon in the hands of Nasser by fostering any level of ties with Israel that could be interrupted as ending the policy of balance. With the benefit of hindsight it is possible to see that this policy of balance was not quite as successful as the Foreign Office hoped. Many in the Arab world, and not only Nasserites, did not believe the terms of the British policy. As the politics of the Middle East developed in zigzag patterns towards the third Arab–Israeli war in 20 years, the maintenance of this policy became almost impossible, and it was this fact that was to lead to changes in British strategy towards the region.

The West Germans go weak at the knees and the water hots up

By the time that the Israeli Ambassador called upon the new Secretary of State, Michael Stewart, on 19 February 1965, a new crisis had started to erupt in the Middle East.[10] The issue concerned the delivery of arms to Israel from West Germany. At this stage, Lourie argued that the Israelis had only taken delivery of some 40 tanks out of a promised figure of 200.[11] West German statements indicated that the remainder of the consignment would not be delivered.[12] The Egyptians had placed pressure on the West Germans to stop the shipment of arms to Israel and, much to the surprise of the British and the Americans, the Germans had complied with Egypt's request and announced the decision to suspend further deliveries. In London, Lourie was pressurizing the Foreign Office to 'try to stiffen the backs of the West Germans'.[13] The deeper Israeli fear, in addition to the impact of the German decision on the balance of arms in the Middle East, was that once Nasser had seen that he had been successful with stopping German arms reaching Israel, he would turn his attention to other countries such as Britain that continued to supply Israel with arms. Israel at this time was feeling particularly isolated and vulnerable, feelings that were exacerbated by the formation of the United Arab Command – a move which Israel took to mean that the Arabs were in the long-term preparing for another round of conflict with Israel.

After lengthy negotiations between Israeli and West German officials the deal that emerged included the establishment of Israeli–West German diplomatic relations. Compensation, which Israel could use to buy the arms from another country, replaced the final part of the arms deal between the two. When all the credits and debits for Israel of the agreement were totalled up, Beith, the British Ambassador in Tel Aviv, thought that the Israelis had done very well out of it, when at one point it looked liked suffering a major reversal of fortunes.[14] Many Israelis, however, did not welcome the establishment of diplomatic relations with West Germany, but Beith correctly argued that at least many Israelis saw the move as a realistic step forward.[15]

In terms of the consequences of Israeli–German problems over the sale of arms for British sales, the Foreign Office noted that the Germans had failed to keep the sale of the weapons a secret. Indeed, the West Germans had appeared keen to let Nasser know of the sale at an early stage of the process.[16] The details of both British and American arms sales to Israel were shrouded in secrecy, which was designed to avoid the kind of Arab pressure that Nasser and the wider Arab world had been able to employ with the Germans. For its part, Israel respected the wishes for secrecy of both Britain and America and there were no handover ceremonies or press conferences when the arms arrived in Israel. In light of the events surrounding the West German arms, the British Embassy in Israel called for a strict adherence to this policy of secrecy over the sale of British weapons to Israel.[17]

As one crisis was successfully resolved, the increasingly bitter struggle over Jordan waters threatened to further escalate during 1965 and lead to a major armed exchange – exactly what the Foreign Office's policy of balance hoped to avoid. Though the various projects appeared to be in a 'state of suspended animation' the potential for future difficulties was clear for all to see. In short, the Israelis appeared to have succeeded in deterring the Syrian efforts to prepare the ground of the northern bank of the channel that would take water from the Hasbani and Banyas rivers down to the Yarmuk.[18] As the Embassy in Tel Aviv reported, this area was within range of Israeli artillery and the Israelis had been able to inflict a lot of damage on Syrian equipment under the cover of border artillery exchanges.[19] This had been backed up by the threat of constant Israeli air patrols. On the Lebanese side, things were moving more rapidly with the plans for water diversion.[20] Israel's own plans to pump water from Lake Tiberias had not gone without a hitch.[21] The cost of the process had increased substantially due to the unexpectedly high salinity of the lake. Given the need to maintain the flow of fresh water to Lake Tiberias, this made the Israelis even more concerned about Arab attempts to divert waters away from it.[22]

Farewell Golda: the new kid in town

During the course of 1966 there were several key changes of personnel at the top of both the British and Israeli Foreign Ministries. The most important were the promotion of Abba Eban to succeed Golda Meir as the Minister of Foreign Affairs in Israel, and in London the Cabinet reshuffle that brought George Brown to the Foreign Office on 11 August.

Brown's 18 months at the Foreign Office was not a totally happy time. Moreover, his personality was clearly not to everyone's taste at the Foreign Office. He was said to be 'abrasive, abusive and ebullient and was considered by some of his Cabinet colleagues not to have precisely the right temperament for the Foreign Office'.[23] In truth, and in terms of style of presentation and diplomatic negotiation, Eban resembled a traditional British Secretary of State more than Brown appeared to do.

Eban couldn't have been a more different type of personality to deal with than his predecessor Meir. Foreign Office officials were already familiar with Eban from his time as Meir's deputy and were quite naturally deeply impressed by his well-documented linguistic skills (as well as Hebrew and English, he spoke fluent Arabic and Persian).[24] While Meir enjoyed a large following of support from within the ruling Mapai Party in Israel, Eban did not enjoy the same support.[25] Indeed, he was often a largely isolated figure in the Israeli Cabinet and there was a sense in the Foreign Office that while he would be in charge of the implementation of foreign policy, Eshkol would set its overall course more than when Meir ran the Ministry.[26]

Eban's first official meeting with British Officials took place on 18 January 1966 when he called on Hadow, the British Ambassador in Tel Aviv. On the main point of his meeting, the question of arms supplied by the Western powers to the Arabs, Eban appeared comparatively relaxed, in contrast to Meir, who usually gave her hosts a lengthy lecture on the subject of Israel's security needs every time the subject was raised.[27] Eban's style was clearly very different. He argued that if the Western powers did not supply the Arabs with modern weapons, the Soviets would. Eban stressed that the arms question in the Middle East was as much psychological as practical.[28] After all, he went on, the whole doctrine of deterrence was a psychological one. The Israeli Government was suffering from the psychological effects and public opinion had become unduly excited.[29] Eban concluded, correctly, that this was largely due to the fact that Western arms deals to the Arabs were publicized, while, for obvious reasons, the British and French supplies to Israel were censored.[30]

This more laid-back attitude was all very new for the Foreign Office. The sense that the management of Anglo–Israeli relations would be easier with the Israelis under the stewardship of Eban was not only apparent to the Foreign Office. The US State Department had grown extremely tired of dealing with Meir during the final part of her time at the Foreign Ministry and there was a belief in the American Embassy in

Tel Aviv that they would have an easier ride with Eban than they had had with Meir.[31] The Foreign Office was extremely happy with Eban's first meeting with the Secretary of State, and especially the fact that he did not complain about not being able to meet with the British Prime Minister, Wilson.[32] By August 1966, the British Embassy in Israel was reporting how much easier life was for them at that end dealing with Eban than Meir.[33] The knock-on effect of Eban's promotion in the short run was that Israel was more popular in general than under Meir.[34]

Ironically, just as the memory of Meir was starting to fade from Foreign Office minds, her named cropped up once more in an unusual context, but one, which the Foreign Office felt could damage the British policy of even-handiness towards the Arabs and the Israelis. Meir had been invited to open the 1966 Labour Party Conference.[35] Although the organizer had asked Meir not to talk about the Middle East, there was deep concern that her invitation would be seen as evidence of pro-Israel bias.[36] As the Foreign Office itself admitted, there was little they could do to stop the visit. As one official noted sarcastically in a memo, 'In this country political parties, like the press, are free.'[37]

Caught in the middle

Back in the real world of politics, it was not long before Eban was dealing with the political fall-out from a number of incidents on the Israeli–Syrian border.[38] On top of this, the Foreign Office was pressing Israel on the question of its nuclear reactor. An inspection by American scientists had not been carried in a way that provided much reassurance to the Foreign Office.[39] The Americans had apparently found no evidence to suggest that Israel was producing nuclear weapons.[40] The winds of the Middle East were starting to shift in the direction of war, with Israel caught in the middle of internal battles in the Arab world. As Hadow, the British Ambassador, put it: 'The widening split between so-called pro-gressive Arab States and the traditionalists, and a more active Soviet policy in favour of the former, has meant that Israel is once more caught up in Great Power and internal Arab politics.'[41] The revolution in Syria in February was too great an opportunity for the Soviets to miss and they quickly returned to their traditional policy of trying to win friends by being hostile to Israel. Since this point, border tensions with Israel had increased, with Syrian attacks being met with traditional IDF retaliatory actions.[42] The British at this time, however, still clung to the belief that Israel was not looking for conflict and that given the strength of Israel's conventional forces, the Arabs would not 'attempt to secure Arab ends by military means'.[43]

In times of war and peace

As we now know from history, the so-called strength of Israel's deterrents did not prove strong enough to deter Nasser from escalating the crisis to a level at which war was unavoidable.[44] Bogged down and slowly losing a war in Yemen, Nasser was able to transfer his troops into Sinai and regain much of the faith that the Arab world had originally put in him. Just as Hadow suggested in January, Israel was the victim of Soviet and Arab internal politics. It is not the object of this book to speculate on Nasser's motives. Did he want war, or was he simply playing a dangerous game of diplomatic brinkmanship? The trigger of the war was the false Soviet reports of massive Israel tank movements near its border with Syria, and from this point on events moved too fast for the opportunity for diplomatic activity to have a chance of success. In truth, if there was ever any real prospect for peace between Israel and the Arabs, it was lost during the first part of the decade.

While Britain retained some influence in the region, this influence was more often than not linked to the Americans. On this occasion it was the American and the Johnson administration that led the diplomatic activity to try to prevent Israel from launching its pre-emptive strike on Egypt on the morning of 5 June 1967. The speed and scale of Israel's military victory in the ensuing war created new realities in the Middle East: a united Jerusalem under full Israeli control, Israeli control over the Golan Heights, the Sinai and the West Bank. For its part, the Foreign Office was extremely keen not to accept these gains as permanent features, but rather viewed them as Israeli bargaining chips that would be used to trade with the various Arab states for a settlement. As we shall see later, the ensuing diplomatic process did not endear the British to the Israelis, and even the usually calm figure of Eden grew increasingly agitated with British stances, particularly during the post-war diplomatic activity at the United Nations.

In terms of the immediate impact of the war on Anglo–Israeli relations, Hadow in his somewhat understated Annual Review of Anglo–Israeli relations suggested that they had had a rather chequered year in 1967.[45] Even before the war broke out, Britain had faced the kind of criticism in the Israeli press which the Ambassador described as only being dished out to those that Israel regarded as being near family.[46] On 29 March,

Hadow had informed the Foreign Office that he feared that there was going to a very stormy period of Anglo–Israeli relations ahead which would take the relationship back to the period before 1958.[47] Hadow's prediction drew an angry response from Morris at the Foreign Office, who accused the Ambassador of using shock tactics.[48] Moreover, Morris claimed that relations between Britain and Israel were 'uncomfortably close' before 1958.[49] Such was the tone of Morris's draft response that he was advised to adopt a less angry tone before the telegram was cleared for issue.[50] It should not be forgotten that this was a time of great tension in the Middle East and in the Foreign Office. The British policy of disengagement and attempts at averting another Arab–Israeli war was clearing not succeeding. To make matters worse for the British, in the month before the war there was another diplomatic crisis between Britain and Israel. The apparent crime that Britain had committed this time was to refuse to attend the Independence Day parade in Jerusalem.[51] The British were also blamed for apparently encouraging the Americans and the French to follow suit.

All of this was soon forgotten with the strong British Government and public support for Israel in the immediate period leading up to the Six-Day War and during the war itself.[52] This support not only wiped the slate clean from Britain's actions over the Independence Day parade in Jerusalem, it also led, as Hadow reported, to a great upsurge in pro-British sentiment in Israel. Unfortunately, disenchantment soon followed after Britain criticized Israel's occupation of Jerusalem and disagreed with Israel on how best to achieve a political settlement to the Arab–Israeli conflict. This difference can best be summarized as follows. The Israeli Government believed that if nothing was done the Arabs would be forced to come to the negotiating table and deal directly with the Israelis.[53] The British believed that the Arabs simply wouldn't do this.[54] The British did claim, however, to have detected a change in the Arab world, which could be taken advantage of to work for peace, but, as they put it, 'this would take time, perseverance and flexibility'.[55] Naturally, the Israelis took this to mean more Foreign Office appeasement of the Arabs.

Before recounting the efforts of the Foreign Office to push for Israeli withdrawals from the lands it had conquered during the course of the Six-Day War, it is worth outlining the attitude of the Israeli Government to calls to return these lands in exchange for peace. In essence, there was no broad consensus within the Israeli Government as to what to do with the conquered lands. The exception to this was of course Jerusalem. On this issue there was a broad consensus that East Jerusalem should be annexed and that the united city of Jerusalem should not be open to any negotiation. The government that had been formed on the eve of the war was a National Unity one, which for the first time included Menachem Begin and Gahal. Begin and his colleagues were against the return of any of the lands which they saw as being part of 'Greater Israel': a Jewish state to include the West Bank. It was within the parties of the Labour Zionist movement where the largest splits occurred. Some senior members of Mapai wished to exchange all the lands for peace; others, such as Moshe Dayan from the breakaway party Rafi, called for a more complex policy, and others wished to retain some lands that were deemed important for national security and hand others back.[56] Eshkol was extremely sensitive to these splits and, at times, his striking out against diplomatic attempts to resolve the conflict had much to do with the deep tensions within his own Cabinet on the issue.

Given the perception in the Israeli press that the hidden hand of the Foreign Office was behind attempts at the United Nations to force Israel to return the lands, it was perhaps only natural that an increasingly frustrated and angry Israeli Prime Minister should strike out at the British Foreign Office and the diplomatic service.[57] Eshkol summoned the British Ambassador, Hadow, for a meeting on 16 October 1967 in Jerusalem.[58] Hadow noted that it was indeed a rare pleasure to be invited for a one-to-one meeting with Eshkol, who did not usually grant such audiences. At the meeting, a clearly emotional Eshkol vented his anger and frustration at the British for about an hour without interruption.[59] There were elements of his predecessor, Ben-Gurion, in Eshkol's long, rambling section on Zionist history (Hadow had already shown himself to be an expert in Israeli history) and understanding of British interests in the region.[60] The key part of the talk was that Israel did not trust the United Nations (of which it had a bad experience) and that Israel would not cave in to pressure to return all the lands it had captured.[61] Eshkol concluded his monologue with a warning for the British that Jews had long memories.[62] Bevin had been an enemy of Israel and used similar phrases to describe the current Foreign Secretary, George Brown. These were strong words from a man who was famed for being rather bureaucratic and dull in his style of leadership.[63] At the conclusion of the meeting, Eshkol handed Hadow a copy of a memorandum to send to Brown outlining the Israeli Government's displeasure at what it saw as the further appeasement of the Arabs which would help bring them to the negotiating table.[64]

The content of the meeting between Eshkol and Hadow caused a great deal of concern in the Foreign Office. It appeared to suggest that a lack of grip and cohesion might be partially responsible for the anti-British attitudes in Israel at the time as well as Israel's inflexibility in dealing with the Arabs.[65] In a subsequent note to the British Prime Minister, Harold Wilson, the Secretary of State added that at this time the Israelis were in a dangerously nervy and unreasonable frame of mind.[66] This, Brown argued, had led some of its leaders to encourage a campaign of hostility towards Britain in the local press.[67] Though on the advice of his officials Brown did not respond directly to Eshkol, he did inform Hadow to let the Israeli Prime Minister know how much he resented the accusation that he was hostile to Israel.[68] Brown then offered a detailed explanation of British policy in the Middle East for Hadow to pass on to the Israeli Prime Minister.[69] Central to the British policy was the belief that President Nasser and King Hussein remained the two Arab leaders most capable of drawing the most realistic conclusions from the post-war situation and be able to act on them. Brown wanted the Israeli Prime Minster to understand that he was under no illusion in dealing with Nasser; he understood his motives and he had not abandoned them. Brown also attempted to dismiss Israeli claims that all that the British wanted to see was the reopening of the Suez Canal. End of story.

When Hadow met with Eshkol on 25 October to communicate the thoughts of the Secretary of State, he found the Israeli Prime Minister in a much more conciliatory mood.[70] By way of explaining his conduct during the first meeting, Eshkol said that it had been a good thing to speak to the Ambassador and get the matter off his chest, and this helped clear the air.[71] As Hadow reported, the tone of the meeting was thoroughly friendly. Eshkol clearly wanted to get relations back onto an even keel and his anxiety and embarrassment were apparent in his being even more incomprehensible than usual in a jumble of English, Yiddish, Russian and German.[72] One of Eshkol's officials told Hadow afterwards that what the Prime Minister was trying to convey, given his inadequate command of English, was to say sorry if he had caused any offence. And so the crisis was over for the time being.[73]

Eshkol's original outburst revealed two important points. The first of these was that while in public the Israel had no objection to the British re-engagement with Nasser, in private they were concerned that the British would sacrifice its relations with Israel in order to achieve this. The French had appeared to have done exactly this and there was a sense that it was impossible not to take sides at this time. There was also a sense that the Israeli felt that the British owed them for the protection of Western interests against the pro-Soviet Nasser. The second point was that despite all the progress made in Anglo–Israeli diplomatic and economic relations since 1948, whenever a crisis arose the Israelis brought up the period of the British Mandate and the record of Bevin in trying to prevent the creation of the state. The past, while not the driving issue in Anglo–Israeli relations, could not yet be consigned to dustbin of history.

In January 1968 Eshkol arrived in London for a meeting with Harold Wilson and the Foreign Secretary. He met with the Prime Minister on 17 January on his way back from talks with President Johnson in America. The meeting opened with the usual question of arms supplies to the Arabs from the Soviet Union and to Israel from the United States. For once, an Israeli Prime Minister said that he had not come with a shopping list for arms.[74] Wilson, no doubt relieved that this was the case, then moved on and pressed Eshkol on the issue of the status of Jerusalem.[75] The Israelis held out little hope of progress on this issue, stating that they were shocked at the damage that had been done to Jewish holy sites in the Old City.[76] Eshkol did agree that Israel would be willing to make King Hussein the keeper of the Islamic holy sites in the Old City.[77] This decision proved not to be to everyone's taste in the Middle East, but it remains in place until today.[78] Eshkol pleased the British by confirming that Israel would be willing to negotiate a separate agreement with Nasser that would allow the Suez Canal to reopen, provided that the passage of Israeli shipping would be guaranteed.[79]

The meeting was calm and businesslike; Eshkol appeared to have got over his displeasure at British efforts in the Arab world. In Israel, much of the attention to Eshkol's trip was devoted to his visit to the United States and to the Jarring diplomatic mission.[80] The Israeli press were satisfied with Eshkol's visit to London. *Haaretz* confirmed that Eshkol's visit reflected the improved atmosphere in Anglo–Israeli relations.[81] *Davar* agreed with this assessment, but still maintained that differences maintained over the best way forward and on the possibility of continued conflict in the region.[82] Most of the Israeli press focused on the discussion of the mediation attempts of the international community by way of the Jarring mission in order to try to broker a deal between Israel and Egypt. British Ministers are reported to have argued that Nasser's apparent moderation couldn't last for ever and that the fear that Arab extremists elements would prevail.[83]

The reduction in Anglo–Israeli tension was confirmed in meetings between British and Israeli Ministers that took place over the course of

1968. At the Foreign Office, Michael Stewart had replaced Brown in March 1968. Stewart returned to become the first head of the newly re-organized Foreign and Commonwealth Office (FCO). The Israelis warmed to Stewart much more than to his predecessor, Brown. The fact that Stewart was a little more reserved in manner than the brash Brown no doubt helped his case enormously. Israeli officials and ministers liked to be listened to and not lectured at.

Among the visitors to London was Israeli Deputy Prime Minister Yigal Allon. Allon was one of the leading candidates to succeed Eshkol and he took a keen interest in foreign policy. Being a senior figure in one of the more hawkish parts of the Israeli Labour Party, which was formed in 1968, his views were of great interest to the Foreign Office officials. During the course of the year he held several meeting with Stewart. On 19 September 1968 he, together with Remez, the Israeli Ambassador, met with Stewart at the Foreign Office. Allon was officially in town to give two lectures at the Institute of Strategic Studies. No change here in the British policy of not officially or formally inviting Israelis for fear of offending the Arabs. Allon's analysis of the situation in the Middle East was rather bleak.[84] He argued that the Jarring mission would ultimately fail and that there was little chance for any successful third-party mediation. He subsequently put the traditional Israeli case for direct bi-lateral talks between Israel and the Arabs, starting with Nasser.[85] Foreign Official officials gleaned from Allon that there was little shift in what it termed Israeli inflexibility.[86] For this reason Allon's meeting simply confirmed the result of all diplomatic contacts with Israel at the time: the Israelis were deeply reluctant to make major concessions. Allon had also noted the Khartoum Summit and the hard line adopted by Nasser with the phrase 'No negotiations with Israel' ringing in everyone's ears.[87]

After all the turbulence of the previous year, 1968 had been rather better for Anglo–Israeli relations. At the heart of this the realization lay the development in both Britain and Israel of a deeper understanding of the realties of the post-war situation in the Middle East. The Israelis were learning that its military victory and occupation brought its own disad-vantages and problems, and the British were realizing its limited influence on Israel on this issue.[88] As Hadow suggested, relations had been on an even keel for the year, despite some over-sensitivity of the Israelis to some of Britain's actions such as the closure of the Hebrew service of the BBC and Britain's actions at the United Nations.[89]

To some degree, Britain's relations with Israel had become more important to the Israelis now that General de Gaulle was considered hostile. French re-engagement in the Arab world, particularly with Nasser, led the General to take a very antipathetic line against Israel.[90] This represented a marked change from the start of the decade when the French had been Israel's closest ally, helping it build its nuclear reactor, which at some point during the decade had allowed Israel to allegedly produce nuclear weapons. Foreign Office officials at the time noted the highly emotional nature of the Franco–Israeli relationship and the potential for it to all fall apart. The state of relations at the end of the decade was simple confirmation that the officials were proved correct. True, the United States had become Israel's closet ally and, more significantly, arms supplier, but with the French out of the picture British influence was at least accepted, if not always welcomed, by the Israelis.

The return of Golda Meir to centre stage

The Israeli Prime Minister, Levi Eshkol, died on 26 February 1969. His death was unexpected and for a time it plunged the ruling Israeli Labour Party into crisis. At the time of his death, an increasingly bitter power struggle was taking place within the party between Moshe Dayan, Yigal Allon and Pinhas Sapir, all of whom came from a political generation below Eshkol.[91] In the end, a compromise was reached and Golda Meir returned to power to become Israel's first female Prime Minister on 17 March 1969.[92] There were two immediate questions that the Foreign Office devoted much time to considering: how long would she remain in office? and what line would she take with the Arabs?[93] Regarding the former question the Foreign Office made much of the internal disputes between Meir and Dayan at the time – not least because, as we shall see, Dayan himself was complaining about her to the British Ambassador. These disputes were said to have become more pronounced in the smoke-filled rooms in which the leadership decisions were taken.[94] To a certain extent, the Foreign Office misread the importance of the dispute between the two, which settled down a little when the government was installed with Dayan serving as Minister of Defence. As a result, officials nearly concluded that Meir might not run in the Knesset elections scheduled for November 1969.[95] Appleyard of the Near Eastern Section argued that Meir had a strong preference for Allon as her successor – something that was not totally true.[96] Her aim would therefore to be to ease him into power in a year or maybe two.[97] Put simply, the Foreign Office was not sure if Meir would remain in power in either the short or medium term.

Regarding the second question, Meir's speech to the Knesset on 17 March outlining the guidelines for her government served as a clear warning that she would take a tough line on the Arab–Israeli conflict.[98] In summary, she rejected any outside attempt to impose a settlement on Israel and restated a call for direct talks with the Arabs. Appleyard suggested that he did not think that we could expect any new concessions towards a Middle East peace settlement from her government.[99] On this issue, Appleyard's judgement proved to be extremely accurate.

Equally worrying for the Foreign Office's diplomatic efforts was the assessment of Meir by Moshe Dayan. At a private family dinner with the British Ambassador, Hadow, in Tel Aviv on 12 March 1969, the notoriously gossipy, and at times bitchy, Dayan had confessed to Hadow that he believed that Meir simply did not understand the Arabs and was completely blind to their needs and welfare.[100] As he put it:

> It was strange how an old time socialist with deeply ingrained ideals about the brotherhood of man, the dignity of labour and so on preferred to leave one section of humanity, the Arabs, out of her calculations. She was always preaching about Hebrew labour but this was as far as it went. When I try to get her interested in Arab labour she said that it was her business to look after the Jews first.[101]

Dayan went on to predict that he saw great difficulties with her about the administration of the West Bank in general, but in particular he said that he found her difficult to deal with on the question of providing work for the Arabs in the Gaza Strip and the West Bank and getting decent wages for those Arabs employed inside Israel. Needless to say, the Foreign Office was extremely grateful for this piece of intelligence on Meir from someone who was the number two ranking Minister in Israel.[102]

Back to the tanks (again!)

A common theme of this book might be based on the old movie phrase, 'Just when you thought it was safe to go back into the water.' The issue of arms sales to Israel, which had dominated the early years of Anglo–Israeli relations, looked to have finally been buried by 1969. The British had supplied the Israelis with pretty much all the arms they had requested for some time, and more importantly the United States had agreed to sell large numbers of weapons to Israel. One fact had, however, not altered. Both the United States and Britain were still keen to use the sale of weapons as a means of attempting to influence the political position of the Israeli Government. In a crude terms, this revolved around the Israelis agreeing to make some kind of concession (major or minor) in order for the arms to be delivered. The British Foreign Office and the American State Department felt that this was all quite right and proper. The Israelis, on the other hand, pointed to the fact that the Soviets did not impose similar conditions on its arms supply to Egypt and Syria.

The issue this time concerned the proposed sale of around 250 Chieftain tanks to Israel. On 21 December 1968, the Secretary of State had informed the Israeli Ambassador in London that there was no objection in principle to the supply of 250 Chieftains to Israel over the next four years.[103] On 1 May 1969, however, the Secretary of State informed the Israeli Ambassador that Britain was putting the deal on hold until the autumn when it would be reviewed again against the backdrop of events in the Middle East.[104]

Consequently, it came as little surprise to anybody that the issue of tanks was at the top of Meir's agenda when she visited Britain in June 1969. Both the Foreign Office and the Israelis noted the importance of this visit, which was Meir's first overseas trip since taking office.[105] Worryingly for the future prospects of Anglo–Israeli relations was the admission that the Israelis viewed the tank issue as the 'touchstone' of its relations with Britain.[106] This was a clear throwback to the 1950s, when the Israelis had adopted a similar litmus test to Anglo–Israeli relations. The Foreign Office was also made aware that the failure to sell Israel the tanks would be viewed as 'a transfer of British weight to the Arab scale'.[107]

An angry Meir argued in meetings with the Prime Minister, Foreign Secretary and the Minister of Defence that Israel should be allowed to buy the tanks.[108] She argued that the British rationale for not selling them, which the Foreign Office had devised, was simply wrong. The Foreign Office had stated that it acted in the interests of a settlement in the Middle East, which would ensure Israel's security.[109] 'Let Israel define its own security interests,' Meir retorted in all her meetings with British Ministers.[110] In her meeting with Wilson on 11 June 1969 Meir had launched into a long plea arguing that Israel needed the tanks to protect the balance of arms in the Middle East.[111] To make matters even more uncomfortable for Wilson, the Israeli Prime Minister asked him about press reports in London that morning that the British Government was about to sell tanks to Libya. Wilson spent much of their meeting on the defensive. Few other issues got a look-in at the meeting.[112] Although Stewart managed to keep much of the focus of his meeting with Meir on the issue of the Four Powers talks on the future of the Middle East, the Israeli Prime Minister again made an urgent plea for the tanks, which she saw as vital in ensuring Israel's security.[113]

The Israelis suspected that the reality was that the British were using the issue of the tanks to apply pressure on the seemingly inflexible Meir-led government in Israel to make concessions towards peace. If the Foreign Office was attempting to convince the Arab world of its good intentions by not selling the tanks, then this strategy was not completely successful. Radio Cairo reported on Meir's talks in London, arguing that even if she did not get the tanks, the fact remained that Britain continued to be (in the view of Radio Cairo) one of the biggest suppliers of arms to Israel.[114] The Arab suspicion of the British was still very much present for all to see, and the cancellation of a single contract was not going to change that very simple fact.

If the British tactics of not agreeing to sell the tanks to Israel was designed to force Meir into concessions, then it clearly failed. The Foreign Office admitted as much after Meir had departed Britain. They accepted that little had changed as a result of Meir's visit.[115] During the course of her stay, Meir had given an interview to the *Sunday Times* in which she outlined her government's hawkish position on the Palestinians, 'There was no such thing as a Palestinian' (referring to them as West Bankers) and her objection to the creation of a Palestinian state ('There are already 14 Arab states').[116] There appeared to be little room for diplomatic manoeuvre here.

Autumn came and the British still had not made an official decision about the tanks.[117] In a meeting between the Secretary of State and the Israeli Minister of Foreign Affairs, Abba Eban, on 6 October, the Foreign Office merely stuck to the line that no decision had yet been taken when the ever-wily Eban raised the subject just as he was leaving the Secretary of State's office.[118] In Britain, the *Daily Mail* ran a story on 30 October. It argued that the deal was indeed off and that it was cancelled at the request of Michael Stewart and the Foreign Office, which had caved in to Arab pressure.[119] The decision was to be kept secret to avoid damaging Anglo-Israeli relations at a sensitive time (George Thomson, the Chancellor of the Duchy of Lancaster, was due to deliver a keynote speech in Israel on Balfour Day commemorating the British pledge of a national home for the Jews).[120] Though the Foreign Office had been firm in its opposition to the sale, which they felt would jeopardize British interests in the Arab world, the Ministry of Defence had called for the sale to go ahead, arguing that it was too good an opportunity to miss.[121]

The seeming inflexibility of Meir and her government, the related issues of a lack of progress in British and international diplomatic efforts, and the non-sale of the tanks to Israel led to a deterioration in Anglo–Israel relations. In Israel, E. Barnes sent a dispatch to the Foreign Office on 18 August outlining in detail the problems facing Anglo–Israeli relations at the time.[122] The report outlined three major issues that stood to damage Anglo–Israeli relations: the Great Power talks, the issue of Jerusalem, and arms sales. Regarding the first, there remained in Israel a sense that British support for the talks was motivated not only by an attempt to keep Britain operating in the big league, but also by the pro-Arab feelings in top corridors of the Foreign Office.[123] The issue of Jerusalem was difficult for it also concerned not only Anglo–Israeli relations, but Israel appeared more sensitive to British criticism of its policy on Jerusalem than similar comments from other countries.[124] The third area of arms sales was perhaps the most important. If Britain was sold the tanks to Israel, then the Israeli comments criticizing the British over the first and second issues would have been more muted.

At the time, with a British active policy on the Middle East being operated mainly out of the United Nations in New York, there was concern in the Embassy in Tel Aviv as to why there wasn't a more active policy in the region itself. It argued that the Great Power talks were mainly an American–Soviet-run show, with Britain only on the fringes of the process.[125] What also worried the Embassy was the debate that was doing the rounds at the Foreign Office at the time on the philosophy of either/or (meaning choose the Arabs or the Israelis but try not to continue to attempt to be balanced). There appeared to be support for a greater shift in balance towards the Arabs among some of the British Embassys based in the Arab world. In Jeddah, the British Ambassador argued that if Britain's policy was based on *realpolitik* then it might well have reached the same decisions as the French Government did in 1967 and given considerably more support to the Arabs.[126] Both public and parliamentary opinion in Britain, however, at the time would never permit the British Government to make this change even if the government's own political and humanitarian views were to change.[127] Calls for a change in emphasis were particularly strong on the questions of arms sales to the region.[128] 'We need a settlement before the rot spreads further . . . and there will be really serious damage to British interests in any new arms sales to Israel,' claimed R. Beaumont, the British Ambassador in Cairo.[129] Clearly, on occasion, Tel Aviv conceded, the Foreign Office had to choose between its relations with the two sides or at least prioritize the relationship with one side or the other.[130] But in general terms there were strong interests linking Britain with both sides and therefore it could not afford to ignore ether side.[131]

In truth, the Foreign Office did not want to adopt an either/or policy. It recognized that its interests in both the Arab world and Israel were too strong for such a decision to be taken. There was also a sense that despite the increased complexities in Anglo–Israeli relations caused by its conquest of new lands in the Six-Day War and the arrival of Meir in power, it was prudent to try to retain as much influence in Israel as possible. The Foreign Office was also receiving very detailed reports into the internal political situation in Israel at the time which indicated that the issue of the conquered lands could tear the ruling coalition apart if the issue was forced too much. In reality, Meir was dealing with these splits on the issue by using a very simple old political tool of agenda fixing. Detailed analysis of the protocol of Cabinet sessions and meetings of the party organs of the ruling Labour Party confirms just how little debate was allowed on the issue. This inertia, while not popular with the Arabs or the international community, at least maintained internal cohesion in Israel.[132]

The era of the Wilson government came to a grinding halt with its electoral defeat at the hands of the Tories on 19 June 1970. In simple terms, Anglo–Israeli relations during the Wilson era can be divided into two distinctive periods: pre- and post-Six Day War. The first period was characterized by a British disengagement from the region and a policy of attempted balance between the Arabs and the Israelis. Central to this policy were Foreign Office attempts to stop the crisis developing into full-scale armed conflicts that posed a threat to British interests in the area. With Nasser initially tied down in Yemen this policy appeared to be relatively successful in areas such as the question of the division of the waters of the River Jordan. During this period Anglo–Israeli relations flourished with the development of strong trade links reinforcing the pace of the political development. The issue of arms supply, which had been such a thorny one during the 1950s, wasn't to be a stumbling block, with Britain supplying Israel with pretty much what it wanted.

The Six Day War transformed Anglo–Israeli relations, with the British Government now pursuing a more active foreign policy in the hope of securing an Arab–Israeli settlement. This policy led even the usually mild-mannered Israeli Prime Minister, Levi Eshkol, to blow a fuse at British attempts to pressurize Israel, and the Foreign Office in particular. The arrival of Meir in power, following the death of Eshkol, further complicated Anglo–Israeli relations. The decision of the Foreign Office not to honour the sale of the tanks to Israel was clearly intended to send a message to the Israeli Government that British interests remained very strong in the Arab world and that if Anglo–Israeli relations were to remain 'on an even keel' she would have to show more flexibility on the Arab question. At the start of the 1970s things on this front did not augur well for both the region and for Anglo–Israeli relations.

6

Profit versus loss: British interests in the Middle East

I cannot conclude these impressions without recording my admiration and sympathy for the Israelis. They have their defects, but they are entitled to them. I hope and believe that Israel is here to stay. It is just that the Jewish people should have a state of their own, and it can only be in Palestine. If we could persuade the Arabs to accept that proposition and its consequences, the problems of the Holy Land could, for once, be regulated not by force but by diplomacy.

W. B. J. Ledwidge, British Ambassador to Israel, 30 April 1973[1]

The period between the arrival of the new British Government led by Edward Heath and the October 1973 war was one in which many in the Foreign Office thought could best be characterized by the phrase 'creeping sanctions and creeping occupation'.[2] Anglo–Israeli relations remained on one level extremely cordial, with Abba Eban and his British counterpart, Alec Douglas-Home, doing their best to paper over the growing cracks in the relationship. On a deeper level, however, at the centre of much of the discord on the Israeli side was the active British diplomatic effort at the United Nations to secure a settlement, which the Israelis felt was primarily motivated by British efforts to secure its interests in the Arab world at the direct expense of Israel.[3]

The mini-submarine litmus test

The Israelis once again used the issue of arms sales from Britain to Israel as the litmus test for the state of Anglo–Israeli relations. Israelis have long memories and its government remained concerned over the failure of the previous British government to sell them the tanks. This despite the fact that the Israelis eventually concluded that they no longer actually wanted to purchase the tanks and bought tanks from America instead. This decision was eventually confirmed in a meeting between the Minister of Defence and General Tsur, the Israel Assistant Minister of Defence, on 17 November 1970.[4] General Tsur had already made it clear to the British Ambassador in Tel Aviv during the summer that this would be the case.[5] Although General Tsur dropped the request for the tanks he raised another issue, which became central to the arms question over this period. The issue at hand was Israel's request to develop and buy mini-submarines from Vickers, possibility in collaboration with the Germans.[6]

For Britain it was a case of 'out of the frying pan and into the fire' as this period was also characterized by increasing concerted Arab pressure on the British Government to stop selling arms to Israel.[7] This pressure was unusually unified. The Arab Ambassadors to Britain jointly wrote to the Foreign Office stating:

> The Ambassador and Heads of Diplomatic missions accredited to the Court of St. James call on the Secretary of State express their deep concern and shock over news published since 9 January 1970, in the British press, and substantiated subsequently through diplomatic and other channels, relating to the size and contribution of British arms supplies in Israel.[8]

To some degree, the Arab pressure was a by-product of the publicity that the debate on the potential sale of tanks to Israel had attracted. The previous Foreign Office policy of selling in secret to Israel was blown apart by newspaper articles and parliamentary lobbying and debates on the issue, as well as a letter to some 80 MPs calling on the then Prime Minister, Harold Wilson, to go through with the sale.[9] Once the cat was out of the bag it became harder for the Foreign Office to deny the stories originating from the Arab world of major British arms sales to Israel. Arms sales to Israel were now largely in the public domain and this made the issue all the more difficult for the Foreign Office to manage. A Foreign Office statement on the issue in July 1970 concluded that there would be problems meeting any of Israel's expected requests for arms in the coming years.[10] On top of this the arms issue had publicly revealed divisions between the Foreign Office and the Ministry of Defence, the latter of which was naturally keener to sell arms on economic grounds. The Ministry of Defence remained none too pleased that the order to sell some 250 British-made tanks to Israel had, in its eyes, been lost.

It is important to note the timing of all these developments as having taking place during the period of the Wilson Government. Israelis do have long memories, but when the need suits they are also known to have very short-term ones as well. As we shall see, when the issue of the supply of supplies to Israel hit rocky waters in Whitehall, the Israelis blamed the Conservative Government of Edward Heath of tightening the policy of arms sales to Israel. This, as we have just seen, was not strictly true; the change took place under the Wilson Government. Indeed, there was a great deal of continuity between Michael Stewart and his successor at the Foreign Office, Sir Alec Douglas-Home, on the issue of British policy towards Israel and the Middle East as a whole.

Regarding the three mini-submarines, the government eventually authorized the go-ahead for the sale in 1971 and the deal was signed in February 1972.[11] Much of the Foreign Office's time was spent first trying to keep the project secret, but also developing strategies for expected Arab backlash if details of the deal were leaked. The hope for secrecy failed when Chapman Pincher ran an article in the *Daily Express* on 7 March 1972, which, though full of mistakes, alerted the world to the decision to agree to Israel's request.[12] Even at this stage, Foreign Office officials argued against issuing a formal statement.[13] Anthony Parsons suggested that if such a statement were issued, the Arabs would feel obliged to react fully.[14] By not issuing a statement, the Foreign Office was giving the Arabs every chance not to react.[15] The arguments that the Foreign Office were ready for the Arabs was that the submarines were being built as a private venture project and that they did not alter the military balance of the Middle East. Moreover, Britain would be ready to consider sympathetically any requests from Arab states for submarines. The deal for the three mini-subs was the exception to the rule. Britain remained extremely reluctant to sell weapons to Israel prior to October 1973 and after the war a strict embargo on arms sales to Israel was implemented: an embargo which naturally did not please the Israelis, whose Ambassador in London, Michael Comay, raised the issue in his meetings at the Foreign Office.[16] Comay also expressed his dissatisfaction at the embargo during his highly published farewell speech at the Anglo–Israel Association Silver Jubilee dinner on 30 October 1973.[17]

Douglas-Home and Eban paper over the cracks

The first meeting between Eban and Douglas-Home since the latter returned to the Foreign Office took place on 1 July 1970. The profile of Eban that the Foreign Office prepared for the Secretary of State said much about the high esteem that many Foreign Office officials felt for Eban. He was almost one of us – or, as Barnes in Tel Aviv put it:

> He has of course a powerful intellect, triple first at Cambridge and all that. English is his mother tongue and he speaks it better than the

English do. We don't know about the Scots. His Hebrew, too, before the normal Israeli can understand it, has to be translated into Hebrew . . . He is a keen cricket fan and will, I am sure, be grateful for any pearls which drop from the lips of a former President of the MCC.[18]

These warm words of reference for Eban could not be in greater contrast to the Foreign Office's view of his boss, Meir, who it blamed for the lack of progress in diplomatic negotiations. Though the meeting, between Douglas-Home and Eban, which took place on 1 July 1970, merely covered the issues of the day, with Eban talking about such issues as the continued Soviet penetration into the region and the ongoing diplomatic efforts for a settlement, the Foreign Office's news department was employed to discourage any speculation that there was any substantive discussion of the Chieftains.[19]

In truth, Eban raised the tanks issue during the meeting as an example of the kind of area in which Anglo–Israeli relations needed to be improved. Eban suggested optimistically that perhaps Britain and Israel could turn the clock back to the day in which arms sales between the two were conducted in secret.[20] In reality, as the later case of the mini-subs confirmed, it was extremely difficult to put the genie back in the bottle again. Once the debate about the Chieftain tanks had gone public there was a much greater degree of scrutiny, not least by the Arabs, of arms deals. Given the Arab focus on this issue the Foreign Office believed that it could not be found out agreeing to new major arms contracts involving Israel in the near future. The risk, in the eyes of the Foreign Office, to British interests in the Middle East was simply too great to chance. If the Foreign Office had to implement a Cabinet decision to sell arms to Israel, as in the case of the mini-subs, efforts to maintain secrecy were doubled, and it was agreed that it would be made clear to the Arabs that they were also entitled to purchase the same or similar equipment.

After Harrogate: are the Tories more restrictive?

Harrogate is a town that is not usually associated with the Arab–Israeli conflict. In a speech at Harrogate in November 1970, the Secretary of State had talked of 'putting Britain's relations with the Arab world on a new footing',[21] although the Foreign Office argued that the speech only contained ideas that the British had been advocating in the Four Power talks for many months.[22] These views covered what was essentially the British view on a fair settlement in the Middle East and included Israeli withdrawal from the lands captured during the 1967 war.[23] This with-drawal was based on the British interpretation of UN Resolution 242, which in essence called for Israel to withdraw from lands captured during the war in exchange for peace. Foreign Office officials saw that, for example on the issue of the Golan Heights, Britain would not think of suggesting that Israel abandon the Golan without assurances about its security, but equally the terms of the UN Resolution 242 included with-drawal from the Golan Heights.[24]

It will come as little surprise that the Israelis did not take the Harrogate speech very well or indeed Britain's continuingly active diplomatic role at the UN and in the Four Powers.[25] The Israeli Ministry of Foreign Affairs argued that these two factors, along with the lack of progress on arms sales to Israel (especially the submarines), meant that the Heath-led Government was becoming 'more restrictive' on Israel than the previous Wilson-led Government.[26] At the very heart of Israel's concerns lay the fear that Britain was going to, as Arthur Lourie (now based in the Israeli Ministry of Foreign Affairs) put it, 'do a France' and disengage from Israel in order to build stronger economic and political ties in the Arab world.[27] Such a scenario would have left Israel, in its opinion, deeply isolated and highly dependent on the United States as the only member of the Four Powers in Israel's camp.[28] The Israeli Ministry of Foreign Affairs launched a major press campaign to express its fears of such a development and to warn of the perils of the allegedly 'more restrictive' policy which the British Government was pursuing on Israel.[29] The timing of the Israeli media campaign 'to win friends and influence people', as the Foreign Office referred to it, was linked to a visit to Britain in December 1970 by Abba Eban for talks with Alec Douglas-Home.[30]

At the meeting between Eban and Douglas-Home, which took place on 16 December 1970, the Secretary of State made it clear to Eban that in his opinion it was not in Israel's interests to stand pat, and that they should get moving in the direction of a settlement based on UN Resolution 242.[31] Eban preferred to shift the focus on to what was rapidly becoming a major issue in British foreign policy (and remains so until the present day), namely the orientation of its foreign policy towards America or Europe, or, as Tony Blair argued in his Guildhall speech of 2006 (see the final chapter of this book), retaining strong links with both. The British Prime Minister of the day, Edward Heath, was a well-known strong Europhile who did much to take Britain into the Common Market. Eban was suggesting that British interests lay in aligning its interests with America rather than with those of Europe. This Israeli belief was stated for the obvious reasons of self-interest – it hoped that if Britain were closer allied with America, it would take a less critical line with Israel. That said, there was a fear that, with Britain heading towards member-ship of the European Economic Community, its foreign policy orientation was going to shift more towards Europe, with all the implications that would have for Israel in the medium to long term.

A meeting between the Secretary of State and his Israeli counterpart that didn't cover the question of arms supplies to Israel? Surely not. On this occasion the Foreign Office, through the Embassy in Tel Aviv, had informed the Israeli Ministry of Foreign Affairs prior to the meeting that the Minister would not be able to discuss specific proposals and arms deals.[32] This was due to the fact that a major Foreign Office review on the question of arms sales to the region was under way. Eban, as a result, quite rightly did not press the Foreign Secretary on the issue during the course of the meeting.[33]

On issues of substance Anglo–Israeli relations did not progress very much in the immediate aftermath of the Secretary of State's meeting with Eban. During the course of 1971 the Foreign Office moved closer than ever to referring in public to UN Resolution 242 as meaning, certainly in terms of the Egyptian–Israeli dispute, a full Israeli withdrawal from the lands captured by it during the course of the Six Day War.[34] This did not please the Israeli Prime Minister, Golda Meir, who argued that the lin-guistic ambiguity of the resolution meant it only required Israel to withdraw from some of the lands in order to comply with UN Resolution 242.[35] Once again, British action at the United Nations in New York, both in terms of its voting record on resolutions about the Middle East and in framing and amending resolutions, greatly disappointed the Israelis.[36]

The charm offensive and the policy of the three Cs

On a more positive note for Anglo–Israeli relations, the Foreign Office embarked on something of a charm offensive aimed at reassuring the Israelis that, despite differences over the diplomatic efforts to secure an Arab–Israeli settlement, and the perception of something of a shift in British policy towards the Arabs, Israel remained an important factor in British Middle Eastern policy. Abba Eban became the first Israeli Minister of Foreign Affairs to visit London as the guest of the British Government. Previous visits by senior Israeli leaders to London had been portrayed as talks while they were in town, giving private talks, or as fund-raising missions for Israel. This notion of some-official talks with Israeli leaders was quite naturally a charade, but nevertheless the Foreign Office believed that it was an important one in order to help appease hostile Arab reaction to the visits. On the one level Eban's visit to London at the end of November was hailed as a great success, which went a long way to at last restoring a degree of trust between Britain and Israel.[37] The Secretary of State had also contributed to this improvement with a series of speeches culminating in a well-received address to the Anglo–Israeli Association, made during Eban's visit to London.[38]

On a deeper level, however, major differences remained over substantive issues that continued to centre on Britain's role in pushing for a settlement of the Arab–Israeli conflict and Israeli feelings on insecurity due to Britain's decision to join the Common Market.[39] The Foreign Office and Diplomatic Service's concerns about Israel were not restricted to matters of policy. Israel's ageing and seemingly out-of-touch leadership came in for criticism. In retrospect, the British Ambassador in Tel Aviv hit the nail on the head when he described Golda Meir as being more concerned about preserving the heritage of past achievements than to embark on new departures.[40] The Minister of Finance, Barnes (who was a possible successor to Meir), still ran the party and the economy out if his little black pocket book, when something more like a bionic computer was needed.[41] Even the Minister of Defence, Moshe Dayan, who passed in Israel for being young, would be one of the older members of the British Cabinet. Barnes also viewed Dayan as an opportunist rather than a systematic policy-maker. Only the Foreign Office's favourite Israeli, Eban, was spared from criticism; though here it was noted that he was the real powerbase in Israel and was becoming Meir's salesman – not an easy job at the best of times.[42]

Barnes' comments said much about the growing frustration in London about the Israeli Government. If Meir was proving inflexible on the issue of an Arab–Israeli settlement, there was no sign of somebody waiting in the wings who would be more supportive of the Foreign Office's vision for such a settlement, which would of course meant substantial territorial concessions by Israel as well as other concessions on the issue of Palestinian refugees. Meir's comments reported in the *Sunday Times* that there was effectively no such person as a Palestinian had exasperated the Foreign Office. The opposition party in Israel was making gains on the Israeli Labour Party, but they were the political descendants of the Revisionist Zionist movement and even more hardline than Meir over the issue of the return of the territories. Its leader, Menachem Begin, was still reviled by the British and had resigned from the National Unity Government in Israel when Meir had made her only concession to the Americans over plans for a settlement with Egypt based on the Rogers Plan.[43]

The frustration in the Foreign Office about the lack of flexibility in the Israeli Government over what it saw as vital concessions that were needed to help secure a Middle East settlement, but also its understanding of the motive of Israeli leaders at the time, was best summed up by Anthony Parsons:

> It seems to me that Israel is in an impregnable position in the short term. If I were an Israeli I doubt whether I would support any government that proposed withdrawal from the Occupied Territories. I would feel much happier with the present situation . . . The Israelis would do well to make peace with the Arabs before the slow tide of history begins to run against them. But people and governments tend to make decisions essentially for short-term reasons, and who can blame them? No one can predict the shape of the distant future. Therefore why risk the bird in the hand?[44]

Meir was clearly basing her political support on just such a rational acceptance of the status quo. The impact of her policies on Britain's ability to protect its interests in the Middle East proved to be a constant worry for the Foreign Office which, despite some calls from its officials to effectively shift towards the Arab world, remained keen to reassure the Israelis that Britain retained strong interests in keeping its links with Israel despite the disagreements.

As part of the Foreign Office's wider campaign to try to repair some of the damage caused by the Israeli perception of change in the emphasis of British policy away from Israel and towards the Arabs, the British Embassy in Tel Aviv recommended in 1971 the pursuit of what it termed the 'three Cs' policy towards Israel: commerce, culture and courtesy.[45] During the course of 1971 this policy was implemented with mixed results. In commerce, Anglo–Israeli trade links continued to grow. British exports to Israel reached record levels of over £100 million, and Israeli exports to Britain also continued to rise as rapidly.[46] In culture the results were less good with the notable exceptions of educational exchanges and television material.[47] There was little in the way of British spectacles reaching Israel shores. A proposed visit by the Royal Shakespeare Company had not come off.[48] In terms of courtesy, this was harder to measure, but there had been several visits to Israel by low-ranking members of the British Government. The real expectation in this area, however were the plans for Sir Alec Douglas-Home to visit Israel in 1972, the first-ever visit to Israel by a British Foreign Secretary.[49]

The Foreign Secretary goes to Jerusalem

The visit to Israel in March 1972 by the Secretary of State, Sir Alec Douglas-Home, was of great symbolic importance to Anglo–Israeli relations.[50] This simple fact tended to obscure the reality that Meir and Eban gave the Secretary of State no evidence of a change in Israel's position towards a settlement to the Arab–Israeli conflict.[51] In fairness the Foreign Office did not expect the visit to lead to any immediate political breakthroughs. The object was rather to improve and develop a greater degree of trust between the two parties and to help foster bi-lateral trade relations. The Israelis remained extremely concerned about the decision of Britain to join the EEC and its implications for Israel trade.[52] Eban also argued that there was alleged trade imbalance, with British exports to Israel far outstripping Israel's exports to Britain.[53] The political aspect of the talks with Meir and Eban focused on general discussions about the chances of success for the Jarring mission ('Not great', thought the Israelis) and the future intentions of the Soviet Union in the region. On a deeper level, both sides agreed to differ on the basis for a settlement in the Middle East, but at least had the effect of reducing the tension on this key issue for a time. The Israeli press gave the visit a good deal of coverage, most of which was extremely positive.[54] The tone of the coverage was essentially that Britain's power to influence a Middle East settlement was limited, but that the Foreign Secretary was given credit for his desire to contribute towards a balanced settlement.[55] In the end the Secretary of State's visit had to be curtailed in order for him to return to London to take part in an urgent Cabinet debate on another conflict closer to home, namely Northern Ireland.[56] Despite Foreign Office concerns about the Jerusalem aspect of the visit (Britain did not recognize Israel sovereignty over Eastern Jerusalem), the visit was judged to have achieved its aims of pleasing and flattering the Israelis.

The Foreign Office's profit and loss definition

With little prospect of a diplomatic breakthrough and the Israeli Government sticking to its line of strongly favouring direct talks with the Arabs, the state of no peace and no war increasingly worried the Foreign Office over the summer of 1972. The murder of the Israeli athletes at the Munich

Olympic Games by the Black September Group had moved the Arab–Israeli conflict back into the public spotlight, but the *impasse* in negotiations still remained. The decision of President Sadat in Egypt to disengage from the Soviet sphere and eventually shift towards the American camp at least appeared to reduce the threat of superpower confrontation, or, as Sir Alec Douglas-Home put it, depolarized the situation.[57] With little sign of progress in the autumn, however, there was a major informal review of policy within the Foreign Office over defining British policy towards the Arabs and the Israelis.

James Craig from the Near Eastern and North African Department put forward a detailed case for a shift in British policy towards aligning itself more with the interests of the Arabs. He summarized the rationale for this change as follows:

> As Lord Janner once said: 'Oil is thicker than Jewish blood.' In our calculations, it will have to remain so. If there is no real settlement of the Arab–Israeli conflict (and no one can be optimistic about the prospects) we cannot afford not to ensure that our very considerable interests in the Arab world are not, as a result, put at risk. This does not require us to abandon the search for ways to promote a settlement, to renege on our commitments to Israel's independence and its need for security, to adopt the Arab (Egyptian) position or even go as far as the French have gone towards doing so; but it does mean that we have to be more sensitive to Arab than to Israeli attitudes towards our policies and postures.[58]

In other words, Craig's view of the British policy on the Arab–Israeli conflict was based in simple terms on profit and loss for British interests.[59] Later in the year, Anthony Parsons attempted to refine and clarify the rational behind Craig's thoughts. Parsons argued that Craig's profit and loss equation remained the best summary judgement that the Foreign Office could manage.[60] He argued that the important question for Britain was not so much which of the parties in the Arab–Israeli dispute was more or less in the right (in so far as this term had any real meaning he admitted) but what effect the overall dispute had on Britain's overall interests in the Middle East.[61] Parsons went on to argue that a peaceful solution to the conflict would suit Britain best of all, but that naturally a fresh eruption of hostilities could seriously damage British interests.[62] In truth, Parson's comments revealed where the heart of the problem lay between Britain and Israel at the time. The Foreign Office felt that it could not reconcile itself as apparently the Israelis could to the situation of no peace and no war. The Israelis believed that their military superiority would sustain them for some time and that eventually the Arabs would be forced to come to the negotiating table. In retrospect, as the October 1973 war confirmed, the judgement of the Israelis proved to be false, but, as we have already seen, it was a very seductive and easy judgement for Israelis to live with at the time.

Many of the arguments for a shift towards the Arabs put forward by Craig and clarified by Parsons were countered by the newly arrived British Ambassador in Tel Aviv, Bernard Ledwidge.[63] The Ambassador argued that the proposed tactical shift away from Israel was already being seen in speeches that had tended to praise the Arabs and criticize the Israelis.[64] More especially, he argued that the Egyptian had only gone up in the eyes of the Foreign Office for ceasing to do things that they should not have been doing in the first place. In terms of what the Foreign Office were now openly referring to as 'creeping consolidation' in the West Bank, the Ambassador had to concur with the views of Craig and Parsons. Both officials argued that it was difficult to criticize Israel on economic grounds for what it was doing in the Occupied Territories, providing jobs and developing infrastructure.[65] In this area Craig had coined another phrase: 'creeping prosperity' in the Occupied Territories.[66] But the Foreign Office, and in particular Colin Crowe, the British Ambassador to the United Nations, believed that the overall creeping consolidation of the Occupied Territories would make a settlement all the more difficult.[67] As time went by without a settlement, the creeping consolidation would be further strengthened. Soon the parameters of this debate would shift towards the question of the building of Israeli settlements on his lands, and new terminology could be employed such as 'putting facts on the ground'. The rationale of the debate, however, has remained the same up to the present day.

Parsons understood Israeli fears and suspicions that British policy on the Middle East had changed.[68] The alleged changes in British policy had been given extensive coverage in the Israeli press.[69] He felt, however, that the British had not changed.[70] In the strictest sense of the word 'change', he was indeed correct. Britain still viewed the settlement to conflicts through UN Resolution 242, and its interpretation of this resolution had not changed.[71] On closer inspection, however, there was at least a sense in the Foreign Office that the Arabs, and in particular the Egyptians, had come a long way since 1967.[72] They had agreed to recognize the existence of Israel, sign a peace treaty with it, accept demilitarized zones, accept international guarantees and dispense with the Soviet advisers.[73] All this was a case, as the British Ambassador in Tel Aviv had pointed out, of looking at the glass being half full or half empty.[74] Parsons thought that if the Israelis feared creeping sanctions, then the Foreign Office feared creeping consolidation.[75]

The apparent shift in balance in British policy towards the Arabs and the related British actions at the United Nations naturally did not please the Israelis very much. Sir Alec Douglas-Home admitted as much when he met Abba Eban in London on 11 December 1972.[76] The Secretary of State then moved on to what was to become a common theme over the ensuing years in meetings between secretaries of state and their Israeli counterparts: Israeli settlements in the Occupied Territories. On this occasion, the Secretary of State merely raised concern that these settlements looked permanent in nature, and this was therefore a very worrying development.[77] Two days later, On 13 December 1972, the new British Ambassador in Tel Aviv had his first official meeting with the Israeli Prime Minister, Meir. Given Meir's well-known ability to dominate meetings, Ledwidge got his key question in early.[78] He enquired as to whether Meir thought that there would be any moves towards negotiations in 1973.[79] Meir replied that it was up to the Arabs. Nothing new here, but given the tension in Anglo–Israeli relations at the time, it was probably a sensible ploy to talk in generalities with Meir.

In reality, the decline in Anglo–Israeli relations was not unique. Governments across the world (and not just the usual suspects) were becoming more critical of Israel and more insistent that it made concessions to break the deadlock in the negotiations.[80] This was reflected in a more hostile attitude towards Israel in both UN debates and the subsequent voting for UN Resolutions.[81] These UN debates worried the Israelis, but they did not make them any more flexible. With regard to British actions the Israelis continued to argue that all that was achieved by British initiatives at the UN and elsewhere was encouragement of Arab illusions about the terms of a peace settlement.[82] In truth, the Israelis were not too concerned about what it continued to see as political bandstanding by a power whose influence on the international stage was clearly now subservient to the United States and soon to Europe (though there was some concern that Britain would be influenced by French foreign policy when it joined the EEC). The real fear of the Israelis was that the British would conclude a major arms deal with the Arabs that would impact on the balance of arms in the region.[83] With President Sadat disengaging from Soviet influence, the feeling in Israel was that its balance of arms weighed heavily in its favour. In its eyes the status quo of no war and no peace could be maintained for some time.

The sands of time and the winds of war

The Foreign Office assessment at the time did not agree with the Israeli belief that time was on its side.[84] In June 1973, some three and a half months before the outbreak of the third major Arab–Israeli war, both Parsons and Craig concluded that Israel would do well to make peace before the tide of history started to run against them.[85] Both Craig and Parsons were responding to a dispatch by Ledwidge from Tel Aviv that had caused a certain amount of concern in the Foreign Office. The dispatch, dated 30 April 1973 and entitled 'My first impressions of Israel', had contained much food for thought for the Foreign Office. Ledwidge started in similar tone to the first report by Britain's first official representative in Israel, Sir Knox Helm, in 1949. Like Helm, Ledwidge couldn't resist commenting on just how ugly he found Tel Aviv. He added that the Jews were never great builders, their genius was verbal, not plastic.[86] He went on to argue that the beauty of Jerusalem was menaced and that too much was being built too fast. International action was as urgent for Jerusalem as it was for Venice.[87]

The main reason for the dispatch, however, was to express Ledwidge's belief that it might suit Israel better to 'live dangerously' than to go for an early peace settlement.[88] Ledwidge went on to suggest that Israel would never go back to its 1967 borders and that Israeli leaders shed no tears over the refusal of the Arabs to offer peace terms that they could be expected to accept.[89] Moreover, not all Israeli leaders would regret another Arab attack, which would justify an Israeli counter-attack. Arab follies, he argued, tempt one to conclude that the only way to peace for Israel was to go on hitting the Arabs hard until they admit that they had had enough.[90] In terms of British policy, Ledwidge argued that, in order to have the correct influence on Israel, the West must condemn Arab terrorism and attempt to persuade Egypt that Israel was here to stay.[91] He concluded by arguing that Israel was largely unassailable for another decade or so and that it might prefer the 'No war, no peace' option.[92]

Back at the Foreign Office, Sir Alec Douglas-Home had minuted Ledwidge's dispatch using the phrase 'This is a very shrewd assessment.'[93] Craig, on the other hand, was none too pleased with its contents. He argued that the Ambassador had clearly been taken over by some of the well-known Israeli disregard for the Arab factor in the Middle East equation.[94] This was code for the Ambassador reflecting Israeli interests too much at the expense of the wider picture of the Middle East. Given the fact that war broke out later that year, some of Craig's comments in response to the report were spot on. Craig argued that Israel had not yet won the war with the Arabs.[95] The 1967 campaign, along with the 1956 and 1948 campaigns, was not so much a war but rather a battle. By Craig's definition, if Israel had won the war it would have been able to dictate the peace just as the Allies had done with Germany in 1945.[96] On this point Craig would appear to be on extremely solid ground. Israel has never been able to dictate the peace with the Arabs and has often suffered political setbacks following its successful military campaigns, notably after the 1956 campaign. Craig went further, however, suggesting that a total Israel victory which would involve taking one or more of the Arab capital would not guarantee victory, given the fact that Israelis were so few and the Arabs so many.[97]

It was of course perfectly possible that Craig and Parsons were reading the detailed reports they received from the intelligence services about the situation on the ground in the Middle East. These reports, as the Israelis would testify, were at the time extremely confused about the intentions of President Sadat and Egypt. During a meeting of the heads of the Levant Departments of the foreign ministries of the EEC member states held in Brussels on 21 May 1973, Craig had discussed the situation on the ground in the Middle East.[98] He noted that he had received reports of troop movements and exercises but these were too circumstantial to arouse anxiety.[99] On the whole, he argued, he thought that it was unlikely that Egypt would start any hostilities. Fighting, however, could not be ruled out.[100] Interestingly the French predictions of a potential war later that year proved to be much more accurate (French intelligence networks in Egypt were stronger at the time given its openly pro-Egypt policy).[101]

In reality, at the time Craig and Parsons were debating with the Ambassador, Egypt and Syria had already concluded their top-secret agreement to launch a joint military attack on Israel. The only question mark remained over its timing, which, for a number of political, military and logistical reasons, was set for October 1973, when the tides would be correct for such an attack. Although Craig, Parsons and Ledwidge did not know it at the time, the opportunity for diplomacy had already been lost. The Egyptians and Syrians had opted to try to regain the lands that they had lost to Israel in 1967 by force. The Israelis, and the British Ambassador, continued to sleep, believing that such an attack was almost unthinkable given Israel's reported military strength. In retrospect, given the failure of diplomacy and the increasingly perilous position of President Sadat in Egypt, such an attack was almost inevitable.

The slide towards cooler times

As we have seen, the change in government in Britain in 1970 was not as significant to Anglo–Israeli relations as the Israelis tried to suggest. The previous Labour Government of Harold Wilson had effectively started to demand that the Israelis make territorial concessions in order to advance the diplomatic process with the Arabs. There was, however, a certain nostalgia in Israel for Wilson's Government – the leaders of the Israeli Labour Party were personally acquainted with their British counterparts through the meetings of Socialist International, of which both parties were members. The arrival of the Conservative Government led to a continuation of the process of sliding away from Israel, whose government was widely viewed by the British as being inflexible. The Foreign Office and the Diplomatic Service were at the centre of much of the diplomatic actions and manoeuvrings. The Harrogate speech caused a certain degree of alarm in Israel, as did Britain's decision to join the EEC. To some degree, as a result, the Foreign Office devoted its attentions to reassuring Israel that it remained a relevant factor in British Middle Eastern policy. That said, there was no mistaking the growing frustration at what it saw as Meir's inflexibility.

The Foreign Office believed that a settlement of the Arab–Israeli conflict was the best way of securing British interests in the region, and it wanted a deal fast, though there was a realization that Britain's contribution to such a deal would be limited and conducted through the Great Power talks and through its actions at the United Nations. There was little interest in the Foreign Office for a process which could eventually lead to peace. Consequently, it disagreed with the Israeli Government on the methodology for achieving peace – the Israelis appeared interested in management rather than resolution – as well as, in the eyes of the Foreign Office, the hopelessly unrealistic Israeli demand for direct negotiations with the Arabs. On top of this, the Foreign Office was completely at odds with the Israeli Government's interpretation of UN Resolution 242, which, after the Conservatives returned to power, the Foreign Office had more clearly articulated that in its eyes it meant a withdrawal from all the territories captured during the Six Day War.

Given all the above, it was perhaps surprising that the Foreign Office, in calculating the profit and loss factors of its Middle East policy, did not shift more towards reflecting Arab interests as Mr Craig, and to a degree Parsons, had recommended. Between 1970 and 1973 the Arab lobby got its act together and operated in a more unified and organized way, picking on the Achilles heel of Foreign Office policy (in its own view) – arms sales to Israel. Once the debate over the sale of the tanks went public, then the danger to British interests in the Arab Middle East became all the greater. Even the subsequent sale of three mini-submarines to Israel, which the Foreign Office had worked hard to keep secret, was leaked to the newspapers, causing a great deal of difficulty. From this point onwards, arms sales to Israel, which the Israelis still regarded as the real litmus test of Anglo–Israeli relations, were extremely hard for the Foreign Office to approve. Ignoring the rights and wrongs of the Arab–Israeli conflict (which was the policy of the Foreign Office) we shall see that the onset of war and the subsequent use of the oil card by the Arabs illustrated the shortcomings of the Foreign Office's policy of trying to retain influence among both the Arabs and the Israelis.

7

The right to remain silent

From now on the Arabs will be watching for our sins of omission as well as our sins of commission and as the present stalemate over the Euro–Arab dialogue suggests, we shall find the Palestine question colouring more and more the whole range of our relations with the Arab world. We shall be forced to take a public position, whether we like it or not, and it will be better for us to do this on ground of our own choosing.[1]

P. G. D. Adams, Cairo, 9 December 1974

In the period prior to the Yom Kippur War the Foreign Office continued its dialogue with the British Ambassador in Tel Aviv, Bernard Ledwidge. The issue at hand continued to be the attitude of the Foreign Office towards Israel and the Arabs. The dialogue took place amid a further rise in tension between the Foreign Office and its Israel counterpart, the Ministry of Foreign Affairs. This was part of the wider deterioration in Anglo–Israeli relations that took place in the months leading up to the war. The worsening of Anglo–Israeli relations continued both during the war itself and in the period following it. Two issues were at the heart of Israeli anger towards Britain, and to the Foreign Office in particular: the reimposition of an arms embargo on sales of weapons from Britain to Israel and the failure of the British Government, in the eyes of the Israelis, to correctly identify the true aggressors in the war. From the perspective of the Foreign Office, its main bone of contention continued to be what it saw as Israel's inflexibility on both the terms and methods of negotiations with the Arabs, which had directly resulted in Anwar Sadat's decision to move towards the military option.

The period of the aftermath of the war was characterized by major political change in Israel with the resignations of Mrs Meir and Dayan and the ushering in of a new generation of Labour Party leaders such as Yitzhak Rabin and Shimon Peres. In Britain there was also a change of power in 1974, with Harold Wilson and the Labour Party defeating the Conservative Party in the general election. The central feature of the post-war period, however, was the nightmare scenario that the Foreign Office had feared would materialize: the use of the oil weapon by the Arabs in order to attempt to gain political advantage.

The 'Craigium Dictum'

Anthony Parsons laid out the bottom line in the Foreign Office's relations with Israel. He argued that Israel's survival and independence could not be compromised, but that because of Britain's interests in the Arab world it had to be more sensitive to Arab attitudes than to Israeli ones.[2] There was also a sense that British interests in the region were more exposed than any of the other powers. At the heart of the reasons for this exposure was the fact that in simple terms the Arabs blamed Britain for the establishment of the state of Israel due to the Balfour Declaration and the decision to hand over the Mandate to the United Nations in 1947.[3] Parsons' argument on British interests was labelled by Ledwidge as the 'Craigium Dictum' after its author James Craig.[4] In essence, Ledwidge accepted the policy but he feared that Israeli interests and attitudes should not be ignored.[5]

In meetings with Israeli officials the Foreign Office continued to try to reassure the Israelis that there had been no change of British policy towards it or the Arabs.[6] The Israelis, however, found this hard to swallow and were keen to list a series of instances in which it felt that the British were becoming increasingly hostile to Israel. Some of these examples were relatively minor issues, such as visits to the West Bank by the British Council representative in Amman, while others were more significant, such as the attitude of the British towards the Mediterranean in the EEC.[7] The Israelis had effectively joined the dots and argued that this was proof of a shift in British policy away from it and towards the Arabs. Not content to rest with this assessment, the Israelis employed its litmus test to the state of Anglo–Israeli relations, a request for arms supplies for the British. At this stage, Israel wanted heavy tanks and strike aircraft (Jaguars and Harriers). In truth, the Israelis did not expect a positive response from the Foreign Office. This was soon confirmed when Parsons outlined the standard policy of the day – that Britain would not agree to supply either side with any items which, in the judgement of the Foreign Office, would enhance the likely risk of further hostilities, or to lessen the prospects of a peaceful settlement.[8] Parsons confirmed that Britain could not therefore supply Israel with any tanks or planes. The Israelis took from this what they wanted: a sign that Anglo–Israeli relations were not, in its eyes, on an even keel.

In Israel, the British Ambassador was feeling the heat from the Israeli officials. Yeshayahu Anug, the Head of the European Division of the Ministry of Foreign Affairs, said that these were very dark days for Anglo–Israeli relations.[9] The Director-General of the Ministry, Avraham Kidron, argued that both government and public opinion in Israel felt that Britain was becoming more critical and that its position was swinging towards a more pro-Arab position comparable to that of France.[10] The Head of the Ministries UN Division, Mordechai Kidron (no relation to Avraham), could not understand why Britain had to be such eager beavers at the UN.[11] In reality, Ledwidge suspected the hidden hand of Eban behind this co-ordinated series of comments by the three senior officials. Eban did not go in for issuing personal rebukes himself, preferring to focus on the bridge building rather than to dish out, as Ledwidge saw it, 'a warning shot across the bows' for the British.[12]

The world according to Moshe Dayan

One man who didn't appear to share the concerns of the Israeli Ministry of Foreign Affairs at the time was Moshe Dayan. Ledwidge had his first meeting with General Dayan on 18 June 1973. What followed was a *tour de force* from General Dayan reflecting his credentials as Israel's most populist politician.[13] When asked about the state of Anglo–Israeli relations, Dayan replied that it did not seem to him that Britain did very much in the Middle East. He went on to suggest that at the UN Britain's line as the UN was pro-Arab, and he understood why.[14] There was, however, a great deal of good feeling towards Britain in Israel and he always retained affection for the British way of doing things. General Dayan was, in truth, focused on the bigger picture in the Middle East; and Britain, in his eyes, was only a very small part of that picture.[15] There were no requests for arms and he openly admitted that Israel no longer needed tanks – he argued that it could probably build better tanks itself.[16] This crude mixture of bluster and dismissiveness, laced with a degree of condescending charm towards the British, was vintage Dayan and of little interest to the Foreign Office.

What was of far greater to Foreign Office officials was General Dayan's take on the big picture in the Middle East.[17] Ledwidge noted that the General appeared to go out of his way to write off President Sadat. 'Hopeless' was Dayan's verdict on Sadat.[18] He would eventually fall, and nobody could judge what his successor would be like. Overall, he felt that the Arab position was hardening towards Israel and the West, and that Colonel Qadhafi of Libya was at the centre of much of this. There were growing calls to use Arab oil as a political weapon.[19] Dayan thought that this would lead to a crisis that would eventually see America move closer to Israel. In retrospect, Dayan was right about US–Israeli relations, but, as we shall see, for all the wrong reasons.

Back in the Foreign Office, James Craig was on equally combatative form, arguing that while General Dayan might be right that the present situation was good for Israel, it was difficult to see how he could be right in the long term.[20] Craig went on to suggest that it was clear that Dayan was right on tactics but wrong on strategy, and that he hoped that the politicians and diplomats would win the day over soldiers such as Dayan.[21] As an aside, Craig recounted a story to the Ambassador that General Dayan had apparently said to Elizabeth Munroe that it was the job of the army to destroy, not construct.[22] Needless to say, the Foreign Office and Diplomatic Service regarded General Dayan as the most dangerous of the current batch of Israeli leaders.[23]

Oil as a weapon

General Dayan's analysis was correct on another score: the threat of the Arabs to use the supply of oil as a weapon. Even prior to the outbreak of the Yom Kippur War, the oil question was focusing the minds of Foreign Office officials. The Prime Minister, Edward Heath, had set up a task force on oil supplies under the chairmanship of Lord Carrington, the Foreign Office being represented on this task force by Minister of State Lord Balniel and Parsons. In its first report the task force recommended:

> Internationally we must pay particular attention to fostering good relations with the Arab world generally and particularly with oil-producing countries. We should consider new commercial and diplomatic initiatives to encourage a degree of economic inter-dependence between us and to provide an outlet for their oil revenues, which will diminish the incentive for them to leave their oil in the ground.[24]

The Foreign Office was asked to prepare a paper on specific diplomatic initiatives. Both Parsons and Craig agreed that Sir Colin Crowe would be an excellent choice to author such a report.[25] Crowe had just finished serving as Ambassador to the United Nations, a job that had involved its share of criticism of Israeli policy. During his time at the UN, Crowe had made it clear that he believed that British interests lay predominantly in the Arab world and there was a need for a shift in focus in this policy away from the Israelis and towards the Arabs. In other words, he sub-scribed to the Craigium Dictum.

The highly detailed report that Crowe and his team of consultants produced was circulated on 2 October 1973, some four days before the outbreak of the Yom Kippur War. Its contents could be divided into two categories: positive initiatives for Anglo–Arab relations and negative proposals for the same purpose, which in effect were at the expense (rightly or wrongly) of Israel.[26] Crowe concluded, probably correctly, that it was unlikely that public opinion in Britain would accept a policy of total opposition to Israel along the lines of the policies that were being pursued by the Soviet Union and France.[27] The report concluded that such a policy would not be needed as Britain already had a clear policy on the Anglo–Israeli conflict that had been set out in the Secretary of State's speech in Harrogate in November 1970, and in Britain's accept-ance of UN Resolution 242.[28]

At the heart of the report, however, lay the issue of the sale of British arms to the region. The report argued that Britain must avoid doing things to help the Israelis.[29] The report, as a result, recommended the stopping of all arms supplies to Israel, even the mini-submarines.[30] The argument essentially centred upon the simple fact that Britain could not offset the damage of arms sales to Israel by similar sales to the Arab world.[31] The report therefore concluded that weapons should be refused to both sides,[32] although in terms of sales of aircraft to Saudi Arabia the report was more positive.[33] Crowe argued that when the Israelis claimed that the arms policy was anti-Israeli the answer was that it was pro-British.[34] Overall, the report concluded that if Britain was to foster better relations with the Arab states and preserve its oil supplies it should intensify its existing policy.[35] British interests lay in a Middle East settle-ment and this would be possible without an Israeli withdrawal and Britain should not hesitate to push for this and be seen to push.[36]

Although the significance of the report was slightly overshadowed by the outbreak of war and the eventual use of the oil weapon by the Arab oil-supplying states during the post-war period, it remained an important report. In essence, the report reflected the arguments of three key official players of the day in shaping British policy towards the Arab–Israeli conflict, Parsons, Craig and Crowe. Their blueprint of British policy towards the Arab–Israeli conflict continued to be the dominant strand of thinking in the Foreign Office during much of the 1970s. The fact that much of the report, and British policy, was based on the relative strength of Israel's military power over its Arab neighbours, which the Foreign Office argued allowed the Israelis to remain inflexible politically, was about to be put to its greatest test. In truth, from the British perspective all the planning for a possible oil embargo by the Arabs failed to alter the simple fact that the largely unforeseen Yom Kippur War placed British oil and other interests in the region in mortal danger.

Foreign Office narrative of the war

The Israeli narratives of the Yom Kippur War have already been widely published and centre upon the failings of its intelligence agencies that allowed the Egyptian–Syrian attack to achieve a degree of surprise, the difficult early days of the war when the Arab armies made rapid gains, followed by the Israeli counter-attack that drove the Egyptians and Syrians back deep into their own countries.[37] The British perspective of the war is similar in places to the Israeli version of the war, but it differs in key places. Ledwidge argued that only with American help did Israel gain the upper hand in the war, and that without this help Israel could not have won the war and would have probably lost.[38] To make matters worse for Israel, during the war it found itself in almost total diplomatic isolation, with only the United States in its corner.

On this occasion, unlike the Six Day War, the Israelis did not launch a pre-emptive military strike on the Arabs when the Israelis learned on the evening of 5 October about the joint Egyptian–Syrian attack planned for the next afternoon. The Chief of Staff of the IDF, General Elazar, had called for an immediate air strike against the newly installed Surface to Air Missile (SAM) system in Syria.[39] It is widely recalled in Israel that Meir and the Israeli Cabinet vetoed calls from the IDF to mount such an attack, for fear of alienating the Americans. The American Secretary of State, Henry Kissinger, had warned Israel in September of making any pre-emptive strike that he argued could have led to America condemning Israel. The British concurred with this view but placed greater emphasis on the fact that Israel, as Ledwidge argued, feared appearing in total diplomatic isolation before the court of the United Nations Security Council, with even the US among its accusers. This was an important factor in deterring the Israeli Cabinet from authorizing a pre-emptive strike.[40] In other words, the pressure exerted upon Israel at the UN over the years by the Arabs and its military supporters had finally paid a military dividend.[41] Prior to the war, the Israelis were fond of saying that the UN resolutions were little more than hot air and changed nothing on the ground; the events of 6 October proved this assumption to be wrong.[42]

On the military front the British argued that the war demonstrated that the Israelis could still fight off the Arabs even if they were taken by surprise.[43] It also demonstrated, however, that it could not fight off the Arabs supported by the Soviet Union without the help of the Americans.[44] It is in this point that Israeli and British analysis of the war diverges. The Israelis argued that the massive American airlift of arms to Israel during the war was an important factor in its victory, but not the decisive one. The British argued that without the airlift the Israelis would have probably lost the war. Put simply, the British understood almost immediately the new military and economic dependence of Israel on the United States from this point onwards.[45] The immediate Israeli reaction to the war was to develop its own Military Industrial Complex (MIC) that would make it self-sufficient in terms of arms. This required a great deal of money and thus this attempt at self-sufficiency actually ended up making Israel even more heavily reliant on America.

Correspondingly, it was a bad year for Anglo–Israel relations, with the Israelis arguing that British policy during the war favoured the Arabs, particularly the arms embargo.[46] The fact that the British had remained largely silent on the question of who started the war did not help Anglo–Israeli relations. A visit to London by the Israeli Prime Minister, Golda Meir, in November 1973 reduced some of the tension. In truth, the Israelis were keen at this stage not to alienate any members of the EEC, which was extremely important to it economically. There was also a feeling in Israel that there could be a backlash against attempts by the Arab states to play the oil card, which would result in some European powers developing closer ties with Israel.

Post-war rebuilding, Foreign Office style

The Foreign Office viewed the Yom Kippur War as confirmation that its policy of pressurizing Israel to withdraw from the territories it had captured during the 1967 war had been the correct one.[47] James Craig was still not very hopeful that Israelis would admit the error of their ways.[48] The Embassy in Tel Aviv appeared to have detected some cracks in the post-war Israeli positions towards the Occupied Territories, but these changes were hard to read.[49] In terms of Anglo–Israeli relations the Israeli

Ministry of Foreign Affairs appeared to be calling for a dual relationship, by which they meant that the Foreign Office should be saying things at a rhetorical level with which the Israelis naturally couldn't agree, while in private confidential exchanges were carried out on a quieter level, and vice versa.[50] This suggestion did not please Craig, who argued that the Foreign Office had grown tired of the Arabs talking to it nicely in private and telling it to forget their hostile public statements.[51] Understandably, Craig clearly did not want a repeat performance of this double act with the Arabs in Anglo–Israeli relations.

In essence, the Yom Kippur War changed very little in the Foreign Office's attitude towards the Arab–Israeli conflict. The decision-making to shift the balance towards the Arabs had already been taken before the war, and with the use of the oil weapon by the Arabs it became clear that this policy was not as successful as the British Government had hoped it would be. In terms of Israel, the basis for a settlement remained the same in the eyes of the Foreign Office: a withdrawal from the Occupied Territories in exchange for secure and permanent borders. The re-election of Golda Meir and the Israeli Labour Party in the Israeli elections held on 31 December 1973 indicated that there would not be much change in Israeli policy towards the Arabs. Indeed, in Tel Aviv, Ledwidge argued correctly that, given the fact that the opposition Likud, led by Menachem Begin, had made considerable gains at the elections (though not enough to win power on this occasion), Meir's room for manoeuvre had become even more limited than before.[52] In essence, she would not be able to agree a settlement if the terms were not acceptable to Begin and the Likud.[53] At this stage, any terms that would be acceptable to the Likud would have in all probability proved unacceptable to the Egyptians and the rest of the Arab world.[54]

The changing of the guard

In the end, Meir's Government was not brought down in elections or by internal splits over the terms of an agreement with the Arabs, but rather by a growing tide of Israeli public opinion that demanded her resignation, along with that of General Dayan, for the Israeli failures at the start of the Yom Kippur War. The political demise of Meir brought to an end the period of rule by the members of the Second and Third Aliyahs (the founding fathers and mothers of the state). Meir was eventually replaced by Israel's first Sabra Prime Minister, Yitzhak Rabin, who had previously served as the Chief of Staff of the IDF during the Six Day War (indeed he gave the war its name), and subsequently as Israel's Ambassador to Washington. Rabin's appointment was largely welcomed by the Foreign Office, who had little doubt about his judgement.[55] In Tel Aviv, Ledwidge suggested that the new Prime Minister had a strong will and a fine record behind him, and that he had made a good start as Prime Minister.[56] The Children, as he put it, were now in charge.[57] In truth, what was most feared in London in terms of Israeli politics was that the actions of the PLO, the continued hostility of the UN and the Arabs would drive Israel towards desperation.[58] If that happened, Ledwidge argued, there would be deep trouble. As he put it:

> The right-wing Likud Opposition, headed by the ex-terrorist Menachem Begin, will join the government in Jerusalem and there may be the devil to pay because peace-making is likely to become impossible. We must work against this. It will be best if the present Israeli Government remains in power with Prime Minister Rabin at its head, and if the present Opposition remains in opposition. In that event the dangers of another Middle Eastern war may yet be averted, unless the Arabs start it.[59]

In other words it was a case of anyone but Begin. It is interesting to note that at this stage much of the speculation about Begin and the Likud from Tel Aviv and London centred upon the chance of it joining a new broad National Unity Government in Israel.[60] Given its electoral performance in the 1973 elections, and the fact that, as Ledwidge suggested, Israel remained in a state of deep gloom, Likud was on the brink of power in its own right.[61]

In truth, Rabin's honeymoon with the Foreign Office, if that is what it ever amounted to, was swiftly over. Not long after assuming office, Rabin held his first meeting with the British Prime Minister, Harold Wilson, at Downing Street on 28 June 1974.[62] The Israeli Prime Minister was in Britain to attend a meeting of the Socialist International and appeared in a relaxed mood.[63] If the Foreign Office had expected Rabin to arrive bearing diplomatic gifts it would have been extremely disappointed. The Foreign Secretary, James Callaghan, who also attended the meeting, pointed out during the meeting that he saw no prospect of President Sadat agreeing a separate peace deal between Israel and Egypt without a Palestinian settlement.[64] The Israeli Prime Minister argued that Egypt would sign agreements with Israel on a gradual phased basis.[65] Even at this relatively early stage of his political career, Rabin enjoyed presenting his strategic blueprint of the Middle East as he saw it to attentive audiences. This blueprint did not endear the Israeli Prime Minister to the British Ambassador in Egypt, David Gladstone. The Ambassador responded to the thoughts of the Israeli Prime Minister in a most robust manner:

> I do not know whether Rabin was relaxing in the company of what he may have assumed to be sympathetic listeners or whether he was trying to sell some rather complex line. But if what he said accurately reflected what he actually thought, then he is surely living in cloud-cuckoo land in which the dominoes are still stacked as much as they were in 1967. The bare bones of his message seem to be: keep Hussein, use Sadat to the extent that he toes the Israeli line, otherwise scrap him. In any case separate Egypt off from the Palestinians (in whose destiny Egypt is not really interested in anyway) and get them to make further substantial concessions to Israel as an earnest of their (Egyptian) good faith (or changed spots).[66]

Put simply, Rabin was acting as if 1973 had not happened and Israeli political and military strength in 1974 was compatible to that of 1967. In the eyes of the Foreign Office this simply wasn't a true reflection of the reality of the day. The question at the back of everyone's minds was 'Is Rabin going to be another Golda?' Gladstone's somewhat veiled criticism of the Wilson Government being the 'sympathetic listeners' revealed the disappointment in the Foreign Office and Diplomatic Service that the new Labour Government had modified British policy towards the Arab–Israeli conflict, or at the very least had stopped the slide away from Israel that had taken place under the previous Conservative Government.

During the course of a parliamentary debate on the Middle East on 18 October 1973, Harold Wilson, then leader of the Opposition, had described the Harrogate Speech, which had formed the basis of the Conservative Party's Arab–Israeli policy, as a total reversal of the policy of the previous [Labour] Government.[67] Back in office, the Foreign Office advised Wilson on the issue of the Harrogate speech that the present was not the time for the outside powers to state positions on territorial issues and that it thought it desirable to avoid comparisons between the present government's view and those of its predecessors or the previous Labour administration.[68] Put simply, it was not helpful for outside parties to produce their own definitions of UN Resolution 242. This, in turn, meant that the shift towards the Arab position of UN Resolution 242 – withdrawal from all the territories – was countered by the new Labour administration, which stated 'Conservative Foreign Secretaries do not adopt our speeches. Neither do we adopt theirs.'[69]

Brainstorming for the Palestinian issue

Questions over the interpretation of UN Resolution 242 and the Labour Government's take on the Harrogate speech were not the only issues attracting the attention of the Foreign Office. In December 1974 there was a debate over the question of the British policy towards the Palestinians. Although the debate was already under way among Foreign Office officials, the impetus to put something more formal down on paper came from a meeting between Ledwidge and James Callaghan, the Foreign Secretary, in London on 17 December 1974. At the meeting Callaghan said that he wanted to keep in close touch with Henry Kissinger on the future of the Palestinians.[70] His idea was to feed the Secretary of State with ideas about a medium- to long-term solution for the Palestinian issue. In short, he was asking his officials for ideas.[71] Luckily for Callaghan, James Craig and others had been busy attempting to see if there was any common ground that could be teased out between the Israelis and the Palestinians. The major catalyst for the debate had been the private suggestion by a senior Israeli figure about Israel talking to the PLO if the PLO recognized Israel and stopped their violence.[72] Although, as Ledwidge reported, Yaariv's suggestions had been shot down, it was nevertheless still of interest to Craig.[73] The initiative which the Foreign was alluding to was actually a joint one by Aharon Yaariv and Victor Shemtov. It showed to the Foreign Office that at least there was some debate with the Israeli Government as to what to do with about the Palestinian question.

In Cairo, Philip Adams favoured the adoption of a two-state solution to the Palestinian problem and called for a 'freshening up' of UN Resolution 242 in the form of a new resolution that would include a just settlement for the refugee issue and the establishment of a Palestinian state within boundaries to be negotiated.[74] He suggested that it should be introduced by Britain. Adams was quite open about his motives for his proposals. As he recounted: 'Any British diplomat in the Middle East must be familiar with the plea: why don't you British do something to bring about a Palestine settlement? After all, you created the problem and you have the experience needed for its solution.'[75] In arguing his case,

Adams said that in the long run it was clear that if the Palestine question were ever to be resolved it could only be in one of two ways: the withering away of Israel into a united secular state of Palestine or by the creation of a separate Palestinian state alongside Israel.[76] The stark alternative was that if the Palestine questions remained unresolved for years there would be a perpetual risk of war, terrorism and oil embargoes.[77] The views of Adams were extremely representative of much of the diplomatic service in the Middle East, and indeed the vast majority of the Near Eastern Department of the Foreign Office. It was all, however, a question of emphasis, with the Foreign Office placing a priority on trying to first secure a deal between Egypt and Israel with the premise that such a deal would include some interim or permanent solution to the Palestine question.

Business as usual as Allon comes to town

Given the increased centrality of the Arab–Israeli conflict to British interests, as a result of the use of the oil weapon by the Arabs, the visits of Yigal Allon, the new Israeli Minister of Foreign Affairs, to London were deemed of heightened importance by the Labour Government.[78] The fact that Allon was seen by the Prime Minister and the Foreign Office as being both personally and politically close to Yitzhak Rabin added further significance to his visits. Rabin, the Foreign Office noted, had served as Allon's deputy when the latter was a General during the 1948 war.[79] On a number of occasions Allon's visits included private meetings with Harold Wilson at Chequers, the weekend home of the British Prime Minister, and at Dorneywood, the county residence of the Foreign Secretary. Allon's visits to Britain were largely private affairs; more often than not he was either on the way to, or coming back from, meetings in Washington. Allon would be collected by the Israeli Ambassador's car at an airport and whisked away to Chequers or Dorneywood far away from the prying eyes of the media. No need to alert the Arabs to the fact that the Israeli Minister of Foreign Affairs was enjoying extended and frequent access to both Wilson and Callaghan.

On 28 July 1974, Allon was invited to Chequers by the Prime Minister. During the course of the private meeting, Allon called for the reinstatement of intelligence sharing between Britain and Israel that had been a feature of relations in the period prior to the Six Day War in 1967.[80] In true form, however, Allon left the arms questions until the end of the meeting, asking about the supply of tanks, to which the Prime Minister replied that they were trying to scrape them together from their own resources.[81] Wilson concluded that Allon went away very happy.[82] No wonder: the Labour Party had shown itself to be more open to arms requests from Israel.

It helped matters no end that the Israeli requests for arms tended to be on a smaller scale than before. Increasingly the theme of discussions on this issue centred upon Israeli attempts to ensure that the British were not selling arms to the Arabs, which could alter the arms balance in the Middle East. In reality, Allon appeared personally fairly relaxed about the arms issue, and indeed the balance of arms in the region. He argued that if Egypt attacked again, Israel would be able to take them from the beginning this time.[83] From time to time minor irritants arose, such as rumours in the Middle East that Vickers had agreed to supply the Libyans with the same mini-submarines that had been promised to the Israelis.[84] This turned out to be false; the Soviets had actually supplied the Libyans with similar mini-submarines at a lower price than the British had offered.[85] That said, the Israelis still introduced the issue at almost every meeting at ministerial level and in the Israeli Ambassador's visits to the Foreign Office. Clearly the notion of Ben-Gurion's litmus test of Anglo–Israeli relations centring on the question of arms sales had been passed down through the political generations in Israel.

On 18 January 1975, Allon was back at Chequers and had one-to-one talks with Wilson for four hours over a private lunch.[86] The talks took the form of a general account of Middle Eastern developments. Allon then gave a repeat performance of his analysis in a private dinner with the Foreign Secretary, James Callaghan.[87] On 1 March 1975, Allon again dined with the Foreign Secretary at Dorneywood. Again, amid all the catching up on Middle East diplomatic gossip, Allon argued that the Israeli Government was becoming afraid that too many arms were being given to the Arabs, and particularly Egypt, by the West.[88]

The Foreign Office reminded Allon that the Israelis had been told in confidence what Britain had in mind over arms deals to Egypt and that no deals had taken place since this original conversation.[89] Allon then made the standard play for second-hand Centurion tanks, which he claimed Israel badly needed.[90] On this point Callaghan was non-committal.[91] The Foreign Office later confirmed that only a very few second-hand Centurion tanks would become available for sale over the next couple of years.[92] This was caused by the slower than expected pace of re-equipping British arms with the Chieftain tank.[93] Worryingly for Israel, the Foreign Office confirmed that there was going to be a delay of at least one year in the delivery of the mini-submarines from Vickers.[94] The reason given was that old 1970s British excuse, 'labour problems'.[95] The Israeli Ambassador, Gideon Rafael, had visited Vickers and had been dismayed at what he had seen and discovered.[96] The Israelis were now openly threatening that they would cancel the order and give it to the South Koreans, who were building submarines of the same design. The first submarine would not be launched until the following year. Ignoring for a moment all the political reasons for the initial delays, this was not a great advert for the British defence sector.

Arms to Egypt: Israel reacts

In June 1975 the Egyptians announced that they were in negotiations with the British over the purchase of new defence equipment. To add to an already difficult situation, the Egyptians had greatly exaggerated the extent of the proposed deal.[97] When they heard the news, the Israelis were furious and listed their complaints in a terse letter from Allon to Callaghan. Callaghan was puzzled by the strong response from Israel. He did not believe that Israel could claim with any justification to have been taken by surprise by the announcement of the negotiations as it had been kept informed well ahead of any potential sale of important military items to Egypt.[98] Callaghan argued that there had been no change in British policy towards the Arab–Israeli conflict in general, which remained as acceptance of UN Resolutions 242 and 338.[99] Callaghan went on to try to reassure Allon that there had also been no change in the British policy towards arms sales to the region.[100] As Callaghan put it:

> I frankly do not believe that the equipment under consideration, which we have already told you we are willing to supply to Egypt, will have the effect of creating the 'material and psychological pre-conditions for war' which you suggest. You may rest assured that I shall continue to exercise the closest personal control over the export of arms to the Middle East, as I have done since taking up office.[101]

Callaghan had already met with Rabin who was passing through London at a hotel near Heathrow on 16 June 1975.[102] The Foreign Secretary argued that Britain was still guided by the principle that it did not wish to upset the balance of power in the Middle East, but that it was very important that Egypt was not unduly dependent on the Soviet Union.[103] Rabin's response was much more low key than that of Allon's.

Rabin argued that the Israelis had indicated in the past that their attitude to arms supplies to Egypt had depended on what had been involved, and in this case press reports had indicated that an enormous number of weapons were under consideration.[104] In truth, as Ledwidge pointed out, to a large extent Allon's response had been promoted by the requirements of Israeli domestic politics rather than by any real concern over British policy.

The response of the Foreign Office to Allon was said by one Foreign Office official to be firm but not impolite. Ledwidge delivered to Allon personally on 19 June. A fairly pleased Allon appeared to confirm Ledwidge's assessment that his action had been taken largely for domestic consumption.[105] Allon pointed out that it was fortunate that he had summed Ledwidge on 14 June because, when he was questioned in the Knesset on 18 June, he had been able to demonstrate that the Israeli Government had taken action.[106] As a result, he had been able to keep the initiative and had been able to transfer the debate to the Foreign Affairs and Security Committee without going into too much detail. His aim, Allon claimed, was to dispose of the issue of the arms sales without damage, or with as little damage as possible, to the friendly Anglo–Israeli relations.[107]

This was not the end of the story. The arms issue continued to cause tension in Anglo–Israeli relations, and in particular with the Foreign Office's relationship with it. During a visit to London by President Sadat from 6 to 9 November 1975 there had been a lot of press speculation that Britain was about to sell British defence equipment to Egypt, including Jaguar aircraft.[108] Following the visit Britain had informed the Israeli Ambassador that no agreement had been reached.[109] Naturally during the course of his meeting with the Foreign Secretary on 3 December, Allon raised the issue of the potential sale of the Jaguar jets, warning that if the sale went through it would put Britain on a collision course with Israel.[110]

In essence, the arms issue remained a deeply difficult problem for the Foreign Office to manage. This had, in all honesty, become much more difficult given the fact that since the start of the decade much of this policy had been forced to be conducted in a more public manner. Gone were the days when arms deals to Israel could be kept quiet and the Israelis could be relied upon to raise objections in private. To some degree, the talks had also become a little easier given the fact that Britain was no longer a prime supplier of arms to Israel, which was heavily reliant on US weapons and, in time, on its own military industrial complex. It was of course no coincidence that the arms issue often developed into mini, or full-scale, diplomatic crises at the very moment that there was significant movement in other Arab–Israel diplomatic issues. The case of the potential sale of jets to Egypt took place at the same time as negotiations over the future of the Sinai between Israel and Egypt.

Despite the testiness at times of Allon, relations between the Foreign Office and Israel improved under the Wilson Government. The Craigium Dictum might still have been in place in the Foreign Office, but the shift towards the Arabs that had characterized the period immediately before and after the Yom Kippur War had been arrested. This shift, and the desire of both Wilson and Callaghan to meet with senior Israeli leaders in secret as the Israelis passed through Heathrow on their way back and forth to America, at the very least improved communications between the British and the Israelis. This made it easier to deal with the various crises as they arose. An interesting feature of Allon's time as Minister of Foreign Affairs was that as the first soldier to hold the portfolio he did not appear to carry the same baggage of suspicion towards the Foreign Office as his predecessors had appeared to have. Allon dealt with the Foreign Office in the present rather than constantly bringing up the unhappy past. For this, and despite his somewhat Israeli directness, he made a significant contribution to developing Israel's relations with the Foreign Office.

A deal at last

The most crucial event in the Middle East in 1975 was the conclusion of an interim agreement between Israel and Egypt, signed on 1 September, and which was implemented pretty much to the letter. In the eyes of the Foreign Office the agreement had led to the start of a new relationship between Egypt and Israel, which was a 'tender plant' and needed nursing. From an Israeli perspective the agreement appeared to signal that Egypt had neither the will nor the means to embark on another war, though as the Foreign Office noted, it also illustrated the growing political and economic dependence of Israel on the United States.[111] The agreement was seen as strategically important in terms of, in the minds of the Foreign Office, making a war between Israel and Syria less likely.[112]

By the end of 1975 the Foreign Office was growing more acutely aware of the increasingly small room left for Rabin to manoeuvre in Israel. The Israeli Prime Minister was viewed as having no real power base in the ruling Israeli Labour Party or enjoying no broad degree of support among the Israelis. His freedom of action, as a result, was, in Foreign Office eyes, more restrained than most of his predecessors.[113] These domestic pressures, Allan Urwick, from the Near East and North Africa Department concluded, correctly, made it very unlikely that Rabin would be able to get into serious negotiations over the West Bank in the fear future.[114] To a certain degree, Yasser Arafat and the PLO's continued attacks against Israel released Rabin from any domestic debates about having to adopt the Shemtov–Yaariv formula for talks with any Palestinian group that pledged non-violence and recognized Israel's right to exist.[115] The major hope from the Americans was for, at the very least, the appearance of progress in terms of Arab–Israeli conflict, and the Foreign Office concurred with this view.[116] Too much pressure on Rabin and his government would split and fall, forcing early elections and diplomatic inertia. Although the Foreign Office believed and understood that the Rabin Government was in deep trouble, there was little it believed it could do to help. Appeals from the British Ambassador for a clearer British policy on Resolution 242 and in other areas were rejected by officials.[117] They argued that ministers would not tolerate such a change and also that it was unwise for Britain to declare its policy before full Middle East negotiations took place.[118]

Corruption and decline of the Israeli Government

In addition to the growing political difficulties for Rabin, the Foreign Office was also aware that something was rotten in the state of Israel at the time. Although much corruption pre-dated the Rabin Government, the impression was that it was not doing enough to deal with it. More to the point, this seemingly domestic affair was having an impact upon the diplomatic by putting Rabin under increasing pressure. The British Embassy in Tel Aviv had kept the Foreign Office fully informed on the increasing number of scandals that surrounded the Israeli Government and the wider economy at this time. On the wider economic issues Ledwidge wrote:

> I think Israel's philosophy has been that it desperately needed money and that, if extra cash could be made in international financial operations such as currency speculation, Israel was entitled to profit by the ingenuity of the international Jewish business community without too close a regard for rules and regulations. It was the philosophy of a

country at war and of a people whose chief weapon of defence against persecution over many hundreds of years has been their skill in money management.[119]

With the onset on an economic recession in 1974 many of the speculations went wrong, and this, taken together with the fact that many of the speculators had been taking a large slice of the profits for themselves and were unable to cover their tracks, created a sense that the Israel economy had been infected.[120] In reality, the Israeli Government tried to cover up the corruption before deciding to come clean and start investigating it and debating its consequences for Israel. The problem for the Israeli Government was this: once you start investigating you tend to uncover more, and in the case of the Israeli Government much of it was very close to home, including a Cabinet Minister and senior government officials. In the end, Rabin was himself tainted by a scandal involving the failure to close bank accounts held in Washington.

The upshot of all this, when taken together with other factors such as the Labour Party's failures at the start of the Yom Kippur War, was that the Foreign Office suspected that this was a government that was in rapid decline.[121] Although it is fair to say that the Foreign Office did not fully comprehend the deeper reasons for the decline of the ruling Israeli Labour Party, it made a correct judgement on the evidence that it could see and understand. With the performance of Likud in 1973 elections, there was a seeming viable alternative government in the wings whose ideology, views and past statements on the Arab–Israeli conflict were of great concern to the Foreign Office that had developed a relatively good working relationship with the Israeli Labour Party over the years. At the heart of Foreign Office fears were the statements from the leader of Likud about Greater Israel – a Jewish state that would include the West Bank. The very real fear among Foreign Office officials was that, if elected, Begin would annex the West Bank, an action that would potentially lead to another round of hostilities in the Middle East, which would put British interests in the region once more in mortal danger. As we recounted earlier in the book, there was also a strong sense of antipathy towards Begin among past senior figures in the Foreign Office. Begin's actions during the British Mandate had not been forgiven or forgotten by the Foreign Office, and his eventual arrival in power in 1977 shifted the focus back on to the difficult period of the Mandate.

8

Menaced and menacing

A dispassionate analysis of Israel's situation in the world today might suggest that time was not on her side and that a policy of anticipating events and flexibility, rather than of holding tightly on to past gains, might best suit her long-term interests . . . Israeli foreign policy often seems rigid, naively defensive and unprepared to take any chances based on a real calculation of risks.

Anthony Elliot, British Ambassador to Israel, 28 April 1976[1]

In traditional accounts of the Arab–Israeli conflict, 1977 is seen as the year of transformation.[2] The man that Foreign Office officials referred to as the ex-terrorist – or the viper – and whose very presence in government they believed would substantially increase the risk of another Middle Eastern war, Menachem Begin, came to power in what Israelis referred to as an electoral earthquake, after 29 years of leading the Opposition. It was also the year of the diplomatic breakthrough with President Sadat's visit to Israel and his address to the Knesset. That said, there is a strong case that, in terms of the Foreign Office's relationship with Israel anyway, 1976 was at least as significant as if not even more important than 1977. In 1976, along with a highly active series of diplomatic contacts, the Foreign Office conducted a major review of its Middle Eastern policy, and specifically its options regarding the Arab–Israeli conflict. The decision of Foreign Office Ministers to adopt some of the findings of the reports compiled by their officials meant that British Middle East policy evolved over the next decade into taking a much more critical line with Israel. Within this policy framework criticism of the various Israeli governments of the day was voiced, mainly over the question of the increased pace in the construction of Israeli settlements in the Occupied Territories. The philosophy behind the policy, and the methods used in its implementation, remained fairly static.

The year of 1976 started fairly quietly, the British Ambassador, Bernard Ledwidge, had retired and departed to London. It is fair to say that Ledwidge had been an extremely shrewd observer of Israel and the Middle East and was not afraid to argue the case for greater weight on the Israeli side of the Foreign Office's set of Middle East balancing scales. In the course of his actions he had often come up against the head of the Near East and North Africa Section, James Craig, who had a fierce intellect and deep-rooted belief that British interests in the Arab world made it difficult to lean towards Israel. Craig also left his office during the course of the year to become Ambassador to Syria, but the Craigium Dictum, as Ledwidge referred to British Middle East policy, remained very much intact in the Near East and North Africa Department.

Ledwidge's valedictory dispatch entitled 'Israel: menaced and menacing' contained the usual dosage of commonsense advice and astute observations. Gone was the confident country that had greeted him upon his arrival in Tel Aviv the year before the Yom Kippur War. Gone also was Israel's economic success story with an economy which, in the pre-war period, grew faster than that of any other country except Japan. Despite all this and the sense of deep depression which surrounded Israel after the war, Ledwidge remained convinced that there was no doubt that Israel was here to stay or, as Golda Meir had told him when saying goodbye, 'Israel lives in a nasty neighbourhood but she means to stay.'[3] Ledwidge argued that there had been a marked improvement in British policy towards Israel since 1974 and that Britain's best chance of restraining and reassuring Israel should be undertaken on a bilateral basis rather than through the EEC, where French pro-Arab interests were the dominant order of the day.[4] Sensible advice no doubt, but Britain's membership of the EEC was an increasingly additional complicating factor in its bi-lateral relations with Israel and the role of the Foreign Office in guiding these relations.

A new man in Tel Aviv

The new British Ambassador, Anthony Elliot, arrived in the winter of 1975–76 and soon produced detailed 'first impressions' that were of great interest not only to the Foreign Office but also to James Callaghan, who had succeeded Wilson as Prime Minister and who had been shown a copy of the dispatch.[5] Given that Elliot was relatively new to the post, there was a certain amount of crystal ball gazing in his impressions, but nevertheless he showed himself to have a good political antenna. At the centre of his impressions was his belief that the majority of Israelis would agree to the return of the vast majority of the Occupied Territories if they could be convinced that Israel would in return get a real settlement.[6] The theme of Elliot's report was that the Israelis would be very hard to move to positions that were more acceptable to the Arabs so long as they believed that the Arabs would attempt to use any returned territories as a springboard for further advances.[7] The Foreign Office largely agreed with the Ambassador's first impressions, but the real issue that officials were addressing was the question of whether Britain should have a clearer vision of what it felt the terms of a Middle East settlement should be.[8]

In January 1976, Elliot had written that British influence in the Arab–Israeli conflict was very limited, but that it would be easier for Britain to play an effective part if it had a clearer conception of the sort of settlement it believed ought to emerge.[9] The Ambassador gave the example of the Palestinian issue and pointed out that as Ambassador he was liable to be asked if the British view was that the best chance of peace lay in the establishment of some form of Palestinian state in the West Bank and Gaza Strip, or did Britain concur with Israeli opinion that King Hussein still had a chance of reasserting his authority in these areas.[10] Foreign Office officials largely agreed with Elliot's analysis plea, but argued that there was little chance of being able to help him at the present.[11] Urwick, from the Near East and North Africa Department, suggested somewhat ruefully that not only did Ministers believe that it could be damaging to the negotiations to spell out a settlement in advance, but that there were obvious dangers in any attempt to outline Britain's position, notably regarding Israeli withdrawal from the Occupied Territories.[12] The official position was to remain simply that it was best if the details of a peace settlement were sorted out between the parties involved.[13]

In truth, what Elliot was suggesting was that the Foreign Office ought to embark on a process of clarifying in its own mind, in private, a position on a final settlement.[14] The Ambassador suggested a planning staff paper that would be strictly for internal use and that would consider the various feasible solutions.[15] This was needed, for, as Elliot put it: 'The point is that one's approach to the modalities of negotiation, which is all one can realistically talk about at this stage, must in large measure be determined by the kind of long-term solution one judges to be desirable.'[16] In arguing the case, the Ambassador used the ultimate weapon: he suggested that there was evidence that the French had already undertaken such an exercise and that the Americans might have as well.[17]

Urwick, however, was initially keen to resist the production of a new planning paper.[18] His rationale for rejecting it said much about the thinking in the Foreign Office at that precise moment and the splits between its officials and ministers, but especially the split between Foreign Office policy and the Prime Minister Harold Wilson's vision of the Middle East just prior to his resignation.[19] Urwick argued that ministers were reluctant to spell out the details of a settlement because such an elucidation would have to take account of the Prime Minister's strongly held views on Israeli withdrawal from the Occupied Territories and his interruption of UN Resolution 242.[20] The point that ministers held strong views in private on the settlement should not be relevant to the production of an internal Foreign Office report, but it would be pointless if the outcome produced a paper whose conclusions were contrary to the Prime Minster's views.[21] As Urwick wrote: 'It would give rise to a very delicate situation if it were to become known that the [Foreign] Office was acting on the basis of assumptions so greatly at variance with Wilson's expressed preferences.'[22] Put simply, the Foreign Office did not want to be responsible for the charge of trying to run a second semi-independent foreign policy, the contents of which the Prime Minister of the day strongly disagreed with. If this had happened, there would, in all likelihood, have been calls for the censure or even for the resignation of the officials involved in the report and its implementation.

Summer activity and reports

Just when the issue of a new planning report appeared to have been put to bed, those at the Foreign Office who were keen to conduct such an exercise got lucky. The unexpected resignation of Harold Wilson on 5 April, and his replacement by James Callaghan, led to a major Cabinet reshuffle, with new ministers arriving at the Foreign Office in addition to the new Foreign Secretary, Anthony Crosland. The Foreign Office, as a result, had the excuse to draft two new major papers on the short- and long-term aspects of the whole Arab–Israeli question.[23] These papers were designed both as background briefing papers for the incoming ministers, who were not previously familiar with the issues, and to launch a 'fundamental reappraisal' of the issues by the Foreign Office.[24] This use of the smokescreen of the incoming ministers was opportunistic and clever and gave the authors of the report a relatively free hand. At the heart was the very basic fact that many in Foreign Office and diplomatic service regarded British thinking on the Arab–Israeli conflict as leaning too much towards the Israelis.[25] The change of Prime Minister and this report provided a golden opportunity in the eyes of officials and diplomats who concurred with this assessment to change British policy.

Foreign Office officials were not the only busy-bees following the departure of Wilson. At the start of the summer of 1976 there was something of an outbreak of the reassessment bug among the diplomatic core based in the Arab states. These calls for changes to Britain's view on the Arab–Israeli conflict reflected those in the Foreign Office and centred upon shifting the balancing scales back towards the Arabs.[26] The catalyst for this paper trail was a letter to the Foreign Office from the British Ambassador in Cairo, William (Willie) Morris on 7 June 1976. Weir agreed the contents, pointing out that 'we are doing our best to work for the sort of changes in our position which you advocate'.[27] At the heart of Willie Morris's proposals was preventing the British from being singled out among the EEC countries for special pressure among the Arabs.[28] The British Ambassador to the United Nations, Ivor Richard, agreed with Morris's viewpoint, arguing that there was a chance that Britain could, as a result, be left isolated during UN votes.[29] He also called for greater co-ordination between the member states of the EEC, with Britain moving more in line with its European counterparts.[30]

Elliot in Tel Aviv thought that Weir's rationale for action was quite strange.[31] For his part, Elliot argued that the prime obligation of the British Government, before taking action which was likely to have a major bearing on the Arab–Israeli conflict, was to consider whether the action would or would not likely help facilitate a settlement.[32] In Damascus the outgoing Ambassador, David Roberts (he was replaced by the irrepressible James Craig of Craigium Dictum fame), argued that British policy needed to be much clearer. He called for a redefinition of UN Resolution 242 by putting in the definite article 'the' to mean an Israeli withdrawal from all the Occupied Territories.[33] This should then be followed, he argued, by a move halfway towards formal relations with the PLO on the grounds that this would help provide the British with practical advantages and also some access to intelligence.[34] Finally, at a later date, Britain should recognize the PLO and adopt a formal position on a Palestinian state.[35]

Morris, who correctly identified the underlying trends in the region but in actual fact ended up misreading the result, completed the round robin of correspondence.[36] He argued that as there appeared so little give in Israel's position then any talk of a negotiated settlement was a waste of words.[37] Israel was well equipped militarily and would not be caught napping twice; the Arabs would know that they had no military option and would consequently be forced to use their economic weapon against the West.[38] This was why, as he argued, Britain should be making sure that it was not out in front of our partners when it was fired at.[39] In retrospect, when faced with all of the above, along with a series of domestic political difficulties, President Sadat did not opt for rallying Arab support for firing the economic weapons. Instead, he took the decision to openly pursue a peace settlement with Israel that led to the signing of the Camp David Accords with the Foreign Office's old foe, Menachem Begin, on 17 September 1978, and a full peace treaty between Egypt and Israel was signed the following year on 26 March 1979.

In truth, the pressure for a change of direction in British policy from the British Embassies was nothing special. They had constantly argued this line for some time. Its timing was, however, important, with the Foreign Office embarking on a full-scale assessment of British policy under the cover of presenting briefing papers for the new ministers in the department. At this point the ambassadors, with the exception of Elliot, were moving in harmony with the general thrust of the Foreign Office's thinking to repair the damage that Wilson's pro-Israel line had caused, or could cause in the future, to British interests in the Arab world.

The first of the reports was completed on 20 February 1976 and dealt with the near future as well as the question of the interpretation of UN Resolution 242.[40] In terms of possible action by Britain, the report concluded that there was very little scope for action.[41] In essence, the report argued that if the Americans could not get things moving then Britain would certainly not be able to do so.[42] There was a sense, however, that if the deadlock in the Middle East continued, Britain might find it necessary to do something in order to provide some kind of appearance of progress.[43] Even allowing for the creation of an illusion of progress, the report warned that it might be necessary to take some steps to protect British interests against Arab retaliation for the lack of diplomatic progress. The recommended method was some kind of pronouncement in favour of a Palestinian homeland or Palestinian self-determination.[44] The latter would bring Britain in line with the majority of the other members of the EEC who had already adopted similar lines towards the Palestinians.[45] In terms of Resolution 242 the report clearly favoured some shift in its interpretation, but with the Prime Minister very heavily in favour of remaining vague on the issue, any new recommendations would simply have been a waste of time in the short term.[46]

The second paper was submitted by the Near East and North Africa Department for discussion on 23 June 1976 and dealt with the situation in the medium term, the prospects of a settlement and implications for British policy.[47] The recommendations made in this report were much more far reaching and reflected the opinion among officials that British policy towards Israel and the Arab–Israeli conflict needed to change.[48] The report argued that the British Government should state publicly that the pre-1967 borders, albeit with some minor ramifications, should provide the basis for Israel's boundaries in any settlement with the Arabs.[49] The report also argued that the British Government should support the establishment of a Palestinian 'homeland'.[50] In terms of style it argued that there must be a change here as well. Instead of maintaining a low profile and saying as little as possible, which might please or annoy either side in the conflict, Britain should state its views more openly.[51] As the report argued, 'the resentment of both Arabs and Israelis for home truths which they find unpalatable in any case tends to be moderated if the home truths are equally shared out'.[52]

The reports reached the desk of the Minister of State, Roy Hattersley, in July 1976.[53] Hattersley agreed with the contents of the reports and in a letter and minute to Anthony Crosland on 3 August 1976 argued that there was no doubt that Britain needed to move to a position which was crudely less pro-Israel than British policy had been in the past.[54] The only concern that Hattersley maintained was whether this shift in British policy should be undertaken in one large leap or in a more staged way within the forums of the EEC.[55]

Perhaps the most interesting aspects of the two reports was the definition of British interests and aims in the Middle East, which lay at the heart of the motivation of the Foreign Office to change British policy towards the Arab–Israeli conflict. As the report put it:

> We have important interests in the Middle East. We need to avoid the outbreak of another conflict which could threaten world peace, split the NATO Alliance and bring a new oil embargo damaging to Western interests as a whole. We want to take advantage of greatly increased Arab wealth by expanding our trade with the Arab states. While our material interest in Israel is much smaller, we have the strongest moral and political obligation to uphold her right to exist and the freedom of her citizens. Finally we want to restrict Soviet influence in the Middle East, which benefits from situations of instability and unrest.[56]

Although the Foreign Office argued that the best way of securing British interests in the Middle East was through a 'just and lasting peace' it was also realistic to understand that this did not look particularly likely at the time.[57] Policy, as a result, was aimed at effectively trying to prevent another conflict from breaking out and, if it did, making sure that British interests in the region were damaged as little as possible.[58] In other words, the Willie Morris philosophy was very much the order of the day: if war did break out, making sure that British interests were not the most exposed of all the European powers to an Arab backlash.

In terms of the question of motive for the policy of the Foreign Office towards Israel and the wider issue of the Arab–Israeli conflict, a question that goes to the very heart of this book, it appears fairly clear what the Foreign Office was attempting to achieve in this review. Officials believed that Harold Wilson's stance on Israel, particularly his reluctance to define UN Resolution 242, had exposed British interests in the Middle East to a further Arab backlash. It is worth remembering that this backlash was not a weapon that was merely used as an idle threat by the Arab oil-producing states. Rather, it had already been used to good effect from an Arab perspective – and who was to say at the time that despite American pressure to prevent it happening again, it would not be deployed for a second time? Given the nature of the threat, the Foreign Office could have gone much further in attempting to shift the balance of the scale towards the Arab side. Its officials believed, however, that Britain still retained a degree of influence in Israel that could be suitably deployed to help the foundering American diplomatic initiative led by Henry Kissinger.[59]

The quiet shift under Callaghan

The resignation of Harold Wilson and the arrival of James Callaghan in Number 10 meant that the Prime Minister of the day was more in line with the Foreign Office's vision of a Middle Eastern policy than his predecessor had been. Callaghan was, however, against any major new initiative or shock announcement, but rather favoured a gentle slide away from the overtly pro-Israel policy of Wilson. On 15 September 1976, the Prime Minister was criticized in the Israeli press as a result of comments he had made on UN Resolution 242 to an Israeli periodical in which he appeared to decline to commit his government to supporting the English language version of the resolution (withdrawal from territories) over the French version (withdrawal from the territories).[60] Callaghan simply avoided committing his government to any of the versions. Rightly or wrongly, the Israelis were deeply concerned by this apparent change from the Wilson era. Wilson, the Israelis argued, had told a meeting of the

Central Committee meeting of the Israeli Labour Party on 27 December 1972 that 'if our government had meant all, we would have said all. We would never have wanted to say it anyway, and if we had, it wouldn't have passed.'[61] As we have seen, Wilson made similar noises about the resolutions back in the UK during the course of a House of Commons debate. To make matters worse for the Israelis, during the course of Callaghan's interview he had talked of the need to recognize the right of the Palestinian people to the expression of their national identity.[62] In truth, the Near East and North Africa Department at the Foreign Office had drafted Callaghan's responses, in which they were keen to illustrate some degree of slide away from Israel.[63]

The Secretary of State, Anthony Crosland, made a similar comment on the Palestinian issue in a speech to the United Nations General Assembly on 5 October 1976.[64] In his speech he made reference to 'a land for the Palestinians', which had caused a great deal of displeasure to the Israelis who by now were beginning to sense a clear shift in British policy on the Arab–Israeli question.[65] It wasn't long before the Israeli Ambassador in London, Gideon Rafael, was bringing up this very point with the Minister for State, David Owen.

Rafael was not one of the Foreign Office's favourite Israelis. While officials admired his intellect and linguistic abilities, he was regarded as sometimes being hard, prickly and awkward as well as something of a loose cannon (meaning he sometimes acted without the formal instructions from his government).[66] Worse still, he had acquired something of a reputation for leaking the details of his meetings with British ministers and officials to the press.[67] Urwick had advised Dr Owen before his first meeting with Rafael to get a pledge from him to keep their discussions private.[68] Ever the smooth operator, Dr Owen used Urwick's suggestion as something of an attempted icebreaker with the Israeli Ambassador during their meeting on 17 September 1976, eliciting a promise from the Ambassador to keep their discussion confidential.[69]

At the meeting on 1 November 1976, Rafael cut straight to the chase by stating that he sensed that there had been a change in the policy of the British Government towards the Arab–Israel question.[70] Dr Owen responded as if he had been accused of some terrible crime, assuring the Ambassador that this was not the case and enquiring why he felt the need to raise the issue.[71] He went on to list other meetings involving British and Israeli politicians and officials that had taken place since the speech and said that not one of them had raised the issue of an alleged shift in British policy.[72]

In a sign of the times, a request by Rafael to have a meeting with the Secretary of State the following month was turned down by the Foreign Office, who offered him a rerun with Dr Owen instead.[73] Internally in correspondence between senior Foreign Office officials, the reason given was that Rafael would be unlikely to have anything new to say.[74] Wheeler from the Near East and North Africa Department argued that the Israelis were trying to counter the recent peace overtures of President Sadat and the PLO and Rafael was probably trying to support the Israeli effort. To a certain extent this snub, for whatever reasons discussed, was part of a broader new culture that was part of the slide away from Israel.

A second feature in the apparent slide was the reduction of the number of official or semi-official visits by Israeli leaders to Britain and by British ministers to Israel. The British Prime Minister cancelled a visit to Israel that had been planned by his predecessor for late 1976 and the Foreign Secretary made it clear that he would be too busy to undertake a visit to Israel in the first half of 1977 (Britain held the presidency of the EEC at this time).[75] Allon, who was a frequent visitor to London on semi-official or private trips (he had two children at school in England), was also informed that there would be no reason for him to be invited on a formal visit by the British Government.[76] Indeed, the access that Allon enjoyed in the era of the Callaghan Government was much more restricted than it had been when Harold Wilson led the government.

To be fair, there was always a price to be paid for the visit of Israeli leaders to Britain, and the Foreign Office was more aware of this fact than anybody. The visit of the Israeli President to London, which included lunch with the Queen, during the course of 1976 had not gone down well with the Arabs, this despite the fact that the visit was not a state one, but rather classified as private. In December 1976, the Israeli Minister of Defence, Shimon Peres, visited London to speak at a function organized by the Joint Israel Appeal. As Minister of Defence, Peres's portfolio also included responsibility for the administration of the Occupied Territories. The Permanent Under-Secretary at the Foreign Office, Sir Michael Palliser, accepted an invitation to attend a lunch in honour of Peres on 3 December 1976. The Foreign Office, as a result, received many complaints, to which Sir Michael responded in robust fashion: 'In my diplomatic business no good purpose is served by a refusal to talk to those with whom one sometimes disagrees.'[77]

Israeli fears and concerns

While the Foreign Office was flying under the radar conducting its internal reassessment of policy options towards the Arab–Israeli conflict and implementing the resulting quiet slide away from Israeli positions, Israel viewed its relationship with Britain with a sense of heightened importance. To be honest, much of the sense of importance Israel placed on Britain was related to the potential damage to Israeli interests if Britain adopted a more pro-Arab line. For Israel in 1976 there were six major issues of concern in which the British, in particular the Foreign Office, could play a role, if they so desired, in limiting the damage to its national interests.[78] These areas were the blocking of the 'Zionism is racism' issue at the UN, stopping the creeping diplomatic legitimization of the PLO, acting as buffer to anti-Israel political and economic issues in the EEC, breaking the Arab boycott of Israel, stopping the supply of weapons (mainly strike aircraft) to the Egypt and the wider Arab world, and helping contain the civil war in Lebanon from developing into a wider regional conflict.[79]

Meetings between British and Israeli officials as well as their counterparts centred upon these issues rather than any major attempt at finding a settlement to the Arab–Israeli dispute. There was a realization both in the Foreign Office and in Israel that the time was not ripe to move towards a settlement, despite an intuitive by President Sadat. In America, 1976 was election year and much of the work of Henry Kissinger had come to a halt. The victory of Jimmy Carter over the incumbent Gerald Ford in the November presidential elections threw the process into further stagnation. At the time, Carter was something of an unknown quantity and had campaigned largely on domestic issues such as clean government. His attitudes to the diplomatic process in the Middle East were far from clear, a point that was compounded by the fact that he was an outsider to Washington and thus had no voting record on Middle East issues in the House or in the Senate.

In terms of the six key issues in Anglo–Israeli relations the Foreign Office's position differed from the Israelis on almost all the issues.[80] In terms of the anti-Zionist moves at the UN there was widespread agreement between the Foreign Office and Israel that such moves were absolutely unacceptable.[81] The Foreign Office believed that given the nature of the UN voting system there was little they could do. On the question of the PLO, the Foreign Office had a track record of abstaining on this issue and would continue with this tactic.[82] Britain's role in the

EEC at blocking potentially damaging proposals aimed at Israel was perhaps the most useful role it could play for the Israelis. As we have seen, there was a general consensus within the Foreign Office and the Diplomatic Service that British policy on the Arab–Israeli question must fall more into line with that of the other member states.[83] In other words, the Foreign Office would not attempt to protect Israeli interests in the EEC as strongly as it had done during the era of the Wilson Government.[84] The Foreign Office's attitude to the Arab boycott was to encourage trade links with Israel but to direct British companies wishing for advice to the Board of Trade.[85]

The key immediate concern for the Israelis about the British, however, once more centred upon the question of arms sales to the region.[86] With the exception of the secondhand tanks and one or two other bits of hardware and ammunition, the Israelis were no longer interested in placing large orders in Britain for arms.[87] By 1976 the Israeli programme of developing its own military industrial complex was well under way and this, taken together with the supply of American weapons, made Israeli requests for arms much less frequent.[88] As we have seen from Allon's previous visits to Britain, the major Israeli fear was that Britain would agree to sell weapons such as Jaguar aircraft to Egypt, which would alter the balance of arms. There was a deep-rooted belief in Israel that President Sadat would only come to the negotiating table on terms agreeable to Israel if it had no real military option. The Foreign Office continued to take the view that it would examine each request for arms on an individual basis. Finally, in terms of Lebanon there was agreement in both the Foreign Office and in Israel that much work needed to be done to stop the civil war from developing into a regional conflict.

Despite outbreaks of Israeli moaning, or the registering of protests, about British attitudes or actions on one or more of the six issues, Anglo–Israeli relations continued to be very cordial.[89] This cordiality continued despite increasing Israeli suspicions that there had been a change in the British attitude towards the Arab–Israeli conflict.[90] There remained strong ties between the British and Israeli Labour Parties, which had been fostered through meeting and exchanges organized by Socialist International.[91] At the senior level, Wilson, Callaghan, Rabin and Allon all got on well, which helped ensure a high level of communication and a good degree of understanding, but importantly not total agreement on the key issues that lay at the core of Israel's conflict with the Arab world. The Israelis naturally remained keen to keep up the pressure on Britain to help moderate the policy of the EEC towards the conflict and to reduce its activity at the United Nations. On top of all this was the very stark fact which Israel had been forced to absorb about the 1973 war: it had been left to stand alone, diplomatically and militarily, with the exception of the United States.[92] Israeli leaders did not want a repeat of this if there was going to be anther round of fighting. Britain, as a result, was given a slightly more elevated role by the Israelis, which in other times it might not have been afforded.

A tale of two plans

Alan Urwick from the Near East and North Africa Department felt that it might well have been this fear of diplomatic isolation that led its Minister of Foreign Affairs, Yigal Allon, to publish his private plan for peace, known as the Allon Plan, on 16 September 1976.[93] In truth, Urwick saw the plan, which was published in *Foreign Affairs*, as a means of appeasing the opinion of world Jewry that Israel should put forward its views on where its eventual borders would be and an opening bid in the next round of negotiations, at which the Israelis expected to come under strong American pressure.[94] At the time of the publication of the plan, Allon was not particularly liked by the Foreign Office, who saw him as a forceful personality and a potential future leader, but claimed that there was a bit of a *'faux bon homme'* about him. This was, however, the first version of the Allon Plan, which had been in existence since 1967, to be published on the future of the territories captured during the 1967 war. For this reason, if no other, the publication of the Allon Plan represented an important development.[95]

The publication of the plan created a great deal of interest in the Foreign Office, not so much because of its contents, which were seen as merely an articulation of an Israeli hard-line position, but rather on the question of motive.[96] There was also the question of whether Rabin had authorized the publication of the plan, and whether or not he agreed with its contents.[97] Officially, the Prime Minister's office in Jerusalem issued a statement claiming that Rabin had not seen or approved of the text.[98] The fact that its publication had led the opposition Likud in Israel to table a debate on its contents in the Knesset, and the deep divisions in ruling coalition on the issue of borders, meant that it was unlikely to have been published for domestic reasons.[99] Indeed, in terms of its contents it led one Foreign Office official to suggest that 'the fact that what is essentially a hard-line thesis can attract so much criticism from within the Israeli Government shows what a super-human task awaits the next mediator in the Arab–Israel problem'.[100] Urwick added that it was difficult to believe that the Arabs would find anything acceptable in the proposals.[101]

The publication of the Allon Plan had been preceded by leaks of details of another Israeli plan in the Hebrew press. On 17 June 1976, Israel Galili, Minister without Portfolio, had outlined his vision of a settlement in *Davar*.[102] The Foreign Office thought that Galili, who officials rather curiously labelled a former Private Secretary of Yigal Allon, was more hawkish than Allon.[103] Again the article was of interest to the Foreign Office as it represented the 'fullest and most explicit exposition' of the position of the Israel Government towards the Palestinian issue.[104] The contents of the article did not make for pleasant reading for Foreign Office officials, who described it in the following way:

> Taken all in, the article represents a tough redefinition of Israel's policy towards the West Bank, the Palestinians and related issues. We can be fairly certain that although the article appeared under Galili's name it would not have been published without the approval of the Prime Minister and probably the rest of the Cabinet . . . It should be taken as a sign that the Israeli Government are not yet ready to admit to any softening in their position.[105]

Although Alan Urwick felt that the publication of such plans, after years of silence, were indeed an indication that the Israelis were fearful of isolation, they also served the purpose of issuing a stark statement to the Americans and the European powers that Israel would not accept an imposed settlement. Israel, in truth, appeared ready to make concessions on Sinai, but not on the West Bank and the related question of the Palestinian issue.

In truth, the position of the Israeli Government, and the belief in the Foreign Office that Rabin's own position towards the Israeli settlements was hardening, provided an increased degree of legitimacy for its policy of a slide away from Israel and towards the Arabs. There was also an awareness that if Britain and America pushed the Rabin Government too hard it would probably implode and that either a National Unity Government would have to be formed that included Likud or fresh elections would be called in which the Israel Labour Party stood a fair chance of losing. Whichever way, the Foreign Office remained convinced that the outbreak of hostilities between Israel and the Arabs could not be discounted, even in the short term, and as a result Britain needed to make sure that its interests in the oil-producing Arab world were protected as much as possible. In this respect, 1976 was a pivotal year which saw the adoption of polices that would eventually become central to British policy towards Israel, the Occupied Territories, the Palestinians and the wider Arab–Israeli conflict.

Part 4

The Thatcher and Major Era:
May 1979 to May 1997

9

Thatcher, Israel and the Foreign Office

You mentioned Golda Meir. Of course, in a way, I follow in her footsteps. I knew her. I greatly admired her. I greatly admired her as a war leader. I greatly admired her tremendous courage. I greatly admired her as a pioneer. I greatly admired her as a human being, warm, thoughtful, kind, for all her fellow citizens and for human kind in the world as a whole.[1]

Margaret Thatcher, Jerusalem, 25 May 1986

Many years before the iconic image of Margaret Thatcher test-driving a new Challenger tank in Germany in September 1988, another photograph, which had been bought by the *Daily Mirror*, caused something of a storm.[2] The photograph featured the then Leader of the Opposition wearing an Israeli General's anorak, complete with badges of rank, to protect herself against the strong wind on an Israeli hilltop lookout post on the Golan Heights.[3] The date was 22 March 1976 and Thatcher was in the middle of a three-day fact-finding visit to Israel.[4] The story behind the photograph gave the Foreign Office and Diplomatic Service an early warning of Thatcher's attitude towards them. Prior to departing Tel Aviv for the Golan Heights, staff at the Embassy had pressed Thatcher to take an overcoat.[5] She robustly declined their advice, and as a result the photographer got his snap of her dressed in an Israeli military uniform looking out from an Israeli military post.

The photograph of 'General' Thatcher would have been seen back home as a PR disaster for most British politicians. Not so for Thatcher, whose brief visit turned out to be one of the most successful by a British politician to Israel.[6] She appeared not to care about following Foreign Office diplomatic guidance that called for avoidance of anything controversial during visits to Israel by British politicians.[7] As the British Ambassador in Tel Aviv pointed out, even the Prime Minister, Rabin, was in an 'unusually expansive' mood and much more relaxed than Elliot had ever seen before when he met with her on 23 March.[8] As the Ambassador concluded, Thatcher's personality here in the meeting with Rabin, as elsewhere in Israel, produced remarkable results.[9] Even at this early stage

Israel's love affair with Thatcher was under way, with the Israeli press and public paying a great deal more attention to her visit than to those of most VIP visitors.[10]

Thatcher and Israel support and contradictions

The superficial narrative of the Thatcher era in terms of foreign policy is more often than not defined in simple black and white as being pro-Israel and anti-Arab, pro-America and anti-Europe, and within Whitehall of being anti-Foreign Office. In the way that most clichéd narratives go, this pro- and anti- list is only a partial reflection of the true picture. In the case of Thatcher, Israel and the Foreign Office, the real story was very much more complex and reveals contradictions with the wider published doctrines of dogma, just as Northern Ireland was the exception to the rule in economic politics.

After assuming power in May 1979, Thatcher was initially heavily dependent on the Foreign Office and her Foreign Secretary, Lord (Peter) Carrington, to brief her for key meetings.[11] Despite her already deep suspicion of the Foreign Office as a bastion of complacency she was politically astute enough to know that she needed it, and in particular its Rolls-Royce of briefing statements and background information on the foreign leaders, many of whom she was meeting for the first time.[12]

Meetings on Israel and the Middle East were not the exception to this rule, despite the fact that the Prime Minister believed that she already knew something about Israel from her time serving as an MP in Finchley, with its large Jewish community. Thatcher often used community events and publications in Finchley to stress her strong emotional support and links to Israel. In a letter to the Finchley Anglo–Israel Friendship League on 6 December 1979 she stated that her government would not recognize the PLO claim to be the sole representative of the Palestinians.[13] The letter went on to stress that there was no question of abandoning her total commitment to Israel's future.[14] On 3 April 1980, Thatcher used a letter to the *Finchley Times* to reassure her constituents that government policy towards the PLO had not changed following comments by Lord Carrington which had indicated a softening in its approach to the PLO.[15] All this was part of the clear strategy of Thatcher to illustrate that her strong commitment to Israel was still intact now that she was serving as Prime Minister. There was a feeling among many in the British Jewish community and in Israel that many leading British leaders had been seen as being very sympathetic towards Israel when out of office, but when in power their beliefs appeared to change.[16]

On a deeper level, Thatcher, while not hostile towards Israel, grew increasingly impatient with Israel's Likud-led governments and in private criticized President Reagan for not putting more American pressure on Israel to make concessions.[17] In respect to the Arab–Israeli conflict Thatcher was not really as out of tune with the Foreign Office as has been suggested. Indeed, had the PLO and Yasser Arafat got their act together sooner and accepted a two-state solution and renounced violence sooner than they did, they might have found Thatcher more receptive towards their demands for a state.[18] There were a number of events and issues that tested Thatcher's patience with Israel: the Lebanon War of 1982 and the events at Sabra and Shatilla refugee camps, the increasing Israeli settlement drive in the Occupied Territories which, she argued, diminished Israel's claim to be the only democracy in the region, and the related issue of the rights of the Palestinians.

Although Thatcher was always careful in public to dress up her criticism of Israel as that coming from a friend, the truth is that she felt that the Israel of the 1980s was becoming increasingly distant from the vision of the country that she remembered from the days when her daughter had spent a summer on a Kibbutz in the early 1970s and from her two visits she had made to country earlier in her career. It is therefore something of an irony that as she moved against the Foreign Office following the Falklands Islands War on the issue of the Arab–Israeli conflict, her vision of a comprehensive and just settlement of the dispute, the methodology used to get there and the importance of the role of European Community in achieving this were all remarkably similar to those of the Foreign Office. In other words, on this issue there was no clear blue water between Number 10 Downing Street and the Foreign Office, as many believed.

The Venice Declaration

The Venice Declaration of 13 June 1980 was the first time that the nine members of the Community agreed to talk of the right of the Palestinians to self-determination.[19] On top of this the nine considered that only the renunciation of force or the threatened use of force by all parties could create a climate of confidence in the area.[20] It will come as little surprise that the Declaration did not go down well in Israel, whose settlements were described as constituting a serious threat to the peace process in the Middle East.[21] The Leader of the Opposition and former Prime Minister,

James Callaghan, was not so impressed by the notion of self-determination.[22] As he put it:

> Of course there are rights for the Palestinian people, but what has been happening, and what has Europe fallen for? Europe's motives are suspect as long as it is so concerned about oil. Both protagonists are always trying to line up allies. The PLO has won a propaganda victory by lining up the Europeans to give it a boost the week after it said that it was going to destroy Israel. That cannot contribute to peace in the Middle East.[23]

Given what had gone before during Callaghan's time as Foreign Secretary and Prime Minister, his comments on self-determination appear much more pro-Israeli in nature than any policy that originated out of his time in office. Perhaps there was something to be said about Yediot Aharonot's comments about leaders being more pro-Israel when not in office.

For the Foreign Office the Venice Declaration represented something of a triumph. It effectively ended the threat of the fears expressed by Willie Morris in Cairo in 1976 that Britain would be signalled out at the head of the queue for Arab retaliation over the Arab–Israel conflict.[24] The Declaration was also very much in line with the Foreign Office internal reports on the subject which were produced in 1976 and called for Britain to fall into line with the policy of the other members of the European Community and also for a stronger lien of the questions of Palestinian rights.[25]

The signing of the Camp David Accords between Israel and Egypt in 1978 and the full peace treaty in 1979 changed much of the dynamics of the Arab–Israeli conflict, but the question of Palestine, which was supposed to be linked to the implementation of the peace agreement, was still up in the air.[26] The Foreign Office viewed the Venice Declaration and the resulting diplomatic process as complementing the American-led Camp David process. This was to be the cornerstone of EC action in the region for the coming years. The fact that it was far from successful said much about the success of Israeli attempts to downgrade European influence in the diplomatic process.

During a visit to the United States the following year to meet with the new American President Ronald Reagan, Thatcher was forced to defend the European initiative set out in the Venice Declaration to an American press which appeared to view it as appeasement of the PLO.[27] Later the same year, on 12 June 1981, Thatcher was put on the defensive in an interview with the *Jewish Chronicle* over the terms of the declarations that related to Palestinian self-determination.[28] The paper asked her if she had handed over the conduct of British Middle Eastern polices to Lord Carrington and the old Arabists in the Foreign Office, and that with her policy of delegation she didn't interfere with how they carried it out.[29] Thatcher naturally denied the charge and did not accept that the Foreign office was Arabist, in the sense that it espoused one cause.[30] She then highlighted the part of the Declaration that was favourable to Israel, its right to live in peace behind secure borders.[31]

The fact that the major British Jewish newspaper appeared to be blaming the Foreign Office for the failings of the Venice Declaration from an Israeli perspective was very interesting. Thatcher's emotional commitment to Israel and praiseworthy statements made in its support appeared to have been successful in shielding her from much of the backlash from Britain's Jewish community. The Foreign Office, on the other hand, with the widely held perception of its Arabist traditions, took the brunt of the blame for the declaration that further shifted the scales of British and European policy towards the Arabs and away from the Israelis. The slide away from Israel that had started under Callaghan was continuing under the Thatcher Government.

As inter-European politics developed around the Venice Declaration, and this naturally meant Franco–British tensions. Thatcher was forced to deal with the question of the PLO once more, arguing that the aim of the Declaration was that Europe should not negotiate with the PLO, but that the PLO should be associated with the settlement.[32] This phrase, of course, fooled no one, not least the Israelis. The major failing of the Venice Declaration, and that at all subsequent European initiatives on the Middle East, was that it played second fiddle to the American diplomacy. Rightly or wrongly, the Israelis were deeply suspicious of the Venice Declaration, of European policy as a whole, and wished to minimize its role in the peace process. The timing of the Venice Declaration had been scheduled in order to fill the political vacuum caused by the 1980 American elections. The subsequent victory of Reagan set American foreign policy on a largely new course. With this change across the Atlantic the Venice Declaration was consigned to being a back-up process or playing understudy to American diplomatic efforts.

As regards the Foreign Office, the Venice Declaration, and the subsequent European diplomatic process, if not successful at least moved British policy in the direction that it had being advising since 1976. To a certain extent, this point was caused not by the brilliance of its thesis, but rather by the perceived continued inflexibility of consecutive Israeli governments towards the Occupied Territories and the related Palestinian issue. At this stage, some Israeli leaders still harboured the view that there was a military solution to the Palestinian problem, and one of them, Ariel Sharon, was about to put such plans to the test in Lebanon.[33]

British patience with Israel runs short

Even before Begin and Sharon gave the orders for the start of Operation Peace for Galilee (known internationally as the Lebanon War) to start on 6 June 1982, Anglo–Israeli relations had not been on an even keel for some time. On top of the already recorded British irritation with the perceived lack of progress in the peace process, two developments had added to the growing tensions: the Israeli bombing of the Iraqi nuclear reactor and the vote in the Knesset to annex the Golan Heights.[34] The critical response of the Foreign Office to both events was largely based on the potential of both incidents to lead to renewed fighting between the Israelis and the Arabs. Avoidance of conflict was still very much at the heart of Foreign Office thinking towards the region. In the eyes of the Foreign Office renewed fighting could have led to a threat to British oil supplies through Arab embargos and an equal threat to British trade links in the Arab world.

Thatcher was in full agreement with the Foreign Office's criticism of the Israeli bombing raid on Iraq.[35] She enquired of the *Jewish Chronicle* whether Israel, or any other country, was saying that because some other country happened to start up a nuclear plant, it warranted a bombing attack by another country. She went on to ask what sort of international law was that?[36] Regarding the Israeli decision to annex the Golan Heights, Thatcher commented in a speech to the British Board of Deputies of British Jews on 15 December 1981 that it was with great concern that she had learnt of the situation and that it was a harmful to the search for peace.[37] The speech was, in truth, vintage Thatcher with the criticism dressed up in long passages outlining her emotional and political connection to Israel.[38] Had the Foreign Secretary, Lord Carrington, delivered the same rebuke in a speech to a similar audience, the chances are that his reception would not have been as warm as the one afforded to Thatcher at the end of her speech by the British Board of Deputies.[39]

It was the Lebanon War, however, that finally broke Thatcher's patience with the Likud-led Government in Israel.[40] In this respect her views were very much in line with the Foreign Office whose wings she tried to clip following the Falklands War. The Foreign Office saw the war as 'Begin's blunder'.[41] The British Ambassador in Damascus argued that President Asad of Syria had played his hand well in minimizing any Israeli military and political gains in Lebanon.[42] Thatcher wrote to President Reagan urging America to do more to deal with the Lebanon tragedy.[43] Thatcher also suggested that America and Britain should consult closely on the Lebanon situation and others in the Middle East, something that President Reagan was in full agreement about.[44] From this point on President Reagan and Thatcher were in regular correspondence about the situation in the Middle East, with the President welcoming the Prime Minister's input and her apparent good relations with King Hussein, whom President Reagan viewed as essential to his peace initiative.[45] On 28 March 1983, President Reagan received a letter from Thatcher urging him to 'weigh in the Arabs' to reinforce the message that America was fully committed to its peace initiative.[46]

Although it was by no means unique for two leaders to communicate directly with each other over a key issue, it nonetheless cut the Foreign Office and Diplomatic Service out of the loop to some degree. In truth, following her re-election in 1983 Thatcher took a very dominant role in the management of Britain's foreign affairs. Sir Geoffrey Howe had succeeded Lord Carrington as Foreign Secretary – something that Thatcher came to have regrets about.[47] She claimed that even then she had had her doubts about the suitability of Howe for the Foreign Office.[48] She argued in a very revealing passage in her memoirs about the Foreign Office that Howe fell under the spell of the Foreign Office.[49] Her view of the Foreign Office was that it was a place where compromise and negotiation were ends in themselves.[50] The Foreign Office, she went on, cultivated a reluctance to subordinate diplomatic tactics to the national interest and an insatiable appetite for nuances and conditions that could blur the clearest vision (but presumably not hers).[51]

It would be a gross over-simplification to suggest that because the Foreign Office felt marginalized from the American–British diplomatic process it concentrated solely on the European track, which had been defined by the Venice Declaration of 1980. In terms of scales of influence, however, the Foreign Office enjoyed a much greater input into the European process than the American–British process, which increasingly became dominated, rightly or wrongly, by Downing Street and the White House.[52] This did not mean that Thatcher and the President were in constant agreement over what to do about Israel and the Arab–Israeli conflict. Indeed, as we shall see, on many occasions they profoundly disagreed, with Thatcher calling for America to take a much tougher line with Israel, which she saw as one of the only ways to move the peace process forward.

Britain gets tough on Shamir and Israel

By early 1984, Anglo–Israeli relations were coming under renewed strains.[53] While the Foreign Office was becoming increasingly concerned about the lack of diplomatic progress, Thatcher let it be known that she had had enough of the policies of the Shamir-led Government towards the Occupied Territories.[54] In meeting with the US Secretary of Defence, Casper Weinberger, on 27 February 1984, Thatcher's remarks on Israel were noted down by Weinberger. He cited her comments as follows:[55]

> Mrs Thatcher asked about Israeli views and policies, noting that the Shamir Government appeared shaky. She wondered whether Israeli policies were acceptable to American Jewish opinion. She recalled that the Sabra and Shatilla massacres had caused Begin to establish a commission of enquiry. She remarked that wherever there was a problem it seemed that Israel annexed what it wanted. She urged that there should be a reappraisal of Israeli policy. She drew the Secretary's attention to Israel's economic problems.[56]

In a covering note Weinberger added that Thatcher had been quite frank and critical of Israeli policies, while at the same time encouraging strong American support for King Hussein.[57] In this respect, Thatcher's views were identical to those of the Foreign Office, who thought that King Hussein remained central to the process (the Americans, however, appeared less convinced about King Hussein).[58]

The 1984 Israeli elections were inconclusive, with a National Unity Government formed as a result of the protracted coalition bargaining process.[59] The key to the government, which contained an equal number of Labour Party and Likud ministers, lay in the rotation of the position of Prime Minister.[60] For the first two years Shimon Peres would serve as Prime Minister, with the Likud leader, Yitzhak Shamir, as the Minister of Foreign Affairs. After two years their respective positions would rotate, with Shamir becoming Prime Minister and Peres Minister for Foreign Affairs. Given the fact that the previous Likud-led Government had a miserable record – Israeli soldiers stuck in Lebanon, and in the economy hyper-inflation which put it on par with Argentina – it came as a surprise to many that the Labour Party was not able to secure a more decisive victory.[61]

Peres was clearly a man with whom Britain felt that it could do business.[62] At a Camp David Summit meeting with President Reagan on 22 December 1984, Thatcher told the Americans that she personally knew the Israeli Prime Minister and thought of him favourably.[63] She added that Peres wanted to be constructive and that if Britain and the United States wanted to get anywhere in the Middle East they should do it while Peres was Prime Minister.[64] Once again the Americans were not as sure about Peres as was Thatcher. Secretary of State George Shultz argued that Peres faced many problems and that he would have to address these first if he was to establish himself as a strong leader.[65] So Thatcher was slightly out of harmony with the Americans over the Middle East. The Foreign Office, however, concurred with her views on Peres over Shamir, having noted the transformation of Peres away from security hawk in the first Rabin Government to leading dove in the mid-1980s.[66] Another fillet for the Foreign Office was that Peres was generally perceived as favouring stronger ties with European diplomacy than any of his immediate predecessors. Peres was quite simply the toast of Downing Street and viewed by the Foreign Office as the best hope for a settlement.[67]

In retrospect, Schulz's analysis of Peres proved to be spot on as the Israeli Prime Minister dealt successfully with getting Israeli soldiers out of Lebanon except for a security zone in the south, and with American help curbed Israel's hyper-inflation.[68] In doing both he showed courage and clever political judgement but he handed over power to Shamir in 1986, keeping the rotation agreement. From this point onwards until the arrival of Rabin in power in 1992 Anglo–Israeli relations suffered a number of setbacks. At the centre of British policy remained the deep-rooted belief that the Americans needed to apply greater pressure on Israel to make political concessions.[69]

Thatcher visits Israel

As she got off the plane at Ben-Gurion Airport on 24 May 1986, Thatcher became the first British Prime Minister to pay an official visit to Israel.[70] She was welcomed by Peres, who talked of the strength of Anglo–Israeli relations, which, he claimed, had never been better.[71] While Peres's bold statement might well have been true at this point, relations, in truth, were much more fragile than the Israeli Prime Minister admitted.[72] Put succinctly, the British view, and especially that of the Foreign Office, was that while Peres was in power Anglo–Israeli relations were far friendlier than when a Likud Prime Minister was in power in Israel. The only trouble for the Foreign Office was that under the terms of the rotation agreement, Shamir was due to return to the Prime Minister's office soon after Thatcher's visit.[73]

During the course of Thatcher's visit, which was part of a wider Middle East tour, she concentrated in public on articulating her emotional commitment to Israel and her physical linkage; her constituency of Finchley was twinned with Ramat Gan near Tel Aviv.[74] Speaking at a dinner given in her honour in Jerusalem on 25 May 1986, she outlined the links between Britain and Israel and called for peace, with security for all countries in the region.[75] The Foreign Office was keen that the Prime Minister kept to political generalities in public comments during the visit, whose major purpose it viewed as helping to increase trade links. Thatcher, however, did go into detail, stating that many Israelis knew that the situation in the Occupied Territories could only be temporary and that steps should be taken in the Occupied Territories as a prelude to an eventual settlement.[76] Thatcher, was, however, a very clever political tactician (perhaps the best of her generation) so she followed the slap in the face for many Israelis with a glowing tribute to Golda Meir's leadership, a leadership that, as we have seen, was heavily criticized by the British for its failure to deal with the Occupied Territories and to recognize the rights of the Palestinians – an example of very clever politics indeed.[77]

The following day Thatcher attended a wreath-laying ceremony at Kibbutz Sde. Boker at the tomb of David Ben-Gurion. Here she alluded to Ben-Gurion's great leadership and compared him to Winston Churchill.[78] As she put it:

> He represented all that was best in leadership. He took the best standards for living, the best things in which he believed, the best traditions and the best heritage, and he brought them to life in the remarkable country of Israel . . . All great men see things that the rest of us do not quite see; indeed they are hidden from us. Winston Churchill, also a great admirer of Israel and Ben-Gurion, was also just such a person.[79]

Thatcher followed this tribute to Ben-Gurion with a similar tribute to the other colossus of the Labour Zionist movement, Chaim Weizmann, whom she described as having made a historic contribution to both Britain and Israel.[80] Later the same day, Thatcher addressed an audience at the King David Hotel. The hotel had been the scene of one of the deadliest attacks on the British during the twilight of the Mandate period.[81] During her speech, which was more ceremonial than political, she once again stressed her strong support of Israel.[82] She stressed:

> There are still problems to be solved, but when I look at the problems which have been solved, when I look at the miracles which have occurred, then I think we have every reason, on that basis, to believe that the problems before us are soluble on a basis of security, freedom and justice and on the basis of the extraordinary talent and ability of this great people, and I hope on your friendship with the United Kingdom, and friendship, of course, always with the United States, our great ally.[83]

At the press conference to mark the end of her trip to Israel on 27 May 1986, Thatcher once more outlined Britain's vision of the peace process.[84] At the centre of this was the fact that Palestinian self-determination should mean some kind of Jordanian–Palestinian federation.[85] There would be no role for the PLO until it accepted the UN Resolution, renounced violence and recognized Israel's right to exist.[86] As for Israel, it was not good for it to continue as an occupying power and it should come to the negotiating table with this fact in mind.[87] When questioned about Britain's continued arms sales to the Middle East, which once more had been causing the Israelis a great deal of concern, she strongly argued that there would be no change to the policy of Britain selling arms to countries in the Middle East.[88] Finally, the Prime Minister was forced to admit that new initiatives had come out of the trip but that, as she put it, this was to be expected.[89]

The Foreign Office and the British Embassy in Israel were relatively pleased with the outcome of Thatcher's visit: good for trade, public remarks of friendship, and some tough words in private for Israeli leaders about the Occupied Territories. In terms of Anglo–Israeli relations, another box had been ticked off towards normality: the first official visit of a serving British Prime Minister to Israel had passed off without huge controversy. This important point was down to both the diplomatic skill of Thatcher and the meticulous planning, negotiations and briefing that the Foreign Office and Number 10 undertook prior to the visit. If Thatcher had hoped that Peres might renege on the rotation agreement with Shamir and try to put together a narrow-based Labour-led coalition, she would have been disappointed.[90] On time, Peres handed over to Shamir, and, from British, European and American perspectives, this made progress in the peace process all the more complicated.

Political realities

In a mild rebuke to his closest ally, President Reagan wrote to Thatcher on 30 September 1987 to remind her that they must face certain realties in the Middle East.[91] Shamir, he argued, had a great deal of political power and this was particularly true on an issue that aroused such strong popular and political feeling as peace and the future of the Occupied Territories.[92] Recent experience, he concluded, had shown that Shamir could not be ignored.[93] The outbreak of the Palestinian Intifada just over a month later, the resulting shift to the right in Israeli public opinion and the eventual narrow but decisive victory of Likud in the 1988 Israeli elections confirmed President Reagan's belief that Shamir was here to stay.[94]

During this time much of the work of the Foreign Office was directed towards helping keep the moderate Arab states engaged in the diplomatic process. The withdrawal of King Hussein from the process following his decision to drop Jordanian claims on the West Bank was a move that made it all but impossible for Israel to deal with the Palestinian issue through negotiations with Jordan. The British still favoured an international peace conference that would lead to bi-lateral negotiations between Israel and King Hussein, together with a Palestinian delegation which rejected violence.[95] Thatcher was lobbying hard in Washington with President Reagan, who appeared much more reluctant to bring the parties together into such a make-or-break event.[96] President Reagan claimed not to be giving up on the idea but argued that they had to face the reality that there was little chance for progress.[97] The President, in short, appeared much more reluctant than the British to apply pressure on Israel.[98]

In reality, the Foreign Office saw pressure on the Israeli Government as the only way forward. It was acutely aware of the failings of the diplomatic process under Golda Meir from 1969 until the Yom Kippur War, and saw this scenario being repeated at the end of the 1980s. Shamir continued to enrage the British with his resolute rejection of any form of meaningful discussion of the West Bank and Gaza Strip.[99] Thatcher argued that time was running out for Israel and that this was the moment for its government to enter into negotiations.[100] One factor that gave the Foreign Office a more hostile approach to Israel was that, as its polices were closely tied with the European diplomatic process (which, as the Venice Declaration illustrated, was critical of elements of Israeli policy), it was often portrayed as calling for greater pressure on the Israeli Government, particularly after the outbreak of the Palestinian Intifada in December 1987.[101] Clearly, if British and European efforts were going to prove more fruitful from their perspective, the pressure that the Foreign Office and Thatcher were attempting to apply on Israel needed to be matched by a similar push from Washington. Two events were to lead to just such a situation arising.

One step forward, two steps back (again)

Thatcher cautiously welcomed the internal debate within the PLO and the eventual decision in 1988 to apparently accept a two-state solution to the Israeli–Palestinian issue and to formally renounce violence.[102] As ever, she was suspicious of the small print, arguing that violence hadn't been utterly renounced nor Israel's right to exist explicitly recognized, but nevertheless saw it as a step forward.[103] The Foreign Office saw it as vindication of the European policy of trying to develop moderate Arab opinion, a task that, it argued, was becoming ever more difficult as the result of the Israeli response to the Palestinian Intifada. On top of this, the Foreign Office was cautiously optimistic that the incoming administration of President Bush, which assumed power in January 1989, would adopt a more critical line towards Israel than had the Reagan administration. The Israelis certainly feared the worst from President Bush, whose record on the Middle East they had closely followed.[104]

It was, however, not until the collapse of the Soviet Union and the emergence of the loosely defined 'New World Order' of the post-Cold War era that the Americans were able to being the parties together for the Madrid Peace Conference of 1991 and the subsequent bi-lateral and multi-lateral negotiations in Washington that followed the conference. In the interim the Persian Gulf War had taken place, which led to profound short- and long-term changes in the region. None of these events and changes took place on Thatcher's watch. She had been forced from office at the end of 1990 and was replaced by the diplomatically inexperienced John Major as Prime Minister. She had, however, laid much of the groundwork with President Bush for what followed.

Thatcher's relations with Israel were full of paradoxes. Her increasingly strained relationship with the Foreign Office following the Falklands War of 1982 and her re-election in 1983 sometimes gave the impression of the notion of dual British policy towards Israel an the Arab–Israeli conflict. This was, however, not the case. The paradox was that while Thatcher disagreed with the methods the Foreign Office used, its style and its elitism, as well in other foreign policy areas, on the Arab–Israeli conflict she was very much on the same wavelength. Like the Foreign Office, her starting point was that pressure must be applied on the Israeli Government to make concessions using the 'land for peace' formula.[105] She viewed the occupation as having a corrosive impact on Israeli democratic values and institutions and, put simply, she felt that it was wrong. While the Foreign Office was still widely viewed to be staffed by Arabists (according to the *Jewish Chronicle* anyway) its influence in the peace process would always suffer from the history of this perception and its links to the European initiative. Thatcher, with a past history articulating her emotional and political commitment to Israel, was another case altogether. She cleverly used the very positive perception of her democratic values and her anti-terrorist rhetoric to put what was an essentially similar message to the Israelis and the Americans to that of the Foreign Office. One thing is clear: Thatcher's relationship was not as black and white as had been presumed up to now. With the release of new papers in future years we will be able to more fully access the extent to which she was willing to pressurize Israel, often via the Americans, to make concessions.

All aboard for the Oslo train

Post-Thatcher British foreign policy

The fall from power of Margaret Thatcher in November–December 1990 had a profound impact upon British foreign policy and the role of the Foreign Office in its formation and implementation. It would be a gross over-simplification to suggest that the arrival of the diplomatically inexperienced John Major in Number 10 led to a return of the glory days for the Foreign Office. Thatcher's departure (and with it all her anti-Foreign Office baggage) did, however, turn the clock back slightly in favour of giving the Foreign Office greater influence in the arena of British policy-making towards the Middle East. Major, as well as being diplomatically a blank canvas so to speak, was heavily reliant on his Foreign Secretary, Douglas Hurd, who was widely regarded both within Whitehall, and on the international stage as a safe pair of hands. As a result, many of the day-to-day policy decisions on the Arab–Israeli conflict were initially left to Hurd and the Foreign Office.

Hurd's own personal attitude to Israel and the Arab–Israeli conflict was based on the underlying philosophy that both sides had faults.[1] He claimed that he always felt uncomfortable visiting Jerusalem to talk to Israeli leaders and the West Bank to talk to Palestinian leaders.[2] In essence, Hurd regarded the strongly nationalist sentiments in the Middle East as an essentially corrupting influence on what he described as otherwise intelligent human beings.[3] For similar reasons, Hurd also had little time for President Asad of Syria, whose infamous long and selective versions of Middle Eastern history he was subjected to each time he visited Damascus.[4] The Foreign Secretary, who regarded himself as something of a gentleman in the old-fashioned sense of the word rather than the toff he was widely perceived to be, was naturally appreciative of King Hussein of Jordan.[5] Hurd was not a natural peacemaker in the Middle East, preferring instead quiet piece-by-piece diplomacy, much of which was aimed at attempting to manage the region's conflicts rather than trying to resolve them.

Part of Hurd's, and the Foreign Office's, attitude towards Israel at the time was based on his perception of the Shamir-led government in Israel constituted a major obstacle to peace in the region.[6] When the National Unity Government in Israel collapsed in 1990 over the future direction of Israeli policy towards and international peace conference and other issues, it looked at first as if the Western powers might get the Israeli government they preferred, a narrow-based Labour-led government under Shimon Peres.[7] This was before the ultra-orthodox parties and their spiritual guiders intervened to effectively block Peres's attempts. The result was a narrow-based Likud-led government under Shamir, which for the first time included the parties of Israel's far (sometimes termed radical) right.[8]

One of the major policies of his government was to create as many facts on the ground as possible in the Occupied Territories to make it impossible for any future Israeli Government to hand over control of these lands. In the West Bank this meant the adoption of the scatter approach to settlements. This plan called for lots of small new settlements situated across the West Bank, often in areas near Arab villages and towns. With each new settlement came an Israeli Army base to guard the settlers and eventual new infrastructure such as roads. In statistical terms, the 2010 Plan aimed at increasing the Jewish population in the Occupied Territories by 2.6 million, involving the construction of some 700,000 building units and 170 settlements at a cost of $140 to $195 billion (at 1992 rates).[9] If the plan had been fully implemented it would have altered the demographic balance in the territories so that the population of the West Bank would have been around 40 per cent Jewish, and Gaza 5 per cent Jewish.[10] As a result of this, the Foreign Office believed that time was running out to reach a settlement with the Palestinians, as did many officials in the US State Department.[11]

The one positive fact that the Foreign Office noted was that the coalition of Shamir started crumbling almost from day one, and that in the Labour Party sitting in the wings there was a viable alternative Israeli Government. Although the British largely did not try to intervene in Israeli politics, the Americans could not resist the temptation and as a result the 1992 Israeli elections featured almost unprecedented levels of American interference.[12]

The politics of decline in Britain

The Shamir-led Government was not the only administration that was crumbling. During the 1990s Europe was the dominant political issue of the day. It was an issue that threatened to destroy the Conservative Party, which, after securing a seemingly improbable election victory in 1992, started to self-combust as new words such as 'Maastricht' and 'convergence' entered the political agenda.[13] Much of Major's time and effort was spent on trying to keep a crumbling party and parliamentary party intact.[14] As a result, the Foreign Office was to some extent given greater freedom of action in the arena of British policy towards the Middle East peace process. In truth, as the decade progressed it became clear that a lot of the Foreign Office's input into the Middle East peace process was being both helped and hindered by the initiatives of the European Union. In terms of policy towards Israel there was basic convergence in the opinions and strategies of the bureaucrats in Whitehall and those in Brussels. As the European Union attempted later in the decade to translate its economic aid to the area (and specially the Palestinians) into a seat at the high table of political influence, so the direct role of the Foreign Office was, at times, somewhat diminished.

A man with whom to do business

Douglas Hurd compared the signing of the Declaration of Principles by Israel and the PLO on the White House Lawn on 13 September 1993 to the falling of the Berlin Wall in Europe some three years earlier.[15] In other words, nothing would ever quite be the same again in the Middle East.[16] For the Foreign Office the signing of the first of the agreements between Israel and the PLO that came to collectively be known as the Oslo Accords led a short-term public readjustment in its policy towards Israel. This shift had started to take place when Yitzhak Rabin became Prime Minister in the summer of the previous year, following the victory of the Israeli Labour Party over Likud in the Israeli general election held on 23 June 1992.[17] This was the first time that the Israeli Labour Party had been able to win an election and put a narrow left-of-centre based coalition together since 1973, and consequently Likud found itself out of office for the first time since 1977.

The Foreign Office made little effort to cover the fact that it was relieved to see the back of Yitzhak Shamir and Likud, which they believed to be one of the biggest obstacles to Middle East peace. The relief at Rabin's victory was all the more acute for the Foreign Office when it became clear that Shamir had intended to use the peace process as a means of buying time in order to allow Israel to build more settlements in the Occupied Territories.[18] Though Shamir denied that he had actually meant this, in the newspaper interview he gave his comments seem to confirm what the Foreign Office had long thought about Shamir's strategy towards the peace process.[19] On a deeper level there was also a sense that the old terrorist had been ousted from power and his hard-line polices towards the Occupied Territories had departed alongside him.

Rabin, on the other hand, was viewed in a much more favourable light by the Foreign Office, who saw him as more likely to be willing to make territorial compromises than his predecessor. Speaking in the House of Commons, Douglas Hogg (then Foreign Office Minister with responsibility for the Middle East) summarized this position by stating that he certainly agreed that there was a greatly improved chance of negotiating a settlement under Rabin 's Government.[20] He also went on to argue that the changed policy on Israeli settlements in the Occupied Territories was extremely welcome.[21] Much of the goodwill that was directed towards Rabin resulted from the perception that Rabin had frozen Israeli settlement activity in the Occupied Territories.[22] The major concern that the Foreign Office initially had about the Rabin Government was the seeming preference it had for reaching an agreement with Syria first rather than with the Palestinians.[23] Douglas Hogg outlined the policy of the Foreign Office towards the Middle East peace process in the House of Commons. As the Minister put it:

> First, talks must proceed on the basis of Security Council resolutions 242 and 338 – the concept of land for peace. Secondly, the security of the state of Israel must be ensured. Thirdly, everybody must recognize that the Palestinians have a right to determine their own political future and have a right to land to make a reality of that self-determination. I believe that an agreement between the Israelis and the Palestinians is a condition precedent to any development between Israel and the Arab states. I do not believe that Israel can secure separate, free-standing agreements with the Arab states unless there is satisfaction about the Palestinians. The Israelis will have to make substantial concessions and it will not be easy for them.[24]

Hogg's comments reflected, in truth, the fear within the Foreign Office that the Rabin Government appeared to prefer leaving the Palestinian track of the peace process until after an agreement had been signed and implemented with President Assad in Damascus. Foreign Office mandarins were acutely aware of the fact that Israeli prime ministers remained extremely reluctant to make concessions on more than one track of the peace process at a time.[25] Clearly any deal between Israel and

Syria at the time would have meant an Israeli withdrawal from the strategically important Golan Heights, which overlooks much of Northern Israel. Such a move would have proved a hard sell to the Israeli public, especially given that during his successful election campaign in 1992 Rabin had stood on the Golan Heights and declared that Israel would never come down from them.[26]

As well as serving as Prime Minister, Yitzhak Rabin had kept the Defence portfolio for himself. This was not without precedent in Israeli politics. Israel's first Prime Minister and founding father, David Ben-Gurion, had also held both portfolios at the same time. Likewise, and more controversially, given his lack of military experience, Levi Eshkol held both portfolios before eventually agreeing to appoint Moshe Dayan as Minister of Defence on the eve of the Six Day War. Much later, Menachem Begin held both portfolios for a time following the resignation of Ezer Weizmann. Rabin, in holding both portfolios, aimed to control as many of the closely related elements of peace and security as possible. In practical terms, Rabin, who spent much of his time in the Prime Minister's office in Jerusalem, was heavily reliant on the Chief of Staff of the IDF, Ehud Barak. Barak, one of Israel's most decorated soldiers having served as head of Israel's special forces, was also a close political confidante of the Prime Minister. Some four years after Rabin's assassination, Barak would become Prime Minister.

The fears of the Foreign Office about a Syria first deal proved to be well founded. General Barak clearly favoured a deal with Syria, which he saw as being less complicated than any deal with the Palestinians. In retrospect, General Barak presumed that a deal with Syria would open up the Arab world to Israel, with several other Arab countries following Syria's lead and reaching an agreement with Israel. From an Israeli perspective Barak correctly presumed that such a scenario would strengthen Israel's position *vis-à-vis* the Palestinians and erode the Palestinian position. As a result, Rabin during the initial phase of his government devoted much effort to downplaying expectations about a potential breakthrough in the Israeli–Palestinian track of the peace process. This strategy caused much growing concern within the Foreign Office along with the emerging picture of continued Israeli settlement activities in the Occupied Territories.

For those who bothered to look at Rabin's pronouncements on Israeli settlements during the 1992 election campaign and in the first year of his administration it was clear that he had not actually put a stop to settlement activity. Most election campaign and outcomes are much more complex than first meets the eye, and the 1992 Israeli election was in this respect no different from other elections. Rabin made a distinction between what he termed 'political settlements' and 'security settlements'.[27] He talked of putting a stop to what he termed 'political settlements'. Rabin, however, deliberately never defined the terms of each definition. He did talk of strengthening the major Israeli settlements blocks, which he presumed would remain a part of Israel following any potential deal with the Palestinians. In effect, Rabin the candidate and Rabin the Prime Minister never really promised a freeze on all Israeli settlements activities. He merely stated that he could not start building any new outlying ones which could not be considered to be part of a natural expansion of existing settlement blocks.

The Foreign Office, and to some extent the US State Department as well, were duped by Rabin. To a large extent, they wanted to be seduced by him and his vision of peace. In other words, the bar was set at a much lower level for Rabin than it had been for Shamir on the question of settlements. In retrospect, the evidence is quite clear: there was a significant increase in the number of Israeli settlers in the West Bank under Rabin. In America, President Bush concluded that Rabin had passed the settlement test and agreed to provide Israel with the $10 billion of loan guarantees that his administration had refused to give to the Shamir Government. On a political level, Bush's decision was important, as Israel badly needed the loans to help finance the absorption of the thousands of Jewish immigrants arriving at Ben-Gurion airport from the former Soviet Union. On a deeper level it sent a signal to the world, and one that the Foreign Office in London was quick to pick up, that Rabin was, in effect, kosher and should be given enough space and time to move on the Palestinian track.

Rabin undertook a series of overseas trips during the autumn of 1992 to help reinforce the view that here was a man who was different from his predecessors, and who was willing to make major concessions in order to reach an agreement with the Syrians and after that with the Palestinians. For once, the Foreign Office did not dread the visit of an Israeli Prime Minister to London. Indeed, Rabin's visit was considered a success by the Foreign Office officials, who found him to have what almost all other Israeli leaders appear to have lacked, namely a world view. Rabin, on the other hand, was slightly troubled by the visit, revealing as it did John Major's lack of a world vision and especially his lack of understanding of the issues that drove the Middle East.

The winter of discontent

As is usual in the Middle East just as the diplomatic process appeared to be inching forward something happened to derail any real or potential progress. On 16 December 1992, following attacks by militants from Hamas in Israel, Rabin, backed by his Chief of Staff and Cabinet, decided to move against individuals they accused of being leading members of Hamas, living in the Occupied Territories. In order to remind Israelis of the reasons why he was affectionately referred to as 'Mr Security' in Israel, Rabin instigated the new and highly controversial punishment of expulsion. The original plan called for some 415 suspected members of Hamas to be ferried out of Israel in a fleet of buses and sent over the border into Lebanon.[28] Barak argued that if they did this quickly and at night it would be completed before Israel's judiciary could challenge the deportation orders or the international community could apply pressure on the Rabin Government to rescind the orders.

From the outset the operation all went wrong for Rabin. The buses didn't get the potential deportees over the border in time, Israeli human rights lawyers intervened and the Israeli courts froze the expulsion orders while they ruled on their legal validity. By this time the world's press were in attendance at the border and a big story became an international incident. The 415 alleged militants were eventually sent over the border into no-man's-land, but the Lebanese authorities refused to allow them to enter the country so they were left stranded between the two countries. It was, at the very least, a PR disaster for Rabin and caused much damage to his own standing outside of Israel. In the long term it was also a strategic mistake as many of the Hamas deportees came into contact with the Lebanese group Hezbollah for the first time and learned crucial lessons from them. Many Israelis criticized Rabin's tactics, but crucially understood his motives. In defending his action, Rabin stated that his policy was built on two pillars: the attainment of Israeli security and a willingness to make concessions in order to secure peace.[29] In retrospect, Rabin's actions deposited some stock at the security bank that would be much needed in 1993 when he had to explain to Israelis why he had authorized secret talks with the still demonized Yasser Arafat and the PLO.

The United Nations led the international condemnation of Rabin's actions, calling for the deportees to be allowed to return home.[30] For the Foreign Office the expulsion issue was a reminder of Rabin as the Israeli Minister of Defence who had ordered the harsh Israeli military response to the Palestinian Intifada. Here an interesting parallel remains with another reforming figure of the same era, Mikhail Gorbachev. Thatcher famously stated after her first meeting with him that he was someone with whom she could do business. As a result, Gorbachev was given a degree of slack to push through his reforms. Reformers (for this was what the Foreign Office considered Rabin to be, dragging a suspicious and reluctant country behind him) do not follow straight lines. Instead, most reformers adopt a zigzag strategy that often includes reminders of former hard-line policies. Hurd appeared to be willing to offer Rabin a similar degree of slack. Speaking in the House of Commons, Hurd was keen to re-emphasize that there had been a radical change in macro Israeli policy towards the peace process since Rabin assumed office.[31] He argued that while damaging to the negotiations with the Palestinians, it was a little local difficulty that could, he hoped, be overcome.[32] Nothing is ever easy to achieve in Israeli–Palestinian negotiations.

Rabin was not the only leader to come under severe domestic pressure and who resorted to some political bandstanding. From his office in Tunis, Yasser Arafat watched the developing events closely. The PLO was nearly bankrupt as a result of Arafat's support for Saddam Hussein during the Persian Gulf War and the resulting cut in funding from the Gulf States for the PLO in the aftermath of the Allied victory in Kuwait. Such was the extent of its financial problems that some of its diplomatic offices across the world were being closed down for failure to pay overdue rents on the premises. With the PLO purse strings being cut by angry Arab leaders and the political door at the White House not yet fully open, Arafat had never been more isolated.

In the Occupied Territories support for the PLO-led Intifada was dwindling. This was partly due to increasing war weariness among many Palestinians, a lack of funds to continue to organize and drive the uprising forward, and new strategies employed by the IDF which centred upon avoiding points of contact or friction between Israeli soldiers and Palestinian youths. The public relations value of the uprising, particularly in the United States, that had proved so important to the Palestinian cause, had all but ceased given the Palestinian support for Iraq in the war.

In the Foreign Office officials were becoming increasingly concerned about what a cornered Arafat would do next. Having renounced violence and accepted a two-state solution in 1988, officials wanted to offer Arafat something of a carrot to counter the stick being waved by the United States and influential parts of the Arab world. As a result, Foreign Office officials started to offer a safety net to Arafat. This took the form of high-lighting the Palestinian cause as well as the offer of some token aid. The Foreign Office feared two potential developments: the collapse of the PLO and its replacement by Hamas, or that Arafat with nothing to lose would return to some form of tactical or all-out armed struggle in order to win political concessions.

In private, Arafat was preparing for one last throw of the diplomatic dice with Israel. Form his Tunis office, Arafat had to first direct a response to the Catch-22 situation he and the PLO leadership found themselves in over the 415 Hamas deportees stuck in no-man's-land on the Israeli–Lebanese border. Arafat, in truth, couldn't have cared less about the fate of the deportees. Indeed, from an internal Palestinian perspective the PLO was none too displeased that some 415 members of its major rival organization found themselves sitting in tents far away from the Occupied Territories. There were two important reasons, however, why Arafat had to do something, or at least be seen to be proactive. The first was that Palestinians of many political persuasions living in the Occupied Territories were angry at Israel's actions and so Arafat needed to find a way to punish Israel for its actions. Never one to miss a trick on the international stage, Arafat quickly understood the public relations damage to Israel that the attempted deportations were causing. In order to deal with all the above factors, Arafat announced that the Palestinian negotiators would not return to the peace talks in Washington following the festive break in December. Arafat, in short, wanted to international-ize the crisis and draw the United States into it as sponsor and host of the peace talks in order to pressurize the Rabin Government into making concessions; in other words, finding a formula for winning the return of the deportees that could be perceived as a political victory for the PLO.

With the official talks between the Israeli and joint Jordanian delegation in Washington suspended, the Foreign Office grew increasingly concerned about a possible deterioration in conditions in the Occupied Territories and the potential for a renewed escalation in the violence. By withdrawing the Palestinian negotiators from Washington, Arafat had sent a clear signal that he was very much in charge of the Palestinian delegation and that little or no progress would be possible without him. This message was not lost on the Foreign Office, which was increasingly trying to help find a formula that would allow Rabin to back down and save face in Israel. To say that the shadow of Hamas loomed over the whole decision-making process at the time would be an over-simplification, but the rise of the organization did focus minds in the Foreign Office on the fact that at some point Israel would have to make a choice between talking to Arafat or to Hamas. Arafat had shown that the Israeli policy of attempting to talk with the local Palestinian leadership in the Occupied Territories had failed.

The secret channel

Unbeknown to the Foreign Office (or anybody else outside a tight group of Israeli and Palestinian leaders and officials) secret talks had started between, at first, Israeli academics and PLO officials in the Norwegian capital, Oslo, in late 1992 and early 1993.[33] The operational story of the secret channel has been recounted many times in the seemingly endless series of memoirs and recollections published by the participants in the channel.[34] As a result, much of the diplomatic activity during the spring and summer of 1993 was based on the false belief that there were no real ongoing negotiations between Israel and the Palestinians. True, a few eyebrows were raised (not least among the Palestinian delegation to the official talks in Washington) when Arafat ordered the delegation to return to Washington without giving a full explanation for his about-turn. There was a palpable sense of relief in the Foreign Office that the deportation issue had been laid to rest and a formula found to return the Hamas members. The Washington talks restarted, not because of any deal on the deportations, but rather because Rabin set this as a condition to Arafat to see if the Palestinian leader was serious about using the Oslo channel. Rabin was, in effect, testing the water with the Oslo channel to see if Arafat was at the other end of it. By sending the Washington delegation back to the talks, Arafat was confirming that he *was* at the other end and that this was his favoured channel.

In retrospect, the secrecy of the Oslo talks was largely maintained not by clever disinformation but by the belief that there was little prospect for direct talks between the Israeli Government and the PLO in the foreseeable future. The Foreign Office, along with the State Department and European governments, welcomed the rescinding of the law in Israel that made contacts between Israelis and PLO officials illegal. The passing of this law in the Israeli Knesset, however, was not expected to lead to direct talks between Rabin and the PLO. Right up until the deal was signed, Rabin poured scorn on any press enquiry about talks with the PLO, preferring to steer people's attention towards Syria and the official Middle East talks in Washington, which were now, unbeknown to the participants, acting as a safety net for the Oslo channel.

When the announcement of the agreement which Israel and the PLO reached in Oslo (and later in Paris) became public there was widespread amazement and a genuine sense of confusion over how the deal had been done, what it involved for each side and, crucially, how it impacted upon the various national interests of the external powers in the Middle East. In London, the Foreign Office saw the deal as a vindication of its policy of pressurizing the Rabin Government into making concessions, and at the same time trying to build up what it termed as the moderate Palestinian leadership. It was clearly a sign of the changing times that the Foreign Office considered Arafat to be a moderate. In truth, the rise of Hamas had changed the dynamics, and Arafat, who only 18 months previously had seemed finished politically, was once more an important player.

Managing the peace in the Middle East

When Douglas Hurd referred to the signing of the Declaration of Principles between the Israeli Government and the PLO as the Middle Eastern equivalent of the fall of the Berlin Wall, he didn't mean that everything would be rosy in the Middle East from this point onwards. On the contrary, Hurd was perfectly aware that the Arab–Israeli conflict was entering uncharted waters, and that the Foreign Office would have to work hard to defend and develop British interests in the region. To be sure, the Foreign Office was publicly extremely supportive of the agreement that was signed with much American pomp and ceremony on the White House lawn in September 1993. In private, some officials raised fears over the terms of the agreement that left the core issues of the Palestinian–Israeli conflict unaddressed and unresolved. The phrase 'historic breakthrough' is often overused, but within the context of the Arab–Israeli conflict the Foreign Office was keen to talk up the breakthrough and the fact that both parties had felt able and compelled to negotiate directly with each other rather than use mediators. Foreign Office Officials understood that the implementation of the interim agreement would be extremely difficult for both sides and that gaining the scheduled future agreements would prove just as difficult as, if not harder than, securing the original breakthrough.

As well as continued concern over the future direction of the Israeli–Palestinian track of the peace process, the Foreign Office understood that there was still a long way to go before the Arab–Israeli conflict could be considered to be resolved. As Douglas Hurd put it in the House of Commons:

The Israel–PLO accord is a dramatic breakthrough, which the House has welcomed, and Israel and the PLO are trying to put it into practice. There will not be comprehensive peace until there are agreements between Israel and Jordan, Israel and Syria, and Israel and Lebanon. While it is right that the sensitivities of Israeli democracy should be understood and respected – we always try to do that – equally, it is important that none of the three other tracks, with Jordan, with Syria and with the Lebanon, should be long neglected.[35]

Hurd's comments, to some extent, reflected a deeper concern held by many in the Foreign Office that Israel would need time to digest the Oslo Accords and would be reluctant to make concessions on other tracks of the peace process, particularly on the issue of the Golan Heights with Syria.[36] There was a sense that the Syrian position was moving in the right direction, with its Foreign Minister, Faraq Al-Shara, calling for total Israeli withdrawal from the Golan Heights for total peace. This was reflected in Washington, where the Clinton administration made it clear that following the signing of the Israeli–Palestinian agreement its priority was to secure an agreement between Rabin and President Assad of Syria.

When the music stopped

It soon became clear in the Foreign Office that the agreement between Rabin's Government and the PLO was extremely fragile and that the agreement would need careful nurturing from the external powers in the Middle East. The certain sense of private glee that the Americans had been effectively bypassed in the negotiations was soon replaced by a sense of how to develop the shape the British and European response to the agreement. This required quick action and rapid political about-turns. Arafat, who had been publicly shunned by the Foreign Office, was moved centre stage. As one official stated in private, it was as if the Persian Gulf War hadn't happened and all that had gone before was removed. In private, as we have discovered, the Foreign Office had contributed to Arafat's political survival in the hope that he would be a better alternative than Hamas.

In Israel, Rabin was struggling to get the agreement with the PLO ratified. Speaking in the Knesset, he was on the defensive. There was one phrase in his speech that everyone noted, including the Foreign Office, which appeared to offer hope for finding a realistic way of implementing the accords:

We cannot choose our neighbors, or our enemies, not even the cruelest among them. We only have what there is. The PLO fought against us, and we fought against them. With them we are searching a path to peace.[37]

The implementation of the Oslo Accords was never going to be easy, but the Foreign Office saw its role as helping to develop the intuitions of the Palestinian Authority into a potentially viable state. On top of this there was a need to donate funds in order to help the wider Palestinian public.

In reality, the Clinton administration became the central focus of the diplomatic process, with Britain and Europe pushed very much into the background. The assassination of Rabin on 4 November 1995 and the succession of Peres to power led, in the short term, to a slight increase in European influence (Peres was keener on European input than Rabin, who favoured the Americans). As Peres's internal troubles grew with the suicide bomb attacks in February and March 1996 by Hamas and Islamic Jihad, the Europeans tried to contribute more, attending a hastily arranged anti-terrorism summit.

The election victory of Benjamin Netanyahu over Shimon Peres in May 1996 was viewed as a step backwards by the Foreign Office. While officials did not believe that Netanyahu would be as inflexible as his predecessor Likud leader, Yitzhak Shamir, there was a realization that Netanyahu's terms for a Middle East settlement would be largely unacceptable to the Arabs. As the Conservatives lost power in the May 1997 elections, Netanyahu had already signed the Hebron Agreement with the Palestinians, but had also announced the start of the construction of a new Jewish settlement in Arab East Jerusalem called Har Homa. The result was that as Major left office the peace process had ground to a standstill and the prospects of a peaceful solution to the Israeli–Palestinian issue appeared to have receded. There was, in reality, little he, or the Foreign Office, could have done to alter this fact.

Part 5

New Labour Era:
May 1997 to May 2007

11

Blair, the FCO and Israel

On the surface, the ten years of the Blair era would appear to have been characterized as a time of generally positive developments in Anglo–Israeli relations. There remain certain parallels between the premierships of Blair and the second brief period in office of Harold Wilson (1974–76). While both Blair and Wilson can be regarded as two of the most pro-Israeli Prime Ministers, the Foreign Office during both periods was not as keen to shift the balance of British Middle East policy towards Israel. The Craigium Dictum of the early 1970s clearly remained an important factor, particularly as the Oslo peace process collapsed and the threat of major new hostilities in the region increased from 2000 onwards. The Craigium Dictum argued, in essence, that Israel's survival and independence could not be compromised, but that because of Britain's interests in the Arab world it had to be more sensitive to Arab attitudes than to Israeli ones.[1] With Blair's decision, along with the United States, to invade a sovereign Arab country in 2003 the need to be even more sensitive to Arab attitudes increased, particularly on the question of Palestine. This need was reflected, at various times, in both the Foreign Office's thinking and, to some extent, 10 Downing Street's.

It is worth recalling that the second Wilson Government had inherited a situation in which the Israeli inflexibility in the negotiations with the Arabs was widely perceived by the Foreign Office as having led to the Yom Kippur War in 1973. Israel's diplomatic isolation, with the exception of the United States, both during the war and its immediate aftermath, appeared to confirm that the Foreign Office was not alone in its analysis. The Wilson Government did not, however, have to deal with the architects of the Israeli policies from 1967 to early 1974 as Golda Meir and Moshe Dayan soon resigned. As we saw previously, the new Prime Minister, Yitzhak Rabin, and Minister of Foreign Affairs, Yigal Allon, were deemed to be more flexible in their approaches to negotiations with the Arabs, the agreement on a partial Israeli withdrawal from the Sinai being the main result. In other words, to some degree both Wilson and Blair were lucky in that their counterparts in Israel concluded with a belief in the need for Israel to offer political concessions in order to advance negotiations.

When Blair came to power in May 1997, most of the world, including the Foreign Office, appeared to largely blame, rightly or wrongly, Israeli inflexibility once more for, on this occasion, the near collapse of the Oslo peace process.[2] This time the guilty culprit in the eyes of the world was the government of Benjamin Netanyahu.[3] Within two years, however the Netanyahu Government was out of power and Ehud Barak installed as Prime Minister. Just as Wilson found common ground with Rabin, so Blair did so with Barak and his apparent willingness to offer major concessions to the Arabs in exchange for peace. Blair got lucky again when Barak's successor, Ariel Sharon, shed his hawkish clothing to also offer, and make, major concessions to the Palestinians.

On a deeper level, during the Blair era there were a number of problems and issues that the Foreign Office had to continue to deal with regarding Anglo–Israeli relations. These problems centred upon the continued construction of Israeli settlements in the Occupied Territories, in particular in the West Bank, the planning and construction of its security fence, and the Israeli shift towards a unilateral settlement through disengagement. All of these issues were extremely emotive in the Arab world, which increasingly viewed Britain under Blair as pro-Israeli and anti-Arab. Naturally the Foreign Office had to attempt to balance the scales in order to repair some of the damage that these polices had on British interests in the Arab world.

In terms of policy towards Israel, the Foreign Office remained consistent. Israeli settlements continued to be viewed as illegal under international law.[4] The Foreign Office called for a total freeze on all settlement activity.[5] In terms of the Israeli policy of disengagement, it argued that negotiations leading to a two-state solution remained the best chance of a settlement.[6] Regarding Israel's security fence, the Foreign Office accepted the right of Israel to construct such a barrier but argued that it must be done so along the green line that divides Israel from the West Bank.[7] The Foreign Office remained critical of the Israeli policy of closures in the Occupied Territories and of Israeli military gains in general in these areas.[8] Finally, it was extremely critical of Israel's policy of targeted killings and said that tool little effort was made to avoid civilian casualties.[9]

A dual British foreign policy towards the Middle East

It is an exaggeration to suggest that during the Blair era there were two quite distinct sets of British policies towards the Middle East, and specifically the Arab–Israeli conflict: one run out of Number 10 Downing

Street, and the other out of the Foreign Office. There were, however, differences and tensions between these two offices regarding British policy towards the Arab–Israeli conflict and more significantly the management of the war in Iraq. These tensions were publicly highlighted in 2004 when 52 leading ex-diplomats took an unprecedented step and published an open leader in which they were extremely critical of Blair's policies in Iraq, in the Israel–Palestine conflict and his relationship with President Bush and America.[10]

More recently, during the Lebanon War in the summer of 2006, while Blair (as the leader of the Israeli opposition, Benjamin Netanyahu, put it), was seen bravely doing the right thing for Israel and understanding the key issues of the conflict, the Foreign Office was adopting a much more sceptical approach towards Israel.[11] This scepticism was illustrated in attempts by the Foreign Office to adopt a more measured response and on the Palestinian track encouraging Israel to make political and economic concessions to the Palestinians.[12] The Foreign Office was concerned that Blair's apparent pro-Israel stance was damaging, or could damage, British interests in the Arab world. At a time of heightened emotiveness in the Arab world due to the war, the Foreign Office judged, correctly, that British interests in the Arab world were being placed at huge risk.[13]

British policy towards the Arab–Israeli conflict under Blair

Having established the Prime Minister's dominance in British Foreign policy-making, it is important to outline and analyse Blair's policies towards the Middle East. In terms of the Arab–Israeli conflict, and specifically the Israel–Palestine track, there are four distinct periods. The first ran from 1997 to 1999, which from a British perspective was defined as being hard on Netanyahu and showing strong opposition to the Israeli creation of facts on the ground – the major focus of diplomatic efforts being on attempts to prevent Har Homa from being built. The second period ran from 1999 to 2001, a period in which both Downing Street and the Foreign Office were generally supportive of Ehud Barak's efforts to secure peace, and post-Camp David and Taba (2000 and 2001) increasingly sceptical about Yasser Arafat and the PA's ability and motivation to end the conflict. The third period ran from 11 September 2001 to the outbreak of the Iraq War in which British policy became strongly linked to US efforts in the region. During this final period the American-termed War on Terror was at the forefront of policy. Downing Street was widely supportive of Bush's non-intervention approach in the Israel–Palestine conflict, while the Foreign Office grew increasingly concerned abut the lack of diplomatic progress of the Israeli–Palestinian front.

During the fourth phase, from the Iraq war onwards, Blair became more defensive and more willing to pressurize Israel into concessions in order to appease his own left-wing domestic support.[14] To put it simply, at times he appeared to address what many in his party saw as double standards regarding his policies on Iraq and Israel. During this period he made much noise about attempting to use his apparent close relationship with President Bush to push for new US-led initiatives on the Arab–Israeli conflict.

Robin Cook and the ethical foreign policy?

After assuming office, the largely inexperienced new Prime Minister attempted to devote the majority of his time to dealing with domestic issues.[15] With the Middle East peace process in increasing crisis, however, Blair was forced to become more involved than he would have liked to at this stage. Blair's involvement in the process could not be divorced from his administration's close relationship with the Clinton presidency. Blair did not carry the same emotional or political attachment to the Oslo Accords as the President, who clearly viewed the implication of the agreements as the legacy of his good friend, the assassinated Israeli Prime Minister, Yitzhak Rabin.[16] He did, however, agree with the Clinton administration's assessment that the Oslo process was the only game in town and that much work was required if the accords were to be successfully implemented.

During the first-term Blair administration, the Foreign Office was led by Robin Cook, who was not a close colleague of the Prime Minister but was extremely popular with the Labour Party faithful. Cook took a strong line with Israel, and blamed the Israeli Prime Minister of the day, Netanyahu, as being the major reason for the increasingly problematic implementation of the various parts of the Oslo Accords. Though Cook's assessment of Netanyahu and his government did not differ widely from his boss's view, he pursued a much more vigorous campaign to highlight what he saw as Israeli intransigence towards the Palestinian Authority. Much of the tension between Cook (the Foreign Office he led) and the Netanyahu administration came to a head with the decision of the Israeli Government to build a new Jewish housing project, Har Homa, in East Jerusalem in 1997.[17]

Cook's visit to Israel in March 1998 marked the low point in

British–Israeli relations. During the visit Cook toured the disputed area of Har Homa and initially wanted to be escorted there by officials from the PA. Despite the fact that a compromise solution was reached in which he visited Har Homa, but was escorted by Israeli officials, the visit marked one of the low points in the recent history of Anglo–Israeli relations. The sight of Cook at Har Homa surrounded by Israeli protestors (some of whom looked as though they were jostling him) and security officials sadly remains one of the definitive images of the first Blair Government's Middle Eastern policy. Later the same day Netanyahu refused to keep a dinner appointment with Cook at the King David Hotel – a deliberate snub to the Foreign Secretary and his *modus operandi*.

In reality, behind Cook's bluster was a real challenge to Israel, and an excellent illustration of the tensions between the Foreign Office and Israel at this time. Central to this was Cook's attempt to try to develop a wider role for the European Union in the peace process, which had been stalled since the decision of the Israeli Government to start building at Har Homa the previous year. On this note the criticism of Cook's visit did not only come from the Israeli Government. In an editorial of the visit *The Times* of London was extremely critical of Cook's visit, arguing that if the stated purpose of Cook's Middle East tour was the promotion of the European Union's role in the peace process, it was difficult to see how this could have been advanced by raising the profile of the most contentious and explosive issue in the region.[18]

Upon his return to the UK, Cook defended his actions in the House of Commons. As Cook put it:

> On my visit to Har Homa, I am absolutely clear that I was right to underline the long-standing opposition of Britain and Europe to the expansion of settlements on occupied territory. I fully agree with Lord Hurd, who said at the time that I was right to proceed with the visit because to abandon the visit would have been to show that I was abandoning the policy . . . My Hon. Friend is right to draw attention to the fact that my visit to the Middle East – and particularly to Har Homa – achieved the full support of my colleagues throughout the EU, and has had much support throughout Europe.[19]

Though Blair publicly offered his total support for Cook's visit to Har Homa, there was anger in Downing Street that his visit had made the Prime Minister's own visit a month later to the region (and particularly Israel) more difficult.[20] It came as little surprise, however, that when Blair was re-elected in 2001, he replaced Cook as Foreign Secretary with Jack Straw. As well as being a relatively close political ally of Blair (something that Cook certainly was not), Straw's style was much less dramatic, and his worldly view much more in line with the Prime Minister's.

The end of the deep freeze

Anglo–Israeli relations warmed considerably with the election of Ehud Barak in the 1999 Israeli elections. Within the Foreign Office there was a sense that Barak was the natural successor to Yitzhak Rabin and that he would reinvigorate the Oslo peace process with the Palestinians, although there was some initial disappointment in the Foreign Office that Barak was not immediately offering major concessions to the Palestinians. Indeed, Barak indicated that he was rather unconvinced about the prospects of implementing the interim stages of the accords. In truth, Barak let it be known that he favoured attempting to reach a deal with Syria first before moving on to deal with the Palestinian final status issues. This came as little surprise to the Foreign Office given the fact that while serving as Chief of Staff at the IDF he had advised Yitzhak Rabin to adopt the same order of priorities when he came to power in 1992. Downing Street in particular was to be seen to accept the widely acknowledged Israeli policy of only making concessions on one track of the peace process at a time. Better one than none, was the feeling within Downing Street.

In retrospect, the treatment and understanding of internal domestic restraints afforded Barak by both Downing Street and the Foreign Office was much friendlier than that dished out to Netanyahu. To some extent, this fitted very much with the then black-and-white vision of consecutive British governments towards Israeli politics and the peace process. To put it succinctly, the Israeli Labour Party was good for peace (willing to make concessions); Likud was bad for peace (much more reluctant to make concessions). The fact that it had been a Likud Prime Minister who authorized the Israeli withdrawal from Sinai as part of the Camp David Accords between Israeli and Egypt mattered little.

At a press conference following Barak's meeting with Blair on 20 July 1999, Blair could hardly contain his enthusiasm for Barak and his seeming willingness to follow the land-for-peace strategy of his Labour Party predecessors.[21] As Blair put it: 'I just wanted to put on record our admiration for what he [Barak] has achieved so far and my 101 per cent support for all that he is doing for Israel and the Middle East peace process.'[22]

Later the same year, in the shadow of potential Israeli–Syrian talks, the two met again in London. Once more, Blair voiced enthusiastic support for Barak, saying that Barak had raised a beacon of hope for people the world over facing conflicts. Blair explained further that it was a beacon of hope that these conflicts could be resolved if there were political leadership and the will to resolve them.[23]

Following the breakdown of the Camp David Summit between Israel and the Palestinian Authority, Blair led the European criticism of Arafat, arguing that the deal on the table at Camp David was the best deal he (Arafat) would ever get. There were also increasing doubts over whether Arafat would ever agree to a peace deal with Israel. As a result of this judgement, more attention was given to what became known as the post-Arafat period, which both Downing Street and the Foreign Office hoped would bring what they termed a more flexible Palestinian leader to power such as Abu Mazen or Abu Ala.

The start of the so-called Second Palestinian Intifada in late September 2000 complicated Anglo–Israeli relations. In some respects, there appeared to be a separation of the two issues of cause and effect. Many in the Foreign Office saw the major cause of the violence as the walk by Ariel Sharon to the Temple Mount. Initially there was little debate in the UK about the central orchestration of the violence and the fact that it appeared to suit the political survival needs of Yasser Arafat. As a result, initially, many key officials in the UK saw the second Intifada as simply a rerun of the first one.

Downing Street was more circumspect, continuing to support Barak, whose political position was weakening by the day, and blaming Arafat for the failure of negotiations. This policy was, however, heavily prefixed by the feeling that Sharon's walk was at best provocative and helped light the fuse for the resulting violence. In political terms, there was a sense within Downing Street that everything should be done to help Barak, but that he was, in reality, a lost cause and was likely to lose the election in Israel that he had been forced to bring forward to January 2001.

Sharon's landslide election victory over Barak in January 2001 was greeted with both a sense of resignation and concern by the Foreign Office and the Blair Government. Comparisons between Sharon and Winston Churchill, which were highlighted in some newspaper articles at the time, fell largely on deaf ears in the Foreign Office. The Lebanon War of 1982, and especially the massacres at the Sabra and Shatilla refugee camps in Beirut, continued to define Sharon's reputation in the Foreign Office.

Changed realities: from 9/11 to the Iraq War

The events of 9/11 led to profound changes in Britain's Middle Eastern policy. Perhaps the most significant development regarding the Arab–Israeli conflict was the real emergence of the debate in Britain as to whether Israel was the front line against global terror or was at the root cause of it.[24] To date, in the UK this debate and the issues that arise from it have dominated the philosophical thinking behind its policy towards Israel and the Middle Eastern region. In terms of the Israeli–Palestinian peace process, it initially appeared to be business as usual with another run-in between an Israeli Prime Minister and the British Foreign Secretary, Jack Straw. The controversy this time was over comments made by Straw in an Iranian newspaper prior to his tour of the region in which he appeared to attribute blame to Israel for the terrorist attacks on it and an understanding of the terrorist attacks against Israeli citizens.[25] Sharon cancelled a planned meeting with Straw and it was only after a personal phone call from Blair that the Israeli Prime Minister agreed to meet with the Foreign Secretary.[26]

Blair appeared to adopt the philosophical line that Israel, in alliance with moderate Arab states, was the best buffer to the rise of radical Islam in the region and beyond. He was strongly supportive of both American-led peace initiatives towards the peace process as well as to European – though these often ran parallel to the US ones. In other words, Blair's growing closeness with President Bush following the events of 9/11 translated into a near merging of British and American policy aims and objectives towards the Middle East in general, and specifically the Arab–Israeli conflict.

From Iraq to Lebanon

The Iraq War and the difficult state of affairs that emerged from it came at almost the same time as the Israeli Prime Minister appeared increasingly flexible in terms of making concessions on the Palestinian track of the peace process. Although there was nervousness about the unilateral nature of the Israeli disengagement plan, there was also a growing sense in the Foreign Office that Sharon was the man to reach an accord with the Palestinians. As Sharon's plans started to emerge in greater detail and his statements and actions confirmed that he was actively pursuing the path of disengagement, so British support for him personally grew, especially in Downing Street. Indeed, Sharon was a welcome guest at Number 10, with routine photo opportunities with Blair at the front door – something that Number 10 would have not granted the Israeli Prime Minister just a few years previously.

Since Ehud Olmert took over from Sharon, Blair had been keen to continue political business as usual, attempting to develop close ties with the Ehud Olmert-led Government (even at times when this made him rather unpopular within the UK). The problem for Blair was that his political strength was rapidly evaporating, partly through genuine unpopularity caused by the Iraq War, and partly because of his decision to announce that he would not see a fourth term in office. This made it all the more difficult to stand next to Israel – particularly at times such as during the Israel–Hezbollah War of 2006 – when Israel was extremely unpopular with the majority of the UK elite and the wider general public. For its part, the Foreign Office remained nervous at Blair's efforts to appear to be politically close to Israel.

It's all about trade

One aspect of Anglo–Israeli relations that flourished during the Blair era was the bi-lateral trade links between the UK and Israel. As a result, bi-lateral business relations between Israel and the UK are, in general, becoming much more important for the UK, and, as the British Embassy in Tel Aviv puts it: 'Trade relations between Israel and the UK continue to flourish. Britain has traditionally enjoyed good trading relations with Israel and is seen as a natural trading partner.'[27] In statistical terms, UK exports to Israel reached £1.35 billion in 2005.[28] Moreover, annual bi-lateral trade between Britain and Israel has exceeded £2 billion for the past five years and is forecast to reach £3 billion by 2010. In exact figures, in 2005 UK–Israeli trade was £2.38 billion – slightly up from 2004 when the total was £2.34 billion.[29] Currently, Israel is the UK's 23rd largest market worldwide, and significantly its largest individual export market and trading partner in the region.[30] This fact of course has political ramifications. Over the years, the Foreign Office has been keen to develop trade links with Israel, but has always remained wary about the impact of such trade on British economic interests in the Arab world.

A return to the Guildhall

On 13 November 2006, Tony Blair came the closest to articulating his vision of a British Middle Eastern policy.[31] This policy contained some very worrying news for the Israelis, who for years had viewed Blair as a strong supporter of Israel and defender of its interests and appeared to bring the Prime Minister's views very much more in line with the thinking of the Foreign Office.[32] The timing of Blair's speech was very interesting given the fact that he had already stated that he would leave office at some point in 2007.[33] In other words, the Prime Minister was clearly attempting to set out a long-term foreign policy framework that would influence the policies of his successor as leader of the Labour Party and Prime Minister. We shall return to this future post-Blair era in the final section of this book.

The wider theme of Blair's speech, at one of the biggest set-piece occasions in the British political calendar, was the importance of Britain's partnership with both America and Europe.[34] As we shall see, Blair's Middle Eastern policies can't be divorced from his perception of the two key relationships for the UK: namely the United States and Europe.[35] He told guests at the Lord Mayor's Banquet that it would be the surest route to the destruction of our true national interest for Britain to give up either relationship, both of which are precisely suited to us.[36]

The key part of the speech, however, focused on the Middle East. This was especially significant as the day before the speech Blair had given evidence via a video link to the James Baker's Iraq Group in the USA.[37] To quote from the text of the speech that covered the Middle East:

> . . . A major part of the answer to Iraq lies not in Iraq itself but outside it, in the whole of the region where the same forces are at work, where the roots of this global terrorism are to be found, where the extremism flourishes, with a propaganda that may be, indeed is, totally false; but is, nonetheless, attractive to much of the Arab street. That is what I call a 'whole Middle East' strategy.
>
> There is a fundamental misunderstanding that this is about changing policy on Syria and Iran. First, those two countries do not at all share identical interests. But in any event that is not where we start. On the contrary, we should start with Israel/Palestine. That is the core. We should then make progress on Lebanon. We should unite all moderate Arab and Muslim voices behind a push for peace in those countries but also in Iraq. We should be standing up for, empowering, respecting those with a moderate and modern view of the faith of Islam everywhere.[38]

In reality, Blair, in declaring Israel–Palestine as the core of the problem of the Middle East, appeared to be siding with elements of the British elite who view Israel and its relationship with the Palestinians as the root cause of the trouble of the Middle East.[39] This group, if one is honest, comprises most of Blair's Cabinet colleagues, the Labour Party he led, many ex-officials and diplomats at the Foreign Office, as well as the so-called intellectual and artistic elites in the UK.[40]

Blair's remarks were also political code for his belief in the creation of a viable Palestinian state, and as a result an Israeli withdrawal to approximately 1967 lines in the West Bank – something that many Foreign Office officials have argued since 1976.[41] From this speech we could also deduce the obvious: Iraq remained the British priority in the Middle Eastern region and everything else revolves around managing the violence at levels that would allow the British to withdraw from the southern parts of the country they currently patrol.[42] In other words, Blair appeared willing to pay for ending the war in Iraq with Israeli currency (political code for pressurizing Israel into making territorial concessions).[43] Again, this was something that, in truth, the Foreign Office would have little trouble with accepting.

In some regards, Blair's speech was similar to Anthony Eden's Guildhall speech in 1955 in which the then Prime Minister discussed Israeli territorial withdrawal from the 1949 Armistice lines as a means to securing peace with the Arabs and specifically President Abdul Gamal Nasser.[44] Moreover, though Blair wouldn't thank us for drawing any parallels with Eden, there are clear linkages of the Suez Crisis of 1956 (a mere year after Eden's Guildhall speech) to the Iraq War.[45] As an aside, it is worth remembering that Israeli reaction to Eden's Guildhall speech was made in public, was hostile and led to a poisoning of relations.[46] This was only put on hold when the two countries found common interest over Egypt that resulted in the Suez War and Crisis of 1956.[47] It also, along with other issues, helped poison Anglo–Israeli relations in late 1956 and early 1957. To date, there has not been a similar official Israeli reaction to Blair's remarks, made almost exactly 51 years later.[48]

In truth, Blair had come under strong pressure from the Foreign Office and his Cabinet colleagues to both change strategy on Iraq and do something about his seemingly pro-Israel policy, which had come under great criticism (particularly from within his own Cabinet) during Israel's war with Hezbollah in the summer of 2006.[49] We should remember that at the time of Israel's war with Hezbollah, Blair's own position and authority were under intense pressure. There were growing signs of an internal revolt within his own Cabinet and party, with calls for him to resign and hand over power to his Chancellor (Minister of Finance), Gordon Brown. Though Blair's apparent pro-Israel policies were not the reason for this rebellion they were highlighted as a prime example of just how much he was personally out of touch with his Cabinet and party.[50]

UK policy towards the Middle East in the post-Blair era

Until recently little was known about Brown's foreign policy leanings, with the exception that he was less keen than Blair on the Iraq War.[51] Though he never publicly criticized the waging or the management of the war, he rarely referred to it in his speeches and writings. Instead, much of Brown's efforts have been concentrated on trying to alleviate Third World debt.[52] At the Foreign Office there is a hope and expectation among some officials that Brown will be something of a blank canvas in terms of foreign affairs, much like John Major, and initially leave the majority of policy to it.

In terms of the Middle East it is fair to say that we can expect Brown to be pragmatic in terms of the Arab–Israeli conflict. In reality, given his love of economics he will devote some attention to finding ways to help the Palestinian economy.[53] He also strongly subscribes to the view that conflict management and resolution come out of economic improvement and will no doubt cite the Northern Irish model as evidence of this argument. There must be a question mark over just how aware he is of poverty levels in Israel, which for a Western-style democracy remain worryingly high.

All of this will naturally put Brown very much in touch with the thinking of the Foreign Office towards the conflict. As a result, there will likely be less tension between it and Downing Street over Middle East policy – particularly if Brown gives an early indication of an accelerated timetable to disengage Britain from Iraq. That said, it is worth remembering that Blair arrived in power with a similar domestic agenda and was soon drawn more and more into foreign affairs.

Opinion polls in Britain conducted in late 2006 and the first part of 2007 put the Labour Party trailing the Conservatives – though not by a margin that is insurmountable.[54] Labour's position in the polls could be attributed to the usual ruling party factors such as electoral fatigue of both Blair and the party, but most of all to the war in Iraq, which remains the single most damaging issue for the government. As previously discussed, much of Blair's Middle East policy was unpopular with key sectors of the Labour Party and its constituency – notably Blair's strong support for Israel. Brown might well be tempted to distance himself from this by taking a more critical approach to Israel. Such a policy would not prove unpopular with the Foreign Office.

Perhaps the key issue, however, is the growing strength (numerically and in terms of organization) of Muslims in the inner-city seats (most of which are traditional Labour strongholds). Though Labour's majorities in these seats are often very large there is evidence of an organized attempt by Muslim groups to target some of these seats: either by attempting to displace the sitting Labour MP or by encouraging Muslims to vote for other candidates at the election. The rise of the influence of Muslim groups both within the party and outside presents perhaps the biggest restraint to a future British Prime Minister developing stronger ties with Israel. In other words, all the indicators point to a period of reduced tension between Downing Street and the Foreign Office on British policy towards Israel, the Arab–Israeli conflict and the Middle East as a whole.

A Tory return to power

In the medium term there is a chance that the Conservative Party will return to power. The current two key figures in foreign policy-making in the Tory Party are the leader, David Cameron, and the Shadow Foreign Secretary, William Hague. In truth, the latter did not endear himself very much to the Israeli Government, or indeed to his own party leader, with his comments criticizing Israel's actions in the war with Hezbollah in the summer of 2006.[55]

In terms of the Middle East, it is possible to identify three groupings within the Conservative Party. I would caution against being too specific about membership of these groups. Also it is worth noting, as in the Labour Party, that just because an individual MP is sympathetic to Israel it does not mean that they will stand up in the House of Commons or even the House of Lords and speak in favour of it. Finally, it is worth pointing out that the centralization of candidate selection for key seats at the next election with the 'A-List' of some 100 centrally sponsored candidates has led to canvassing by both sides of the Arab–Israeli lobbying divide of these newly selected candidates.

- The Arabists – strong links to the old public school – similar to Foreign Office. Others simply view the Arab states as more important.
- The non-committed – people such as Douglas Hurd view the conflict as a dirty little civil war. Do not enjoy dealing with either side and rather wish that the conflict would go away.[56]
- Pro-Israel group – often with links to business. Many old grades of the party are Jewish, along with a significant number of donors to the party.

Even if the Tories do return to power it is difficult to foresee Cameron adopting a similar line towards Israel as Blair. Given this fact, there would in all likelihood not be any deep divisions between a Tory-led government and the Foreign Office over Israel. In other words, both Wilson and Blair were the exceptions to the rule in their strong support for Israel that led to tensions with the Foreign Office. We are unlikely, as a result, to see a repeat scenario for some years to come.

The judgement

In truth, it is too soon to judge how successful Blair's Middle Eastern policies have been. He has left Whitehall deeply divided over his Middle Eastern policy. Just as Thatcher viewed the Foreign Office as a bastion of complacency, Blair identified it with two dirty 'E' words in the New Labour vocabulary: 'empire and elitist'. For its part, the Foreign Office naturally tried to resist the shift away from it and towards Downing Street in terms of foreign policy-making. Relations between the two, as a result, were never great. The battleground between the Foreign Office and Downing Street just happened to be the Middle East, which as a region came to dominate the agenda during Blair's decade in power.

It is rather stating the obvious to suggest that in the short to medium term Iraq will dominate Blair's legacy. In historical terms, however, it is still early days for the rebuilding of Iraq. Despite the well-documented criticism of Blair, the former Prime Minister can point to some achievements in the region. In Israel, with Foreign Office help, Blair appears to have at last cast off the shadow of the British Mandate period that led to tensions in Anglo–Israeli relations. Blair and the Foreign Office can point to strong trade links between the two countries. On the Palestinian side, Blair, while not exactly flavour of the month, was at least respected as perhaps the major European statesman of the day. If truth were told, Blair could not have really done much more for Middle Eastern peace than he managed to do. The increasingly apparent failure of US policy in the region was not his fault – it is questionable just how much influence he had in the US. Finally, Blair's successor, Brown, and the Foreign Office face, in addition to the Arab–Israeli conflict, increasing challenges in Iraq and Iran as well as in the so-called war on terror. As a result, Israel and Middle Eastern-related issues will continue to take up much of the time and effort of the Foreign Office during the era of Brown.

Conclusions:
A long road to normalization

In the Introduction to this book I suggested five rather crude reasons why the Foreign Office has for nearly 60 years been perceived as having a difficult relationship with Israel. This book has attempted to get beneath these rather clichéd, almost schoolboyish ideas and look at the very complex set of events and issues that the Foreign Office had to deal with over the years with regard to Anglo–Israeli relations and the Arab–Israeli conflict. For those, however, who prefer simple 'Guilty' or 'Innocent' verdicts then this book must conclude that the Foreign Office is not guilty of being systematically anti-Israeli. It is equally clear that it is not institutionally pro-Arab either. The truth is that over the last 60 years, the Foreign Office has defended British interests in the Middle East region in the best way it has seen fit. To a large degree, this has meant identifying British interests primarily with the Arabs rather than with the Israelis. As one Foreign Office official noted in this book, it would have all been different if oil had been found in Israel.

Of course, in institutions such as the Foreign Office and the related Diplomatic Service there have been, and still are, individuals who are extremely sympathetic to the Arab cause, and in recent times to specifically that of the Palestinians. This has also been true about Foreign Secretaries and Prime Ministers of the day. What has remained constant, however, is an institutional set of values that has governed the Foreign Office's vision of just what could be termed in the 'British interest'.

When I started researching this book a colleague of mine suggested that I should investigate what key Foreign Office officials did after they left the Service. Look at the Arabist institutions they joined and the books they wrote, he argued. To me, this misses the point. Yes, of course, ex-officials over the years have joined Arab think-tanks and Arabist-dominated academic departments, and have even become full-time lobbyists for Arab causes. Although I haven't fully investigated this, it is highly unlikely that many ex-officials took on similar positions among the pro-Israel lobbies in Britain. Another colleague suggested that I should research the last retreat of the Foreign Office Arabists, the gentlemen's clubs of St James, where, sipping tea and reading the *Daily Telegraph*, they recount stories of the golden eras of Lawrence of Arabia, and, later, Glubb Pasha.

On a deeper level, it is clear that for much of the nearly 60 years of Israel's existence, the Foreign Office set of balancing scales has been tilted towards the Arabs. The identification of British interests laying with the Arab world, fears over oil supplies and Arab hostility to any sign or signal of deepening Anglo–Israeli ties saw to that. Israel has, as a result, come a pretty poor second when it came to efforts by the Foreign Office to win friends and influence people. The theme of Foreign Office paranoia over the Arab world and its subsequent appeasement of the Arabs at the expense of the Israelis has been a constant theme in this book. Arab ambassadors and statements were fond of reminding Foreign Office officials that the Arab world held Britain responsible for the creation of the Israeli problem, citing the Balfour Declaration and the British decision to hand over the Mandate to the United Nations in 1947 as the prime cause of the creation of the state of Israel. 'You caused it, you fix it' was their rather crude message to the British in the period up to the Six Day War in 1967. This fact quite naturally made the Foreign Office rather nervous and at times prone to over-compensation towards the Arab cause.

More often than not, the Foreign Office's prime reason for developing and maintaining ties in Israel was to attempt to gain influence to persuade the Israeli Government to adopt a moderate line on a key issue of the day. This strategy was occasionally successful, but as in the case of Golda Meir and others, it proved largely ineffective from a British perspective. Central to British interests in the region has been the avoidance of conflict (with the exception of the 1956 Suez Campaign) and talks with Israeli leaders have centred upon the avoidance of another round of Arab–Israeli fighting that would close the waterways and threaten the supply of oil to the Western powers.

Following the débâcle of the Suez operation in 1956, Britain largely withdrew from the Middle East, preferring to adopt a low-key approach to diplomacy. During this time, and with the notable exception of the thorny question of arms sales to Israel, Anglo–Israeli ties developed towards a degree of normalization hitherto unseen. It was only after the Six Day War in 1967 and the subsequent conquest of land by Israel during that war that relations started to become more complicated. Almost from day one of the post-war period, the Foreign Office believed that in order to secure peace, Israel would have to return all the lands it had conquered back to the Arabs. The Conservative Government led by Edward Heath and with Alec Douglas-Home as Foreign Secretary largely concurred with this viewpoint. The subsequent government led by

Harold Wilson, however, did not agree with this reading of UN Resolution 242, and for a time Anglo–Israeli relations were on a more even keel. Wilson's departure and the subsequent policy review conducted by the Foreign Office in 1976 led to a more critical approach towards Israel that has remained in place until the present day.

In its dealings with Israel, particularly up to 1974, the Foreign Office dealt with a highly impressive Israeli Ministry of Foreign Affairs. Given the difficult diplomatic hand that its officials had to play, the Ministry between 1948 and 1974 remained one of the most impressive in the world. Relations between the Foreign Office, both direct and via the British Embassy in Tel Aviv, with the officials of the Ministry were interesting. Over the years the Foreign Office has had its preferred list of Israeli officials and also those whom it regarded as being dogmatic. In terms of Israeli politicians it will come as little surprise that the Foreign Office, as we saw in Chapters 1 and 2, had a clear preference for Moshe Sharett over David Ben-Gurion. The Foreign Office saw Sharett as not having much of the baggage of Ben-Gurion, not only towards the Arabs, but also towards the Foreign Office. It came as some relief to the Foreign Office when the old departed the Israeli political scene for good. Likewise, Golda Meir gave the Foreign Office headaches, particularly during her time as Prime Minister.

Of all Israelis, it would be fair to say that Abba Eban was perhaps the only one that the Foreign Office liked dealing with: 'triple first from Cambridge and all that'. Eban's enjoyment of cricket also helped. Even here, however, the Foreign Office was acutely aware that while they almost regarded Eban as one of their own, in Israel he was seen for the same reasons as something of an outsider. Of the latter-day Israeli leaders, Rabin was admired and respected (even during his difficult first term in office between 1974 and 1977). Peres from the late 1970s onwards was viewed to use Thatcher's line, 'a man with whom to do business'.

The four Likud Prime Ministers to hold power (Begin, Shamir, Netanyahu and, pre-Kadima, Sharon) were all treated with great suspicion by the Foreign Office. Cries of 'Repel the viper from our bosom' rang out from the Foreign Office when Begin first tried to visit Britain. Even after he signed the peace agreements with Egypt, he was still treated with a degree of suspicion and at times contempt by the Foreign Office. Shamir was, in simple terms, seen as an unmovable roadblock to peace, while Netanyahu was seen as scheming and distrustful. Only Sharon, once he had committed Israel to disengagement and carried out the withdrawal from Gaza, was given plaudits by the Foreign Office. If there is a major criticism of the Foreign Office it would be in this area, still seeing Israeli politics black and white or in equally simple terms as divided into two camps: a peace camp and a nationalist camp.

The Foreign Office's relationship with Israel was naturally not a one-sided affair. For Israel, the major role that the Foreign Office has played in bi-lateral relations between Britain and Israel and in regional multi-lateral relations has been in sanctioning, or not, the sale of weapons. As we have seen, this issue was used by Ben-Gurion as the 'litmus test' of the state of Anglo–Israeli relations. During the early years of the state, Israel's need for weapons was at the very centre of the state's struggle for survival. Much of the tension that characterized the early years of Anglo–Israeli relations was caused by the refusal of the Foreign Office to sanction major arms sales to Israel (tanks and planes), while at the same time supplying many of the Arab states who were lined up against Israel with the same military equipment. The fact that Britain continued to supply Egypt with military after President Nasser had turned nasty towards Britain was seen as further proof in Israel of the Foreign Office bias against it.

Israeli diplomacy with the Foreign Office until the mid-1970s was to a large extent dominated by the issue of trying to persuade it to sell arms to Israel, and if this was not possible to at the very least convince the British to stop selling arms to the Arab states. At various times, Israeli diplomacy was successful in this respect, but in the vast majority of cases it failed. Today, as the critics of Israel beat their drums about continued arms sales to Israel, the reality is that these sales annual sales constitute only 0.1 per cent of Israel's total arms imports.[1] At times, the Foreign Office had to override the objections of other Whitehall departments who were keener to sell arms to Israel. Over the years it had several disagreements with the Ministry of Defence, where Israeli lobbying tactics had proved much more successful.

When major arms deals with Israel did take place, there was co-operation and agreement between the Foreign Office to keep the deals secret. No press conferences were held by the Israelis to announce the arrival of new equipment, and any intelligence reports claiming that a sale had taken place were denied. When this system broke down it became much harder for arms sales to go ahead. Even the sale of the mini-submarines, which this book has examined in detail, caused a storm in the Arab world, with official-led press campaigns denouncing Britain and threatening British interests in the Arab world. In retrospect, as a result, it is not difficult to see why the Foreign Office said no to arms sales to Israel more often than it said yes.

To those who see the relationship between the Foreign Office and Israel as being warm and cosy and who look for conspiracy theories, the revelations about the sale of heavy water to Israel in the 1960s added fuel to their fire. In reality, the cock-up theory appears the most likely explanation for such actions. Yes, the Foreign Office got it wrong, but more often than not it did its job, to protect British interests.

The history of the Arab–Israeli conflict has never moved forward in straight lines. In reality, it moves in zigzags, and this has also been true of Anglo–Israeli relations. For anyone not convinced by the development in Anglo–Israeli relations, look at the language used in the quotation at the top of Chapter 1 and compare it to the language that Jack Straw and lately Margaret Beckett routinely employed when holding talks with an Israeli leader. It would be wrong to exclude the Foreign Office from the reasons as to why Anglo–Israeli relations have reached the point of normalization after nearly 60 years of zigzagging. In other words, despite Israel suffering from a case of loaded dice against it in its relations with the Foreign Office, the relationship evolved beyond recognition from the era of Bevin to that of Beckett. Credit for this improvement needs to be given to both the Foreign Office and the Israeli Ministry of Foreign Affairs, as well as to their respective diplomatic services.

A note on sources

The vast majority of research for this book took place in the Public Records Office, now called the National Archives, in London during 2006 and early 2007. As the charge of being anti-Israeli had been laid at the door of the Foreign Office, the vast majority of files looked at were those that related to the Foreign Office's dealings with Israel and the Arab–Israeli conflict. These files produced many surprises and confirmed quite a few widely held beliefs. This book was not intended to be a definitive guide to Anglo–Israeli relations, which would require an even greater investigation and would be difficult to keep to a single volume.

For the more recent chapters on the Thatcher, Major and Blair Governments I have attempted to use primary source material wherever available. There have been a number of interesting document releases in America that cover the Reagan–Thatcher era and which provided a useful insight into Thatcher's views and policies on the Arab–Israeli conflict. A number of documents were also requested under the Freedom of Information Act relating to the period 1977 to 1997.

At the start of this project I decided that interviews with British and Israeli officials and diplomats would not form the major part of the research. A number of officials very kindly gave their time to talk about specific issues that arose from the documents. I remain extremely grateful to these officials, and their advice and direction proved to be very useful.

Finally, I started the book with a confession and have to end it with another one. Whatever the rights and wrongs of Foreign Office policies reviews, minutes of meetings, memorandums and correspondence, it was an absolute pleasure to read more often than not beautifully written prose. As a friend of mine told me, whatever you might think of the Foreign Office, its officials don't half write well. Amen to that.

Notes

Introduction

1 MTF/Mrs Thatcher interview with *Jewish Chronicle*, 12 June 1981.
2 See, for example, Hugo Young, *One of Us: A Biography of Margaret Thatcher*, Macmillan, London, 1991; John Campbell, *Margaret Thatcher: Volume One, The Grocer's Daughter*, Jonathan Cape, London, 2000.
3 Hugo Young, *One of Us*, p. 173.
4 Hugo Young, *One of Us*, p. 172.
5 Peter Hennessy, *The Prime Minister: The Office and Its Holders Since 1945*, pp. 413–4.
6 John Nott, *Here Today Gone Tomorrow: Recollections of an Errant Politician*, Politicos, London, 2002, pp. 254–5.

Chapter 1

1 Public Records Office (PRO)/FO/371/82506/Report on the State of Israel 1949, p. 1.
2 The report was prepared by Colin Crane, British Delegation in Tel Aviv.
3 PRO/FO/371/82506, p. 1.
4 PRO/FO/371/82506, p. 1.
5 PRO/FO/371/82506, p. 4.
6 PRO/FO/371/82506, p. 4.
7 PRO/FO/371/82526/British Labour Party's Delegation Visit to Israel.
8 PRO/FO/371/111065/Memorandum, Visit by Menachem Begin, Tripp, 21 October 1954.
9 PRO/FO/371/12366/Collected Files on Menachem Begin's Trip to the United States, 1948.
10 Ibid.
11 Ibid.
12 PRO/KV/2/2252/Conclusion in Memo on Menachem Begin, 17 April 1953.
13 PRP/KV/2/2252/Letter from George Rendel, British Embassy in Brussels to Bernard Burrows, Eastern Department, Foreign Office, 1 November 1949.
14 PRO/KV/2/2252/Letter from Bernard Burrows, Eastern Department, Foreign Office, 15 November 1949.
15 Ibid.
16 PRO/KV/2/2252/'Old Foe Boasts: I Beat Britain', Press Cutting, *News Chronicle*, 23 July 1955.
17 PRO/FO/371/111065/Letter from Mr A. Abrahams, Zionist Revisionist Organization in Great Britain to Mr Clement Davies MP, 18 October 1954.
18 PRO/KV/2/2252/Letter from Passport Control, Foreign Office to W. McCallum, Home Office, 20 September 1954.
19 PRO/FO/371/111065/Memorandum, Suggested Visit of Mr Begin to United Kingdom, Mr P. Falla, 29 October 1954.
20 Ibid.
21 PRO/FO/371/111065/Memorandum, Suggested Visit of Mr Begin to United Kingdom, Handwritten Comment by Mr J. Ward, 29 October 1954.
22 PRO/FO/371/111065/Letter from Lord John Hope, Foreign Office to Mr C. Davies, 3 November 1954.
23 Ibid.
24 John Campbell, *Margaret Thatcher: Volume Two, The Iron Lady*, Jonathan Cape, London, 2003, p. 335.
25 Margaret Thatcher, *The Downing Street Years*, HarperCollins, London, 1993, p. 510.
26 PRO/FO/371/68699/Reply to Cable No. 1116, Mr O'Leary Requests Guidance on his Personal and Social Relations with Israeli Officials, 4 December 1948.
27 Ibid.
28 PRO/FO/371/75048/Foreign Office Conference of H. M. Representatives in the Middle East, 13 July 1949.
29 Ibid.
30 Ibid.
31 PRO/FO/371/71686/Israeli Government's Investigation into the Stern

Gang's Assassination of Count
Bernadotte.

32 PRO/FO/371/71686/Letter from S. J.
Balfour, 12 October 1948.

33 PRO/FO371/82506, p. 4.

34 PRO/FO/371/75064/Press Cutting,
Daily Telegraph, 24 January 1949.

35 PRO/FO/371/75064/Letter from Lyall
Wilkes to Ernest Bevin, 8 January 1949.

36 PRO/FO/371/75064/Letter from Ernest
Bevin to Lyall Wilkes, 2 February 1949.

37 Ibid.

38 PRO/FO/371/82506/Report on the State
of Israel 1949, p. 2.

39 PRO/FO/371/75205/Cable No.14 from
Tel Aviv to Foreign Office, 19 May 1949.

40 PRO/FO/371/75205/Cable No. 15 from
Tel Aviv to Foreign Office, Summary of
Israeli Press, *Palestine Post*, 19 May 1949.

41 Ibid.

42 PRO/FO/371/75205/Cable from British
Consulate General in Haifa to Foreign
Office, Extract of Speech by Mr
Agronsky (Editor of *Palestine Post*) in
USA, 20 April 1949.

43 Ibid.

44 Ibid.

45 Ibid.

46 Ibid.

47 Ibid.

48 PRO/FO/371/75205/Cable No. 15 from
Tel Aviv to Foreign Office, Summary of
Israeli Press, *Haaretz*, 19 May 1949.

49 Ibid.

50 Ibid.

51 Ibid.

52 PRO/FO/371/75205/Cable No. 3 From
A. K. Helm to Ernest Bevin, 23 May
1949.

53 Ibid.

54 Ibid.

55 Ibid.

56 Ibid.

57 For more on the attitudes of British
Officials to their American counterparts,
see Neil Caplan, *Futile Diplomacy Volume
Four, Operation Alpha and the Failure of
Anglo-American Diplomacy in the
Arab–Israeli Conflict*, Frank Cass, London
and Portland, 1997, p. 6.

58 PRO/FO/371/75205/Cable No. 3 from
A. K. Helm to Ernest Bevin, 23 May 1949.

59 PRO/FO/371/75206/'The British Drop
Balfour', *Maariv*, 25 May 1949.

60 Ibid.

61 PRO/FO/371/75206/Cable from
Mr Helm to Mr Burrows (FO), 28 May
1949.

62 PRO/FO/371/75206/Handwritten Draft
of FO Reply to Cable from Mr Helm to
Mr Burrows (FO), 28 May 1949.

63 Ibid.

64 PRO/FO/371/75206/Cable No. 202
from Mr Helm to Foreign Office, 16 July
1949.

65 PRO/FO/371/75206/Cable No. 206
from Mr Helm to Foreign Office, 16 July
1949.

66 Ibid.

67 Ibid.

68 PRO/FO/371/75206/Handwritten
Comments from FO Officials About
Cable No. 202 from Mr Helm to Foreign
Office, 16 July 1949.

69 Ibid.

70 Ibid.

71 Ibid.

72 Ibid.

73 PRO/FO/371/75206/Record of Meeting
Between Mr Helm and Dr Eliash, 5
August 1949.

74 Ibid.

75 PRO/FO/371/75206/Press Cutting of
'Reconciliation with Britain Aids Israeli
Case at Lausanne', *Guardian*, 1
September 1949.

76 PRO/FO/371/75206/Handwritten
Comments Next to Press Cutting of 'Reconciliation with Britain Aids Israeli Case
at Lausanne', *Guardian*, 1 September
1949.

77 PRO/FO/371/75206/Cable from Paris
to East Department, Paris 'Figaro' Article
on Improvement in Anglo–Israeli
Relations, 2 September 1949.

78 PRO/FO/371/75206/Letter from British
Embassy Paris to Eastern Department
Foreign Office, 2 September 1949.

79 PRO/FO/371/75206/Correspondence
from E. Tomkins in Foreign Office to
R. Barclay in Washington, 21 September
1949.

80 Ibid.

81 PRO/FO/371/75206/Cable from

B. Burrows Foreign Office to H. A. Clarke, British Embassy Paris, 19 September 1949.

82 Ibid.

83 Ibid.

84 PRO/FO/371/75206/Memorandum on Relations with Israel Prepared by Mr Burrows to Mr Helm, 15 September 1949.

85 Ibid.

86 Ibid.

87 PRO/FO/371/75207/Cable No. 107 from Mr Helm to Mr Bevin, 23 September 1949.

88 PRO/FO/371/75207/British Policy Towards the Arabs: Interview with Israel Minister of Foreign Affairs, 23 September 1949.

89 Ibid.

90 Electoral results from BBC News website.

91 Ibid.

92 PRO/FO/371/82528/Cable No. 16 from Mr Helm to Foreign Office, 28 February 1950.

93 Ibid.

94 PRO/FO/371/82528/Minister of State's Conversation with Israeli *Chargé d'Affaires*, 11 April 1950.

95 Ibid.

96 PRO/FO/371/82528/Foreign Office Brief for Minister of State's Conversation with Israeli *Chargé d'Affaires*, 11 April 1950.

97 PRO/FO/371/82528/Minister of State's Conversation with Israeli *Chargé d'Affaires*, 11 April 1950.

98 Ibid.

99 Ibid.

100 Ibid.

101 Ibid.

102 Ibid.

103 Ibid.

104 PRO/FO/371/82528/Memorandum of Meeting Between British Air Attaché in Tel Aviv, Wing Commander J. A. O'Neill and Israeli Chief of Staff, Yigal Yadin in Ramat Gan, 13 April 1950.

105 The meeting was also attended by Colonel Chaim Herzog (Director of Military Intelligence) who later served as President of Israel.

106 PRO/FO/371/82528/Cable from Mr Helm to Mr Furlonge, Eastern Department, Foreign Office, Report of Conversation with the Israeli Minister of Foreign Affairs on Anglo–Israeli Relations, 20 April 1950, p. 2.

107 PRO/FO/371/82528/Cable from Mr Helm to Mr Furlonge, p. 2.

108 Ibid.

109 PRO/FO/371/82528/Cable from Mr Helm to Mr Furlonge, p. 4.

110 Ibid.

111 PRO/FO/371/82528/Cable from Mr Helm to Mr Furlonge, p. 3.

112 PRO/FO/371/82528/Cable No. 202 from Mr Helm to Foreign Office, Israel's MFA Conversation with Mr Helm After *de jure* Recognition by HMG, 28 April 1950.

113 PRO/FO/371/82528/Cable No. 212 from Mr Helm to Foreign Office, Conversation with Mr Helm and Israeli MFA on UK Arms Supply and Middle East Settlement, 2 May 1950.

114 Ibid.

115 Ibid.

116 Ibid.

117 Ibid.

118 Ibid.

119 PRO/FO/371/82528/Cable No. 213 from Mr Helm to Foreign Office, Mr Helm's Comments on his Interview with Israeli MFA, 3 May 1950.

120 Ibid.

121 Ibid.

122 Ibid.

123 Ibid.

124 For more on this see Neill Lochery, *The Israeli Labour Party: In the Shadow of the Likud*, Ithaca Press, Reading, 1997.

125 PRO/FO/371/82528/Four Papers on Matters Concerning Anglo–Israeli Relations Handed to Mr Wright by Mr Neville Blond, 14 June 1950, The Implications of British Middle East Policy, 28 February 1950, p. 4.

126 Ibid.

127 Ibid.

128 Ibid.

129 136 PRO/FO/371/82528/The Implications of British Middle East Policy, 28 February 1950, p. 5.

130 Ibid.
131 PRO/FO/371/82528/Four Papers on Matters Concerning Anglo–Israeli Relations Handed to Mr Wright by Mr Neville Blond, 14 June 1950, Middle East Policy, 11 April 1950.
132 Ibid.
133 Quoted from PRO/371/FO/82529/Israel Parliamentary Delegation: Points for Speeches by the Minister of State and the Parliamentary Under Secretary of State, 18 July 1950.
134 PRO/371/FO/82529/Israel Parliamentary Delegation, pp. 2–3.
135 Ibid.
136 PRO/371/FO/82529/Cable No. 168 from Mr Helm to Foreign Office, Conversation between Mr Helm and Israeli Prime Minister, 29 June 1950.
137 PRO/371/FO/82529/Cable No. 168 from Mr Helm to Foreign Office, p. 2.
138 Ibid.
139 Ibid.
140 Ibid.
141 PRO/371/FO/82529/Cable No. 168 from Mr Helm to Foreign Office, p. 1.
142 Ibid.
143 Ibid.
144 Ibid.
145 PRO/371/FO/82529/From Mr Chadwick in Tel Aviv to Foreign Office, Summary of Article by D. R. Elston in *Haaretz* on Anglo–Israeli Relations and the Achievements of Sir K. Helm, 25 July 1950.
146 PRO/371/FO/82529/Foreign Office Background Notes on Mr Elath, 15 September 1950.
147 Ibid.
148 PRO/371/FO/82529/Conversation Between Israeli Minister and Parliamentary Under-Secretary on Anglo–Israeli Relations, 15 September 1950.
149 PRO/371/FO/82529/Conversation Between Israeli Minister and Parliamentary Under-Secretary, p. 3.
150 Ibid.
151 PRO/371/FO/82529/Conversation Between Sir William Strang and Mr Elath, Israeli Minister, on Anglo–Israeli Relations, 14 November 1950.
152 PRO/371/FO/82529/Conversation Between Sir William Strang and Mr Elath, p. 1.
153 Ibid.
154 Ibid.
155 Ibid.
156 Ibid.
157 PRO/371/FO/82529/Conversation Between Sir William Strang and Mr Elath, p. 2.
158 Ibid.
159 Ibid.
160 PRO/371/FO/82529/Brief for Secretary of State on Israel and Future of UK Policy to Israel, Prepared by Mr Furlonge, 1 November 1950.
161 PRO/371/FO/82529/Record of Conversation Between Mr Davies and Mr Burstein, 19 December 1950.
162 Ibid.
163 Ibid.
164 Ibid.
165 Ibid.
166 For more on Bevin see Alan Bullock, *The Life and Times Of Ernest Bevin*, Politicos, London, 2002.
167 PRO/FO/371/91705/Israel Annual Review for 1950, p. 1.
168 PRO/371/FO/82529/Cable No. 168 from Mr Helm to Foreign Office, Conversation between Mr Helm and Israeli Prime Minister of 29 June 1950.

Chapter 2

1 PRO/FO/371/104778/Secret Memorandum, A Note on Refugee Vagrancy, Sir John Glubb (Glubb Pasha), March 1953.
2 PRO/FO/371/98251/Confidential Report on the Re-establishment of the British Position in the Middle East, undated, p. 1.
3 Orna Almog, *Britain, Israel and the United States 1955–58: Beyond Suez*, Frank Cass, London and Portland, 2003, p. 34.
4 PRO/FO/371/91716/1092/1/51/From Mr Helm to Mr Furlonge, Eastern Department, Foreign Office, 8 January 1951, p. 3.
5 Ibid.
6 PRO/FO/371/91716/1092/1/51/From Mr Helm to Mr Furlonge, Eastern Department, Foreign Office, 8 January 1951, p. 2.

7   Ibid.

8   Ibid.

9   PRO/FO/371/98251/Confidential Report on the Re-establishment of the British Position in the Middle East, undated, point 19.

10   Ibid.

11   Ibid.

12   PRO/FO/371/104733/Annual Review for Israel 1952, p. 2.

13   189 PRO/FO/371/98251/Confidential Report on the Re-establishment of the British Position in the Middle East.

14   PRO/FO/371/98786/The Annual Review for Israel for 1951.

15   On this see Neill Lochery, *The View from the Fence: The Arab–Israeli Conflict from the Present to Its Roots*, Continuum International, London and New York, 2005, pp. 59–62.

16   PRO/FO/371/98490/Cable from Mr Chadwick, Tel Aviv to Mr Wardrop, Eastern Department Foreign Office, 14 January 1952.

17   PRO/FO/371/98786/Israel Annual Review for 1951, p. 2.

18   PRO/FO/371/91716/Cable from Mr Wardrop to Foreign Office, 26 February 1951.

19   Ibid.

20   PRO/FO/371/91716/Cable from Mr Helm to Mr Furlonge, Foreign Office, 17 May 1951.

21   PRO/FO/371/91716/1033/12/Internal Foreign Office Memorandum, 6 March 1951.

22   Ibid.

23   PRO/FO/371/91716/Memorandum from Mr P. Johnson, Eastern Department, Foreign Office, 2 March 1951.

24   Ibid.

25   PRO/FO/371/121855/From Mr Hadow, Foreign Office, to Washington, March 1956.

26   Orna Almog, *Britain, Israel and the United States 1955–58: Beyond Suez*, p. 35.

27   PRO/FO/371/98807/Conversation Between the Secretary of State and the Israeli Foreign Minister, 11 March 1952.

28   PRO/FO/371/98799/Letter from Mr Sharett to Mr Eden, 11 March 1952.

29   PRO/FO/371/98799/Internal Memoran-

dum on Mr Sharett's Visit, undated.

30   Ibid.

31   Ibid.

32   Ibid.

33   PRO/FO/371/98799/Letter from Mr Sharett to Mr Eden, 24 March 1952.

34   Ibid.

35   PRO/FO/371/98799/Conversation Between the Secretary of State and the Israeli Foreign Minister, 11 March 1952.

36   Ibid.

37   Ibid.

38   PRO/FO/371/98807/Letter from Foreign Office to Mr G. Wheeler, Ministry of Defence, 28 March 1952.

39   PRO/FO/371/98807/1193/12/From Mr J. C. Wardrop, Foreign Office, 3 April 1952.

40   PRO/FO/371/98807/Letter from Mr M. Fleet, Treasury to Sir James Bowker, Foreign Office, 16 April 1952.

41   PRO/FO/371/98807/From Mr A. D. Ross, Foreign Office, 16 May 1952.

42   Ibid.

43   Ibid.

44   Ibid.

45   PRO/FO/371/98807/From Mr A. D. Ross, Foreign Office to Mr G. Wheeler, Ministry of Defence, 28 May 1952.

46   PRO/FO/371/98807/1193/18/From Foreign Office, 25 June 1952.

47   PRO/FO/371/98807/1193/18/Handwritten Note by R. G. Bowden (acting in the name of Sir William Strang) in Memorandum on Placing of United Kingdom Orders in Israel, 20 June 1950.

48   PRO/FO/371/98807/Letter from Mr G. Wheeler, Ministry of Defence to Mr A. D. Ross, Foreign Office, 17 June 1952.

49   PRO/FO/371/98799/Cable No. 337 from British Embassy, Tel Aviv to Foreign Office, 6 December 1952.

50   PRO/FO/371/98799/Memorandum from Mr Ross on Israel Visit, 6 December 1952.

51   Ibid.

52   Ibid.

53   Ibid.

54   Ibid.

55   Ibid.

56   PRO/FO/371/104215/Unnumbered Cable from Tel Aviv to Foreign Office,

31 December 1952, p. 2.
57 Ibid.
58 Ibid.
59 Ibid.
60 PRO/FO/371/104215/From Tel Aviv to Mr A. Ross, Eastern Department, Foreign Office, London.
61 Ibid.
62 PRO/FO/371/104215/Record of Meeting Between Mr W. Strang and the Israeli *Chargé d'Affaires*, 7 January 1953.
63 PRO/FO/371/104215/From Mr J. Chadwick, Tel Aviv to Mr J. Wardrop, Eastern Department, Foreign Office, 2 January 1953.
64 Zach Levey, *Israel and the Western Powers 1956–59*, The University of North Carolina Press, Chapel Hill and London, 1997, p. 35.
65 PRO/FO/371/104215/From Mr J. Chadwick, Tel Aviv to Mr J. Wardrop.
66 Ibid.
67 Zach Levey, *Israel and the Western Powers 1956–59*, p. 35.
68 PRO/FO/371/104215/From Mr J. Chadwick, Tel Aviv to Mr J. Wardrop.
69 PRO/FO/371/104215/*Aide Mémoire*, Requested Oral Communication to the Israeli Ambassador, 23 January 1953.
70 PRO/FO/371/104215/Requested Oral Communication to the Israeli Ambassador, 23 January 1953.
71 PRO/FO/371/104733/Annual Review for Israel for 1952, p. 1.
72 PRO/FO/371/98799/Cable No. 337 from British Embassy Tel Aviv to Foreign Office, 6 December 1952, p. 2.
73 PRO/FO/371/98792/10110/2-3/Internal Memorandum on Jerusalem, Mr A. D. Ross, 17 May 1952
74 Ibid.
75 Ibid.
76 Ibid.
77 Ibid.
78 PRO/FO/371/98792/Cable No. 10801/40/52 from Mr J. E. Chadwick in Tel Aviv to Mr A. D. Ross Foreign Office, 30 June 1952.
79 Ibid.
80 PRO/FO/371/104739/Press Cutting, Israel Foreign Office: Move to Jerusalem from Tel Aviv, *The Scotsman*, 14 July 1953.
81 PRO/FO/371/104739/Confidential Memorandum, Arab Protests at Move of Israeli Ministry of Foreign Affairs to Jerusalem, Mr P. S. Fala, 7 August 1953, p. 1.
82 PRO.FO/371/104739/Press Cutting, Jerusalem, *The Economist*, 18 July 1953.
83 PRO/FO/371/98792/Cable No. 1141, Foreign Office to Alexandria, 22 July 1952.
84 PRO/FO/371/104739/Cable No. 118 from Mr F. Evans, Tel Aviv to Lord Marques of Salisbury, Foreign Office, 22 September 1953.
85 PRO/FO/371/104778/Secret Memorandum, A Note on Refugee Vagrancy, Sir John Glubb (Glubb Pasha), March 1953.
86 PRO/FO/371/104778/Confidential Correspondence from Mr Furlonge, Amman to Mr Ross, Eastern Department, Foreign Office, 12 February 1953.
87 Ibid.
88 Ibid.
89 Ibid.
90 Ibid.
91 PRO/FO/371/104778/Secret Memorandum, A Note on Refugee Vagrancy, Sir John Glubb (Glubb Pasha), March 1953, p. 9.
92 Ibid.
93 Ibid.
94 Comment on Glubb's prolific nature by Mr Furlonge, Confidential Correspondence from Mr Furlonge, Amman to Mr Ross, Eastern Department, Foreign Office, 12 February 1953.
95 PRO/FO/371/111057/Cable No. 262 from Mr Evans, Tel Aviv to Foreign Office, 8 December 1953, p. 2.
96 Ibid.
97 Ibid.
98 PRO/FO/371/111065/Record of Discussion Between General Horrocks and David Ben-Gurion, 18 December 1953.
99 Ibid.
100 PRO/FO/371/111057/Cable No. 262 from Mr Evans, Tel Aviv to Foreign Office, 8 December 1953, p. 5.
101 PRO/FO/371/111057/Cable No. 262 from Mr Evans, Tel Aviv to Foreign Office, 8 December 1953, p. 5.
102 PRO/FO/371/111057/1041/1/65/From

Mr A. Moore, *Chargé d'Affaires*, Tel Aviv
to Mr P. Falla, Levant Department,
Foreign Office, 19 January 1954.

103 Ibid.

104 Ibid.

105 PRO/FO/371/111065/Memorandum,
Support of Mr Sharett's New Government, Mr C. Thompson, Foreign Office,
26 January 1954.

106 Ibid.

107 Ibid.

108 Ibid.

109 PRO/FO/371/111065/1041/1/54/From
Mr A. Moore, Tel Aviv to Mr P. Falla,
Levant Department, Foreign Office,
19 January 1954, p. 2.

110 PRO/FO/371/111065/Confidential
Memorandum from Mr Fala, Foreign
Office to Mr D. Serpell, Treasury,
6 February 1954.

111 PRO/FO/371/111065/Briefing Paper for
Mr Kirkpatrick for Meeting With Israeli
Ambassador by Mr Falla, Foreign Office,
11 May 1954.

112 PRO/FO/371/111065/Record of
Meeting Between Mr Kirkpatrick and the
Israeli Ambassador, 12 May 1954.

113 Ibid.

114 PRO/FO/371/111065/Confidential
Memorandum, from Mr Dodds-Parker
to Mr Tilney MP, 10 September 1954.

115 Ibid.

116 PRO/FO/371/111065/Record of Conversation Between Mr Fitzpatrick and
Mr Gazit, 16 September 1954.

117 Ibid.

118 Ibid.

119 Ibid.

120 Ibid.

121 Sir Francis Evans was subsequently
appointed British Ambassador to
Argentina in 1954 where he remained for
three years before retiring.

122 PRO/FO/371/111065/Cable No. 169
from Mr Evans to Mr Eden,
30 September 1954.

123 Ibid.

124 PRO/FO/371/111065/Cable No. 169
from Mr Evans to Mr Eden,
30 September 1954, p. 5.

125 Ibid.

Chapter 3

1 PRO/FO/371/115825/1041/6/55/From
Mr J. Nicholls, Tel Aviv to Mr Evelyn
Shuckburgh, Foreign Office, 8 March
1955, p. 2.

2 PRO/FO/371/98251/Confidential
Report on the Re-establishment of the
British Position in the Middle East,
undated, p. 12.

3 PRO/FO/371/111095/Cable No. 5512
from Foreign Office to Washington,
4 November 1954.

4 Ibid.

5 Ibid.

6 PRO/FO/371/111095/Cable No. 2380
from Washington to Foreign Office,
5 November 1954. Also
PRO/FO/371/111095/Letter from Mr
Harold Beeley, British Embassy, Washington to Mr Paul Falla, Foreign Office,
8 November 1954;
PRO/371/FO/111095/From Mr Beeley
to Mr Fala, 17 November 1954.

7 PRO/FO/371/111095/Confidential
Memorandum, United Kingdom/United
States Talks on Palestine, from Mr Fala,
Foreign Office, 12 November 1954.

8 PRO/FO/371/111095/Cable No. 580
from Mr Shuckburgh to Foreign Office,
undated.

9 PRO/FO/371/111095/1079/6/Confi-
dential Memorandum, United
Kingdom–US Talks About Arab–Israeli
Problem, Mr J. Ward, Sir I. Fitzpatrick,
30 November 1954. See also,
PRO/FO/371/111095/Cable No.
5881/From Foreign Office to Beirut for
Mr Shuckburgh, 30 November 1954. The
contents of this telegram were also sent
to Washington with advice to emphasize
to the State Department to prevent a
leakage of the plans to either Arabs or
Israelis.

10 PRO/FO/371/111095/Cable No. 814
from Secretary of State in Paris to
Foreign Office, 16 December 1954.

11 Ibid.

12 PRO/FO/371/111095/Cable No. 2749
from Washington to Foreign Office,
18 December 1954.

13 PRO/FO/371/111095/Secret Memorandum, Notes on Arab–Israeli Dispute,

Mr Shuckburgh, 15 December 1954.

14 Ibid.
15 Ibid.
16 Ibid.
17 Ibid.
18 Ibid.
19 PRO/FO/371/111095/Annex 1, The Elements of a Settlement, Secret Memorandum, Notes on Arab–Israeli Dispute, Mr Shuckburgh, 15 December 1954.
20 PRO/FO/371/111095/Letter from Sir John Sterndale-Bennett to Mr Shuckburgh, 13 December 1954.
21 Ibid.
22 On the complexities of Operation Alpha and British–US diplomatic efforts see W. Scott Lucas, *Divided We Stand; Britain, the US and Suez Crisis,* Hodder and Stoughton, London, 1991; and Neil Caplan, *Futile Diplomacy Volume Four: Operation Alpha and the Failure of Anglo-American Coercive Diplomacy 1954–1956,* Frank Cass, London and Portland, 1997.
23 Neil Caplan, *Futile Diplomacy,* p. xviii.
24 Ibid.
25 On the Suez Crisis and War from a British perspective see Keith Kyle, *Suez,* St Martin's Press, New York, 1991.
26 Evelyn Shuckburgh, *Descent to Suez Diaries 1951–56,* Weidenfeld and Nicolson, London, 1986.
27 PRO/FO/371/115480/Written Reply by Mr Fitzpatrick to Policy in the Middle East, Mr E. Shuckburgh, 15 October 1955.
28 PRO/FO/371/115480/Policy in the Middle East, Mr E. Shuckburgh, 14 October 1955.
29 Ibid.
30 Ibid.
31 Ibid.
32 PRO/FO/371/115480/Written Reply by Mr Fitzpatrick to Policy in the Middle East, Mr E. Shuckburgh, 15 October 1955.
33 Almog, p. 51.
34 The events in Egypt are generally referred to in Israel as the Lavon Affair. The Minister of Defence, Pinhas Lavon denied that he had given the authorization for the operation to take place. Mr Sharett claimed that he was totally in the

dark about it until after it had happened. The affair came to dominate Israeli politics for over a decade with Mr Ben-Gurion not accepting Lavon's version of events. The fall out from the affair initially helped Ben-Gurion return to power, but eventually it caused a major split in the ruling party, Mapai, with Mr Ben-Gurion and his close allies leaving to form a new party, Rafi. Once he had left Mapai, Mr Ben-Gurion never held power again following a major electoral defeat to Mapai, the party he had helped found.
35 For more details of British arms sales to the region at this time, see Zach Levey, *Israel and the Western Powers 1956–59.*
36 The review contained an extended section in which the Ambassador outlined his view of events. Mr Nicholls's written style was not to everyone's taste at the Foreign Office, where the report was described as being a little longer than it should be. PRO/FO/371/121692/Note by Mr P. Laurence, Foreign Office, 28 February 1956.
37 PRO/FO/371/121692/Annual Review for Israel 1955.
38 PRO/FO/371/121692/Annual Review for Israel 1955, p. 4.
39 Ibid.
40 The Sherman tanks had only been secured through French intermediaries, PRO/FO/371/121692/Annual Review for Israel 1955, p. 4.
41 Ibid.
42 Ibid.
43 Ibid.
44 Sir Knox Helm was born in Dumfries and educated at Dumfries Academy. Sir Francis Evans was born in Belfast and educated at Belfast Academy.
45 PRO/FO/371/121233/1054/13/Briefing Paper for Secretary of State, 30 December 1955.
46 PRO/FO/371/121233/1054/13/Defence Policy, Briefing Paper for Secretary of State, 30 December 1955.
47 Ibid.
48 PRO/FO/371/121233/From British Embassy, Amman to Mr Rose, Levant

Department, Foreign Office, 12 January 1956.

49 PRO/FO/371/121322/Report of Meeting Between Mr Gazit, Israeli Embassy and Mr Hadow, Foreign Office, 2 January 1956.

50 Ibid.

51 Ibid.

52 PRO/FO/371/121322/Foreign Office Minute, Arms for Israel, Mr Rose, 2 January 1956.

53 Ibid.

54 PRO/FO/371/121705/Record of Meeting Between Mr Shuckburgh, Foreign Office and Mr Elath, Israeli Ambassador, 9 January 1956.

55 Ibid.

56 PRO/FO/371/121705/Record of Meeting Between Secretary of State, Mr Lloyd and Israeli Ambassador, Mr Elath, 6 April 1956.

57 Ibid.

58 Ibid.

59 Ibid.

60 Ibid.

61 Ibid.

62 PRO/FO/371/121705/Confidential Letter from Mr Nicholls, Tel Aviv, to Mr Rose, Foreign Office, 30 January 1956.

63 Ibid.

64 Ibid.

65 Ibid.

66 PRO/FO/371/121705/Minute from Mr P. Laurence, Foreign Office, 9 April 1956.

67 Ibid.

68 PRO/FO/371/121705/1041/56/From Mr Nicholls, Tel Aviv to Mr Rose, Foreign Office, 9 April 1956.

69 Ibid.

70 Ibid.

71 PRO/FO/371/121705/Record of Meeting between Unnamed Foreign Office Official and Mr Paget, undated.

72 Ibid.

73 Ibid.

74 Keith Kyle, 'Britain's Slow March Towards Suez', in David Tal (ed.), *The 1956 War: Collusion and Rivalry in the Middle East*, Frank Cass, London and Portland, 2001, p. 98.

75 Keith Kyle, 'Britain's Slow March Towards Suez', p. 99.

76 The Suez Crisis and resulting war has thrown up a whole industry of accounts from both the participants and historians. From a British perspective, one of the most enlightening remains Keith Kyle, *Suez*, St Martin's Press, New York, 1991.

77 There are many accounts of the events at Sevres. See Avi Shlaim, 'The Protocol of Sevres: An Anatomy of a Plot' in David Tal (ed.), *The 1956 War: Collusion and Rivalry in the Middle East*, Frank Cass, London and Portland, 2001, pp. 119–44.

78 Avi Shlaim, 'The Protocol of Sèvres: An Anatomy of a Plot', p. 121.

79 Keith Kyle, 'Britain's Slow March Towards Suez', p. 106.

80 Keith Kyle, 'Britain's Slow March Towards Suez', p. 107.

81 Keith Kyle, 'Britain's Slow March Towards Suez', p. 108.

82 Keith Kyle has revealed the source for Mr Gaitskell. It was the Tory backbencher, William Yates, who had been approached by a Lebanese businessman. He had heard a French Senator in a Paris nightclub talk about a meeting between French, British and Israeli representatives who had worked out the plan for Israel to attack Egypt and then allow Britain and France to intervene. As Kyle recounted, Mr Yates first took his story to Edward Hath, the Tory Chief whip, but could not get a meeting with him so took his story to Mr Gaitskell.

83 Motti Golani, 'The Sinai War 1956' in David Tal (ed.), *The 1956 War: Collusion and Rivalry in the Middle East*, Frank Cass, London and Portland, 2001, p. 188.

84 PRO/FO/371/121706/Correspondence Between Mr Ross, Tel Aviv and Mr Logan, Foreign Office, 3 November 1956.

85 PRO/FO/371/121706/Final Report on Suez by Mr Ross, Foreign Office, undated.

86 PRO/FO/371/121804/Israeli Government Press Office, 6 December 1956.

87 Ibid.

88 PRO/FO/371/121706/From Tel Aviv to Foreign Office, 8 December 1956.

89 PRO/FO/371/121706/Reply to Parliamentary Question, 22 November 1956.

90 PRO/FO/371/121804/Foreign Office Minute on Question in HoC by Dennis Healey, Mr Laurence, 6 December 1956.
91 Ibid.
92 PRO/FO/371/121804/Note on Parliamentary Questions about the Alleged Collusion, 12 December 1956.
93 PRO/FO/371/121804/Memorandum from Mr Rose, Foreign Office, 12 December 1956.
94 PRO/FO/371/121804/Memorandum on Ultimatum from Mr Rose, Foreign Office, 18 December 1956.
95 Ibid.
96 Ibid.
97 PRO/FO/371/121804/Confidential Cable from Tel Aviv to Levant Department, Foreign Office, 13 December 1956.
98 401 PRO/FO/371/121804/The British Ambassador Accused of Conspiracy has the Perfect Alibi, *Yediot Aharonot*, 25 December 1956.
99 Ibid.
100 Ibid.
101 Zach Levey, *Israel and the Western Powers 1956–59*, The University of North Carolina Press, Chapel Hill and London, 1997, p. 101.
102 PRO/FO/371/128107/Cable No. 8 from Tel Aviv to Foreign Office, 4 January 1957.
103 Ibid.
104 Ibid.
105 Ibid.
106 PRO/FO/371/128107/R1052/2/C/Confidential Minute by Mr Rose, 9 January 1957.
107 PRO/FO/371/128107/Cable No. 2 from Tel Aviv to Foreign Office, 4 January 1957.
108 PRO/FO/371/128107/The Arab Disease, *Maariv*, 4 January 1957. Quotation slightly modified from Foreign Office's translation for grammatical reasons.
109 Ibid.
110 Mr Eden had served as the Secretary of State on three separate occasions, 1935–38, 1940–45 and 1951–55.
111 PRO/FO/371/128107/Cable No. 59 from Tel Aviv to Foreign Office, 14 January 1957.

112 Ibid.
113 PRO/FO/371/128107/Record of Meeting Between Mr Ross, Foreign Office and the Israeli Ambassador and Mr Shneerson, the Head of the Commonwealth Division of the Israeli Foreign Ministry, 7 February 1957.
114 Ibid.
115 Ibid.
116 Zach Levey, *Israel and the Western Powers 1956–59*, p. 103.
117 PRO/FO/371/128107/Record of Conversation Between Secretary of State and Israeli Ambassador, 5 April 1957.
118 Ibid.
119 PRO/FO/371/128107/Record of Conversation Between Mr Hayter, Foreign Office and Israeli Ambassador, 18 June 1957.
120 PRO/FO/371/128107/Minute by Mr Laurence to the Record of Conversation Between Mr Hayter, Foreign Office and Israeli Ambassador, 27 June 1957.
121 Ibid.
122 Ibid.
123 PRO/FO/371/128107/Record of Meeting Between Mr Hayter and the Israeli Ambassador, 16 June 1957.
124 Ibid.
125 PRO/FO/371/128107/Record of Meeting Between Secretary of State and Mr Aneurin Bevin, 17 July 1957.
126 Levey, p. 104.
127 Ibid.
128 PRO/FO/371/128107/Record of Meeting Held in the Prime Minister's Room, House of Commons, 1 August 1957.
129 Ibid.
130 Ibid.
131 Ibid.
132 Ibid.
133 PRO/FO/371/128107/Records of Conversation Between Secretary of State and Israeli Ambassador, 11 September 1957.
134 Ibid.
135 Ibid.
136 PRO/FO/371/128107/Record of Conversation Between Secretary of State and Israeli Ambassador, 10 December 1957.
137 Ibid.
138 PRO/FO/371/134267/Annual Review

for Israel in 1957, p. 4.

139 PRO/FO/371/134284/Conversation Between Secretary of State and Israeli Ambassador, 2 May 1958.
140 Ibid.
141 PRO/FO/371/134284/Cable No. 348, From Foreign Office, 16 July 1958.
142 Ibid.
143 PRO/FO/371/134284/Cable No. 352, From Mr Rundall, Tel Aviv to Foreign Office, 19 July 1958.
144 Ibid.
145 PRO/FO/371/134284/Cable No. 353, From Mr Rundall, Tel Aviv to Foreign Office, 19 July 1958.
146 Ibid.
147 Ibid.
148 Ibid.
149 PRO/FO/371/134284/Cable No. 352 from Mr Rundall, Tel Aviv to Foreign Office, 19 July 1958.
150 Ibid.
151 PRO/FO/371/134284/Cable No. 353 from Mr Rundall, Tel Aviv to Foreign Office, 19 July 1958.
152 PRO/FO/371/134284/Record of Meeting Between the Secretary of State and the Israeli Ambassador, 21 July 1958.
153 PRO/FO/371/134284/Cable No. 102 from Mr Rundall, Tel Aviv to the Secretary of State, 28 July 1958.
154 Ibid.
155 Ibid.
156 Ibid.
157 Ibid.
158 PRO/FO/371/134286/Foreign Office Minute, 26 July 1958.
159 PRO/FO/371/134285/Brief for Secretary of State for the Visit of Mrs Meir, the Israeli Minister of Foreign Affairs, 9 August 1958.
160 Zach Levey, *Israel and the Western Powers 1956–59*, p. 112.
161 Zach Levey, *Israel and the Western Powers 1956–59*, p. 113.
162 PRO/FO/371/142271/The Annual Review of Events in Israel for 1958, 8 January 1959.
163 Ibid.
164 Ibid.
165 Ibid.

Chapter 4

1 PRO/FO/371/157284/Letter from Mr C. W. Hart-Jones to Mr Croome, United Kingdom Atomic Energy Authority, 11 January 1961.
2 Speaking in 2006 the Israeli Prime Minister appeared to admit that Israel was a nuclear power. His office later argued that his comments had been misinterpreted and that he had made no such admission.
3 PRO/FO/371/142304/Record of Conversation Between Secretary of State and the Israeli Ambassador, 10 February 1959.
4 Ibid.
5 Ibid.
6 Ibid.
7 Ibid.
8 Ibid.
9 PRO/FO/371/142304/From Mr Rundall, Tel Aviv to Mr Hadow, Foreign Office, 14 January 1959. Regarding the final point, Mr Ben-Gurion and Mr Begin were involved in a bitter dispute over the Altalena Incident in 1948, when a ship carrying arms for Revisionist forces was scuppered off the coast of Tel Aviv on the orders of the Provisional Israeli Government led by Mr Ben-Gurion. Mr Rundall noted that the two had clashed in the Knesset the day before the letter was received.
10 Ibid.
11 PRO/FO/371/142304/Memo from Mr R. Tesh, Foreign Office, 23 January 1959 and Mr Hadow, 30 January 1959.
12 Ibid.
13 PRO/FO/371/142304/Record of Conversation Between Secretary of State and the Israeli Ambassador, 10 February 1959.
14 PRO/FO/371/151164/Annual Review for Israel for 1959.
15 The Israelis were particularly disappointed given the Financial Agreement signed by Britain and Egypt in 1959, one of the aims of which was to improve British–Egyptian relations. PRO/FO/371/142304/From Mr Hadow, Foreign Office to Mr Rundall, Tel Aviv, 16 February 1959.

16 PRO/FO/371/142364/Minute from Mr J. Beith, Foreign Office, Disposal of South African Tanks, 6 July 1959.

17 PRO/FO/371/142364/Additional Minute from Mr J. Beith, Foreign Office, 7 July 1959.

18 PRO/FO/371/150856/Report on Visit to Middle East by Mr Beith, 14 April 1960.

19 PRO/FO/371/150856/From Mr P. Hancock, Tel Aviv to Mr Beith, Foreign Office, 26 February 1960.

20 Ibid.

21 Ibid.

22 Ibid.

23 Golda Meir's comments. Reported in PRO/FO/371/150856/From Mr P. Hancock, Tel Aviv to Mr Beith, Foreign Office, 26 February 1960.

24 Ibid.

25 PRO/FO/371/151269/Minute on Adolf Eichmann, 13 June 1960.

26 PRO/FO/371/157811/Press Cutting, *Daily Telegraph*, 6 April 1961.

27 PRO/FO/371/157811/Memorandum on the Legality of the Eichmann Trial, 13 April 1961.

28 PRO/FO/371/157811/Cable No. 1661/61 from Tel Aviv to Eastern Department, Foreign Office, 11 April 1961.

29 PRO/FO/371/157762/Foreign Office Minute, Mr R. Crawford, 24 May 1961.

30 PRO/FO/371/157762/Cable No. 176 from Mr Hancock, Tel Aviv to Foreign Office, 27 May 1961.

31 Ibid.

32 PRO/FO/371/157762/Record of Meeting Between the Secretary of State and Mr Ben-Gurion, 2 June 1961.

33 Ibid.

34 Ibid.

35 Ibid.

36 PRO/FO/371/157762/Record of Conversation Between the Prime Minister and Mr Ben-Gurion, 2 June 1961.

37 Mr Ben-Gurion had held a private meeting with Sir Winston Churchill, also on 2 June 1961. It will come as little surprise that during the course of their meeting Mr Ben-Gurion raised the issue of the missiles.
PRO/FO/371/157762/Letter from Mr Montague Brown to Foreign Office,

2 June 1961.

38 PRO/FO/371/157762/Cable No. 55 from Cairo to Foreign Office, 3 June 1961.

39 Ibid.

40 Ibid.

41 PRO/FO/371/157762/1081/61/From Baghdad to Eastern Department, Foreign Office, 8 June 1961.

42 PRO/FO/371/157762/From Rabat to Foreign Office, Translation of Article in *Al-Fayr*, 10 June 1961.

43 PRO/FO/371/157768/Record of Conversation Between Dr Yahil, Director General of the Israeli Ministry of Foreign Affairs, and Mr Hancock, Tel Aviv, 13 June 1961.

44 Ibid.

45 Ibid.

46 PRO/FO/371/157760/Record of Meeting Between the Israeli Ambassador, Mr Lourie and Mr Stevens, the Foreign Office, 8 June 1961.

47 Ibid.

48 Ibid.

49 Ibid.

50 PRO/FO/371/157760/Foreign Office Minute, Meeting with Israeli Ambassador, 17 August 1961.

51 PRO/FO/371/157793/Cable 1478 from Washington to Foreign Office, 16 June 1961.

52 PRO/FO/371/157793/Foreign Office Minute, Arms for Israel, 13 June 1961.

53 PRO/FO/371/157286/Record of Meeting Between Secretary of State and Israeli Prime Minister, 2 June 1961.

54 PRO/FO/371/157286/Letter from Mr Fowler to Mr Pritchard, Commonwealth Relations Office, 8 June 1961.

55 PRO/FO/371/157286/From Beirut to Foreign Office, Israel Nuclear Programme, 23 June 1961.

56 PRO/FO/371/157286/Foreign Office Minute, 23 June 1961.

57 PRO/FO/371/157286/Top Secret Foreign Office Memorandum, Israeli Nuclear Development, March 1961.

58 Ibid.

59 Ibid.

60 Ibid.

61 PRO/FO/371/157286/Handwritten

Minute from Mr Brooke Turner, 8 March 1961.

62 Ibid.

63 PRO/FO/371/157286/Letter from Mr M. Michaels, The Office of the Minister of Science to Mr Croome, 13 January 1961.

64 PRO/FO/371/157286/Letter from Mr M. Michaels, The Office of the Minister of Science to Mr Croome, 13 January 1961.

65 PRO/FO/371/157286/Letter from Mr Croome, UNAEA to Mr Hainworth, Foreign Office, 13 January 1961.

66 PRO/FO/371/157286/Letter from Mr C. Hart-Jones to Mr Croome, 11 January 1961.

67 PRO/FO/371/149586/Cable No. 542 from Paris to Foreign Office, 20 December 1960. Foreign Office officials mocked French denials. One stated that the formal French denial of involvement in the project would be reassuring were it true. PRO/FO/371/149586/Minute by Mr Hainworth, 20 December 1960.

68 PRO/FO/371/149586/Draft by Mr J. Beith on Arab Reactions to Reports about Israel's Nuclear Activities, 22 December 1960.

69 PRO/FO/371/149586/From Mr Beith, Foreign Office to Mr C. Crowe, Cairo, 23 December 1960.

70 PRO/FO/371/149586/Draft by Mr J. Beith on Arab Reactions to Reports about Israel's Nuclear Activities, 22 December 1960.

71 PRO/FO/371/163971/From Mr Hancock, Tel Aviv to Mr Beith, Foreign Office, 5 February 1962.

72 Ibid.

73 Ibid.

74 PRO/FO/371/163971/Reply from Mr Beith to Mr Hancock, undated.

75 PRO/FO/371/164290/Annual Review for Israel for 1961.

76 Ibid.

77 PRO/FO/371/164290/Annual Review for Israel for 1961, pp. 7–8.

78 PRO/FO/371/164309/Correspondence From Mr W. Morris, Amman to Mr Pakenham, Tel Aviv, 8 May 1962.

79 Ibid.

80 PRO/FO/371/164309/Correspondence From Mr Hancock in Tel Aviv to Mr Morris in Amman, 17 May 1962.

81 Ibid.

82 Ibid.

83 PRO/FO/371/164309/Correspondence from Mr Morris to Mr Hancock, 25 May 1962.

84 PRO/FO/371/164309/Briefing Paper for Lord Privy Seal for Meeting with Israeli Ambassador, 12 June 1962.

85 Moshe Gat, *Britain and the Conflict in the Middle East 1964–67: The Coming of the Six-Day War*, Praeger, Westport, Connecticut and London 2003, p. 30.

86 Ibid.

87 PRO/FO/371/164309/Briefing Paper for Lord Privy Seal.

88 Moshe Gat, *Britain and the Conflict in the Middle East*, pp. 32–3.

89 For a detailed history of the political dimension of the water issues that surrounded the River Jordan see the work of Moshe Gat, *Britain and the Conflict in the Middle East 1964–67: The Coming of the Six-Day War*.

90 PRO/FO/371/164309/Briefing Paper for Lord Privy Seal.

91 Ibid.

92 Ibid.

93 PRO/FO/371/170516/Annual Review for Israel for 1962, p. 6.

94 Ibid.

95 PRO/FO/371/170531/Record of Conversation Between Mr H. Pakenham, Tel Aviv and Mr Levavi, Assistant Director General of the Israeli Ministry of Foreign Affairs, 20 February 1963, Report in correspondence with Mr G. Hiller, Eastern Department, Foreign Office, 21 February 1963.

96 Ibid.

97 Ibid.

98 Ibid.

99 PRO/FO/371/170531/Correspondence from Mr Hiller, Foreign Office to Mr Pakenham, Tel Aviv, 19 March 1963.

100 In his pursuit of what he thought was justice in the Lavon Affair, Mr Ben-Gurion had increasingly alienated large sections of the party he had created. His resignation and eventual decision to

leave Mapai (along with Moshe Dayan and Shimon Peres) transformed the internal politics of Israel. Mr Ben-Gurion's new party, Rafi, ran in the 1965 elections but did not do as well as expected. There was to be no second political comeback for Israel's first and longest serving Prime Minister.

101 PRO/FO/371/170531/Cable No. 164 from Tel Aviv to London, Record of Meeting Between Mr Beith and Mr Ben-Gurion, 22 May 1963.

102 Ibid.

103 Amos Oz, *A Tale of Love and Darkness*, Chatto and Windus, London, 2004, p. 420.

104 Ibid.

105 Ibid.

106 PRO/FO/371/170531/Cable No. 164 from Tel Aviv to London, 22 May 1963.

107 Ibid.

108 Ibid.

109 Ibid.

110 Ibid.

111 In defence of Mr Ben-Gurion it is important to point out that for much of the time he served as Prime Minister he simultaneously held the portfolio of Minister of Defence. At varying times he appeared to speak to the British as either Prime Minister of Minister of Defence. The later is formally charged with making sure that the IDF had all the military equipment that it needed to fight both potential and real wars.

112 PRO/FO/371/170531/Record of Conversation Between Secretary of State and Israeli Ambassador, 22 July 1963.

113 Ibid.

114 PRO/FO/371/170531/Briefing Paper for Secretary of State for Meeting with Israeli Ambassador, 18 July 1963.

115 PRO/FO/371/170531/Record of Conversation Between Secretary of State and Israeli Ambassador.

116 Ibid.

117 PRO/FO/371/170531/Extract from Record of Conversation Between Foreign Secretary and Mrs Meir, 2 October 1963.

118 Ibid.

119 Ibid.

120 PRO/FO/371/170531/Foreign Office Minute, 2 October 1963.

121 Ibid.

122 PRO/FO/371/170531/Talking Points for the Israeli Ambassador's Call on the Secretary of State on 3 December 1963.

123 Ibid.

124 PRO/FO/371/170531/Briefing Paper for Lord Carrington's Meeting with Yigal Allon, undated.

125 http://www.fco.gov.uk.

126 PRO/FO/371/170531/Talking Points for the Israeli Ambassador's Call on the Secretary of State on 3 December 1963.

127 Ibid.

128 Ibid.

129 PRO/FO/371/175793/The Annual Review for Israel for 1963.

130 Ibid.

131 PRO/FO/371/175557/Draft Letter from Foreign Office For the Prime Minister's Meeting with Mrs Meir on 3 March 1964.

132 Ibid.

133 Ibid.

134 Ibid.

135 PRO/FO/371/175557/Record of Meeting Between the Prime Minister and Mrs Meir, 3 March 1964.

136 Ibid.

137 PRO/FO/371/175557/Record of Conversation Between the Foreign Secretary and Mrs Meir, 3 March 1964.

138 PRO/FO/371/175557/Foreign Office Minute by Mr Morris, Mrs Meir's Press Conference, 6 March 1964.

139 Ibid.

140 PRO/FO/371/180846/Annual Review for Israel for 1964.

141 PRO/FO/371/175557/Record of Conversation Between Secretary of State and Israeli Ambassador, 2 July 1964.

142 Ibid.

143 Ibid.

144 Ibid.

145 PRO/FO/371/180846/Annual Review for Israel for 1964.

Chapter 5

1 PRO/FCO/17/468/6382502/The Annual Review for Israel for 1967, 22 January 1968.

2 PRO/FO/371/180865/Minute from Mr Morris on Anglo–Israeli Relations,

12 January 1965.
3 Ibid.
4 Ibid.
5 Ibid.
6 Ibid.
7 PRO/FO/371/180865/United Kingdom's Relations with Israel, Mr R. Crawford, Under-Secretary of State, 1 March 1965.
8 Ibid.
9 Ibid.
10 Harold Wilson had originally appointed Mr Patrick Gordon Walker as his Secretary of State in October 1964. Mr Walker, however, lost his seat in the House of Commons in the 1964 election. He resigned as Secretary of State on 22 January 1965 when he failed to win a by-election that would have seen his return to the House of Commons. Despite his short stay in office he was genuinely liked by many Foreign Office officials who noted that he was the first SoS of the twentieth century who could converse with the German Ambassador in German, http://www.fco.gov.uk/servlet.
11 PRO/FO/371/180865/Record of Conversation Between the Secretary of State and the Israeli Ambassador, 19 February 1965.
12 Ibid.
13 Ibid.
14 PRO/FO/371/180846/Review of Events in Israel for First Half of 1965, 12 July 1965.
15 PRO/FO/371/180846/Review of Events in Israel for 1965, 18 January 1966.
16 PRO/FO/371/180846/Review of Events in Israel for First Half of 1965.
17 Ibid.
18 On the debate as to what Israeli military might be taken if the Arabs went ahead with the diversion schemes see Moshe Gat, *Britain and the Conflict in the Middle East 1964–67*, pp. 94–7.
19 Ibid.
20 PRO/FO/371/180846/Review of Events in Israel for 1965, 18 January 1966.
21 PRO/FO/371/180846/Review of Events in Israel for First Half of 1965.
22 Ibid.

23 For his profile see www.fco.gov.uk.
24 PRO/FO/371/186825/Foreign Office Profile of Abba Eban.
25 Ibid.
26 PRO/FCO/17/471/3907328/Foreign Office Memorandum, Mr Eshkol, Mr Eban and Israeli Foreign Policy, 19 January 1968.
27 PRO/FO/371/186825/Cable No. 27 from Mr Hadow, Tel Aviv to Foreign Office, 19 January 1966.
28 Ibid.
29 Ibid.
30 Ibid.
31 PRO/FO/371/186825/Correspondence from Mr Hadow, Tel Aviv to Mr Morris, Foreign Office, 21 January 1966.
32 PRO/FO/371/186825/Correspondence from Mr Hadow, Tel Aviv to Mr Morris, Foreign Office, 3 March 1966.
33 PRO/FO/371/186825/Correspondence from Mr Hadow to Mr Morris, Foreign Office, 12 August 1966.
34 PRO/FCO/468/Annual Review for Israel for 1966, 24 January 1967.
35 PRO.FO/371/186893/Foreign Office Memorandum, Mrs Golda Meir and the Labour Party Conference, Mr Morris, 3 August 1966.
36 Ibid.
37 Ibid.
38 PRO/FO/371/186825/Correspondence from Mr Hadow, Tel Aviv to Sir Roger Allen, Foreign Office, 21 January 1966.
39 PRO/FO/371/186864/Internal Memorandum, The Dimona Reactor, 9 May 1966.
40 PRO/FO/371/186864/From Mr A. Goodison, Foreign Office to Mr C. Everett, Washington, 27 April 1966.
41 Quoted from PRO/FCO/468/6382502/Annual Review for Israel for 1966, 24 January 1967.
42 Ibid.
43 Ibid.
44 PRO/FCO/468/6382502/Annual Review for Israel for 1967.
45 Ibid.
46 Ibid.
47 PRO/FCO/17/548/3907412/Cable No. 176 from Mr Hadow, Tel Aviv to Foreign

Office, 29 March 1967.

48 PRO/FCO/17/548/3907412/Foreign Office Memorandum, Anglo–Israeli Relations, Mr Morris, 30 March 1967.

49 Ibid.

50 PRO/FCO/17/548/3907412/Foreign Office Minute by Sir D. Allen, Anglo-Israeli Relations, 31 March 1967.

51 PRO/FCO/468/6382502/Annual Review for Israel for 1967.

52 Ibid.

53 PRO/FCO/17/548/3907412/Cable No. 1130 from Mr Hadow, Tel Aviv to Foreign Office, 16 October 1967.

54 Ibid.

55 Ibid.

56 For more details of the splits see Neill Lochery, *The Israeli Labour Party: In the Shadow of the Likud*, Ithaca Press, Reading, 1997.

57 PRO/FCO/17/548/3907412/Cable No. 1130 from Mr Hadow, Tel Aviv to Foreign Office, 16 October 1967.

58 PRO/FCO/17/548/3907412/Cable No. 1127 from Mr Hadow, Tel Aviv to Foreign Office, 16 October 1967.

59 Ibid.

60 PRO/FCO/17/548/3907412/Cable No. 1129 from Mr Hadow, Tel Aviv to Foreign Office, 16 October 1967.

61 Ibid.

62 Ibid.

63 Ibid.

64 PRO/FCO/17/548/3907412/Cable No. 1128 from Mr Hadow, Tel Aviv to Foreign Office, 16 October 1967.

65 PRO/FCO/17/548/3907412/Cable No. 2188 from Foreign Office to Tel Aviv, 20 October 1967.

66 PRO/FCO/17/548/3907412/Memorandum from Mr Brown to Mr Wilson, 24 October 1967.

67 Ibid.

68 PRO/FCO/17/548/3907412/Telegram from Mr Brown to Mr Hadow, Tel Aviv, undated.

69 Ibid.

70 PRO/FCO/17/548/3907412/Cable No. 1183 from Tel Aviv to Foreign Office, 25 October 1967.

71 Ibid.

72 Ibid.

73 Ibid.

74 PRO/FCO/17/548/3907412/Cable No. 21 from Foreign Office to Certain Missions and Dependent Territories, Visit of Mr Eshkol to the United Kingdom, 19 January 1968.

75 PRO/FCO/17/548/3907412/Record of Meeting Between the Prime Minister and the Prime Minister of Israel, 17 January 1968.

76 Ibid.

77 Ibid.

78 During the failed negotiations at Camp David in 2000 between Israel and the PLO, the Israeli Prime Minister, Ehud Barak, offered the Palestinians control of the old city. This caused a storm not only in Israel, but also in Jordan which saw its influence being clipped in Jerusalem.

79 PRO/FCO/17/548/3907412/Cable No. 21, Visit of Mr Eshkol to the United Kingdom, 19 January 1968.

80 PRO/FCO/17/548/3907412/Press Review, 4 January 1968.

81 PRO/FCO/17/548/3907412/Cable No. 74 from Tel Aviv to Foreign Office, 18 January 1968.

82 Reported in 696 PRO/FCO/17/548/3907412/Cable No. 74 from Tel Aviv to Foreign Office, 18 January 1968.

83 Ibid.

84 PRO/FCO/17/618/3907423/Record of Meeting Between the Foreign Secretary and Deputy Prime Minister of Israel, 19 September 1968.

85 PRO/FCO/17/618/3907423/Summary of Meeting Between Secretary of State Mr Thorp and Mr Allon at D. E. A., 19 September 1968.

86 PRO/FCO/17/897/3907632/The Annual Review for Israel for 1968, 21 January 1969.

87 PRO/FCO/17/618/3907423/Record of Meeting Between the Foreign Secretary and Deputy Prime Minister of Israel, 19 September 1968.

88 PRO/FCO/17/897/3907632/The Annual Review for Israel for 1968, 21 January 1969.

89 Ibid.

90 Ibid.

91 On this, see, Neill Lochery, *The Israeli Labour Party: In the Shadow of the Likud.*
92 PRO/FCO/17/896/3907796/From Tel Aviv to London, New Israel Government, 8 March 1969.
93 PRO/FCO/17/896/3907796/Correspondence from Mr M. Mandel to Mr L. Appleyard, Near Eastern Department, Foreign Office, 2 April 1969.
94 Ibid.
95 PRO/FCO/17/896/3907796/Foreign Office Memorandum, The New Israeli Government, Mr L. Appleyard, 19 March 1969.
96 Ibid.
97 Ibid.
98 Ibid.
99 Ibid.
100 PRO/FCO/17/896/3907796/Correspondence from Mr M. Hadow, Tel Aviv to Mr G. Arthur, Foreign Office, 13 March 1969.
101 Ibid.
102 In Israel the Minister of Defence tends to outrank the Minister of Foreign Affairs or the Deputy Prime Minister.
103 PRO/FCO/17/906/3907638/Foreign Office Briefing Paper, Chieftains, 30 October 1969.
104 Ibid.
105 PRO/FCO/17/947/3907786/Cable No. 269 from Tel Aviv to Foreign Office, 12 June 1969.
106 Ibid.
107 Ibid.
108 PRO/FCO/17/947/3907786/Foreign Office Memorandum, Mrs Meir's Visit, 20 June 1969.
109 PRO/FCO/17/947/3907786/Record of Meeting Between Secretary of State for Defence and Mrs Meir, 13 June 1969.
110 Ibid.
111 PRO/FCO/17/947/3907786/Record of Meting Between the Prime Minister and Mrs Meir, 11 June 1969.
112 Ibid.
113 PRO/FCO/17/947/3907786/Record of Meeting Between the Foreign Secretary and the Prime Minister of Israel, 13 June 1969.
114 PRO/FCO/17/947/3907786/Comment on Mrs Meir's London Visit, Voice of the Arabs, 16 June 1969.
115 PRO/FCO/17/906/3907638/Memorandum from Mr G. Arthur, Foreign Office, Chieftains and Mrs Meir's Visit, 20 June 1969.
116 PRO/FCO/17/906/3907638/Interview with Golda Meir, *Sunday Times*, 15 June 1969
117 PRO/FCO/17/906/3907638/Foreign Office Briefing Paper, Chieftains.
118 PRO/FCO/17/906/3907638/Secretary of State's Meeting with Mr Eban on 6 October 1969.
119 PRO/FCO/17/906/3907638/Tanks to Israel Deal Off, *Daily Mail*, 30 October 1969.
120 Ibid.
121 Ibid.
122 PRO/FCO/17/908/3907779/Dispatch from Mr Barnes, Tel Aviv to Foreign Office, Anglo–Israeli Relations, 18 August 1969.
123 Ibid.
124 Ibid.
125 Ibid.
126 PRO/FCO/17/908/3907779/From Mr A. Craig, Jeddah to Mr J. Tripp, Eastern Department, Foreign Office, 28 August 1969.
127 Ibid.
128 PRO/FCO/17/908/3907779/Correspondence from Mr R. Beaumont, Cairo to Mr G. Arthur, Foreign Office, 5 September 1969.
129 Ibid.
130 PRO/FCO/17/908/3907779/Dispatch from Mr Barnes, Tel Aviv to Foreign Office, Anglo–Israeli Relations, 18 August 1969.
131 Ibid.
132 On this see Neill Lochery, *The Israeli Labour Party: In the Shadow of the Likud.*

Chapter 6
1 PRO/FCO/93/124/3909360/Diplomatic Report, 266/73, First Impressions of Israel, Mr Ledwidge, 30 April 1973.
2 PRO/FCO/17/1749/3909268/Foreign Office Minute, Mr Craig, 12 December 1972.
3 Behind much of the Israeli thinking on this issue was that Britain was a power

in decline in the Middle East. In other words, in order to gain favour or influence in the Arab world, Britain would pay with Israeli currency (working towards pressuring Israel into making political concessions to the Arabs). In the past, Britain had bought favour with the Arabs using economic inducements along with defence treaties. Clearly, Britain at the start of the 1970s was no longer in a position to use these tried and tested methods. The Israelis believed that selling Israel down the river in order to curry favour with the Arabs must have been very tempting to the British Government.

4 PRO/FCO/17/1308/3909190/Record of Meeting Between Minister of State for Defence and General Tsur, 17 November 1970.

5 PRO/FCO/17/1299/3909124/Cable No. 38 from Tel Aviv to Foreign Office, 15 July 1970.

6 PRO/FCO/17/1308/3909190/Record of Meeting Between Minister of State for Defence and General Tsur, 17 November 1970.

7 PRO/FCO/17/1299/3909124/Cairo Radio on British Arms for Israel, 21 January 1970.

8 PRO/FCO/17/1299/3909124/Cable No. 162 from Foreign Office to Cairo, 11 February 1970.

9 PRO/FCO/17/1299/3909124/Press Cutting, Wilson Turns down Pleas By 81 MPs on Israel, 26 March 1970.

10 PRO/FCO/17/1299/3909124/Memorandum on Arms for Israel: General Policy, 23 July 1970.

11 PRO/FCO/17/1752/3909269/Foreign Office Minute, Small Submarines for Israel, Mr Pike, Near Eastern Department, 1 March 1972.

12 PRO/FCO/17/1752/3909269/Press Cutting, Yes, Two Subs, *Daily Express*, 7 March 1972.

13 PRO/FCO/17/1752/3909269/Foreign Office Minute, Mr Laver, Near Eastern Department, 6 March 1972.

14 PRO/FCO/17/1752/3909269/Foreign Office Minute, Mr Parsons, 6 March 1972.

15 Ibid.

16 PRO/FCO/93/144/3909917/Farewell Call by Israeli Ambassador, 31 October 1973.

17 PRO/FCO/93/144/3909917/Press Cutting, Israeli Envoy Puts Case, *Guardian*, 31 October.

18 PRO/FCO/17/1337/3909191/Cable No. 614 from Mr Barnes, Tel Aviv to FCO, 29 June 1970.

19 PRO/FCO/17/1337/3909191/Cable No. 325 from Foreign Office, Record of Meeting Between Foreign Secretary and Mr Eban on 1 July 1970, 2 July 1970.

20 Ibid.

21 PRO/FCO/17/1337/3909191/Brief for the Secretary of State's Meeting with the Israeli Foreign Minister, 16 December 1970.

22 Ibid.

23 Ibid.

24 Ibid.

25 PRO/FCO/17/1337/3909191/Correspondence from Mr Barnes, Tel Aviv to Foreign Office, 1 December 1970.

26 Ibid.

27 Ibid.

28 PRO/FCO/17/1337/3909191/Press Cutting, Israel's Fear of Growing Isolation Heightened by Shift in British Policy in Middle East, *The Times*, 14 December 1970.

29 The above article was an example of this campaign. The Foreign Office were so concerned that the Israelis would continue this campaign using the details of Mr Eban's meeting with Mr Douglas-Home that they suggested that the Secretary of State try, at the start of the meeting, to secure a promise from Mr Eban that the details of their talks would not be passed on to the media, except to say that they had discussed the issues of the day. Even if Mr Eban agreed, the Foreign Office felt that other Israelis would still leak out details. In short, there was distrust and mutual suspicion all round.

PRO/FCO/17/1337/3909191/Internal Memorandum From Mr R. Evans, Near Eastern Department, Secretary of State's Meeting with Mr Eban, 15 December 1970.

30 Comments made by Mr R. Evans, PRO/FCO/17/1337/3909191/Internal Memorandum From Mr R. Evans, Near Eastern Department, Secretary of State's Meeting with Mr Eban, 15 December 1970.

31 PRO/FCO/17/1337/3909191/Correspondence from Mr Philip Adams, Foreign Office to Mr Barnes, Tel Aviv, 18 December 1970.

32 PRO/FCO/17/1337/3909191/Correspondence from Mr Barnes, Tel Aviv to Foreign Office, 1 December 1970.

33 PRO/FCO/17/1337/3909191/Correspondence from Mr Philip Adams, Foreign Office to Mr Barnes, Tel Aviv, 18 December 1970.

34 PRO/FCO/17/1735/3909193/The Annual Review for Israel for 1971, 1 January 1972.

35 The ambiguity lay in the absence of the definite article (the) from the English wording of the resolution. The phrase 'from lands captured in 1967' was taken to mean 'not all the lands' by the Israelis. The Arabs took a contrary view to this, arguing that in Arabic the resolution implied a withdrawal from all the lands. To this day the debate over the meaning of Resolution 242 continues.

36 PRO/FCO/17/1735/3909193/The Annual Review for Israel for 1971, 1 January 1972, p. 2.

37 PRO/FCO/17/1735/3909193/The Annual Review for Israel for 1971, p. 3.

38 Ibid.

39 Ibid.

40 PRO/FCO/17/1735/3909193/The Annual Review for Israel for 1971, p. 4.

41 PRO/FCO/17/1735/3909193/The Annual Review for Israel for 1971, p. 5.

42 Mr Eban had little power within the ruling Israeli Labour Party. He was a prime example of an Israeli who was more popular abroad (particularly in the Foreign Office and US State Department) than he was at home. Some Israelis argued that he simply wasn't Israeli enough. The three potential successors to Mrs Meir were Mr Dayan, Mr Sapir and Mr Allon. The Foreign Office was not particularly impressed by any of the three successors or alternatives to Mrs Meir.

43 For more on the Rodgers Plan and its various versions, see Neill Lochery, *The View From the Fence: The Arab–Israeli Conflict from its Present to its Roots.*

44 PRO/FCO/93/124/3909360/Foreign Office Minute, Anthony Parsons, 25 June 1973.

45 This policy was originally recommended in the Annual Review for Israel for 1970, produced by the Embassy in Tel Aviv in January 1971.

46 PRO/FCO/17/1735/3909193/The Annual Review for Israel for 1971, 1 January 1972.

47 Ibid.

48 Ibid.

49 Ibid.

50 Although Sir Alec Douglas-Home was Foreign Secretary, he was also an ex-Prime Minister, and this gave his visit even greater significance to Israeli eyes. This was not the Foreign Secretary's first visit to Israel; he had visited the country in a private capacity on the eve of the Six Day War. This fact was widely reported in the Israeli press and added to the warmth of the Israeli welcome for him.

51 In reality, nobody expected any diplomatic progress prior to President Nixon's visit to Moscow. PRO/FCO/17/1748/3909267/Diplomatic Report No. 264/72, Your Visit to Israel, 27 March 1972, p. 3.

52 PRO/FCO/17/1748/3909267/Record of Meeting Between the Foreign Secretary and the Israeli Ministry of Foreign Affairs, 22 March 1972.

53 Ibid.

54 PRO/FCO/17/1748/3909267/Diplomatic Report No. 264/72, Your Visit to Israel, 27 March 1972, p. 2.

55 Ibid.

56 PRO/FCO/17/1748/3909267/Diplomatic Report No. 264/72, Your Visit to Israel, 27 March 1972, p. 1.

57 PRO/FCO/17/1749/3909268/Speech by Secretary of State, 18 September 1972.

58 PRO/FCO/17/1749/3909268/Correspondence From Mr Craig, Near East

and North Africa Department, Foreign Office to Mr Sydney Gifford, British Embassy, Tel Aviv, 13 October 1972.

59 The phrase was used later by Anthony Parsons to summarize Mr Craig's letter. PRO/FCO/17/1749/3909268/Correspondence from Anthony Parsons, Foreign Office to Bernard Ledwidge, Tel Aviv, 29 December 1972.

60 PRO/FCO/17/1749/3909268/Correspondence from Anthony Parsons, Foreign Office to Bernard Ledwidge, Tel Aviv, 29 December 1972.

61 Ibid.

62 Ibid.

63 PRO/FCO/17/1749/3909268/Correspondence from Mr Ledwidge, Tel Aviv to Mr Parsons, Foreign Office, 20 December 1972.

64 PRO/FCO/17/1749/3909268/Correspondence from Mr Ledwidge, Tel Aviv to Mr Parsons, Foreign Office, 20 December 1972, p. 1.

65 PRO/FCO/17/1749/3909268/Correspondence from Mr Ledwidge, Tel Aviv to Mr Parsons, Foreign Office, 20 December 1972, p. 2.

66 PRO/FCO/17/1749/3909268/Foreign Office Minute, Mr Craig, 12 December 1972.

67 Reported in PRO/FCO/17/1749/3909268/Correspondence From Anthony Parsons, Foreign Office to Bernard Ledwidge, Tel Aviv, 29 December 1972.

68 PRO/FCO/17/1749/3909268/Correspondence from Mr Parsons, Foreign Office to Mr Ledwidge, Tel Aviv, 15 December 1972.

69 PRO/FCO/17/1749/3909268/Press Cutting, UK Quietly Unhappy with Israel, *Jerusalem Post*, 5 December 1972. See also Britain is Waiting to Jump on the Band Wagon of Pressure Against Israel, *Maariv*, 30 November 1972.

70 Ibid.

71 Ibid.

72 Ibid.

73 Ibid.

74 PRO/FCO/17/1749/3909268/Correspondence from Mr Ledwidge, Tel Aviv to Mr Parsons, Foreign Office, 20

December 1972, 1–2.

75 PRO/FCO/17/1749/3909268/Correspondence from Mr Parsons, Foreign Office to Mr Ledwidge, Tel Aviv, 15 December 1972.

76 PRO/FCO/17/1749/3909268/Record of Meeting Between the Secretary of State and the Israeli Minister of Foreign Affairs, 11 December 1972.

77 Ibid.

78 PRO/FCO/17/1749/3909268/Record of Meeting Between the Israeli Prime Minister and the British Ambassador, 13 December 1972.

79 Ibid.

80 PRO/FCO/93/123/3909359/The Annual Review for Israel for 1972, 1 January 1973, pp. 2–3.

81 Ibid.

82 Ibid.

83 Ibid.

84 PRO/FCO/93/124/3909360/Foreign Office Minute, Mr Craig, 22 June 1973.

85 PRO/FCO/93/124/3909360/Foreign Office Minute, Mr Parsons, 25 June 1973.

86 PRO/FCO/93/124/3909360/Diplomatic Report, 266/73, First Impressions of Israel, Mr Ledwidge, 30 April 1973, p. 1.

87 Ibid.

88 Ibid.

89 Ibid.

90 Ibid.

91 PRO/FCO/93/124/3909360/Diplomatic Report, 266/73, First Impressions of Israel, Mr Ledwidge, 30 April 1973, p. 2.

92 Ibid.

93 PRO/FCO/93/124/3909360/Foreign Office Minute, Mr Craig, 22 June 1973.

94 Ibid.

95 Ibid.

96 Ibid.

97 Ibid.

98 PRO/FCO/93/197/3909526/Record of Meeting, Political Co-operation in Europe, Brussels, 21 May 1973.

99 PRO/FCO/93/197/3909526/Record of Meeting, Political Co-operation in Europe, Brussels, 21 May 1973, p. 2.

100 Ibid.

101 PRO/FCO/93/197/3909526/Record of Meeting, Political Co-operation in Europe, Brussels, 21 May 1973, p. 3.

Chapter 7

1 PRO/FCO/93/548/3912063/Correspondence from Mr P. Adams, Cairo to Mr A. Campbell, Foreign Office, 9 December 1974.
2 PRO/FCO/93/132/3909524/Correspondence from Mr Parsons, Foreign Office to Mr Ledwidge, Tel Aviv, 15 February 1973.
3 Ibid.
4 PRO/FCO/93/132/3909524/Correspondence from Mr Ledwidge to Mr Parsons, 24 January 1973.
5 Ibid.
6 PRO/FCO/93/132/3909524/Record of Meeting Between Mr Parsons and Mr Ruppin, Israeli Embassy, 9 February 1973, p. 1.
7 Ibid.
8 PRO/FCO/93/132/3909524/Record of Meeting Between Mr Parsons and Mr Ruppin, Israeli Embassy, 9 February 1973, p. 4.
9 PRO/FCO/93/132/3909524/The Middle East Conflict and Anglo–Israeli Relations, from Mr Ledwidge to Mr Parsons, 9 May 1973.
10 Ibid.
11 Ibid.
12 Ibid.
13 PRO/FCO/93/132/3909524/From Mr Ledwidge, Tel Aviv to Mr Craig, Foreign Office, 20 June 1973.
14 PRO/FCO/93/132/3909524/Record of Meeting Between Mr Ledwidge and General Dayan, 18 June 1973.
15 Ibid.
16 Ibid.
17 PRO/FCO/93/132/3909524/Correspondence from Mr Craig, Foreign Office to Mr Ledwidge, Tel Aviv, 28 June 1973.
18 PRO/FCO/93/132/3909524/Record of Meeting Between Mr Ledwidge and General Dayan, 18 June 1973.
19 Ibid.
20 868 PRO/FCO/93/132/3909524/Correspondence from Mr Craig, Foreign Office to Mr Ledwidge, Tel Aviv, 28 June 1973.
21 Ibid.
22 Ibid.
23 PRO/FCO/93/132/3909524/Record of Meeting Between Mr Ledwidge and General Dayan, 18 June 1973.
24 PRO/FCO/93/297/3912377/Quoted from Memorandum by Mr Craig, 10 August 1973.
25 PRO/FCO/93/297/3912377/Memorandum by Mr Craig, 10 August 1973.
26 PRO/FCO/93/297/3912377/Memorandum, Oil and Anglo–Arab Relations, Mr C. Crowe, 2 October 1973.
27 PRO/FCO/93/297/3912377/Memorandum, Oil and Anglo–Arab Relations, Mr C. Crowe, 2 October 1973, p. 7.
28 Ibid.
29 PRO/FCO/93/297/3912377/Memorandum, Oil and Anglo–Arab Relations, Mr C. Crowe, 2 October 1973, p. 9.
30 Ibid.
31 Ibid.
32 Ibid.
33 PRO/FCO/93/297/3912377/Memorandum, Oil and Anglo–Arab Relations, Mr C. Crowe, 2 October 1973, p. 10.
34 Ibid.
35 PRO/FCO/93/297/3912377/Memorandum, Oil and Anglo–Arab Relations, Mr C. Crowe, 2 October 1973, p. 13.
36 PRO/FCO/93/297/3912377/Memorandum, Oil and Anglo–Arab Relations, Mr C. Crowe, 2 October 1973, p. 14.
37 On this, see Chaim Herzog, *The War of Atonement: The Inside Story of the Yom Kippur War*, Greenhill Books, London, 1998.
38 PRO/FCO/93/444/3911968/The Annual Review for Israel for 1973, 16 January 1974, p. 1.
39 PRO/FCO/93/444/3911968/The Annual Review for Israel for 1973, p. 4.
40 Ibid.
41 PRO/FCO/93/444/3911968/The Annual Review for Israel for 1973, p. 5.
42 Ibid.
43 Ibid.
44 Ibid.
45 Ibid.
46 PRO/FCO/93/444/3911968/The Annual Review for Israel for 1973, p. 2.
47 PRO/FCO/93/132/3909524/Correspondence from Mr Craig, Foreign Office to Mr C. Giffard, Tel Aviv, 13 December 1973.

48 Ibid.
49 PRO/FCO/93/132/3909524/Correspondence from Mr Giffard, Tel Aviv to Mr Craig, Foreign Office, 28 November 1973.
50 PRO/FCO/93/132/3909524/Correspondence from Mr Craig, Foreign Office to Mr C. Giffard, Tel Aviv, 13 December 1973.
51 Ibid.
52 PRO/FCO/93/444/3911968/The Annual Review for Israel for 1973, p. 2.
53 Ibid.
54 For more details on the internal politics of Israel during this period, see Neill Lochery, *The Israeli Labour Party: In the Shadow of the Likud.*
55 PRO/FCO/93/704/4499360/Minute by Mr G. Williams, Near East and North Africa Department, 30 January 1975.
56 PRO/FCO/93/704/4499360/The Annual Review for Israel 1974, 8 January 1975.
57 Ibid.
58 Ibid.
59 Ibid.
60 Ibid
61 Ibid.
62 Harold Wilson and the Labour Party had defeated the Conservatives in the British general election held on 4 March 1974. Mr Wilson served until 5 April 1976, when he resigned unexpectedly and was replaced by James Callaghan.
63 PRO/FCO/93/448/3912066/Cable No. 255 from Tel Aviv to Foreign Office, 28 June 1974.
64 PRO/FCO/93/448/3912066/Record of Meeting Between the Prime Minister and the Prime Minister of Israel, 28 June 1974, p. 2.
65 PRO/FCO/93/448/3912066/Record of Meeting Between the Prime Minister and the Prime Minister of Israel, 28 June 1974, p. 3.
66 PRO/FCO/93/448/3912066/Correspondence from Mr D. Gladstone, Cairo to Mr D. Gore-Booth, Near East and North Africa Department, 15 July 1974.
67 PRO/FCO/93/447/3911971/Correspondence from Mr N. Williams, Near East and North Africa Department, Foreign Office to Private Secretary, 10 Downing Street, 28 March 1974.
68 PRO/FCO/93/447/3911971/Background Note, Supplementary No. 4, the Harrogate Speech, 28 March 1974.
69 PRO/FCO/93/447/3911971/Notes for Supplementaries for Foreign Secretary, Point 11 Harrogate Speech, undated.
70 PRO/FCO/93/548/3912063/Record of Meeting Between Mr B. Ledwidge and the Secretary of State, 17 December 1974.
71 Ibid.
72 PRO/FCO/93/548/3912063/Correspondence from Mr Ledwidge, Tel Aviv to Mr Campbell, Foreign Office, 20 November 1974.
73 922 PRO/FCO/93/548/3912063/Correspondence from Mr Craig to Mr Ledwidge, 31 December 1974.
74 PRO/FCO/93/548/3912063/Correspondence from Mr P. Adams, Cairo to Mr A. Campbell, Foreign Office, 9 December 1974.
75 Ibid.
76 Ibid.
77 Ibid.
78 Mr Allon also held the title of Deputy Prime Minister of Israel.
79 PRO/FCO/93/447/3911971/Record of Meeting Between Israeli Minister of Foreign Affairs and the Prime Minister, 28 July 1974.
80 Ibid.
81 Ibid.
82 Ibid.
83 PRO/FCO/93/708/3912079/Record of Meeting Between the Foreign Secretary and the Israeli Minister of Foreign Affairs, 1 March 1975.
84 PRO/FCO/93/708/3912079/Israeli Foreign Minister's Call on the Prime Minister, 14 April 1975.
85 Ibid.
86 PRO/FCO/93/708/3912079/Israeli Foreign Minister's Meeting with the Prime Minister, 18 January 1975.
87 Ibid.
88 PRO/FCO/93/708/3912079/Record of Meeting Between the Foreign Secretary and the Israeli Minister of Foreign Affairs, 1 March 1975.
89 Ibid.
90 Ibid.

91 Ibid.
92 PRO/FCO/93/708/3912079/Foreign Office Minute, Anglo–Israeli Bi-lateral Matters, Mr A. B. Urwick, Near East and North Africa Department, 25 March 1975.
93 Ibid.
94 Ibid.
95 Ibid.
96 Ibid.
97 PRO/FCO/93/789/3912257/Cable No. 114 from Mr Callaghan, Foreign Office to Tel Aviv, Washington and Cairo, 18 June 1975.
98 PRO/FCO/93/789/3912257/Cable No. 113 from Foreign Office to Tel Aviv, 18 June 1975.
99 PRO/FCO/93/789/3912257/Cable No. 114 from Mr Callaghan, Foreign Office to Tel Aviv, Washington and Cairo, 18 June 1975.
100 Ibid.
101 Ibid.
102 PRO/FCO/93/789/3912257/Cable No. 112, Meeting with Rabin, From Mr Callaghan, Foreign Office to Tel Aviv, Washington and Cairo, 16 June 1975.
103 Ibid.
104 Ibid.
105 PRO/FCO/93/789/3912257/Cable No. 206 from Mr Ledwidge, Tel Aviv to Foreign Office, 19 June 1975.
106 Ibid
107 Ibid.
108 PRO/FCO/93/710/3912255/Background Briefs for Meeting with Israeli Ambassador, 19 December 1975.
109 Ibid.
110 Ibid.
111 PRO/FCO/93/916/4499362/The Annual Review for Israel for 1975, 8 January 1975, p. 2.
112 Ibid.
113 PRO/FCO/93/916/4499362/The Annual Review for Israel for 1975, 8 January 1975, p. 3.
114 PRO/FCO/93/916/4499362/Correspondence from Mr A. Urwick, Near East and North Africa Department to Mr T. Elliot, 2 February 1976.
115 Ibid.
116 PRO/FCO/93/916/4499362/Correspondence from Mr A. Elliot, Tel Aviv to Secretary of State, 8 January 1975.
117 PRO/FCO/93/916/4499362/Correspondence from Mr T. Elliot, Tel Aviv to Mr A. Urwick, Foreign Office, 18 February 1975.
118 PRO/FCO/93/916/4499362/Correspondence from Mr A. Urwick to Mr T. Elliot, 2 February 1975.
119 PRO/FCO/93/705/3912251/Correspondence from Mr Ledwidge, Tel Aviv to Mr A. Urwick, Near East and North Africa Department, Foreign Office, 30 April 1975.
120 Ibid.
121 The reasons for both the timing of the Labour Party's electoral defeat in 1977 and the deeper reasons for its longer-term decline are complex. On this, see Neill Lochery, *The Israeli Labour Party: In the Shadow of the Likud*, pp. 23–62.

Chapter 8
1 PRO/FCO/93/918/4499493/Diplomatic Report No. 323/76, First Impressions of Israel, Mr A. Elliot, 28 April 1976, p. 5.
2 See, for example, Martin Gilbert, *Israel: A History*, Doubleday, London, 1998.
3 PRO/FCO/93/706/Report from Mr Ledwidge, Tel Aviv to Mr Callaghan, Foreign Office, undated.
4 Ibid.
5 PRO/FCO/93/918/4499493/Correspondence from Private Secretary, Downing Street to Mr Fergusson, Foreign Office, 10 September 1976.
6 PRO/FCO/93/918/4499493/Diplomatic Report No. 323/76, First Impressions of Israel, Mr A. Elliot, 28 April 1976.
7 Ibid.
8 PRO/FCO/93/918/4499493/Correspondence from Mr A. Urwick, Near East and North Africa Department, Foreign Office to Mr A. Elliot, Tel Aviv, 11 August 1976.
9 PRO/FCO/93/916/4499362/The Annual Review for Israel for 1975, 8 January 1976, p. 2.
10 PRO/FCO/93/916/4499362/The Annual Review for Israel for 1975, 8 January 1976, p. 9.
11 PRO/FCO/93/916/4499362/Correspondence from Mr Urwick, Foreign Office to

Mr Elliot, Tel Aviv, 2 February 1976.
12 Ibid.
13 Ibid.
14 PRO/FCO/93/916/4499362/Correspon-
    dence from Mr Elliot to Mr Urwick,
    18 February 1976.
15 Ibid.
16 Ibid.
17 Ibid.
18 PRO/FCO/93/916/4499362/Correspon-
    dence from Mr Urwick, to Mr Elliot,
    27 February 1976.
19 Ibid.
20 Ibid
21 Ibid
22 Ibid.
23 PRO/FCO/93/954/4499763/Correspon-
    dence from Mr Weir, Foreign Office to
    Mr W. Morris, Cairo, 25 June 1976.
24 Ibid.
25 Ibid.
26 Ibid.
27 Ibid.
28 PRO/FCO/93/916/4499362/Correspon-
    dence from Mr Elliot, Tel Aviv to
    Mr Weir, Foreign Office, 23 July 1976.
29 PRO/FCO/93/916/4499362/Correspon-
    dence from Mr I. Richard, UN, New
    York to Mr Weir, Foreign Office, 28 June
    1976.
30 Ibid.
31 PRO/FCO/93/916/4499362/Correspon-
    dence from Mr Elliot, Tel Aviv to
    Mr Weir, Foreign Office, 23 July 1976.
32 Ibid.
33 PRO/FCO/93/916/4499362/Correspon-
    dence from Mr D. Roberts, Damascus to
    Mr Weir, Foreign Office, 28 June 1976.
34 Ibid.
35 Ibid.
36 PRO/FCO/93/916/4499362/Correspon-
    dence from Mr W. Morris to Mr Weir,
    Foreign Office, 28 June 1976.
37 Ibid.
38 Ibid.
39 Ibid.
40 PRO/FCO/93/953/Foreign Office
    Report, Arab–Israel: The Next Few
    Months, 20 February 1976.
41 Ibid.
42 Ibid.
43 Ibid.

44 Ibid.
45 Ibid.
46 Ibid.
47 PRO/FCO/93/954/4499763/Foreign
    Office Report, Arab–Israel, Mr Weir,
    Near East and North Africa Department,
    23 June 1976.
48 PRO/FCO/93/954/4499763/Minute by
    Mr A. Urwick to Mr A. Duff, 23 June
    1976.
49 PRO/FCO/93/954/4499763/Foreign
    Office Report, Arab–Israel, Mr Weir,
    Near East and North Africa Department,
    23 June 1976.
50 Ibid.
51 Ibid.
52 Ibid.
53 Mr Hattersley left the Foreign Office
    after Mr Callaghan became Prime
    Minister. He was given his first cabinet
    post as Secretary of State for Prices and
    Consumer Protection.
54 PRO/FCO/93/954/4499763/Minute by
    Minister of State to Secretary of State,
    3 August 1976.
55 Ibid.
56 PRO/FCO/93/954/4499763/Report of
    Arab–Israel, Part Three: UK Interests and
    Policy, Mr M. Weir, 27 July 1976.
57 Ibid.
58 Ibid.
59 Ibid.
60 PRO/FCO/93/920/4499498/BBC Moni-
    toring Service, Untitled, *Jerusalem Post*,
    Joshua Brilliant, 15 September 1976. A
    short pre-publication account of the
    interview was broadcast on Israel Radio
    on 4 August 1976.
61 Ibid.
62 Ibid.
63 PRO/FCO/93/920/4499498/Migwan
    Questionnaire, Draft Responses, Mr F.
    Wheeler, Near East and North Africa
    Department, 2 July 1976.
64 PRO/FCO/93/920/4499498/Reported
    in Record of Meeting Between Minister
    of State and the Israeli Ambassador,
    1 November 1976.
65 Ibid.
66 PRO/FCO/93/920/4499498/Foreign
    Office Brief, Gideon Rafael, 6 July 1976.
67 PRO/FCO/93/920/4499498/Correspon-

dence from Mr Urwick to Mr Westbrook, 15 September 1976.

68 Ibid.

69 PRO/FCO/93/920/4499498/Record of Meeting Between Minister of State and the Israeli Ambassador on 17 September 1976.

70 PRO/FCO/93/920/4499498/Reported in Record of Meeting Between Minister of State and the Israeli Ambassador, 1 November 1976.

71 Ibid.

72 Ibid.

73 PRO/FCO/93/920/4499498/Foreign Office Minute, Mr Wheeler, 8 December 1976 and Response from Mrs M. Turner, 13 December 1976.

74 Ibid.

75 PRO/FCO/93/920/4499498/Briefing Paper for the Secretary of State's Meeting with the Israeli Minister of Foreign Affairs, UN, New York, 30 September 1976.

76 Ibid.

77 PRO/FCO/93/920/4499498/Correspondence from Mr M. Palliser to Mr W. Whitehead, 9 December 1976.

78 The Foreign Office identified these issues in its briefing papers for it's Ministers meetings with Israelis. PRO/FCO/93/920/4499498/Foreign Office Briefing Papers, 2 December 1976.

79 PRO/FCO/93/920/4499498/Foreign Briefing Paper, 30 September 1976.

80 PRO/FCO/93/920/4499498/Foreign Office Briefing Papers, 2 December 1976.

81 PRO/FCO/93/920/4499498/Foreign Briefing Paper, 15 September 1976, p. 1.

82 PRO/FCO/93/920/4499498/Foreign Briefing Paper, 15 September 1976, p. 10.

83 PRO/FCO/93/954/4499763/Report of Arab–Israel, Part Three: UK Interests and Policy, Mr M. Weir, 27 July 1976.

84 Ibid.

85 PRO/FCO/93/920/4499498/Foreign Briefing Paper, 30 September 1976, p. 2.

86 PRO/FCO/93/920/4499498/Foreign Briefing Paper, 30 September 1976, pp. 1–2.

87 A lot of the Israeli orders were simply for spare parts or ammunition for existing equipment.

88 On the impact of this decision on the long-term future of the ruling Israeli Labour Party see, Neill Lochery, *The Israeli Labour Party: In the Shadow of the Likud*.

89 PRO/FCO/93/920/4499498/Foreign Office Briefing Papers, 2 December 1976.

90 Gideon Rafael stated as much though the real change was much more subtle than Mr Rafael thought.

91 The importance of these ties was expressed in interviews conducted by the author with Israel Gat, Head of the International Section of the Israel Labour Party, 11 August 1994.

92 PRO/FCO/93/444/3911968/The Annual Review for Israel for 1973, 16 January 1974.

93 PRO/FCO/93/952/4499652/Correspondence from Mr A. Urwick to Mr M. Newington, Tel Aviv, 30 September 1976.

94 Ibid.

95 PRO/FCO/93/920/4499498/Foreign Office Briefing Paper on Yigal Allon, 30 September 1976.

96 PRO/FCO/93/951/4499649/Foreign Office Minute, Mr Allon's New Proposals, Mr Urwick, 22 September 1976.

97 Ibid.

98 Ibid.

99 PRO/FCO/93/951/4499649/Cable No. 300, from Mr Newington, Tel Aviv to Foreign Office, 21 September 1976.

100 PRO/FCO/93/951/4499649/Minute from Mr Weir, 23 September 1976.

101 PRO/FCO/93/951/4499649/Foreign Office Minute, Mr Allon's New Proposals, Mr Urwick, 22 September 1976.

102 PRO/FCO/93/951/4499649/Correspondence from Mr J. Poston, Tel Aviv to Mr D. Blatherwick, Near East and North Africa Department, Foreign Office, 30 June 1976.

103 Ibid.

104 Ibid.

105 Ibid.

Chapter 9

1 Thatcher Foundation Archive (MTF), Speech by Mrs Thatcher at dinner given

by Israel Prime Minister (Shimon Peres), 25 May 1986.

2 A copy of the photograph of Mrs Thatcher test driving the Challenger tanks can be found in Margaret Thatcher, *The Downing Street Years,* HarperCollins, London, 1993.

3 PRO/FCO/93/924/4499531/Cable No. 78 from Tel Aviv to Foreign Office, 25 March 1976.

4 Ibid.

5 PRO/FCO/93/924/4499531/Cable No. 78 from Tel Aviv to Foreign Office, 25 March 1976.

6 PRO/FCO/93/924/4499531/Correspondence from Mr Elliot, Tel Aviv to Mr Urwick, Foreign Office, 30 March 1976.

7 In the speeches that Mrs Thatcher gave during her visit, she was careful not to balance her comments. PRO/FCO/93/924/4499531/Cable No. 78 from Tel Aviv to Foreign Office, 25 March 1976.

8 PRO/FCO/93/924/4499531/Record of Meeting Between Mrs Thatcher and the Israeli Prime Minister, 23 March 1976.

9 Ibid.

10 Ibid.

11 John Campbell, *Mrs Thatcher: The Iron Lady,* Jonathan Cape, London, 2003, p. 56.

12 Ibid.

13 MTF/Letter from Mrs Thatcher to Anglo–Israel Friendship League, Published in *Finchley Times,* 6 December 1979.

14 Ibid.

15 MTF/Letter to *Finchley Times,* 3 April 1980.

16 The Israeli paper *Yediot Aharonot* raised this point in an interview with Mrs Thatcher. MT/Interview with Mrs Thatcher and *Yediot Aharonot,* 20 November 1987.

17 RL/original number 291836z Feb 84, Record of Meeting Between Casper Weinberger and Mrs Thatcher, 27 February 1984.

18 Mrs Thatcher made it clear that the PLO had to renounce violence and accept UN Resolution 242 before she would have any dealings with it. Despite this, from

time to time British Ministers did meet people with links to the PLO through the European Community.

19 MTF/Statement by Mrs Thatcher to House of Commons on Venice Declaration, 16 June 1980.

20 Ibid.

21 For the full text see http://ec.europa.eu/external_relations/mepp/decl/index.htm.

22 MTF/Response by Mr Callaghan to the statement by Mrs Thatcher to House of Commons on Venice Declaration, 16 June 1980.

23 Ibid.

24 Willie Morris's viewpoint was mirrored among the senior members of the Near East and North Africa Department in the Foreign Office.

25 PRO/FCO/93/954/4499763/Report of Arab–Israel, Part Three: UK Interests and Policy, Mr M. Weir, 27 July 1976.

26 On this, see Neill Lochery, *The View From the Fence: The Arab–Israeli Conflict from Its Present to Its Past.*

27 MTF/Press Conference for the Washington Press Club, Blair House, Washington DC, 26 February 1981.

28 MTF/Mrs Thatcher Interview with *Jewish Chronicle,* 12 June 1981.

29 Ibid.

30 Ibid.

31 Ibid.

32 MTF/Press Conference After European Summit, Luxembourg, 30 June 1981.

33 On this, see Neill Lochery, *The View From the Fence.*

34 Mrs Thatcher was extremely angered by both actions, raising them in future talks as examples of where Israel did whatever it wanted.

35 Mrs Thatcher was very strong in her condemnation of the Israeli strike on Iraq. She also told the *Jewish Chronicle* that it was a major breach of international law. MTF/Mrs Thatcher Interview with *Jewish Chronicle,* 12 June 1981.

36 Ibid.

37 MTF/Speech by Mrs Thatcher to Board of Deputies of British Jews, London, 15 December 1981.

38 Ibid.

39 Ibid.
40 John Campbell, *Mrs Thatcher: The Iron Lady*, Jonathan Cape, London, 2003, p. 337.
41 FCO/NFY/014/1/The Annual Review for Syria for 1982.
42 Ibid.
43 Reagan Library (RL), F96/107/129/Correspondence From President Reagan to Mrs Thatcher, 18 June 1982.
44 Ibid.
45 RL/F96/107/173/Correspondence from President Reagan to Mrs Thatcher, 7 March 1983.
46 RL/F96/107/183/Correspondence from Mrs Thatcher to President Reagan, 23 March 1983.
47 Margaret Thatcher, *The Downing Street Years*, p. 309.
48 Ibid.
49 Ibid.
50 Ibid.
51 Ibid.
52 Mrs Thatcher had appointed Sir Anthony Parsons as her Special Adviser in Foreign Policy and had started to build a foreign policy unit at Downing Street.
53 These strains were mainly originating from London over the future of the Occupied Territories.
54 For much of the previous year, Mrs Thatcher had been going out of her way to call for an Israeli freeze on building new settlements in the Occupied Territories and to stop expanding existing ones. See, for example, MTF/MRS Thatcher Radio Interview with IRN, 22 March 1983.
55 RL/original number 291836z Feb 84, Record of Meeting Between Casper Weinberger and Mrs Thatcher, 27 February 1984.
56 Ibid.
57 Ibid.
58 RL/NLS/F97/013/16/Memorandum of Conversation Between President Reagan and Mrs Thatcher, Camp David, 22 December 1984.
59 On this, see Neill Lochery, *The Israeli Labour Party: In the Shadow of the Likud*.
60 Ibid.
61 On the detailed reasons for this, see Neill Lochery, *The Israeli Labour Party*.
62 RL/NLS/F97/013/16/Record of Conversation between President Reagan and Mrs Thatcher, Camp David, 22 December 1984.
63 Ibid.
64 Ibid.
65 Ibid.
66 On the transformation of Mr Peres, see Shimon Peres, *Battling For Peace: Memoirs*, Weidenfeld and Nicolson, London, 1995.
67 Mrs Thatcher had also been extremely impressed by how Mr Peres had dealt with Israel's economic crisis and the use of a strong austerity programme to bring hyperinflation under control.
68 For more detail on this, see Neill Lochery, *The Israeli Labour Party*.
69 Despite the attempts to undermine him by Mrs Thatcher, Mr Shamir remained a fan of the British Prime Minister and her style of leadership, calling her a tough woman. Interview conducted by the author with Mr Shamir.
70 Harold Wilson had planned to undertake an official visit to Israel in the second part of 1976, but resigned from office earlier in the year.
71 MTF/Welcoming Remarks by Mr Peres at Ben-Gurion Airport, 24 May 1986.
72 Mr Peres had made a state visit to London in January of the same year. During the course of his visit he argued that Anglo–Israeli relations were improving due to a slight down-swing in British enthusiasm for the PLO. He saw relations as improving not rapidly, but rather in a gradual manner. MFA/9-10/141/Interview with Mr Peres on Israel Radio, 23 January 1986.
73 On the terms of the rotation agreement, see Neill Lochery, *The Israeli Labour Party: In the Shadow of the Likud*.
74 MTF/Speech by Mrs Thatcher at Dinner given by the Israeli Prime Minister, 25 May 1986.
75 Ibid.
76 Ibid.
77 Ibid.
78 MTF/Speech by Mrs Thatcher at Wreath

Laying Ceremony at Ben-Gurion's Tomb, 26 May 1986.

79 Ibid.

80 MTF/Speech by Mrs Thatcher at Weizmann Institute, 26 May 1986.

81 For more details on this, see Martin Gilbert, *Israel: A History*.

82 MTF/Speech by Mrs Thatcher at the King David Hotel, Jerusalem, 26 May 1986.

83 Ibid.

84 MTF/Press Conference Ending Visit to Israel, 27 May 1986.

85 Ibid.

86 Ibid.

87 Ibid.

88 Ibid. She also stated that the question of arms sales had not come up during her meetings with Israeli officials.

89 Ibid.

90 Many of Mr Peres' s own supporters hoped that he would renege on the deal and set up a new government. They argued that he had been one of the most successful Prime Minister's in Israel's history and that the outside world wanted him and not Mr Shamir to lead Israel into peace talks.

91 RL/S98/101/300/Correspondence Between President Reagan and Mrs Thatcher, 30 September 1987.

92 Ibid.

93 Ibid.

94 For more details on the 1988 election campaign and results, see Neill Lochery, *The Israeli Labour Party*.

95 MTF/Interview with Mrs Thatcher in *Jewish Chronicle*, 22 December 1987.

96 Mrs Thatcher expressed this in the House of Commons, Hansard/131/673/78/House of Common Questions, 19 April 1988.

97 RL/S98/101/300/Correspondence from President Reagan to Mrs Thatcher, 30 September 1987.

98 Ibid.

99 On this, see Neill Lochery, *The Israeli Labour Party: In the Shadow of the Likud*.

100 MTF/Interview with Mrs Thatcher in *Jewish Chronicle*, 22 December 1987.

101 To some degree this pressure paid off with the publication of an Israeli peace plan put together by Mr Shamir and Mr Rabin.

102 Hansard/142/869/74/Prime Minister's Question's, House of Commons, 1 December 1988.

103 Ibid.

104 Interviews conducted by the author with Yitzhak Shamir (Prime Minister) and Moshe Arens (Minister of Foreign Affairs, later Minister of Defence).

105 Mrs Thatcher referred to land for peace as 'peace with security'.

Chapter 10

1 Douglas Hurd, *Memoirs*, Little, Brown, London, 2003, p. 269.

2 Douglas Hurd, *Memoirs*, p. 269.

3 Douglas Hurd, *Memoirs*, p. 269.

4 Douglas Hurd, *Memoirs*, pp. 267–8.

5 Douglas Hurd, *Memoirs*, pp. 268–9.

6 This was very much a continuation of the belief of the Foreign Office about Mr Shamir during the Thatcher era.

7 On the coalition collapse, see Neill Lochery, *The Israeli Labour Party: In the Shadow of the Likud*.

8 Ibid.

9 The figures are from *Jewish Settlement in the West Bank and Gaza Strip: Profile 1992*, The International Centre for Peace in the Middle East, Tel Aviv, 1993, p. 29.

10 Ibid.

11 In reality, despite all the rhetoric from the Shamir Government only seven new settlements were built between 1990 and 1992. The major restraining factor appeared to be finance.

12 On this, see Asher Arian and Michal Shamir (eds), *The Elections in Israel 1992*, State University of New York Press, Albany, 1994.

13 For more on this decline, see Alan Clark, *The Tories: Conservatives and the Nation State, 1922–97*, Phoenix, London, 1999.

14 This is a constant theme in his memoirs, John Major, *The Autobiography*, HarperCollins, London, 2000.

15 Douglas Hurd, BBC Radio News, 13 September 1993.

16 Ibid.

17 On the 1992 election see Neill Lochery, *The Israeli Labour Party*; and Asher Arian

and Michal Shamir (eds), *The Elections in Israel 1992.*

18 Douglas Hurd, Column 846, House of Commons, Hansard Debates for 1 July 1992.

19 Author's interview with Yitzhak Shamir.

20 Douglas Hogg, Column 1007, House of Commons, Hansard Debates for 28 October 1992.

21 Ibid.

22 Douglas Hurd, Column 858, House of Commons, Hansard Debates for 25 November 1992.

23 Ibid.

24 Douglas Hogg, Column 1157, House of Commons, Hansard Debates for 27 November 1992.

25 On this, see Neill Lochery, *The View From the Fence.*

26 For more on Mr Rabin's campaign statements, see Neill Lochery, *The Israeli Labour Party.*

27 Interviews conducted by the author with Chaim Asa and Professor Gideon Doron, Members of Mr Rabin's Strategic Team for 1992 Election Campaign.

28 Ministry of Foreign Affairs (MFA)/13-14/41/Cabinet Declaration on Removal of Hamas Activists and Inclusion of Three Organizations as Terrorist Organizations, 16 December 1992.

29 MFA/13-14/44 Statement by Prime Minister Rabin on the Removal of Hamas Activists, 20 December 1992.

30 MFA/13-14/42/Security Council Resolution 799 (1992), Removal of Hamas Activists, 18 December 1992.

31 Douglas Hurd, Column 899, House of Commons, Hansard Debates for 13 January 1993.

32 Ibid.

33 See Shimon Peres, *Battling for Peace.*

34 See for example, Uri Savir, *One Thousand Days.*

35 Douglas Hurd, Column 329, House of Commons, Hansard Debates for 3 November 1993.

36 John Cunningham, Column 331, House of Commons, Hansard Debates for 3 November 1993.

37 MFA/13-14/110, Statement in the Knesset by Prime Minister Rabin on the Israel–PLO Declaration of Principles, 21 September 1993.

Chapter 11

1 PRO/FCO/93/132/3909524/Correspondence from Mr Parsons, Foreign Office to Mr Ledwidge, Tel Aviv, 15 February 1973.

2 On this, see Neill Lochery, *The Difficult Road to Peace: Netanyahu, Israel and the Middle East Peace Process*, Ithaca Press, Reading, 1999.

3 Neill Lochery, The Netanyahu Era: From Crisis to Crisis 1996–99, *Israel Affairs*, Volume 3 Numbers 3–4, Spring–Summer, 2000, pp. 221–37.

4 Middle East Peace Process: Israeli Issues and Actions, http://www.fco.gov.uk.

5 Ibid.

6 Ibid.

7 Ibid.

8 Ibid.

9 Ibid.

10 *The Independent,* 27 April 2004.

11 http://news.bbc.co.uk/1/hi/uk_politics/5256222.stm.

12 Middle East Peace Process: Israeli Issues and Actions, http://www.fco.gov.uk.

13 British participation in the Iraq War rekindled the Willie Morris fear from 1976, that Britain was out of touch with the Middle East policy of its European partners. The result of this was that its interests became vulnerable to Arab political and economic retaliation.

14 This was clear in Mr Blair's statements in the House of Commons as well as in his remarks during visits to Washington.

15 It should be remembered that, due to the extended period of Conservative Party rule in the UK (1979–97), none of the leading members of Mr Blair's Cabinet had any previous experience in government.

16 President Clinton's memoirs revealed the depth of his emotional and political commitment to the Middle East Peace Process. Bill Clinton, *My Life,* Hutchinson, London, 2004.

17 See Neill Lochery, *The Difficult Road to Peace: Netanyahu, Israel and the Middle*

East Peace Process, Ithaca Press, Reading, 1999.

18 *The Times,* 18 March 1998.

19 Robin Cook, House of Commons, Column 139, Hansard, 7 April 1998.

20 *Dispatch,* 19 March.

21 Comments by Tony Blair at Press Conference with Ehud Barak, 20 July 1999.

22 Ibid.

23 Comments by Tony Blair at a Press Conference with Ehud Barak, 23 November 1999.

24 On this question, see Neill Lochery, *Why Blame Israel,* Icon Books, Cambridge, 2005.

25 *Guardian,* 25 September 2001.

26 Ibid.

27 See www.britmb.org.il.

28 Reply to question given by Ian Pearson, Trade and Industry Minister, 4 May 2006, House of Commons, Hansard, 5 May 2006

29 Ibid.

30 Figures from British Embassy in Tel Aviv, www.britemb.org.il/ukisrael/bilateral.htm.

31 *Financial Times,* 16 November 2006.

32 For the text of the speech see http://www.number10.gov.uk/output/Page10409.asp.

33 Blair's decision on the timing of his exit was largely forced by internal party politics in Summer/Autumn 2006.

34 Speech by Tony Blair, Lord Mayor's Banquet, City of London, 13 November 2006.

35 Ibid.

36 Ibid.

37 On the findings of the Iraq Study Group, see The US Institute of Peace, www.usip.org/isg.

38 Ibid.

39 *The Scotsman,* 6 January 2007.

40 Often the reasons for anti-Israel sentiment differ from group to group and from individual to individual.

41 In his first press conference with the Israeli Prime Minister, Ehud Olmert, Mr Blair markedly refused to answer the question from the BBC's Middle East editor of the question of an Israeli withdrawal to 1967 lines. *Guardian,* 12 June 2006.

42 *Observer,* 25 September 2005.

43 On the notion of paying with Israeli currency, see Neill Lochery, *The Israeli Labour Party: In the Shadow of the Likud,* Ithaca Press, Reading, 1997, p. 186.

44 This speech was the seen as the defining moment of British policy towards the State of Israel and the lack of an Arab–Israeli settlement following the end of the first Arab–Israeli War.

45 See proceedings of a one-day conference, 'Suez, 50 Years On', University College London, 8 November 2006 (forthcoming).

46 The strong negative reaction to Eden's speech was articulated by both the Israeli government and in its newspapers.

47 See Neill Lochery, Anglo-Israel Relations Before and After Suez, Conference Proceedings (forthcoming).

48 *Jerusalem Post,* 20 November 2006.

49 *Observer,* 30 July 2006.

50 *Independent,* 26 September 2006.

51 For a general sweep of Mr Brown's views on the Middle East, see Interview with Gordon Brown, *The Politics Show,* BBC Television, 24 September 2006.

52 *New Statesman,* 18 December 2006.

53 An example of this was the joint British Treasury–World Bank Conference on the Economy of the Palestinian Territories, BBC News, 13 December 2005.

54 See *Daily Telegraph,* 19 January 2007. All major polls confirm a slight to moderate Conservative lead over Labour.

55 *Daily Telegraph,* 3 August 2006.

56 See Douglas Hurd's memoirs on his unease with dealing with the Israeli–Palestinian leaderships. Douglas Hurd, *Memoirs,* Little, Brown, London, 2003.

Conclusions

1 Statistics supplied by the Foreign Office, Middle East Peace Process: Israeli Issues and Actions, http://www.fco.gov.uk/.

Bibliography

Primary sources

Archival material

British Public Records Office (National Archives), Kew.
Central Bureau of Statistics, Jerusalem.
Central Zionist Archives, Jerusalem.
European Union, Brussels.
Knesset Archives, Jerusalem.
Library of Congress, Washington DC.
Mapai Archives, Beit Berl, Israel.
Ministry of Foreign Affairs, Jerusalem (MFA).
Ministry of Defence, Tel Aviv.
President Bush Presidential Library Archive.
President Carter Presidential Library.
President Clinton Presidential Library Archive.
President Eisenhower Presidential Library.
President Kennedy Presidential Library.
President Reagan Presidential Library Archive.
President Truman Presidential Library.
State Department, Foreign Relations Series, Truman to Nixon, Washington DC.
State Department Library, Washington DC.
UN General Assembly – Official Records, New York.
UN Secretary General – Official Records, New York.
UN Security Council – Official Records, New York.
UN Security Council – Supplementary Records, New York.

Autobiographies and memoirs

Abbas, Mahmoud, *Through Secret Channels: The Road to Oslo*, Garnet Publishing, Reading, 1995.
Albright, Madeline, *Madam Secretary: A Memoir*, Macmillan, London, 2003.
Arens, Moshe, *Broken Covenant: American Foreign Policy and the Crisis Between the US and Israel*, Simon and Schuster, New York, 1995.
Beilin, Yossi, *The Path to Geneva: The Quest for a Permanent Agreement, 1996–2004*, RDV/Akashic, New York, 2004.
Bentsur, Eytan, *Making Peace: A First-Hand Account of the Arab–Israeli Peace Process*, Praeger, Westport, 2001.
Boutros-Ghali, Boutros, *Egypt's Road to Jerusalem: A Diplomats Story of the Struggle for Peace in the Middle East*, Random House, New York, 1997.
Clinton, Bill, *My Life*, Hutchinson, London, 2004.
Clinton, Hilary Rodham, *Living History: Memoirs*, Headline, London, 2003.
Dayan, Moshe, *Breakthrough: A Personal Account of Egypt–Israel Negotiations*, Weidenfeld and Nicolson, London, 1981.

Dayan, Moshe, *Diary of the Sinai Campaign*, Da Capo Press, New York, 1966.
Dowek, Ephraim, *Israeli–Egyptian Relations 1980–2000*, Frank Cass, London and Portland, OR, 2001.
Eban, Abba, *Personal Witness: Israel Through My Eyes*, Jonathan Cape, London, 1993.
Eban, Abba, *The New Diplomacy: International Affairs in the Modern Age*, Weidenfeld and Nicolson, London, 1983.
Eban, Abba, *My Country*, Weidenfeld and Nicolson, London, 1972.
Farid, Abdel Magid, *Nasser: The Final Years*, Ithaca Press, Reading, 1994.
Govrin, Yosef, *Israeli–Soviet Relations: From Confrontation to Disruption*, Frank Cass, London and Portland, OR, 1998.
Heath, Edward, *The Autobiography: The Course of My Life*, Hodder and Stoughton, London, 1998.
Heseltine, Michael, *Life in the Jungle: My Autobiography*, Hodder and Stoughton, London, 2000.
Herzog, Chaim, *Living History: The Memoirs of a Great Israeli Freedom-Fighter, Soldier, Diplomat and Statesman*, Weidenfeld and Nicolson, London, 1997.
Hurd, Douglas, *Memoirs*, Little, Brown, London, 1993.
Jenkins, Roy, *Churchill*, Macmillan, London, 2001.
Kissinger, Henry, *Years of Renewal*, Weidenfeld and Nicolson, London, 1999.
Kissinger, Henry, *Diplomacy*, Touchstone, New York, 1994.
Kissinger, Henry, *Years of Upheaval*, Phoenix Press, London, 1982.
Kissinger, Henry, *White House Years*, Phoenix Press, London, 1979.
Major, John, *The Autobiography*, HarperCollins, London, 1999.
Meir, Golda, *My Life: The Autobiography*, Futura, London, 1976.
Nott, John, *Here Today: Gone Tomorrow*, Politico's, London, 2002.
Peres, Shimon, *Battling for Peace: Memoirs*, Weidenfeld and Nicolson, London, 1995.
Rabin, Yitzhak, *The Rabin Memoirs*, University of California Press, Berkeley, 1996.
Raviv, Moshe, *Israel at Fifty*, Weidenfeld and Nicolson, London, 1998.
Ross, Dennis, *The Missing Peace: The Inside Story of the Fight for Middle East Peace*, Farrar, Straus and Giroux, New York, 2004.
Shultz, George, *Turmoil and Triumph: My Years As Secretary of State*, Charles Scribner's Sons, New York, 1993.
Thatcher, Margaret, *The Downing Street Years*, HarperCollins, London, 1995.
Thatcher, Margaret, *The Path to Power*, HarperCollins, London, 1995.
Weizmann, Ezer, *The Battle for Peace*, Bantam Books, London, 1981.

Newspapers

Daily Telegraph (London).
Davar (Tel Aviv) – no longer published.
Guardian (London and Manchester).
Haaretz (Tel Aviv).
Jerusalem Post (Jerusalem).
Maariv (Tel Aviv).
Middle East Times (Cairo).
New York Times.
Syria Times (Damascus).
The Times (London).
Washington Post.
Yediot Aharonot (Tel Aviv).

Secondary sources: books and articles

Abu-Amr, 'Hamas: a Historical and Political Background', *Journal of Palestine Studies*, Volume 22, Number 4, Summer 1993, pp. 5–19.

Aburish, Said, *Nasser: The Last Arab*, Duckworth, London, 2004.

Al-Haj, Majid, 'Strategies and Mobilisation Among the Arabs in Israel', in Keith Kyle and Joel Peters, *Whither Israel: The Domestic Challenges*, I. B. Tauris, London, 1993, pp. 140–60.

Al-Khazender, Sami, *Jordan and the Palestine Question: The Role of Islamic and Left Forces in Shaping Foreign Policy-making*, Ithaca Press, Reading, 1997.

Allen, Roger and Chibli Mallat (eds), *Water in the Middle East*, British Academy Press, London, 1995.

Almog, Orna, *Britain, Israel and the United States 1955–58: Beyond Suez*, Frank Cass, London and Portland, OR, 2003.

Arian, Asher and Michal Shamir (eds), *The Elections in Israel 1996*, State University of New York Press, Albany, 1999.

Arian, Asher and Michal Shamir (eds), *The Elections in Israel 1999*, State University of New York Press, Albany, 2002.

Arian, Asher, *Security Threatened*, Cambridge University Press, Cambridge, 1995.

Arian, Asher, *The Second Republic: Politics in Israel*, Chatham House, Chatham, 1998.

Aronoff, Myron, *Israeli Visions and Divisions*, Transaction Books, New Brunswick, 1991.

Aronson, Shlomo, *Israel's Nuclear Programme: The Six-Day War and its Ramifications*, Kings College London Mediterranean Studies, London, 1999.

Ayubi, Nazih N., *Over-stating the Arab State: Politics and Society in the Middle East*, I. B. Tauris, London and New York, 1995.

Azmon, Yael and Dafna Izraeli (eds), *Women in Israel*, Transaction, New Brunswick, 1993.

Bailer, Uri, *Between East and West: Israel's Foreign Policy Orientation, 1948–1956*, Cambridge University Press, Cambridge, 1990.

Bailey, Sydney, *Four Arab–Israeli Wars and the Peace Process*, Macmillan, London, 1990.

Bar-On, Mordechai, *The Gates of Gaza: Israel Road to Suez and Back 1955–1957*, St Martin's Press, New York, 1994.

Bavly, Dan and Eliahu Salpeter, *Fire in Beirut: Israel's War in Lebanon with the PLO*, Stein and Day, New York, 1984

Begin, Menachem, *The Revolt: The Story of the Irgun*, Steimatzky, Tel Aviv, 1952.

Beilin, Yossi, *Israel: A Concise Political History*, Weidenfeld and Nicolson, London, 1992.

Beilin, Yossi, *Touching Peace: From the Oslo Accord to a Final Agreement*, Weidenfeld and Nicolson, London, 1999.

Ben Zvi, Abraham, *Decade of Transition: Eisenhower, Kennedy and the Origins of the American–Israeli Alliance*, Columbia University Press, Chichester, West Sussex, 1998.

Ben-Meir, Yehuda, 'Civil–Military Relations in Israel', in Keith Kyle and Joel Peters, *Whither Israel: The Domestic Challenges*, I. B. Tauris, London, 1993, pp. 223–43.

Ben-Meir, Yehudah, *Israeli Public Opinion, Final Status Issues: Israel–Palestinians, No. 6*, Jaffee Centre for Strategic Studies, Tel Aviv, 1995.

Ben-Zvi, Abraham, *The United States and Israel: The Limits of the Special Relationship*, Columbia University Press, New York, 1993.

Bernstein, Deborah (ed.), *Pioneers and Homemakers: Jewish Women in Pre-State Palestine*, State University of New York Press, Albany, 1992.

Biswas, Asit K. (ed.), *International Waters of the Middle East*, Oxford University Press, Oxford, 1994.

Blumenthal, Sidney, *The Clinton Years*, Farrar, Straus and Giroux, New York, 2003.

Bobbitt, Philip, *The Shield of Achilles: War, Peace and the Course of History*, Penguin, London, 2002.

Boutros-Ghali, Boutros, *Egypt's Road to Jerusalem*, Random House, New York, 1996.

Bulloch, John and Adel Darwish, *Water Wars: Coming Conflicts in the Middle East*, London, 1993.

Caplan, Neil, *Futile Diplomacy Volume Four, Operation Alpha and the Failure of Anglo–American Diplomacy in the Arab–Israeli Conflict*, Frank Cass, London and Portland, 1997

Carter, Jimmy, *The Blood of Abraham: In sights into the Middle East*, Houghton-Mifflin, Boston, 1985.

Clark, Alan, *The Tories: Conservatives and The Nation State 1922–1997*, Weidenfeld and Nicolson, London, 1998.

Cohen, Avner, *Israel and the Bomb*, Columbia University Press, New York, 1998.

Cohen, Michael, *Churchill and the Jews*, Frank Cass, London and Portland, OR, 2003.

Cohen, Mitchell, *Zion and State: Nation, Class and the Shaping of Modern Israel*, Blackwell, Oxford and New York, 1987.

Corbin, Jane, *Gaza First: the Secret Norway Channel to Peace Between Israel and the PLO*, Bloomsbury, London, 1994.

Cordesman, Anthony, *The Arab–Israeli Military Balance and the Art of Operations: An Analysis of Military Trends and Implications for Future Conflicts*, American Enterprise Institute, Lanham, MD, 1987.

Cordesman, Anthony, *Perilous Prospects: the Peace Process and the Arab–Israeli Military Balance*, Westview Press, Boulder, 1996.

Cordesman, Anthony, *The Military Balance in the Middle East*, Praeger, Westport, CT and London, 2004.

Dallek, Robert, *John F. Kennedy: An Unfinished Life, 1917–1963*, Penguin, London, 2003.

Dallek, Robert, *Lyndon B. Johnson: Portrait of a President*, Oxford University Press, New York, 2004.

Darboub, Leila, 'Palestinian Public Opinion and the Peace Process', *Palestine–Israel Journal*, Volume 3, Number 3–4, 1996, pp. 109–17.

Dershowitz, Alan M., *Why Terrorism Works: Understanding the Threat, Responding to the Challenge*, Yale University Press, New Haven, CT and London, 2002.

Diskin, Abraham, *Elections and Voters in Israel*, Praeger, New York, 1991.

Dowek, Ephraim, *Israeli–Egyptian Relations 1980–2000*, Frank Cass, London and Portland, OR, 2001.

Eban, Abba, *The New Diplomacy: International Affairs in the Modern Age*, Weidenfeld and Nicolson, London, 1983.

Edelman, Martin, *Courts, Politics and Culture in Israel*, University Press of Virginia, Charlottesville, 1994.

Eisenstadt, Shmuel, *Israeli Society*, Weidenfeld and Nicolson, London, 1968.

Eisenstadt, Shmuel, *Israeli Society Transformed*, Weidenfeld and Nicolson, London, 1985.

Elazar, David, *Building a New Society*, Indiana University Press, Bloomington, 1986.

Feldman, Shai and Abdullah Toukan, *Bridging the Gap: A Future Security Architecture for the Middle East*, Rowman and Littlefield, Oxford, 1997.

Feldman, Shai, *US Middle East Policy: The Domestic Setting*, Westview Press, Boulder, CO, 1988.

Feldman, Shai and Ariel Levite (eds), *Arms Control and the New Middle East Security Environment*, JCSS Study Number 23, Westview Press, Boulder, CO, 1994.

Fisk, Robert, *Pity the Nation: Lebanon at War*, Oxford University Press, Oxford, 1990.

Flamhaft, Ziva, *Israel on the Road to Peace: Accepting the Unacceptable*, Westview Press, Boulder, CO, 1996.

Freedman, Lawrence and Efraim Karsh, *The Gulf Conflict 1990–1991*, Faber and Faber, London and Boston, 1993.

Freedman, Robert, *The Middle East and the Peace Process: The Impact of the Oslo Accords*, University Press of Florida, Gainesville, 1998.

Friedland, Roger and Richard Hecht, *To Rule Jerusalem*, Cambridge University Press, New York and Cambridge, 1996.

Friedman, Isaiah, *Palestine: A Twice Promised Land – The British, the Arabs and Zionism*, Transaction Publishers, New Brunswick and London, 2000.

Fromkin, David, *A Peace to End All Peace: The Fall of the Ottoman Empire and the Creation of the Modern Middle East*, Phoenix Press, London, 2000.

Frum, David, *The Right Man: An Inside Account of the Surprise Presidency of George W. Bush*, Weidenfeld and Nicolson, London, 2003.

Garfinkle, Adam, *Politics and Society in Modern Israel: Myths and Realities*, M. E. Sharpe, Armonk, New York, 1997.

Gat, Moshe, *Britain and the Conflict in the Middle East 1964–67: The Coming of the Six-Day War*, Praeger, Westport, CT and London, 2003.

Gilbert, Martin, *Jerusalem in the Twentieth Century*, Chatto and Windus, London, 1996.

Gilbert, Martin, *Israel: a History*, Doubleday, London, 1998.

Gilbert, Martin, *The Routledge Atlas of the Arab–Israeli Conflict*, Routledge, London and New York, 2003.

Gilmour, David, *Lebanon: The Fractured Country*, Sphere Books, London, 1987.

Giuliani, Rudolph W., *Leadership*, Little, Brown, London, 2002.

Golan, Galia, *Yom Kippur and After*, Cambridge University Press, Cambridge, 1977.

Golan, Galia, *Soviet Policy in the Middle East: From World War II to Gorbachev*, Cambridge University Press, Cambridge, 1990.

Gordon, Haim, *Looking Back at the June 1967 War*, Praeger, Westport, CT and London, 1999.

Gorst, Anthony and Lewis Johnman (eds), *The Suez Crisis*, Routledge, London, 1997 (collection of documents).

Govrin, Yosef, *Israeli–Soviet Relations from Confrontation to Disruption*, Frank Cass, London and Portland, 1998.

Gresh, Alain, 'Turkish–Israeli–Syrian Relations and their Impact on the Middle East', *Middle East Journal*, Volume 52, Number 2, Spring 1998, pp. 188–203.

Grossman, David, *Sleeping on a Wire: Conversations with Palestinians in Israel*, Jonathan Cape, London, 1993.

Gruen, George, 'Dynamic Progress in Turkish–Israeli Relations', *Israel Affairs*, Volume 1 Number 4, Summer 1995, pp. 40–70.

Hahn, Peter, *The United States, Great Britain and Egypt 1945–1956: Strategy and Diplomacy in the Early Cold War*, The University of North Carolina Press, Chapel Hill and London, 1991.

Halberstam, David, *War in a Time of Peace: Bush, Clinton and the Generals*, Bloomsbury, London, 2003.

Hammel, Eric, *Six Days in June: How Israel Won the 1967 Arab–Israeli War*, Charles Scribner's Sons, New York, 1992.

Harkabi, Yehoshafat, *Israel's Fateful Hour*, Harper and Row, Philadelphia, 1986.

Hashem, Talhami Ghada, *Palestinian Refugees: Pawns to Political Actors*, Nova Science Publishers, New York, 2003.

Hattis-Rolef, Susan (ed.), *Political Dictionary of the State of Israel*, The Jerusalem Publishing House, Jerusalem, 1993.

Heikal, Mohammed, *Autumn of Fury: The Assassination of Sadat*, André Deutsch, London, 1983.

Held, Corbert, *Middle East Patterns Places, People and Politics*, Westview Press, Boulder, CO, 1994.

Heller, Joseph, *The Birth of Israel, 1945–1949*, University of Florida Press, Gainesville Florida, 2000).

Heller, Mark, *A Palestinian State*, Cambridge University Press, Cambridge, 1983.

Hennessey, Peter, *The Prime Minister: The Office and its Holders Since 1945*, Allen Lane, London, 2000.

Herzog, Chaim, *The Arab–Israeli Wars*, Vintage Books, New York, 1984.

Herzog, Chaim, *The War of Atonement: The Inside Story of the Yom Kippur War 1973*, Greenhill Books, London, 1998.

Hillel, Dan, *Rivers of Eden: The Struggle for Water and the Quest for Peace in the Middle East*, Oxford University Press, New York, 1994.

Hinnebusch, Raymond, 'Syria and the Transition to Peace', in Robert Freedman (ed.), *The Middle East and the Peace Process: The Impact of the Oslo Accords*, pp. 134–53, 1998.

Hinnebusch, Raymond, *The International Politics of the Middle East*, Manchester University Press, Manchester, 2003.

Hiro, Dilip, *Dictionary of the Middle East*, Macmillan, London, 1996.

Holbrooke, Richard, *To End a War*, Random House, New York, 1998.

Hourani, Albert, *A History of the Arab Peoples*, Faber and Faber, London, 1991

Hroub, Khaled, *Hamas: Political Thought and Practice*, Institute for Palestine Studies, Beirut, 2000.

Huntington, Samuel P., *The Clash of Civilizations and the Remaking of World Order*, Simon and Schuster, New York, 1996.

Hurwitz, Harry, *Begin: a Portrait*, B'nai B'rith books, Washington, DC, 1994.

Inbar, Efraim and Shmuel Sandler (eds), *Middle East Security: Prospects for an Arms Control Regime*, Frank Cass, London and Portland, OR, 1995.

Johnson, Paul, *A History of the Jews*, Phoenix Books, London, 1995.

Jones, Clive, *Soviet Jewish Aliyah 1989–92: Impact and Implications for Israel and the Middle East*, Frank Cass, London and Portland, OR, 1996.

Joyce, Miriam, *Kuwait 1945–1996: An Anglo–American Perspective*, Frank Cass, London and Portland, OR, 1998.

Kaplan, Robert D., *The Arabists: The Romance of an American Elite*, Free Press, New York, 1993.

Karsh, Efraim (ed.), *From Rabin to Netanyahu: Israel's Troubled Agenda*, Frank Cass, London and Portland, OR, 1997.

Karsh, Efraim, *Fabricating Israeli History*, Frank Cass, London and Portland, OR, 1997.

Katz, Shmuel, *Lone Wolf: A Biography of Vladimir Ze'ev Jabotinsky* (two volumes), Barricade Books, New York, 1996.

Kavanagh, Dennis and Anthony Sheldon, *The Powers Behind the Prime Minister: The Hidden Influence of Number 10*, HarperCollins, London, 1999.

Kedourie, Elie, *The Chatham House Version and Other Middle Eastern Studies*, Weidenfeld and Nicolson, London, 1970.

Kedourie, Elie, *The Crossman Confessions and Other Essays*, Mansell, London and New York, 1984.

Kedourie, Elie, *Politics in the Middle East*, Oxford University Press, Oxford, 1992.

Keegan, John, *The Iraq War*, Hutchinson, London, 2004.

Kelly, Saul and Anthony Gorst (eds), *Whitehall and the Suez Crisis*, Frank Cass, London and Portland, OR, 2000.

Khadduri, Majid and Edmund Ghareeb, *War in the Gulf, 1990–1991: The Iraq–Kuwait Conflict and its Implications*, Oxford University Press, Oxford and New York, 1997.

Kimche, David and Dan Bawly, *The Sandstorm, the Arab–Israeli War of June 1967: Prelude and Aftermath*, Secker and Warburg, London, 1968.

Kimmerling, Baruch and Joel Migdal, *The Palestinians: The Making of a People*, Harvard University Press, Cambridge, MA, 1994.

Kinross, Lord, *The Ottoman Empire*, Folio Books, London, 2003

Kretzmer, David, *The Legal Status of the Arabs in Israel*, Westview Press, Boulder, CO, 1990.

Kumaraswamy, P. (ed.), *Revisiting the Yom Kippur War*, Frank Cass, London and Portland, OR, 2000.

Kurzman, Dan, *Genesis 1948: The First Arab–Israeli War*, Da Capo Press, New York, 1992.

Kyle, Keith, *Suez*, St Martin's Press, New York, 1991.

Landau, Jacob, *The Arabs in Israel*, Oxford University Press, Oxford, 1969.

Laqueur, Walter, *A History of Zionism*, Schocken Books, New York, 1989.

Laqueur, Walter and Barry Rubin (eds), *The Arab–Israeli Reader: A Documentary History of the Middle East Conflict*, Facts on File Publications, New York, 1985.

Levey, Zach, *Israel and the Western Powers 1956–59*, University of North Carolina Press, Chapel Hill and London, 1997.

Levran, Aharon, *Israeli Strategy after Desert Storm: Lessons of the Second Gulf War*, Frank Cass, London and Portland, OR, 1997.

Lewis, Bernard, *The Middle East: 2000 Years of History from the Rise of Christianity to the Present Day*, Phoenix, London, 1996.

Lewis, Bernard, *The Multiple Identities of the Middle East*, Weidenfeld and Nicolson, London, 1998.

Lewis, Bernard, *The Crisis of Islam: Holy War and Unholy Terror*, Weidenfeld and Nicolson, London, 2003, p. 71.

Lewis, Bernard, *From Babel to Dragomans: Interpreting the Middle East*, Weidenfeld and Nicolson, London, 2004.

Liebman, Charles and Eliezer Don-Yehiya, *Civil Religion in Israel*, University of California Press, Berkeley, 1983.

Lochery, Neill, *The Israeli Labour Party: In the Shadow of the Likud*, Ithaca Press, Reading, 1997.

Lochery, Neill, *The Difficult Road to Peace: Netanyahu, Israel and the Middle East Peace Process*, Ithaca Press, Reading, 1999.

Lucas, Noah, *The Modern History of Israel*, Weidenfeld and Nicolson, London, 1974.

Mahler, Gregory, *Israel: Government and Politics in a Maturing State*, Harcourt, Brace Jovanovich, San Diego and New York, 1999.

Makovsky, David, *Making Peace with the PLO*, Westview Press, Boulder, CO, 1996.

Makovsky, David, 'How to Build a Fence', *Foreign Affairs*, March/April 2004, pp. 50–64.

Malki, Riad, 'The Palestinian Opposition and Final-Status Negotiations', *Palestine–Israel Journal*, Volume 3, Number 3–4, 1996, pp. 95–9.

Mansfield, Peter, *A History of the Middle East*, Viking, London and New York, 1991.

Ma'oz, Moshe, *Syria and Israel: From War to Peacemaking*, Oxford University Press, Oxford and New York, 1995.

Masalha, Nur, 'A Critique of Benny Morris', in Illan Pappe (ed.), *The Israel–Palestine Question: Rewriting Histories*, Routledge, London, 1999, pp. 211–20.

Massalha, Omar, *Towards the Long Promised Peace*, Saqi Books, London, 1992.

Mazzawi, Musa, *Palestine and the Law: Guidelines for the Resolution of the Arab–Israeli Conflict*, Ithaca Press, Reading, 1997.

Medding, Peter, *Mapai in Israel: Political Organisation and Government in a New Society*, Cambridge University Press, 1972.

Medding, Peter, *The Founding of Israeli Democracy 1948–1967*, Oxford University Press, Oxford, 1990.

Miller, Rory, *Divided Against Zion: Anti-Zionist Opposition in Britain to a Jewish State in Palestine 1945–48*, Frank Cass, London and Portland, OR, 2000.

Milton-Edwards, Beverley, *Islamic Politics in Palestine*, Tauris Academic Press, London, 1996.

Milton-Edwards, Beverley, *Contemporary Politics in the Middle East*, Polity Press, Cambridge, 2000.

Morris, Benny, *Righteous Victims: A History of the Zionist–Arab Conflict, 1981–1999*, John Murray, London, 1999.

Morris, Benny, *The Birth of the Palestinian Refugee Problem Revisited*, Cambridge University Press, Cambridge, 2004.

Morris, Edmund, *Dutch: A Memoir of Ronald Reagan*, HarperCollins, London, 1999.

Mutawi, Samir A., *Jordan in the 1967 War*, Cambridge University Press, Cambridge, 1987.

Neff, Donald, *Warriors at Suez: Eisenhower Takes the US into the Middle East in 1956*, Amana Books, Brattleboro, VT, 1988.

Netanyahu, Benjamin, *Fighting Terrorism: How Democracies Can Defeat Domestic and International Terrorists*, Allison and Busby, London, 1995.

Newman, David (ed.), *The Impact of Gush Emunim*, Croom Helm, London, 1985.

O'Brian, Conor Cruise, *The Siege: The Story of Israel and Zionism*, Paladin–Grafton Books, London, 1988.

Oren, Michael, *The Origins of the Second Arab–Israeli Conflict*, Frank Cass, London and Portland, OR, 1992.

Oren, Michael B., *Six Days of War: June 1967 and the Making of the Modern Middle East*, Penguin Books, London, 2003.

Ovendale, Ritchie, *The Origins of the Arab–Israeli Wars*, Longman, London, 1992.

Owen, Roger, *State Power and Politics in the Making of the Modern Middle East*, Routledge, London, 1992.

Oz, Amos, *In the Land of Israel*, Flamingo, London, 1984.

Pappe, Ilan (ed.), *The Israel/Palestine Question: Rewriting Histories*, Routledge, London and New York, 1999.

Peres, Shimon, *The New Middle East*, Henry Holt, New York, 1993.

Peretz, Don and Gideon Doron, *The Government and Politics of Israel*, Westview Press, Boulder, CO, 1997.

Quandt, William B., *Peace Process and the Arab–Israeli Conflict Since 1967*, The Brookings Institution, University of California Press, Berkeley, 2001.

Rabinovich, Abraham, *The Yom Kippur War: The Epic Encounter that Transformed the Middle East*, Schocken Books, New York, 2004.

Rabinovich, Itamar, *The War for Lebanon 1970–85*, Cornell University Press, Ithaca, NY and London, 1985.

Rabinovich, Itamar, *The Brink of Peace: The Israeli–Syrian Negotiations*, Princeton University Press, Princeton, NJ, 1998.

Ramsden, John, *An Appetite for Power: A History of the Conservative Party Since 1830*, Harper-Collins, London, 1988.

Randall, Jonathan, *The Tragedy of Lebanon*, The Hogarth Press, London, 1990.

Ranstorp, Magnus, *Hezbollah in Lebanon*, Macmillan, London, 1997.

Reich, Bernard and Gershon Kieval, *Israel: Land of Tradition and Conflict*, Westview Press, Boulder, CO, 1993.

Reinharz, Jehuda and Anita Shapira (eds), *Essential Papers on Zionism*, Cassell (New York University Press), London, 1996.

Richards, Alan and John Waterbury, *A Political Economy of the Middle East: State, Class and Economic Development*, Westview Press, Boulder, CO and Oxford, 1990.

Rubin, Barry, Joseph Ginat and Moshe Ma'oz (eds), *From War to Peace: Arab–Israeli Relations 1973–1993*, New York University Press, New York, 1994.

Rubin, Barry, *Revolution Until Victory: The Politics and History of the PLO*, Harvard University Press, Cambridge, MA, 1994.

Rubinstein, Amnon, *The Zionist Dream Revisited: From Herzl to Gush Emunim and Back*, Schocken Books, New York, 1984.

Sachar, Howard, *A History of Israel: From the Rise of Zionism to Our Time*, Knopf, New York, 1979.

Sachar, Howard, *Israel and Europe: An Appraisal in History*, Knopf, New York, 1999.

Said, Edward, *The Politics of Dispossession: The Struggle for Palestinian Self-Determination, 1969–1994*, Chatto and Windus, London, 1994.

Said, Edward, *Orientalism: Western Conceptions of the Orient*, Penguin, London, 1995.

Said, Edward, *Peace and Its Discontents: Gaza–Jericho, 1993–1995*, Vintage, London, 1995.

Sandler, Shmuel, *The State of Israel, the Land of Israel: Statist and Ethnonational Dimensions of Foreign Policy*, Greenwood Press, Westport, CT, 1993.

Sayigh, Yezid, *Armed Struggle and the Search for State: The Palestinian National Movement, 1949–1993*, Oxford University Press, Oxford, 1997.

Schiff, Ze'ev and Ehud Ya'ari, *Israel's Lebanon War*, George Allen and Unwin, London and Sydney, 1984.

Schiff, Ze'ev and Ehud Ya'ari, *Intifada: The Palestinian Uprising, Israel's Third Front*, Simon and Schuster, New York, 1990.

Seale, Patrick, *Asad: The Struggle for the Middle East*, University of California Press, Berkeley, 1988.

Seldon, Anthony (ed.), *The Blair Effect: The Blair Government 1997–2001*, Little, Brown, London 2001.

Shadid, Mohammed, 'A Housing Strategy for the Palestinian Territories', in A. B. Zahlan (ed.), *The Reconstruction of Palestine: Urban and Rural Development*, Kegan Paul International, London and New York, 1997.

Shalev, Michael, *Labour and the Political Economy in Israel*, Oxford University Press, Oxford, 1992.

Shapira, Anita, *Land and Power: The Zionist Resort to Force 1881–1948*, Stanford University Press, Stanford, CA, 1992.

Shapiro, Yonathan, *The Road to Power: Herut Party in Israel*, State University of New York Press, Albany, 1991.

Sharkansky, Ira, *The Political Economy of Israel*, Transaction Books, New Brunswick, 1987.

Sheffer, Gabriel (ed.), *US–Israeli Relations at the Crossroads*, Frank Cass, London and Portland, OR, 1997.

Shepherd, Naomi, 'Ex-Soviet Jews in Israel: Asset, Burden or Challenge', *Israel Affairs*, Volume 2, Number 1, Winter 1994, pp. 245–66.

Shepherd, Naomi, *Ploughing Sand: British Rule in Palestine, 1917–1948*, John Murray, London, 1999.

Sherman, Martin. *The Politics of Water in the Middle East: An Israeli Perspective on the Hydro-Political Aspects of the Conflict*, Macmillan Press, London, 1999.

Shimoni, Gideon, *The Zionist Ideology*, Brandeis University Press, Hanover and London, 1995.

Shlaim, Avi, *Collusion Across the Jordan: King Abdullah, the Zionist Movement and the Partition of Palestine*, Clarendon Press, Oxford, 1988

Shlaim, Avi, *The Iron Wall: Israel and the Arab World*, W. W. Norton and Company, New York and London, 2000.

Shulewitz, Malka Hillel (ed.), *The Forgotten Millions: The Modern Jewish Exodus from Arab Lands*, Cassell, London and New York, 1999.

Smooha, Sammy, *Israel: Pluralism and Conflict*, Routledge and Kegan Paul, London, 1978.

Smooha, Sammy, 'Jewish Ethnicity in Israel', in Kyle Keith and Joel Peters, *Whither Israel: The Domestic Challenges*, I. B. Tauris, London, 1993, pp. 161–76.

Sofer, Sasson, *Zionism and the Foundations of Israeli Diplomacy*, Cambridge University Press, Cambridge and New York, 1998.

Stein, Kenneth W., *Heroic Diplomacy: Sadat, Kissinger, Carter, Begin and the Quest for Arab–Israeli Peace*, Routledge, New York and London, 1999.

Stephanopoulos, George, *All Too Human: A Political Education*, Hutchinson, London, 1999.

Swirski, Barbara and Marilyn Safir (eds), *Calling the Equality Bluff: Women in Israel*, Pergamon, New York, 1991.

Swirski, Shlomo, *Israel: The Oriental Majority*, Zed Books, London, 1989.

Tal, David (ed.), *The 1956 War: Collusion and Rivalry in the Middle East*, Frank Cass, London and Portland, OR, 2001

Tessler, Mark, *A History of the Israeli–Palestinian Conflict*, Indiana University Press, Bloomington and Indianapolis, 1994.

Teveth, Shabtai, *Moshe Dayan: The Soldier, the Man, the Legend*, Quartet Books, London, 1974.

Thatcher, Margaret, *Statecraft: Strategies for a Changing World*, HarperCollins, London, 2002.

The Middle East and North Africa, Europa Publications, London, published annually.

Vatikiotis, P. J., *The History of Modern Egypt: From Muhammad Ali to Mubarak*, Weidenfeld and Nicolson, London, 1991.

Vital, David, *The Origins of Zionism*, Clarendon Press, Oxford, 1975.

Vital, David, *Zionism: The Crucial Years*, Oxford University Press, Oxford, 1987

Vital, David, *Zionism: The Formative Years*, Oxford University Press, Oxford, 1988.

Woodward, Bob, *The Commanders*, Simon and Schuster, New York, 1991

Woodward, Bob, *Bush at War*, Pocket Books, London, 2003.

Woodward, Bob, *Plan of Attack*, Simon and Schuster, New York, 2004.

Wright, J, *The Political Economy of Middle East Peace: The Impact of Competing Trade Agendas*, Routledge, London, 1999.

Yapp, Malcolm, *The Near East Since the First World War: A History to 1995*, Longman, London and New York, 1996.

Yishai, Yael, *Between the Flag and the Banner: Women in Israeli Politics*, State University of New York Press, Albany, 1997.

Young, Hugo, *This Blessed Plot: Britain and Europe From Churchill to Blair*, Macmillan, London, 1988.

Young, Hugo, *One of Us*, Macmillan, London, 1991.

Zak, Moshe, 'Israel and Jordan: Strategically Bound', *Israel Affairs*, Volume 3, Number 1, Autumn 1996, pp. 39–60.

Ziberfarb, Ben-Zion, 'The Israeli Economy in the Era of Peace', *Israel Affairs*, Volume 3, Number 1, Autumn 1996, pp. 1–12.

Index

consecrated ground. At Ivelet, the coffins were put down to allow the pallbearers to have a rest. A large coffin-shaped stone on the north bank of the river marks the traditional resting spot.

It is widely believed in Wharfedale that Barguest has his lair in Trollers Gill, high up on the moors north of Appletreewick. It is there that he rests up during the day, before setting out at dusk to roam over Yorkshire to bring misfortune, misery and death to those he makes eye contact with.

In 1881 the local scholar James Dixon recorded a verse that relates to the fearsome Barguest of Troller's Gill. It was not clear whether he had collected as a local traditional poem or if he had written it himself:

On the steep fell's crest did the moonlight rest, The beams illumined the dale;
And a silvery sheen clothed the forest green, As it swayed to the morning gale.
From Burnsall's tower the midnight hour, Had tolled; and all was still,
Save the music sweet, to the tiny feet, Of the elfin band, from the fairy land,
That tripped on the rounded hill.
From his cot he stepped, while the household slept, And he caroll'd with boisterous glee;
But he no hied to the green hill side, The fairy train to see.
He went not to stray with his own dear May, Along by a pine-clad scar:
And loving gaze on the dazzling rays, That shot from the Polar-star.
On what intent is the Troller bent?, And where is the Troller bound?
To the horrid gill of the eerie hill, To call on the Spectre Hound.
And on did he pass, o'er the dew-bent grass, While the sweetest perfumes fell
From myriad flowers, where forest bowers, O'ershadow that fairy dell.
And before his eyes did the dark gill rise, No moon-ray pierc'd its gloom;
And his steps around, did the waters sound, Like a voice from a haunted tomb.
And there as he slept, a shuddering crept, O'er his frame, scarce known to fear,
For he once did deem the sprite of the stream, Had loudly called "Forbear!"
An aged yew in the rough cliffs grew, And under its sombre shade,
Did the Troller rest, while with charms unblest, He a magic circle made.
Then thrice did he turn, where the streamers burn, And thrice did he kiss the ground;
And with solemn tone in that gill so lone, He called on the Spectre Hound.
And a whirlwind swept by and stormy grew the sky, While the torrent louder roared;
And a lurid flame o'er the Troller's stalwart frame, From each cleft of the gill was poured.
And a dreadful thing from the cliff did spring; Its wild bark thrilled around;
And a fiendish glow flashed forth I trow, From the eyes of the Spectre Hound.
When on Barden's height glowed the mountain light, And borne on the mountain air,
The priory bell did the peasants tell, 'Twas the hour of the matin prayer.
By shepherd men, where the lurid glen Doth its rugged jaws expand,
A corse was found, where a dark yew frown'd, And marks were imprest on the dead man's
breast,
But they seemed not by mortal hand.
In the evening calm a funeral psalm, Slowly stole o'er the woodland scene;

The hare-bells wave o'er a new-made grave, In Burnstall's churchyard green.
That funeral psalm in the evening calm, Which echo'd the dell around,
Was his dirge o'er whose grave blue hare-bells wave, Who call'd on the Spectre Hound.

Also in the 1880s, a man in Threshfield, west of Troller's Gill, had a large black goat that he kept chained in a small paddock. One time, it broke loose and trotted down the lanes with its chain dragging behind it, looking and sounding for all the world like Barguest. The village miller was returning on his cart from a long day at Kettlewell Market came across the goat and was terrified. He fell to his knees and began praying fervently for spiritual salvation, which is where he was found by the goat's owner a few minutes later.

One of the towns that Barguest invaded was Ossett. In the 1860s the creature was seen more than once patrolling the lane that led down to Horbury Bridge. Barguest has also been seen in the streets of Cowling, Colton and Haworth. All three places are relatively small, but Barguest has also been reported in the centre of York itself. The fatal dog is said to prowl the narrow alleys, known as snickleways, in search of human prey.

Barguest has also been reported at Baildon, where it has the curious feature of having webbed feet. It prowls along the Esk Valley, announcing a death in the family of those who see it. At Grassington Barguest is said to have coloured rings around its eyes. No such colourful features are to be seen on the Barguest of Longshaw Moor above Grindlesford, although it can be frightened off by a loud shout — something that would not be wise to try on the great hound reported at Milnsbridge. The spectral hound has also been reported on Ilkley Moor, Norton, Sedbergh, Sheffield, Skipton and Todmorden. At Thornton the Barguest had a mission, that of guarding a spring.

Not all encounters with Barguest bring bad luck, at least not for all. A Methodist minister named Thomas Reynard was walking home from Keighly to Silsden one evening in the February 1893. When he reached Spring Crag Wood he was puzzled when a large black dog trotted out of the trees and regarded him silently. As Reynard continued, the dog fell in beside him. On the far side of the wood, Reynard could see two men lurking in a rather sinister fashion by the roadside. The dog now moved in front of the minister instead of by his side, and when it reached the two men it stopped and glared at them. The two men stood to one side and Reynard passed on without a word.

Later that evening, a farm boy walking along the same road was attacked by two burly men, who beat him and stole what little money he had. The minister, at least, had reason to thank the great black dog.

Nor do all sightings of the spectral hound belong in the distant past. At just gone 9 o'clock one summer's evening in 2001, two women were driving along the A684 from Northallerton to Leeming Bar when a large black dog bounded onto the road in front of them. The driver slammed on the brakes, but did not stop in time. As the car juddered to a halt, the driver was about to get out to look for the dog's body, but the passenger stopped her. The passenger had seen the dog pass through the bonnet like a shadow. The hound was described as having floppy ears, no clear face and to be large and black.

The main street of Kirkby Overblow is haunted by a ghostly hound — the phantom of a real dog that died here some three centuries ago.

During the 1960s several residents of Hillsborough reported seeing an odd, large black dog. Then a policeman patrolling Taplin Road sighted the hound. He approached carefully so as not to frighten the dog away, and managed to get it backed into a corner. The dog glared at him with almost human emotion, then vanished into thin air.

Opinion is divided as to what the Barguest might be. The 'guest' part of his name is almost certainly derived from a Yorkshire dialect form of the word 'ghost', meaning spirit or phantom. The 'bar' element may come from 'bear', 'burh' (town), 'berg' (mountain), 'bier' (as used in a funeral) or from some other source; nobody is really certain. Some think that he is a real ghostly dog of some kind, although the wide range over which he wanders would indicate that he is no conventional spectre.

Others are of the opinion that the Barguest does not really exist at all. They suggest that he is instead a dimly remembered deity of pagan days, converted by early Christian missionaries into a demon dog. This would certainly account for the vast territory over which he wanders and the consistent themes in stories about him. On the other hand, if Barguest did not exist and never had, one would hardly expect people to see him.

Some scholars link Barguest to a theory that might underpin a wide range of supernatural phenomena. It has been theorised that the human mind is capable of inadvertently creating paranormal events by the sheer strength of willpower. So, if enough people believe that something exists – such as a huge black dog with glowing red eyes – then one will be called into existence from time to time. In other words, the Barguest really does exist, simply because people believe that it does. Such a theory is scorned by conventional scientists, but that does not necessarily mean that it is untrue.

The Barguest is not the only phantom dog to be found in Yorkshire. In the 1970s an old house near Whitby was converted into a nursing home. It was soon obvious that it was haunted by a ghostly collie dog that would enter the rooms of sleeping staff members, but only if they were unmarried women. Local talk had it that this was the ghost of a collie that had been the pet of a serving girl in the house in Victorian days. The girl had fallen sick and died one winter, and the collie had refused to leave her body. It had sat beside her body while it was laid out, then followed it first to the undertakers and then to the graveyard. There the faithful collie stayed, until one morning it was found frozen to death.

At Kirkby Overblow the locals have their own ghostly hound. Back in the late 17th century a shepherd was out on the hills when he fell suddenly ill. He left his sheepdog to guard the flock and staggered back to the village to take to his bed. A fever struck, and for days he was bedridden, too sick even to talk. When he was well enough to sit up, he sent a man up to the hills to bring in the flock of sheep. During the time that the man had been unconscious his poor dog had starved to death. Its phantom now patrols the hills around Kirkby Overflow and on occasion has been seen padding into the village, perhaps seeking its long-dead master.

Just west of Brigham on the River Hull is a crossroads where Brigham Lane crosses the B1249. This crossroads was, in the second half of the 19th century, the home of a local tramp named Willie Sled, who had a white dog as his constant companion. One day in the 1880s Willie Sled was gone. Nobody knew where he had gone, nor why he had left, but his little hut

was empty and his few meagre belongings had vanished. A few months later the white dog came back, or at least so the locals thought. The dog was seen often, but nobody could ever approach it, as it ran off out of sight whenever anyone got too close. As the months and then years passed, it dawned on the good folk of Brigham that the dog was a ghost. Willie Sled's dog haunts the crossroads still, but what became of Willie Sled remains a complete mystery.

CHAPTER 10

Mysterious Unknown Beasts

While dragons, Barguest and spectral hares belong to the realms of the supernatural, the Yorkshire animals in this chapter might belong to the world of flesh and blood. Reports of the Loch Ness Monster, Yeti, Bigfoot and Spotted Lion occasionally hit the news headlines. The study of such mysterious animals is known as cryptozoology, meaning 'the study of hidden animals', while the animals themselves are known as cryptids, meaning 'the hidden ones'. While these animals are as yet unknown to science, it is not common knowledge that new species of animal turn up all the time; in 2010 a new species of lemur was found on Madagascar. Nor are all these new animals small; a previously unknown type of antelope turned up in Vietnam in 1992.

It might seem bizarre to suggest that large creatures could exist in a county as populated as Yorkshire without being seen, captured and identified within a very short time. A cautionary tale comes from Strathglass, near Inverness. In 1978 local farmers began reporting that their sheep were being killed and eaten by some wild animal that inflicted injuries entirely unlike those caused by a dog. A few months later a farmer spotted some tracks and photographed them. Undeniably, these came from a big cat of some kind. The police and scientists were dismissive; there were no big cats in Britain.

In the summer of 1980 sightings of the killer cat began. It was described as being about 2ft tall and 8ft long, having a light-brown coat and a thick tail of a slightly darker colour. Local farmers got out their books about wild cats and soon identified the creature they were seeing as a cougar, sometimes called the puma, a wild cat native to North America. Still, scientists were dismissive, and the local press became more jocular in its reporting of sightings and sheep killings. One farmer, Ted Noble, got annoyed by this attitude. He read up on accounts of cougar-hunting techniques and decided that the safest method was to set a baited trap in an area where he had seen the cougar more than once. This he did, and on 29 October 1980 he caught the mysterious sheep-killer.

To everyone's amazement, except those who had been reporting seeing the cat for so long, it turned out to be a genuine cougar. When sent to a zoo for study, the cat was found to be a six-year-old male. Nobody suggests that the cougar is native to Scotland, so presumably the cat had escaped or been released from a private collection. The incident does show, however, that large animals can survive in Britain for considerable periods of time without any difficulty, and that unless somebody makes seriously determined efforts to catch them, they can remain at large. The scientists who dismissed the sightings were wrong, and the locals who saw the cougar were right.

Turning now to sightings in Yorkshire, we enter the world of the animals dubbed 'Out Of Places' (OOPs) or 'Anomalous Big Cats' (ABCs) by researchers. Whether these animals are escapees from zoos, beasts set loose by animal rights campaigners, or beasts supernaturally transported from foreign climes is very much a matter of opinion.

When the police are called in to deal with sightings of potentially dangerous animals, they invariably assume that the animal has escaped from somewhere. Since the Dangerous Animals Act of 1976, anyone keeping such a creature must register the fact with the police and keep it in secure conditions approved by animal experts. The police can therefore contact anyone in the area who keeps an animal such as that reported. Invariably, it turns out that no such animal has escaped, so the police usually fall back on the explanation that the witness was mistaken. Undoubtedly, some might turn out to be cases of mistaken identity, but some sightings are at close quarters and in conditions of good visibility, so that explanation does not always hold true.

Having started with the undeniably true Inverness Cougar of 1979, it is probably best to start with the big cats reported in Yorkshire. Since the 1960s there have been no less than 127 sightings of big cats in Yorkshire. Some of these could be dismissed as sightings of poor quality, given the light conditions and fleeting nature of the sightings, but others are much more reliable.

The fearsome fangs of a cougar, or puma, the largest wild cat of North America. Persistent reports of sightings of a large cat identical to one of these beasts have been made across Yorkshire for most of the later 20th century.

In 2009 Helen Morris of Dobcross was driving on the A640 from Denshaw towards Rochdale when she came across a big cat. It was 6 o'clock in the morning and the weather was clear and bright. She later reported:

At first I thought it was a sheep, so I slowed down, but the car didn't phase the animal – it wasn't frightened at all. When I got up close I could see the animal was a cat-like creature, almost like a female lion with a long tail. It had huge green eyes, a tawny coat and was the size of a large dog. I kept beeping my horn to try and get it to move. It was quite scary because I didn't really know what it was or how it would react. It was only when I drove right up to it that it calmly walked off onto the moorland. I told the police about it and they said it wasn't the first time sightings of the creature had been reported. I just wanted to make people aware that it was out there. Farmers should also be aware, as should ramblers using the moors. I drive that way every morning and I have never seen it before. There is lots of space round there for it to roam.

There is indeed a lot of space up on the moors, and plenty of food for a carnivore to find. Of course, the weather is not always kind to animals native to warmer climes. The police were quite right to tell Mrs Morris that they had already had similar reports.

A tiger was seen in several places around Church Fenton in 2006. Police mounted detailed searches for the beast, but it was never found.

On 16 June 2006, for instance, a woman was driving from Ryther to Ulleskelf along the B1223 at 10 o'clock in the morning in conditions of clear air and bright sunshine. Coming around the corner by Ozendyke Farm, she saw standing by the side of the road a strange creature. She braked to a halt, with the animal some 50 yards ahead of her. The animal turned to look at her, then pushed through a hedge into a field and vanished from sight. When the animal was gone, the woman drove to her home and called the police. She described the animal as having been a cat about 6ft long. It was, she said, a tawny-orange colour with thick, black stripes running vertically from the back to the belly.

When the police arrived they carried out a search of the area, but found nothing. They were just about to write it off as mistaken identity when a second telephone call came in. Two miles south west of the first sighting, another motorist had spotted a large cat with a striped coat. This sighting was in Common Lane, Church Fenton. It was this second sighting that was the first to reach the press, and so the animal became known as the Church Fenton Tiger. Next day a third sighting was made, although not in such good conditions, alongside the A1 south of Bramham. The police launched a major hunt, calling in a light aircraft from RAF Church Fenton to join the hunt.

The tiger hit the local headlines, but no other sightings were made. Inspector Steve Ratcliffe of North Yorkshire Police summed up the official view of events a few days later, when he said, 'We deployed some units to make a search of the area. Unfortunately, we were unable to confirm this sighting or locate the tiger.'

Four years earlier it had been Kirkheaton that had been the centre of attention. It was Jim Gibb of Cockley Hill Lane who first reported the big cat to the press. On 22 January he had got up early to go to work on his market garden. It was just before dawn that he stepped out of his front door and stopped in amazement at what he saw. Illuminated by the street light a few feet away he saw a large cat-like animal with a short tail and tufted ears. The colour of the coat was difficult to determine in the lighting, but it was a pale colour. The cat looked at him, apparently also having been taken by surprise, then slunk off to the farmland that adjoined the garden.

Once the sighting hit the press, others came forward with their own stories. Darren Green had been visiting his allotment on Town Road when he came across a dead fox with deep, narrow scratch marks on its neck. The fox was only recently dead. Darren and his girlfriend Claire were speculating what could have caused the injuries when they saw a spotted cat dash off from the allotment to nearby fields.

The press contacted the police for a statement. Chief Inspector Chris Hardern said, 'We have had a report from someone who thought he saw a big cat, so we are aware of it, but we have not been told of any further sightings since.'

The animal that most closely matched the descriptions of this animal was the lynx. Unlike the tiger, the lynx is native to Europe. It is about 4ft long and may grow to be 2ft tall at the shoulder. As Mr Gibb observed, it has a short tail and tufts of hair on its ears. It prefers densely forested habitats – of which there is not much around Kirkheaton – where it hunts rabbits, hares, mice and, although only rarely, foxes. The lynx has been extinct in Britain for centuries, and the nearest resident populations are in Norway.

In 2000 the lush acres around Denby Dale saw a number of killings of sheep and lambs. Whatever killed them left signs identical to those made by a big cat.

In 2000 Denby Dale, to the south-east of Kirkheaton, saw a rash of unusual killings of lambs and sheep. The bodies showed the clear marks of long, thin claws, quite unlike those of domestic dogs. What was presumed to be the killer was seen by Denby Dale postmaster, John Radley, who reported that it was 'a long, black cat, but not as big as a puma.'

Meanwhile, Chris Crowther, who was farming 12,000 acres between Meltham and Greenfield, had found the macabre remains of savaged lambs. The coats of the animals had been ripped off and the bones, including the ribcages, picked clean of flesh. Mr Crowther stated, 'They were stripped clean. It was as good a job as a butcher would do. I don't think a fox did this. The lambs would have been far too heavy and big to drag.'

Another farmer at Wessenden reported similar killings, but he had seen a creature that he thought might be the killer. 'I saw it in the dusk when I was checking sheep and it was there. It seemed more scared of me, and turned and ran away. It looked like a puma.'

The Church Inn at Saddleworth Church became the centre of speculation about the beast. Landlord Michael Taylor spotted the creature with his grandson Ayrton. 'It was ferocious-looking and had a broad face and was about four times the size of a domestic cat. It looked quite nasty and had elfin ears. I think there's more to the moors than meets the eye.'

This time, it was the RSPCA, not the police, that was contacted by the press. Heather Holmes of the RSPCA stated, 'Eight times out of 10 from the description we know it is not a wild animal. There are some big cats in the wild who are descended from animals who were let loose

The woods near Warter where, in 2001, a large black cat leapt out on to the path in front of a man walking his dog.

after the 1976 Dangerous Wild Animals Act came in. Some people who did not wish to apply for a licence set them free.' This was an interesting theory.

In 2001 a man out walking his dog in woods near Warter stopped dead when a large black cat leapt out onto the path in front of him. The animal was about 60ft away as it turned to face the man and his dog. It gave a snarl and trotted off with an unmistakeably cat-like gait. Very sensibly, the man and his dog turned around and went back the way they had come.

The mysterious big cats of Yorkshire could produce lighter moments. After a number of sightings around Meltham in 2005, the police launched a search. Unaware of these events, local resident Andy Gallacher took his big black dog for a walk at 6 o'clock one morning down Red Lane, heading for the open land of Deer Hill Moss. He came across two policemen standing still and staring across the open land. The policemen had not noticed Gallacher and his dog approaching. When the dog barked, one of the policemen jumped out of his skin; 'He seemed very nervous,' said Mr Gallacher.

The Meltham press found a big game hunter who was living in Pontefract and asked him for his advice. 'Nine out of 10 times the public will be safe,' he said. 'My advice is not to look the cat in the face. They will see this as a challenge. The best advice is simply to stay still.'

Some of the big cats are treated almost affectionately by the humans who live in their hunting range. The big cat of Whitby is known locally as 'The Beast of the Bay'. It is generally described as being a black panther.

On 12 July 2010 a retired schoolteacher was quite unphased to come across the Beast of the Bay on Whitby Golf Course while out for a walk. Annabel Smith reported that she came across it at around 10 o'clock in the evening. The big cat loped past her with a definite cat-like stride, very different from that of a dog. It passed by and out of sight into a thicket. In 2009 John Bradley came out his front door on a snowy winter's morning to find prints of a large cat across his front lawn.

On 15 July 2008 the Beast of the Bay was seen by Alan Murie and his wife as they were driving on the A171 over Fylingdales Moor. A large black cat crossed the road about 75 yards ahead of the car and then trotted off over the moor. It was only in sight for a few seconds, but Murie was quite certain that he had seen a black panther, not a large dog. The cat has been seen on and off in the Whitby area since 2003.

What the government hoped was the last word on big cats in Yorkshire came in 2010. The government agency Natural England spent some time probing dozens of reported sightings of cougars, pumas and other exotic animals nationwide. A spokeswoman then called a press conference and said, 'Big cats do escape from zoos or other collections, [but] are usually recaptured very quickly. We are confident there is no breeding population in this country, and it is very unlikely that there are any at large in the English countryside.' Others are not quite so confident.

It is not only lions, cougars and tigers that have been seen in Yorkshire. In 1989 a kangaroo was spotted bounding down Hollings Road in Guiseley, while it was a bear that was seen on Skipworth Common in the spring of 1989. In 1982 and 1983 a series of sightings of a bat with a 10ft wingspan were made in the Bradford area. The biggest bats in the world have a wingspan of only 5ft, so what this was is something of a mystery. Some have suggested that it may have been a pterodactyl, although where one of those extinct reptiles would have come from is unclear.

The Yorkshire coast would be a fertile hunting ground for cryptozoologists in search of the sea serpent, for there have been several sightings of that most elusive of marine creatures.

On 28th February 1934 the local coastguard, Wilkinson Herbert, was walking along the rocky shoreline at Filey Brigg. He later reported that, 'Suddenly I heard a growling like a dozen dogs ahead. Walking nearer, I switched on my torch and was confronted by a huge neck, six yards ahead of me, rearing up 3ft high! The head was a startling sight – huge tortoise eyes glaring at me like saucers. The creature's mouth would be a foot wide and the creature's neck would be a yard around.' The body of the beast was less clear to see, but Herbert reckoned that some 30ft of it was in sight and more lay beneath the water surface.

In August 1945 a man named Baylis was loitering on the shore at Hilston when he heard a loud splash and looked out to sea. About 100 yards away was a large, rounded object moving through the water. As they watched, what looked to be a neck with a small head perched on top of it came up from the sea a short distance in front of the object. A few seconds later some smaller objects broke surface to the rear. They presumed that they were looking at an animal composed of a large, rounded body with a neck and head in front, followed by an undulating tail behind.

In 1927 a steamship heading into the Humber, on a voyage from Hamburg to Hull, ran into a dense bank of fog. The ship slowed down for fear of colliding with another vessel, and double lookouts were posted in the bow. One of them spotted what he took to be a mast sticking about 10ft up out of the water. The helmsman was alerted, and he steered around the object. As it passed alongside the port side of the ship, the crew realised that it was a neck with a smallish head on top of it. At the base of the neck a large, blackish-coloured body could be seen slightly awash. The creature gave a jerk as if it had only just realised the ship was there, then dived out of sight.

It is beyond doubt that there are some large creatures in the sea that are not yet recognised by science. It is thought that there are about 21 species of beaked whale, but nobody is certain.

One of the best sightings of a sea serpent was reported by officers and sailors of HMS Daedalus. The captain later produced this sketch of the creature he had seen. It is almost identical to the unknown beast seen off the Yorkshire coast.

Several have not yet been properly described in the scientific literature, as they are known only from a single skull. Others have never been seen alive and a few may not actually exist at all. Others probably do exist, but nobody knows anything about them. The problem is due to the fact that beaked whales dive deep and long, prefer homes off the shipping lanes and have no commercial value. These creatures can grow up to 40ft in length and weigh over 14 tons. If such large creatures can exist in numbers large enough to maintain a breeding population, and yet be so rarely seen as to be almost invisible, it is likely that other large creatures exist in the oceans.

In the case of the sea serpent, the animal in question is, in contrast to some of the beaked whales, fairly well known. It must first be stated that a good many sightings of mysterious marine animals can be explained quite simply. As with all sightings of apparent cryptids, some witnesses were looking at distant objects in poor light conditions and could easily be mistaken about what they were looking at. Other sightings can be seen to be an animal known to science, but not known to the witness. The basking shark, for instance, is well known, but when seen for the first time can seem to be larger than it really is, and is of bizarre enough appearance to give rise to all sorts of misidentifications.

Other apparently legendary sightings have since turned out not to be so wide of the mark. For centuries, sailors told stories about gigantic squid or huge octopus that were said to be over 70ft long and to be voraciously aggressive. A good number of fictional stories were written about these animals attacking ships, overturning boats and devouring humans. Since no squid bigger than around a metre long was known, and perhaps because the more lurid tales were so obviously fictional, science rejected the giant squid as a real animal. Then in 1981 a Russian trawler pulled up a squid that was 13ft long. When it was studied it emerged that this was a juvenile, meaning that the adults would be even bigger. The species was dubbed *Mesonychoteuthis*, or the colossal squid. Over the years that have followed, bigger and bigger examples have been caught. In 2007 a specimen 33ft long and weighing half a ton was found. Perhaps even larger examples remain to be found. The squid is now known to be a voracious hunter of fish. The old stories were not so far off the mark as scientists thought.

Once false sightings of sea serpents are eliminated, there remain a core of witnesses who have reported seeing large animals in good conditions that cannot be explained as known animals. The Filey Brigg sighting of 1934 would seem to be of the cryptid that cryptozoologists have dubbed the 'carapace'. The reports of this creature come from people as respectable as the captain of the Royal Yacht Osborne, who sighted the creature along with several members of his crew on 2 June 1877. This beast is generally described as being akin to a giant turtle, some 50ft long. The head, as coastguard Herbert reported, is held on a neck that can extend up to 6ft from the body. The shell is sometimes said to be jointed and may carry a row of spines.

The Hilston and Humber sightings may be of the creature dubbed variously 'the serpent' or 'the giant eel'. This creature has a long, thin body like that of a snake, and is able to hold its head up out of the water for as much as 8 or 10ft. The body is overall said to be around 60 or 80ft long and to be generally devoid of fins or flippers, although some think that it may have fins.

Quite what these creatures might be is unknown. Some cryptozoologists have suggested they may be marine reptiles left over from the age of dinosaurs, others that they might be sea-going

The famous Craven heifer of the late 18th century was a roan shorthorn cow, like this modern example, but of truly prodigious proportions. Credit: Robert Scarth.

mammals. It may be more likely that they are truly marine animals that do not need to surface to breathe, as this would explain why they are so rarely seen.

One Yorkshire beast that was undoubtedly real was the famous Craven Heifer. In the later 18th century some gentlemen farmers were experimenting with selective breeding of their livestock. The idea was to separate out those animals that had specific qualities – such as hardiness on moors, quick growth or great weight – and to allow them to breed only with each other. The idea had been pioneered by Robert Bakewell in Leicestershire, but was taken up Thomas Bates of Kirklevington, John Booth of Killesby and Reverend William Carr of Bolton Abbey. Together they produced the Shorthorn breed of cattle.

In 1807 a calf was born on Carr's farm that was to prove to be truly spectacular. The roan cow did not seem to be anything special when it was born, but as it grew it became simply enormous. By the time it was adult the heifer stood 5ft 2in at the shoulder and was 11ft 2in long. Its girth was a stunning 10ft 2in. The animal had a prodigious appetite, eating its way through fodder at a stupendous rate. Carr was delighted by his animal and showed it with pride. It was then purchased by a fairground showman, who took it on tour around much of northern England under the name of the Craven Heifer. The showman exaggerated the already-impressive size of the animal, and when reports of the beast reached London many refused to accept that it could be a real animals. To this day, many pubs in Yorkshire are called The Craven Heifer. It is good to see one of the peculiar animals of Yorkshire commemorated in such a sensible fashion.

CHAPTER 11

Mysterious Saints

For some mysterious reason, Yorkshire has always managed to be on a religious borderland. Quite why this should be so is rather unclear, but it has been a factor that has dominated the life of Yorkshire folk as far back as records go.

When the Romans arrived in what is now Yorkshire in the middle of the first century, they found the area divided religiously. The peoples of the area were pagan Celts, but there were important differences between them. The Parisii tribe of the area around the River Derwent were undiscriminating pagans, worshipping the broad range of Celtic gods, as did the Corieltauvi to the south of the Humber. But the rest of Yorkshire, and most of what is now northern England, was the territory of the Brigantes and they had a very distinctive religious life.

The Brigantes were hugely enthusiastic in their worship of the goddess Brigantia; indeed, they took the name of their tribe from her. The name Brigantia means 'The High One', which may be a reference to her importance or to her physical height. She was undoubtedly a warrior goddess, and is often depicted wearing a helmet sporting an animal crest and holding a spear. The Brigantes were a famously warlike tribe – proving difficult for the Romans to subdue and being allowed to manage many of their own affairs even after they became part of the Roman empire – so Brigantia would have been a most appropriate deity.

The Romans were well known for their relaxed attitude to local religions, as long as they did not pose a threat to Rome. As a warlike goddess of a warlike people, Brigantia may have been viewed as something of a threat. The Romans therefore made huge efforts to identify Brigantia to their own goddess, Victoria. The two were not identical, for while Brigantia was a goddess connected to the actual fighting business of war, Victoria was the deity linked to the celebrations held after a victory in battle, hence her name.

Tenuous though the link was, it was good enough for the Romans. There are two surviving Roman inscriptions found in Yorkshire that specifically refer to the goddess 'Victoria Brigantia', as if the two deities were one being.

One of the enduring mysteries surrounding Brigantia is what happened to her when Christianity came to Britain. The new religion began to creep into Britain c.AD 150 or thereabouts, and was fairly well established by the time the successful general Constantine was proclaimed Emperor at York in AD 306. It does not seem to have been the religion of the majority of the population, even when the Emperor Theodosius I made Christianity the official state religion of Rome in 380. It is assumed the worship of Brigantia continued throughout Roman times and beyond.

After the Roman Empire withdrew from Britain, telling the local authorities to look after themselves, Britain entered the Dark Ages. Very little is known about these years, and most of what is known is subject to controversy. In Yorkshire there was a significant, but not overwhelming influx of invaders from northern Germany. These pagan Angles took over the territory of the

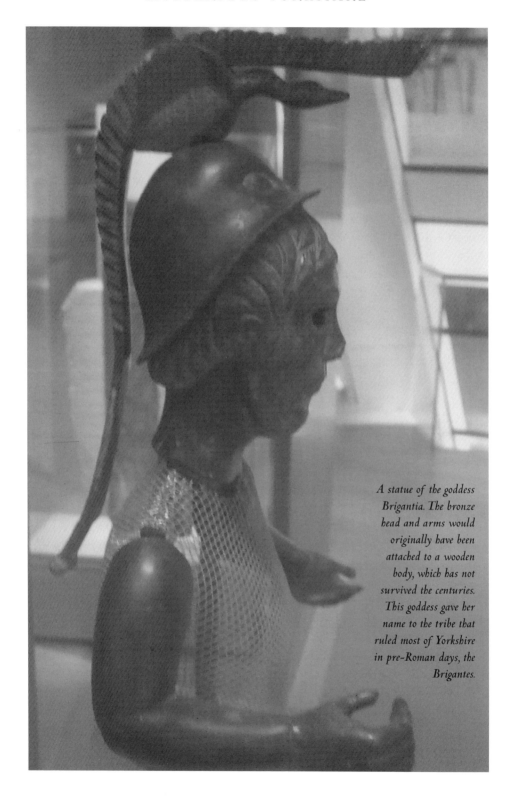

A statue of the goddess Brigantia. The bronze head and arms would originally have been attached to a wooden body, which has not survived the centuries. This goddess gave her name to the tribe that ruled most of Yorkshire in pre-Roman days, the Brigantes.

Parisii *c*.550, turning it into the Kingdom of Deira, with an English ruling class and extensive settlement by English farmers.

The Brigantes seem to have held out longer. By around 580 the lands of the Brigantes east of the Pennines had fallen to the English Kingdom of Bernicia, but the lands west of the mountains remained under Brigantian control, and in time became the Kingdom of Rheged. By 730 Bernicia, Deira and Rheged had become united as the Kingdom of Northumbria under English rule.

Sometime before the unification of Northumbria, the people of Rheged had been converted to Christianity by missionaries from Ireland and Wales. Officially, Brigantia had been displaced and gone to wherever defunct deities go, but some scholars have suggested that the goddess Brigantia survived the Christianisation of her homeland. One of the earliest British Christian saints was St Brigid, or Brigette. She is also one of the most mysterious; the early accounts of her life contradict themselves on nearly every detail and there is no way of knowing which of them, if any, contains any truth at all.

Some aspects of early veneration of St Brigid is distinctly unchristian. In Kildare there was a chapel dedicated to St Brigid in which burned a perpetual flame tended by a rota of female priests. The chapel was surrounded by a hedge that men were not allowed to cross. Any who did cross the hedge would be sent insane by St Brigid. Her feast day is on I February, the same date as the pagan fire festival of Imbolc. This link has persuaded some scholars that St Brigid is, in reality, a Christianized version of Brigantia, although the theory remains controversial.

What is undoubtedly true is that by the 7th century Yorkshire was once again straddling a religious dividing line. To the north and west were lands converted to Christianity by the Celtic missionaries from Wales and Ireland. To the south were lands converted to Christianity by missionaries from Rome. Because the two forms of Christianity had distinct traditions, there was often some friction between the two, and that friction came to a head in Yorkshire where the two forms met.

Some of the differences between the two forms of Christianity were relatively trivial. Roman monks, for instance, shaved their head in a small circle on the top; Celtic monks shaved the entire front half of their head. Other differences were more important. The rites of baptism were distinct and the Romans did not recognise Celtic baptism as valid. The Celtic church was organised on a monastic basis, with the abbot of a monastery being the senior cleric in his area, while the Roman church had bishops as the senior cleric in an area. Celtic monasteries followed the Rule of St Columbanus, laid down by that saint in Ireland in the 590s. This was a much stricter set of rules than the Rule of St Benedict used by the Roman Church. Celtic monks tended to view their Roman counterparts as being less devoted to the monastic ideal than themselves.

Among the laity in Yorkshire, however, the key dispute was over the date of Easter. The date of Easter changes each year, depending on the interrelationships between the solar and lunar cycles. The Celtic Church continued to use the calculations of St Jerome, while the Roman Church had changed to the calculations of St Victorius. Both were convinced that they were

The West Front of Ripon Minster. The monastery here was founded by one of the holiest men in England: St Eata. His sanctity did not stop him from becoming embroiled in a mysterious dispute that saw him being chased out of Ripon at swordpoint.

right and that the other was wrong. The differences meant that while the followers of one date were fasting for Lent, their neighbours were getting stuck into the feast of Easter. Understandably, it led to tension.

In 661 one of the holiest men in England fell foul of the ongoing dispute. St Eata had been born c.620, and as a boy had been taken to the monastery of Lindisfarne to become a monk. His intelligence and devotion to God earned him rapid promotion at the monastery, and in 651 he was chosen to lead a small group of monks tasked with establishing a new monastery at Ripon. He did his job well, and the church of the monastery he founded survives as Ripon Minster. But, after 10 years of success, disaster struck. King Oswiu of Northumbria appointed his son Alfrith to be King of Deira. Alfrith came to Ripon and had a heated argument with Eata. What the dispute was about is a mystery, but it must have been serious, for Alfrith forced Eata out of Ripon at swordpoint. Eata later become Bishop of Hexham and died there in 686, but he never returned to Ripon.

The various disputes between the two schools of Christianity came to a head in the 660s, when King Oswiu of Northumbria (who followed the Celtic Church) married Eanfeld from the Kentish royal family (who followed the Roman Church). The royal court was thus divided into two factions when it came to celebrating Easter. In 664 Oswiu summoned together the leading clerics of his kingdom to discuss the matter and come to a decision. The meeting was held at Whitby, in the monastery of St Hilda.

The debates and arguments went on for days, involving complex views on the phases of the moon and how calculations should be made. Eventually, Oswiu seems to have lost patience and used his authority as King to push for a decision. As Oswiu saw it, the actual calculations were of less importance than the authority of those suggesting them. The Celtic Church drew its inspiration for calculating Easter from St Columba, who in turn had used as inspiration the writings of St John the Apostle, referred to in the Bible as the Apostle whom Jesus loved best. The Roman Church, on the other hand, was following rules laid down by the Pope, successor as Bishop of Rome to St Peter the Apostle, identified in the Bible as the rock on which Jesus would build his church.

Oswiu decided that being a rock was more important than being loved, and came down on the side of Rome. The Synod of Whitby proved to be instrumental in the defeat of the Celtic Church. Within a generation the Celtic practices had virtually ceased to exist across Britain, and the supremacy of the Pope in religious matters had been accepted – something that would cause all sorts of problems to future generations of British rulers.

If the Synod of Whitby was of great importance, it is also something of a mysterious event. For a start, the contemporary accounts say that it took place at the monastery of St Hilda at Streonshalh. Although St Hilda is most closely linked to Whitby, Strensall is just outside York and it may be that the Synod was held there instead. The date of the synod is also disputed. Most accounts say it took place in 663, but one of the earliest accounts place it in the year 664. Nor is it entirely clear what went on there; there are differing accounts of who was present, what they said and even why the synod had been called. Only Oswiu's decision is relatively certain.

The Synod of Whitby was a rather mysterious affair, but it settled the path of Christianity in Yorkshire for centuries after it was held in 664.

Whatever the truth about the Synod of Whitby (or Strensall), there are tales aplenty about St Hilda. She was born *c*.614 into a noble Northumbrian family, and as a young woman joined the abbey at Hartlepool. It was in 657 that she founded her monastery at Whitby. This was one of those odd double monasteries that housed both monks and nuns. The living accommodation was kept separate, but the two sexes shared the same church and other religious facilities.

According to a local legend, Hilda was given the headland above Whitby for her abbey because it was so overrun by snakes as to be useless to the local farmers. Undaunted, Hilda produced a sacred whip with which she rounded up all the snakes, then drove them over the cliff. As she did so, Hilda prayed aloud for the snakes to be turned to stone. This was done and the petrified snakes have continued to be found along the shoreline ever since. In fact, the stone snakes are fossil ammonites, a sort of coiled shellfish that was common some 300 million years ago. Scientists have named one genus of ammonite *Hildaceros* in her honour.

In the 1760s visitors to the ruined Abbey began to notice an odd apparition. During the summer months the sun fell on the ruined choir in such a way that at about 11 o'clock in the morning on sunny days the figure of a woman wearing a shroud appeared in one of the high windows. This was confidently said to be an appearance of St Hilda and became something of a tourist attraction. It ceased appearing in the mid-19th century. Presumably, the shadows cast by the ruined walls created the illusion, and when some rock or other fell or eroded away the illusion ceased. It is still said, however, that the seagulls that whirl around Whitby dip their wings in homage to St Hilda as they pass over the Choir.

The double abbey founded by Hilda flourished until 870, when it was looted and pillaged by Vikings. The buildings seem to have continued to have been inhabited by monks or hermits for some years and were still known as 'priesthouses' in the 11th century. In the 1080s a retired Norman soldier named Rheinfrid decided to become a monk and persuaded local nobleman William Percy to give him the ruins, plus some 240 acres of arable land. The small monastery that he founded grew rapidly, and by the 1300 it was rich enough to afford the mighty church, the ruins of which can be seen to this day. This second abbey was closed by King Henry VIII in 1540.

The abbey ruins were left to fall apart slowly, serving as a landmark for sailors off the coast. During the 1870s and 1880s the seaside town drew a large number of holidaymakers, among them a theatrical manager named Bram Stoker. Some years later Stoker wrote a horror story about a vampire, and set much of it in and around Whitby. The book, *Dracula*, was an immediate success and boosted the tourist business. The town has since become a focus for the Goth subculture, a movement with horror film-inspired fashion and a growing number of adherents. All a very long way from the blessed St Hilda.

Rather more to St Hilda's taste would have been the young man who joined her abbey when she was an old woman. John of Beverley, as he would later become known, is a mysterious figure. He was born in Harpham, although nobody knows quite when, and was highly educated, although nobody knows where. He spent time with St Hilda at Whitby, although nobody knows when. He seems to have sprung fully formed into history when he was made Bishop of Hexham in 687. In 705 he became Bishop of York, then retired in 717 to be a monk in the monastery

Beverley Minster was founded by St John of Beverley, whose remains are still buried here. Despite his later fame, St John remains a shadowy figure about whom surprisingly little is known for certain.

at Beverley that he had founded, although nobody knows when. When a monk named Folcard was commissioned to write a biography of John of Beverley in 1066, he could find almost no facts about him and had to fall back on conjecture and rumour.

Despite the obscurity of his life, John of Beverley rapidly became one of the greatest saints in northern England. His relics at Beverley gained a reputation for curing illness of almost any kind, and by 1266 it was traditional for the men of Yorkshire to march to war under the sacred banner of St John of Beverley, which was kept in the monastery church when not being used to supervise bloodshed. In 1292 a new tomb was made for the bones of the saint: it was 5ft long, 1ft wide and made of pure silver, decorated with figures of pure gold. King Henry V gave credit for his victory at Agincourt to the intervention of St John of Beverley in the slaughter, and promoted the saint to become the patron saint of the royal household.

The great shrine was removed during the reformation, with the gold and silver being melted down and sent to the royal treasury. The relics themselves were buried in the nave, and in 1738 the spot was marked by a great marble slab on which is engraved 'Here lies the body of Saint John of Beverley, founder of this church. Bishop of Hexham AD 687–705. Bishop of York AD 705–718. He was born at Harpham and died at Beverley AD 721.'

St John's feast day is 7 May. On the Thursday closest to the day, the choir, clergy and congregation of Beverley go to Harpham for a church service, after which a procession goes to the village well. On the following Sunday, Beverley holds a great service attended by the mayor,

Rievaulx Abbey is now in ruins, but it was once home to St Ailred of Rievaulx. In later life St Ailred often bemoaned the colourful sins of his youth, and the exact nature of those sins has led to some equally colourful modern debates and disputes.

council and other dignitaries, who process through the town to the minster for a service. The highlight of the service comes when children from Harpham scatter primroses on the saint's tomb. Not bad for a man about whom almost nothing is known.

Another Yorkshire monk around whom mystery revolves is St Ailred of Rievaulx. Compared to St John of Beverley, his life story is fairly well known. Ailred was born in Hexham in 1110, served in the household of King David I of Scotland for some years, and in 1134 entered the Abbey of Rievaulx as a monk. He later rose to be abbot, supervising the rapid growth of Rievaulx to be one of the premier religious houses of northern England, with 100 monks and 400 lay brothers. He travelled widely, and died at Rievaulx in 1167. It is his writings that have lead to the mystery.

Unlike many medieval monks and scholars, Ailred seems to have been almost obsessed with sex. He wrote extensively on the importance of faithfulness in marriage, the celibacy of clergy and the varieties of sexual sins open to mankind. In his writings, St Ailred makes several references to his life of sin as a young man before he entered Rievaulx. Although he nowhere states exactly what these sins were, some scholars have put the various clues together and concluded that he was an active homosexual. This is disputed by others who have studied his works, but the idea of St Ailred as a homosexual saint became firmly fixed in the later 20th century. He is now the patron saint of a number of Christian organisations that minister to homosexuals or admit homosexuals to the priesthood. There is even an Order of St Ailred in the Philippines.

While Ailred was in Rievaulx, a mysterious incident took place at the Abbey of Watton. In about 1141 a toddler was admitted to the abbey to become a nun. As the girl grew older, however, it gradually became clear that she was not really interested in a spiritual life and would have much rather been out in the secular world. She then fell pregnant, much to the outrage of the nuns in the abbey. At a meeting of the nuns called to debate what should be done, the ideas put forward ranged from the relatively mild whipping, to branding, roasting or skinning alive.

The older nuns, however, decided that the guilty party was not the nun, but the man who had made her pregnant. They arranged for the errant nun to meet her lover, supposedly to say goodbye to him, but in reality to lure him into a trap. The man turned out to be one of the lay brothers who did the heavier agricultural work of the abbey. When he appeared he was pounced on by the nuns, who proceeded to castrate him with a knife. The poor man was then thrown out of the abbey grounds. The nun then suffered a miscarriage, which the senior nuns took as a sign that God had forgiven her for her sins. She was taken back into the abbey, but what became of her later is unrecorded. It is a barbarous story and one that has never quite been believed by historians.

One final mystery about saints in Yorkshire concerns St Margaret Clitherow. She was born Margaret Middleton in York in 1556, and in 1571 married a butcher named John Clitherow. The couple were Catholics at a time when England was rapidly becoming Protestant, and their son Henry went to France to train as a Catholic priest. In 1586 she was arrested on charges of aiding and harbouring Catholic priests sent to England from Spain. This was not just a religious matter, but a criminal one as well. The Spanish priests did not only minister to Catholics, but

The church at Watton, once part of a nunnery where mysterious events led to torture, castration and bloodshed.

also sought to organise the murder of Queen Elizabeth I so that she could be replaced by the Catholic and pro-Spain Mary, Queen of Scots.

When brought for trial, Margaret refused to plead. Whether she did this to avoid having members of her family brought to testify, to avoid providing evidence that would have betrayed Spanish priests or for some other reason, has never been discovered. As was then the custom, she was 'pressed' to try to extract a plea so that the trial could go ahead. She was laid on the ground with a wooden door placed on top of her and heavy stones were laid on the door. Margaret still refused to plead, and died. Queen Elizabeth herself wrote a strong letter to the York magistrates, condemning them for their actions and stating that a woman should not have been pressed.

Margaret Clitherow was thereafter regarded as a martyr by the English catholics. Her hand was removed before burial and is preserved as a relic. Her home in The Shambles was turned into a shrine to her memory. In 1929 she was beatified, and then canonised in 1970.

Mystery has always surrounded exactly how closely linked Margaret was to the underground Catholic movement in England at the time. Opinions on her have varied from seeing her as an cruelly martyred innocent, to viewing her as a devious and cunning traitor to her Queen. Recent scholarship has now established that her son, the priest Henry, was deeply involved with the most extreme Catholics in Europe and was actively working for the death of Queen Elizabeth, the forcible return of Catholicism to England and the persecution of Protestants. It seems that the authorities actually wanted Henry, and that his mother's death was a tragic accident. It has also emerged that the shrine is actually in the wrong place. Margaret Clitherow lived two doors down the street.

The disputes between Catholic and Protestant Christians have now lessened, although they have not quite vanished in the way that disputes between Catholic and Celtic Christians have done, or those between the Parisii and the Brigantia worshipping Brigantes. But Yorkshire still finds itself on something of a religious fault line; this time it is between the nominally Christian, but largely secular, bulk of the population and the immigrant communities in some of the cities, who tend to follow the Muslim or Hindu faith.

Being Prepared

Boy Scout - Sailor - Commando

The remarkable wartime adventures of
Lt Cdr Philip Humphries RNVR

In his own words

Edited by his son, Richard Humphries

Being Prepared

Cover photo: Dad's Boy Scout whistle and Royal Navy 'bosun's call'.

This is the story of my Dad, told mainly in his own words. However, although he painstakingly wrote his memoirs at my request, by his own admission he was more used to writing official reports (particularly during his Royal Navy career) than to turning out scintillating prose. Where necessary I have added explanatory comments or given him what I consider to be a helpful nudge, just to get the plot going, as he had requested I should do. I hope I have not detracted from his original narrative.

When the war came it was the start of his big adventure. He turned 18 in May 1940 and signed-up for the Royal Navy a few month before his birthday. Like so many others of his generation, he was just an ordinary bloke. War service meant that he, and others, were called upon to do extraordinary things. They gave up what was left of their youth to go and serve their country and to create the world we live in today.

FOREWORD

We are all shaped by our background. For my dad the saving grace was the Boy Scout movement. As a Cub, then as a Scout, he fully subscribed to the ethos of service to others, of striving to be self-sufficient and of doing a good deed every day. The Scout motto 'Be Prepared' stood him in good stead all his life. He was a remarkable man in his own way and representative of a remarkable generation. As an example he would regularly take himself off on camping holidays, as a teenager, either with Scouting friends or on his own. He was quite at ease in his own company. On one occasion, I guess it was probably 1938 or 1939, he had cycled all the way from London to North Wales for a summer camping trip. A couple of weeks later he cycled back to his home in Cranford, near what is now Heathrow airport, arriving on a Saturday afternoon to find a note on the kitchen table from his father: "Gone down to Folkestone on holiday. Join us there." After making himself a cup of tea, he jumped back on his bike and then cycled all the way down to Folkestone on the south Kent coast. The journey from his Welsh camp site down to Kent was a total cycle ride of well over 300 miles.

But how did it all begin? Here follows, in his own words, a summary of his early life before the world was disrupted by the war of 1939-45.

In addition to this there is an account of his last camping holiday, which took place in the summer of 1940. This came to light purely by chance. By then he had already volunteered for war service with the Royal Navy; he had completed his basic training and he was allowed two weeks leave before taking up his posting to his first ship.

Although he - and everyone else in the United Kingdom - probably didn't realise it at the time, that balmy summer of 1940 was about to change their world for ever. We may have suffered a defeat at Dunkirk but the rescue of our army by the fleet of small boats, coupled with Prime Minister Winston Churchill's rousing speeches, proved we would never be beaten.

It was in this frame of mind that British people seem to have been completely unfazed by the fact that Hitler and his Nazi hordes were massing just across the Channel, ready to invade our shores. The British were determined to enjoy that summer as they always had.

My dad's account of his 1940 holiday lay forgotten in an exercise book stashed away on a shelf in the garden shed of his home in Bexhill, until I discovered it while clearing out his possessions following his death in 2009. His book opens a window onto a world we have left far behind. It was a world of very little traffic, with open roads that meandered across the English countryside, through little towns and villages. A cyclist's paradise.

Immediately after that holiday he embarked on the greatest adventure of his life, first as a sailor, then volunteering for the newly-formed Commandos. He played a part in some of the great military dramas of the age: the sinking of the Bismark; the disastrous 1942 raid on Dieppe; the seaborne invasions of North Africa, Sicily and then Italy, where he was badly wounded and his Commando troop was wiped-out (largely as a result of a blunder by an American general); he had a key role in the D-Day landings; he was in India and caught-up in the infamous mutiny by the Royal Indian Navy; he was there at the Japanese surrender in Singapore; he then became one of the youngest commanders of a major warship - and all by the time he was just 23 years old.

But it didn't end there. He was recalled to the Royal Navy for the Korean War; he was a key witness at probably the most infamous court martial of the era; he took part in top secret operations during the Cold War, dodging Russian 'spy' ships. And all the while he maintained strong links with the Scout troop he had joined as a boy. To the very end he was the epitome of the Scouting ethos. He was prepared for anything. But let him put you in the picture in his own words...

1   Early life

I was born at 52 Whellock Road, Bedford Park, Chiswick, London W4 at 0630 on 27 May 1922, a Saturday. My first recollection was of standing in my cot, which was alongside my parents' bed, and looking at my parents sleeping.

Opposite our back gate was the Southfields Road School and in the morning I always wanted to see the children going to school, so my brother Will made a platform for me to stand on, to look over the back gate.

Eventually I went to the school, progressing through the Infants and Junior schools. At the age of 11 I went to St Clement Dane's (Holborn Estate) Grammar School at Ducane Road, Shepherd's Bush, originally going by bus, then by bicycle.

My brother Will married Gladys about 1930 and my brother Frank married Dorothy Lyons in 1936.

My early life was rather strict, as my mother did not allow me to speak at the meal table. In fact, she kept a cane on the table, so that if I said anything during the meal I got a whack with the cane. I had to eat everything that was put before me and if I left anything I got it for the next meal.

I was never allowed to have a party or to go to a party. On one occasion I was invited to a friend's party, so did not say anything to my mother. I went to the party but, unfortunately, my mother got to hear about it, went and dragged me out of the party and took my back home, where I got a real thrashing.

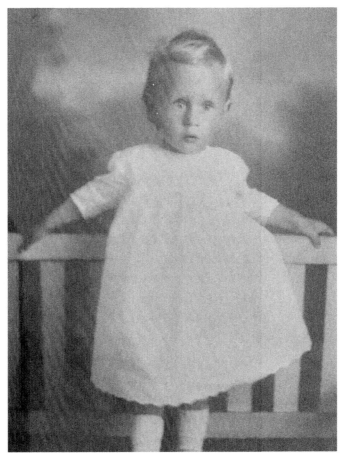

Philip in 1923, looking rather startled!

When I was about seven years old a great friend of mine who lived next door but one died from diphtheria and his mother gave me a model of an airplane which he had. My mother promptly burned it, apparently in case there was any trace of the disease on it.

At the weekend I had to do my chores, which consisted of cleaning all the brass in the house. And in those days, all the taps, finger plates, door knobs and handles were all brass, so it took me quite some time to do this. Then I had to go to the Wall's sausage factory in Acton Vale, which was about a mile away, to get the sausages for Sunday breakfast. Then, having completed all the chores I got my week's pocket money - of one penny!

The house at Whellock Road was a terraced house and was divided into two flats, obviously to help with the purchase price. We had the upstairs flat and a family named Cook had the downstairs. Our flat had the front bedroom, which my parents occupied, a second bedroom just behind, which we boys slept in; a lounge/dining room and a kitchen at the back.

The toilets were in the garden at the back of the house, at the bottom of a flight of stairs going into the back garden. These were rather cold and draughty in the winter.

The Cooks moved out around 1930 and we then occupied the whole house. Upstairs my parents still had the front bedroom. My mother took-in a lodger to help with the finances and he had the bedroom that we boys used to occupy. By this time my brother Will had moved out, so Frank and I had what used to be the lounge as our bedroom. The old kitchen was then turned into a bathroom, which we had not had before.

Downstairs, the front room was our lounge; the room behind was used by another lodger; the kitchen/dining room was behind that and we had a scullery at the back.

The lodger who had the upstairs bedroom was a man, co-incidentally called Cook, who was a musician and used to play the cornet professionally in The Ivy Benson Band. This was rather funny, because the Ivy Benson Band was supposed to be an all-girl band. 'Cookie', as he was called, had to dress up in female clothing when he got to the venue where they were playing that week.

We always went on holiday for the first two weeks of August and always to the same place, a guest house in Sandgate High Street, near Folkestone, Kent. Invariably the other guests were the same ones we had met the year before. However, it was a very nice holiday. Our trunk was sent off a couple of weeks before by rail. On the morning of the holiday we went to Victoria Coach Station and caught the coach down to Sandgate. As all our clothes had already gone down in the trunk, we only had a small amount of hand luggage.

In 1935 my brother Frank had bought a car and he hired a caravan. He, his then-girlfriend Dorothy, my parents and I went on a tour of the West Country. We went along the south coast and came back along the north coast.

When we got to Bossington, which was between Porlock and Minehead, we camped in a field. Having watched what my brother did when he drove the car, I decided to have a go myself. In those days you did not have an ignition key but just switched on – so I got in the car, started it up and drove it round the field, much to the surprise and consternation of everyone else – especially as I had to double de-clutch, as it was a 'crash' gearbox. I have never had any driving lessons and have never had to take a driving test.

When I was old enough I got a morning job as a paperboy, working seven days a week for the (to me) princely sum of three shillings and six pence per week [*17½p in today's currency*]. I was known then as 'Priory', as my round commenced at Priory Road. This, of course, I had to relinquish when we later moved house. Amazingly, when I was in the area after the war, I called-in at the newsagent's shop and the same people were still there. The owner said to me "Aren't you Priory?" – so I must have made an impression!

At the age of eight I joined the 14th Acton Wolf Cubs, which met locally. Then at 11 I joined the 12th Acton Scouts, which were attached to our Methodist Church in Acton and of which my brother Frank was a member.

I had quite a good time with them, going to many camps, including Berkhampstead, Sark, Chideok and many other places. The troop had a permanent camping site at Uxbridge and I used to spend a lot of time there. I remained in contact with some of the surviving old Scouts from that time.

By the age of ten I had also joined the choir of St Michael and All Angels Church, which was our local Church of England church at Bedford Park.

At age 12 I was sent to the Gunnersbury School of Music, which was at Chiswick, at the weekend, to learn piano and this continued for about two years.

Photo: Philip at Scout camp, aged about 13

In 1936 we moved to 8 Westwick Gardens, Cranford, Middlesex. This was very close to where London Heathrow airport is now situated. At that time, however, Heathrow was just a collection of farms and market gardens. The local airport then was at Heston, which is where I went to see Neville

Chamberlain, then Prime Minister, when he returned from his historic meeting with Adolf Hitler in Munich. I saw him wave the famous 'peace in our time' piece of paper.

The house at Cranford was then in a very rural position. Behind the house was just fields. In time these were built-over with rows of houses, so it eventually became quite urban.

Our Whellock Road house remained in my father's ownership and was let out. He had bought the house at Cranford for £600. In those days a good weekly wage was £5.

I still continued my schooling at St Clement Dane's but now I had to cycle down the Great West Road, then through to Ducane Road, a distance of about ten miles. This I did in all weathers until I left the school in 1938.

I started work for the Milk Marketing Board at Thames House, Millbank, which was near the Houses of Parliament, going there by Underground from Hounslow West station. I usually did the journey with my father, who worked at Clough's Correspondence College in Temple Chambers, Temple Avenue, in The City.

The Milk Marketing Board were having new premises built at Thames Ditton. On the declaration of war in 1939 they moved down there, even though the building works were not completed.

It was around this time, when I started work, that I was encouraged to go for an audition for the Oscar Rabin Band at Hammersmith Palais. Much to my amazement, I passed the audition and was accepted.

The interviewer, who was a Geordie, said that I had to change my name as it was too long. He said to me "By jimmy, you're young!" Then suddenly he said "That's it! That will be your name: Jimmy Young!"

When I left the band, on joining the Royal Navy, a Royal Air Force serviceman, who had been invalided-out, asked if he could take over the name. So he became the Jimmy Young of hit-record and radio fame.

My difficulty at that time was how to tell my mother that I

would be singing with the band in the evenings. She disliked intensely what she called "that horrible new racket." And she thought Bing Crosby was terrible.

However, at that time and with the prospect of war breaking out, the Civil Defence Force had been started, so I volunteered as a messenger. One of the regulations for this was that you had to sleep in the basement of Hounslow Town Hall at night.

Our commander there was a man called Mr Sid Pordage. I arranged with him that I would go to Hammersmith Palais in the evening, leaving my bike at the town hall, and going by tube from Hounslow Central. I returned to the town hall to sleep, then went home for breakfast in the morning. This worked perfectly. My mother never did realise what was going on.

Eventually, in May 1940, I joined the Royal Navy as a signalman. I thought I would go in for something I already knew, as I had already gained signalling knowledge in the Scouts.

As explained later on in more detail, I was drafted to *HMS Royal Arthur* – in peacetime it was Butlin's holiday camp at Skegness. I was there for just a week before, on interview, I was made a 'CW' candidate *[Commissions and Warrants – in other words, selected for officer training]*. This meant a transfer to *HMS Collingwood* in Fareham, Hampshire, to train as an ordinary seaman. From there I went to Chatham and joined my first ship, *HMS Sunflower.* I took my commission in 1942. In early 1944 I found myself at another shore establishment, *HMS Lizard* in Hove, where I met my future wife, Wren Marie Presant.

From there I was appointed to *HMS Glenroy* based in Southampton. Every Wednesday I caught the train from Southampton to Hove, to spend the evening with Marie – usually going to a dance.

Being Force G1 Signal Officer at the time, of course I had all the details for the Normandy landings. On the Wednesday before D-Day I told Marie that I would not be seeing her the following week. Of course, she wanted to know why but I could not tell her. I suspect she thought I had found another girl. When D-Day arrived, she knew the reason why!

We were married on Saturday 14 October 1944. We went on honeymoon to Cornwall, staying with Mr and Mrs Cowling at Coxford Farm, Crackington Haven. I was at home for a short while before being sent to Helensburgh in Scotland, to join a tank landing ship, *HMLST 373*, where we took over the ship from the Yanks and sailed to the Far East.

It was while I was in the Far East at the end of the war that my father died in St George's hospital at Hyde Park Corner, whilst undergoing an operation *[for bowel cancer]*. He was 68.

Then, on my way home, when we got to Gibraltar I heard that my mother had also died. *[In fact, his grief-stricken mother, unable to cope with the death of her husband, had hanged herself at the family home]*.

When we arrived at Plymouth I phoned Marie to tell her I had arrived back and asked her to try and get a van to meet me at Paddington Station, as I had ten cases of various goods to bring back. She couldn't get a van – but turned up in a Rolls Royce! We packed as much as possible into the Rolls, which left Marie sitting on my lap in the front. The rest we put in the Left Luggage office at the station.

I found out that my parents had left me our house at Cranford, as my brothers already had their own homes. However, I discovered that they had stripped everything out, so that we had to build a home from scratch. The only trouble was that it was virtually impossible to obtain any furniture in those immediate post-war days. So we had to make-do and get what we could – even ending up making furniture from old boxes.

Our son, Richard, was born at the house in Cranford in October 1947.

P H Humphries

2   Being prepared

Editor's explanatory note:

In those few months of the summer of 1940 between the evacuation of Dunkirk and the commencement of The Blitz, we drew-up the drawbridge, sat back to lick our wounds (all metaphorically speaking) and tried to collect our thoughts. We were alone against the Third Reich. We had become Fortress Britain.

Fortunately, few people outside the Government and the Military realised just how precarious our position had become. The new Prime Minister, Winston Churchill, had given his three rousing speeches to the nation in May and June (1:"Blood, toil, tears and sweat", 2: "We shall fight on the beaches" and 3: "This was their finest hour"). We were a whisker away from being invaded and over-run. If that unhappy circumstance had come to pass, I would be sitting here now writing this in German and not in English.

However, all of this was an improbability in the minds of most British people in that summer of 1940. With Hitler's troops just a few miles away, on the other side of the English Channel, you might be forgiven for thinking that the English in particular would be running around in a state of panic, preparing to be overrun imminently by the Nazi horde. Not a bit of it. Judging by my father's wartime diary, people went about their everyday business; they went on holiday as usual; they went blackberrying; they went fishing. The general tenor of life was unchanged. Defeat in war was not going to happen. Churchill had said so. In the face of adversity the general population really did follow the spirit of the wartime slogan and advice to "Keep calm and carry on."

So… to carry on: In a suburban semi in the West London suburb of Cranford (now unhappily finding itself on the perimeter of London Heathrow airport, which was then just a small, insignificant airfield with no commercial traffic) wartime planning was in full flow. An 18-year old newly-qualified Royal Navy rating and perennial Boy Scout, Philip Harry Humphries, had found himself considerably inconvenienced by Hitler's summer campaign. Young Philip had planned a campaign of his own – and the two were at odds.

Philip's plan was to undertake his annual cycling and camping holiday in the West Country, using up a valuable two weeks' leave following completion of his Royal Navy training, while he waited to take up his first shipboard posting and play his part in the war.

He had volunteered for war service just before his 18th birthday, thereby throwing away the promising alternative careers of a clerical post at the Milk Marketing Board, or (more excitingly) as a crooner with the Oscar Rabin Band at Hammersmith Palais.

While the Admiralty waited for him to join his first ship, Philip was obliged by Herr Hitler to re-plan his holiday. Following the Dunkirk evacuation large parts of the south coast of England had been closed-off to the public while we anticipated the German invasion. An alternative route was needed – and it has survived, carefully folded into the tour log book Philip had opened for the holiday. Good map-reading skills were essential to find your way around England in those days.

With the fear of impending invasion, all signposts had been removed, to confound any invading forces. And towns and villages, generally, did not then advertise themselves with nameplates or signs. If you were travelling anywhere in England in the 1940's, you had to know where you were going and how to get there.

In the following pages he takes up the story – but bear in mind that this was a diary of events for his personal satisfaction and was not intended for general public consumption, so at times the narrative may need interpretation or expansion. It should be explained that Philip already knew the West Country reasonably well. With his parents, his older brother Frank, and sister-in-law Dorothy, he had already enjoyed at least one previous holiday in the area, where they had made good friends and acquaintances who would be useful contacts for Philip during his 1940 holiday.

His tour was planned meticulously. He would be travelling alone, as usual, which is something that in modern times we may find difficult to comprehend.

On the other hand he was always very self-sufficient, thanks to his Scout training, and he enjoyed his own company. The lessons he had learned as a Boy Scout were to stand him in good stead throughout his naval career and beyond. He remained, essentially, an eternal Scout, clinging proudly to the standards laid down by Lord Baden Powell. His entire life was lived on the basis that he should *Be Prepared*, the motto of the Scout movement. He was never found wanting.

Setting the scene: *Before Philip's journey, this was the state of affairs as far as the war was concerned: The war had been a long time coming. When it arrived on 3 September 1939 there was a brief flurry of excitement as air raid sirens and air raid drills were practised. Young children were evacuated to safety outside London and there was an extended 'phoney war', when apart from a few naval and air engagements, not much happened by way of fighting. That is...until the Nazis decided to invade Western Europe in May 1940. As it happens, that was the month that the young Philip Humphries began his naval career, starting with his basic training at*

HMS Royal Arthur, *a navy 'stone frigate' shore establishment – in* *this case, the former Butlin's holiday camp at Skegness. Apart from* *the brief holiday interlude between this and joining his first ship,* *there would be no chance of a holiday for some years to come.*

Alongside Philip's war, the rest of the world was also struggling *for survival. We can only see history from the point of view of* *the ultimate victor. But alongside the heroism and victories there* *were some dark times that, with hindsight, we can say were pretty* *shameful episodes in British history. Here is the timeline that set the* *scene for Philip's wartime progress:*

April 1940
Germany invaded Denmark and Norway.

May 1940
In February 1940, just three months shy of his 18th birthday, Philip *had pitched up at the Territorial Army Centre in Horn Lane, Acton,* *and volunteered for active service as a signalman with the Royal* *Navy. He passed his medical, then returned home to continue to* *await his call-up. It came on 7 May.*

On 10 May, Germany invaded Western Europe. Holland *and Belgium fell quickly, leaving the French and the British* *Expeditionary Force to fight a retreating campaign back to Dunkirk.* *It was from here, at the end of May, that 300,000 British troops, plus* *allies, were evacuated back to Britain in a fleet of small boats.*

Also on 10 May, a lesser-known and much-less publicised invasion *was taking place. Under Operation Fork, Britain invaded Iceland, a* *neutral country with a population of around 150,000 and without* *a standing army. Until the Nazi invasion of Scandinavia, Iceland* *had been in 'personal union' with Denmark. Foreign forces occupied* *Iceland for the remainder of the war, ostensibly to prevent an* *invasion by the Nazis, which could have threatened the safety of* *shipping convoys coming from the United States and Canada to* *Britain. This shameful episode was met with protests from Icelandic* *politicians, who said the nation's neutrality had been 'flagrantly* *violated.'*

A small fleet of Royal Navy ships, carrying an invasion force of

746 recently-recruited British Royal Marines entered the harbour at Reykjavik on 10 May and landed, to be met by a crowd of largely female Icelanders. Over the war years Iceland was occupied by 30,000 British, Canadian and then American troops. It led to an episode known in Iceland as 'The Situation' – the situation being that Icelandic women were throwing themselves at the invading servicemen with the inevitable disastrous consequences. More than 500 local women were said to have had affairs with foreign servicemen, leading to the birth of 255 children. Many of the women and girls – some of whom were said to have been as young as 12 - were falsely accused of either prostitution or of having been raped, until it transpired that any relationships were consensual and eventually led to more than 300 happy marriages. On the positive side, the occupying forces did manage to build a substantial road network and airfields around an otherwise undeveloped country. The initial invasion was without any casualties on either side. The only casualty as such was a young British marine who sadly took his own life during the outward voyage. To be fair, the only resistance likely to have been put up by the Icelandic people would have been from a small group of 60 armed police and 300 reservists who wisely chose to hold their fire against the larger invading force.

The entire episode, apart from its dubious legality, was little short of a farce. The British troops were so poorly trained at that stage that many of the new recruits had not even had the experience of firing a rifle. No one in the British invading force could speak more than a few words of Icelandic. There were few maps of Iceland to share amongst the invaders. Much of the equipment they should have taken with them was actually left on the quayside when the ships left Scotland. Planning of the invasion was pretty much a 'back of a fag packet' effort carried out while they were at sea en route.

The invasion of Iceland took place less than a month after British forces had also invaded another former Danish territory - the Faroe Islands between the Shetlands and Iceland - under Operation Valentine. Then in June 1940 British army and navy forces occupying the Faroes seized a small fleet of destroyers of the Royal Swedish Navy – another neutral country – that happened to arrive in port. Britain refused to hand them back to Sweden for many months. During this time the ships were stripped of equipment by British troops and, basically, trashed before being handed over. The British Government had to pay a substantial amount to Sweden by way of compensation.

It is worth bearing these British invasions in mind when we consider the understandable outrage the British people felt about the German invasion of the Channel Islands in June 1940. In all cases – Iceland, the Faroes and the Channel Island - occupying forces remained on the islands until 1945.

The following *is Philip's account of his journey, which he logged in the form of a daily diary in a hard-backed exercise book. Where necessary I have added explanatory notes in italics. The title of the following chapter is mine, not his. As far as he was concerned, it was a straightforward daily log of his excursion. Bear in mind that by the time he set off for the West Country, the Battle of Britain had been under way for more than two weeks, the official start date now being recognised as 10 July.*

Photo: Philip on a camping trip - probably in 1939.

With hindsight we may now question the wisdom of Philip's parents in allowing their youngest son to travel alone across country in wartime, during bombing raids and with invasion likely at any time. It says much for their faith in him and their faith in England. It was such that they could treat any threat of invasion as a trivial inconvenience. They were very strict Methodists and their faith in the protection of the Almighty was unshakeable.

3 The summer of lost innocence

Summer 1940

Philip writes...

The intended route to be taken was via Chideock, near Bridport, Colyford, Exeter, Ashburton, Tavistock and Liskeard. But owing to the imminent threat of German invasion, all the south coast up to Plymouth was declared a restricted area, so the route had to be changed to run along the north coast of Somerset, Devon and Cornwall.

KIT LIST

Sleeping bag	Comb
Mug	Hair Oil
Plate	Shaving kit
Knife	Stockings
Fork	Scout Jersey
Spoon	Camp hat
Sandals	Torch
Soap	Pencil
Towel	Mirror
Groundsheet	Tea cloth
Handkerchiefs	Permanganate of Potash
Toothbrush	Billy
Toothpaste	Tent

Hairbrush	Swimming trunks
Dubbin and cloth	Matches

27th July 1940 SATURDAY

Started off from Cranford at 9.15am and made steady progress until I was about one mile outside Reading when it started to rain, so I had to stand up underneath a tree for about half an hour until it had stopped raining.

Reached Reading about 12 noon but I lost my way going out of the town and found that I had gone about seven miles out of my way, so I got back again onto the main Bath Road, where I had my lunch.

During this respite I was asked the way to Reading by an RAF officer in a lorry and I promptly told him that he was going entirely in the wrong direction. In fact he was heading for Newbury.

Went through Newbury, Hungerford and Marlborough and then turned out of my way slightly to see the stone circles at Avebury. These circles are a really magnificent sight but they are cut into by the roads.

This circle is nearly four times as big as Stonehenge and it has an enormous ditch and rampart round it.

I then went back and crossed the Bath Road and went along the Devizes Road. After I had got about two miles along the road it started to rain – of course it would be in the middle of the plain with no trees about, so I had to make a dash for the nearest shelter, which was about a mile away.

The stone circle at Avebury, seen from the air

Then I passed through Devizes, Trowbridge and then reached Frome, which is built on a terribly steep hill.

I lost myself again getting out of Frome but was redirected and about two miles out of Frome I found a camp site, which was next to the main GWR line *[Great Western Railway]*.

[Note: The distance from Cranford to Frome is more than 100 miles – not a bad distance to cycle in one day! At this time, following the Dunkirk evacuation from 26 May - 4 June, the Germans were conducting 'Kanalkampf' – Channel War - taking on the Royal Navy in the English Channel, in preparation for the invasion of England. On 27 July 1940 the destroyer HMS Codrington was sunk by the Luftwaffe at Dover and another destroyer, HMS Wren, was sunk off the Suffolk coast at Aldburgh.]

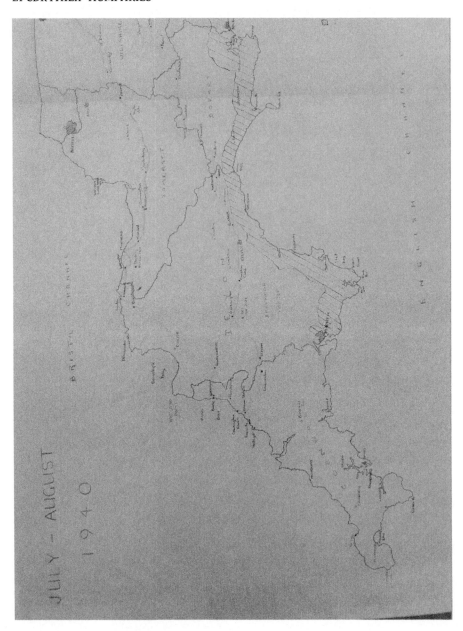

Map illustration: Philip's hand-drawn route map

Saturday night
About 11.53pm I was woken up by the sound of the air raid sirens in Frome. The planes could be plainly heard and were passing northwards but they did not drop any 'eggs'.

At 12.10 the planes could be heard coming back again and at 12.13am there were two terrific explosions from the direction of Frome.

The planes could be heard overhead two or three times later and at 3.10am the 'All Clear' went.

[*Note: Although it was a relatively harmless market town and not an obvious military target, Frome suffered more than most from German bombing. This was on account of the fact that it lay on the route taken by German bombers flying from France to Bristol and Cardiff, where aircraft factories and the docks were important targets. As an example, between July and December 1940, no less than 121 bombs were dropped on Frome. It was no doubt a dumping ground for bombers who had not released their full load on Bristol and found it convenient to release their remaining bombs on any suitable targets on their way home, as Philip's narrative suggests. The bombing continued for much of the war. Quite what Frome had done to deserve this unwelcome attention is not clear but as if the town hadn't suffered enough already, on one day later in the war two German Focke Wulf fighter-bombers spent an afternoon strafing and bombing the town at their leisure.*]

28th July. SUNDAY

Got packed up and started off at 10.15. Had a good journey to Shepton Mallet but just outside there my carrier slipped and put my back brake half on (I did not notice this till later, although I felt the slowing up effect at the time).

Just outside Glastonbury I met one of the Glastonbury Scouts and he told me that they had been having on the average three Air Raid warnings a day.

After leaving Glastonbury I had a very steep climb right up on to the hills and then had a fairly good journey to Bridgwater.

Just outside Bridgwater I had something to eat and while I was having this I was overtaken by a charabanc containing Jack Payne and his Band.

[Jack Payne and his Band were amongst the UK's top jazz stars of the dance band era in the 1930's. Jack made his name as a regular broadcaster on BBC radio and from 1932 onwards he and his band toured Britain regularly. In 1941 he was appointed Director of Dance Music at the BBC, remaining in that post until 1946. After this he became a disc jockey and made occasional appearances on BBC TV's 'Juke Box Jury' in the 1950s.]

On arriving in Minehead I promptly lost my way but I soon found it again and after a five mile ride I arrived at Allerford, which was looking as pretty as ever it did, with the quaint old packhorse bridge and its marvellous gardens.

I found the farmhouse, got permission to camp and was just in the middle of tea when the farmer visited me, so we had quite a long talk. But the main subject was the War on the Welsh coast.

Medieval packhorse bridge at Allerford

Went down to Porlock in the evening but all the shops were shut. Coming back to camp I ran into some London Scouts, who were a very cheerful crowd.

[*Note: Sunday 28 July 1940: RAF involved in dog-fights with the Luftwaffe between Plymouth and Dover.*]

29th July. MONDAY

Went up the Oare valley in the morning, which I reached after a very steep climb up Porlock Hill.

Visited Oare church and saw the window through which Lorna Doone of the novel was supposed to have been shot through (sic).

On the return trip I cycled all the way down Porlock Hill and then did some shopping in Porlock village at the bottom, during which I met the troop of Scouts again.

The 'Lorna Doone' window at Oare church

In the afternoon I decided to go into Minehead and if the

tide was right to have a swim. But when I got there the tide was full out so I just cycled along the front, had a look at the harbour and the bathing pool and then went into the town and did some shopping.

Got to camp and had my tea and then wandered down to the beach but I did not like the look of the extremely large pebbles so I went back and turned into bed early.

[Note: Monday 29 July 1940: Mass German bombing raid on Dover. Intercepted by the RAF. Fierce fighting during the defence of Dover, following which four George Medals were awarded to Dover port personnel. The destroyer HMS Delight was sunk off Portland.]

30th July. TUESDAY

Got up early and got my kit packed ready to go to Bude; had my card filled-in and paid the farmer.

Started off at 9.30am and took three-quarters of an hour to walk up Porlock Hill. When I had just passed the Oare valley a motor coach overtook me with Mrs Godden, nee Eileen Reah in it.[Unable to establish who she was, or her importance}

Went down Countisbury Hill to Lynmouth and then had a stiff climb up the other side.

When I had got about ten miles outside Holdsworthy I was given a lift in a milk lorry for about 14 miles. I then went down to Stratton and along the main Bude-Camelford road to Wainhouse Corner where I enquired the way for Coxford Farm. On arriving there I was given a field to camp in and after putting my tent up I went with Ruth and Jean to feed the chickens.

[Note: On this day shipping convoys were being attacked by the Luftwaffe off Orfordness, Clacton and Harwich. The RAF shot down an Me.110 off Southwold.]

31st July. WEDNESDAY

Got up fairly early and then went down to the farm and watched John and Mr Cowling milking the cows, then went with Jean and helped with the duck (sic), chickens etc and gave a general helping hand round the farm.

In the afternoon I sat with Mrs Cowling, Ruth, Molly and Jean under a haystack and had a talk about different things including a discussion on the Milk Marketing Board.

Went down to Crackington Haven with Edward in the evening and met Mr Crabb and most of the local boys, who are a very friendly crowd.

Had a bathe with the boys and then went up to the farm again and had supper in the farmhouse with the Cowling family.

Crackington Haven, Cornwall

1st August. THURSDAY

I went into Bude in the morning and did several odd jobs for the Cowling family, then put an inner tube in Ruth's cycle.

Did the journey to Bude in 23 minutes from Wainhouse Corner.

In the afternoon I was asked if I would help the Cowling family pick peas. I agreed, so we started off but were given a lift by Mr Crabb, who helped us pick 30 pounds. We then got back into the car, went down to Wainhouse Corner and gave the peas to Molly to sell. We then sat and drank quarts of water.

When we got back to the farmhouse we collected our bathing costumes and went to Crackington Haven and had a swim with Ruth, Jean and Mr Crabb.

Went down to Crackington Haven again in the evening and had a bathe with the local boys, afterwards having a game of sardines on the cliff side, the idea of the game being that one person goes out and hides (usually among the gorse bushes) and then the rest go out and try to spot him.

When you have spotted him you try to get in with him without being spotted by the rest, so that by the time you have finished you are all cramped together in a very small space and getting lots of complaints from the people sitting on the gorse bushes.

[Elsewhere in Europe on this day, the Luftwaffe was directed to achieve air superiority over the RAF, with a view to incapacitating RAF Fighter Command.]

2nd August. FRIDAY

Gave a general helping hand with the farm work in the morning. Mrs Cowling, Fred Cole, Jean Cowling and Edward Cowling had to go into Bude in the afternoon (Edward to have his teeth out and Jean to go for a week's holiday), so I went down to Crackington Haven and found Mr Crabb already there.

Had a swim with Mr Crabb in the afternoon and then took Fred Cole down to Crackington Haven on the back of my bike and waited for the local boys, then had a swim with them, afterwards walking back up the hill and picking blackberries on the way up.

3rd August. SATURDAY

Went down to Crackington Haven in the morning and saw

Henry Hall's family (ie, wife, daughter and son), then went down to have a swim in the sea.

[Note: Henry Hall was another famous band leader of the time. He made regular broadcasts on BBC radio. In 1932 he took over from Jack Payne as leader of the BBC Dance Orchestra, and with them broadcast every weekday at 5.15 pm, attracting a huge following. Henry Hall is best remembered these days for his famous recording of 'The Teddy Bears' Picnic', which sold over a million copies.]

Then went back and had dinner afterwards, going down to Crackington Haven and having another swim and sun bathe. Whilst I was having this, the local boys joined me and we had some grand fun.

Had another turn in the evening and then went up the stream with the boys and they taught me how to catch trout with the bare hands. The way to do this is to search under the stones until you feel a trout 'kick' and then start tickling it under the belly. When it pushes its body into your hand you then start working your way up its body towards its gills and then get the fins in your hand and the thumb and forefinger in its gills, then you can just lift it out of the water.

After catching four trout we had another game of 'sardines'.

[Note: On this day Italian forces began their invasion of British Somaliland.]

Coxford Farm, Crackington Haven, in the 1940's

4th August. SUNDAY

Got up and cooked the trout over the fire and had them for breakfast. They were really delicious.

Got ready for chapel and went there about 11am, afterwards being invited by Mrs Cowling to dinner in the farmhouse and had a really good dinner there.

Changed into shirt and shorts and had a bathe at Crackington Haven in the afternoon and on returning I was invited to tea with Mrs Cowling and family and really blew myself out.

Went to chapel in the evening and then went down to Crackington but we did not bathe as it was too dull. Instead I sat and talked with the local boys for a long while, afterwards going back to camp and turning in.

5th August. MONDAY

Went to the shop and got some stores in, then went round the apple orchard picking up all the windfalls which I cooked for dinner with some blackberries that I had picked previously.

While this was cooking I went down to have a look at the

cattle fair at Wainhouse Corner.

Went down to Crackington Haven in the afternoon and took my tea with me, so I stopped for the evening.

Had a bathe in the evening but the sea was quite rough so I had to give the local boys some help in getting through the breakers until the calmer waters were reached further out.

Had a game of sardines and then caught three trout for my breakfast.

6th August. TUESDAY

Went down to Wainhouse Corner Post Office in the morning for Mrs Cowling. I then went down to Crackington Haven and had a bathe.

Saw the Hall family again and missed listening to the Eisteddfod on the wireless in the morning, so I went down again to have a bathe in the afternoon.

Caught one trout in the afternoon and was then met by Ruth on the beach, afterwards going back and having tea in the farmhouse with the Cowling family.

Had an early bathe in the evening and then went up to watch the local boys being drilled for the LDV. *[Local Defence Volunteers – the forerunner of the Home Guard. Just a week or two previously, the new Prime Minister, Winston Churchill, had announced that the LDV would formally be changing its name to The Home Guard.]*

The Cowling family, pictured in 1944

7th August. WEDNESDAY

Went down to have a bathe and met a girl from Sutton, Surrey, in the water. Mr Crabb came down with the Hall family so I watched them bathe.

Came up for dinner and then went down in the afternoon to catch four trout for Mr Crabb and taught Michael to 'tickle' trout, which he tried unsuccessfully to do.

Went down again in the evening to find Mr Crabb, Betty and Michael Hall there, so I stopped with them for a time.

Came back to the tent and changed into uniform, afterwards going down to the beach and speaking to Jean Cowling over the telephone.

Watched the sun go right down into the sea, which was a really glorious sight.

8th August. THURSDAY

Rained in the morning but it left off for a little while, so I went down to the beach and watched the people swimming.

Got my dinner at a cafe near the beach, for which I had roast chicken, three vegetables and blackberries, apples and cream and a cup of coffee for 1/6d. *[just under 8p in current currency]*

Bathed with Betty and Michael Hall and Mr Crabb in the afternoon; met the girl from Sutton in the water.

Had tea with Mr Crabb, Betty and Michael Hall at which we could not stop laughing at Mr Crabb's friend who was with us.

I had another bathe after tea and then waited about down there. Met the Sutton girl in the evening at 7.30 and I learned that she was training to go on the stage; agreed then to correspond with her, her address being Miss Jean Smith, Trevone, Crackington Haven, Bude, Cornwall.

Said goodbye to the local boys and then went back to bed.

9th August. FRIDAY

Packed up my tent etc and said goodbye to the Cowling family, then started off about 10 o'clock. Made steady progress to Otterham Station going through a watersplash on the way and then went towards Launceston with the wind behind me.

Passed a cattle fair just before I got to Launceston, then passed through Launceston and went down a fairly steep hill towards the country again.

Went through Okehampton and then on to Exeter, which seems to be built entirely on a hill.

Was directed through Exeter and then went on towards Honiton. When I was about five miles outside Honiton I met an RAF man who cycled to Honiton with me.

Had to stop and mend a puncture (my first since I started), then reached Honiton where I put in supplies.

Went on towards Chard and stopped to pick some blackberries by the road, then tried several farms for camping, eventually stopping just outside Chard.

The diary stops abruptly here. We can only assume that the final leg of the journey back to London was never recorded simply because the demands of the Royal Navy were too pressing. Within a few days of this final entry Philip had joined his first ship as a naval Rating. Whether Miss Jean Smith ever received a letter from him, or he from her, was never recorded.

That was not, however, the end of his association with Crackington Haven. He had first gone there with his parents, brother Frank and sister-in-law Dorothy on a caravan holiday in the late 1930's. He was to return again to stay with the Cowlings at Coxford Farm in October 1944 on honeymoon. The final pilgrimage to the Cowling's farm was made in 1961 during a family holiday to Bude.

The holiday in Cornwall was a pleasant but brief interlude in the commencement of Philip's naval service. So to take a step backwards (and in his own words), this is what happened shortly before the West Country episode...

4 Volunteers take one pace forward

Philip writes:

I volunteered for service in the Royal Navy at the Territorial Army centre in Horn Lane, Acton, in February 1940 as a signalman. I thought that as I had been in the Scouts for many years and knew all my signal work backwards it would be better to go in for something that I knew rather than have to start a new trade. Having passed my medical I was then called up on 7 May and told to report to the RTO *[Regional Transport Office]* at King's Cross station in London for onward routing to *HMS Royal Arthur* as a trainee signalman.

On arrival at King's Cross I found that there were six of us going to *Royal Arthur* and I was put in charge of them and handed the tickets with orders to report to the RTO at Skegness.

Having reported, we were then placed in a lorry and driven to *HMS Royal Arthur*, which turned out to be Butlin's Holiday Camp at Skegness, which had been taken over by the Navy for the War as a signal training base.

The next morning we were kitted up and given our service numbers - mine was C/JX234430 – and started our training. I found that in the camp was one of our Scouts, Reg Endacott, so I made my number with him – but this was a rather short-lived meeting.

The following day we had to be interviewed by an officer and I was told that I was going to be made a C.W. candidate *[Commissions and Warrants – in other words, officer training]* for eventual training for a Commission. However, I was told that this could not be done in the Signal Branch and that I would have to do my training as a Seaman. So much for my hope of an easy entry into the Navy!

I was sent to *HMS Collingwood* at Fareham in Hampshire on 14 May to start my training. I found that this was not as onerous as I had first thought, as I had already carried out most of the work in the Scouts, so once again that training came in handy.

One amusing thing happened whilst I was there. On the first day that we were allowed a run ashore, three of us decided to go to Fareham and there we were walking down the High Street when we saw a man resplendent in a gold braid-filled uniform. Being absolutely new, we chopped him off a smart salute as we went past, only to find that it was the Fire Chief standing outside the fire station!

HMS Collingwood, 1940. Philip is back row, centre

My training was eventually completed and on 14 July I was sent to Chatham barrack for drafting to a ship.

After a very short spell in the barracks, which took some getting used to, I received a draft chit to join *HMS Sunflower*. The time in barracks was the only time that I spent there and apart from the rather sparse conditions in the barracks themselves I was rather surprised to find that the toilets, or 'heads' as they are called in the Navy, were outside at the end of the building.

They consisted of a wall about five feet high, then an open gap about two feet high, with a roof over the top.

The ablutions themselves were just a long trough with running water going down it, with a long board over the top with a lot of holes in it.

Of course, when it was full in the morning you had some wag at the top end put a screwed-up newspaper down the trough and light it and let it float down the trough, with the obvious shouts of pain as it progressed down.

So my time in the barracks came to an end and at the end of July I was sent to join *HMS Sunflower*. *[According to naval records, HMS Sunflower was launched on 19 August 1940, although Philip's recollection is that this is the date she was commissioned. She was the most successful of the Flower Class corvettes and spent her entire war career in and around the North Atlantic. Later in the war she was responsible for sinking two German U-boats.]*

5 Atlantic convoy duty

***HMS Sunflower* was built** at Smith's Dock in Middlesborough. She was a Flower Class corvette, built on the hull design of an ocean-going trawler. She was 925 tons, 205 feet long, with a beam of 33 feet. She had a single propeller, giving her a speed of 16 knots, although she regularly exceeded 18 knots.

She had a complement of 85, which included four officers. Her armament was one 4" gun on the forecastle, one Oerlikon gun just abaft the funnel; two Hotchkiss guns on the wings of the bridge, ten depth-charges in rails on the stern; two depth-charge throwers each side and 40 depth-charges in racks placed around the upper deck. Her pennant number was K41.

The ship's crew was mainly H.O officers *[Hostilities Only - in other words, temporary commissions for the duration of the war]* and ratings. The commanding officer was Lieutenant Commander John Treasure Jones, RNR, who, pre-war, was a Liverpool stevedore. He later went on to become the last captain of the *RMS Queen Mary.*

First Lieutenant was Lt Fanshaw, RN, and the other two officers were Sub.Lt Brown, RNVR, and Sub.Lt Lilley, RNVR.

HMS Sunflower

We had to go to Tobermoray on the island of Mull for working-up for convoy escort duties. The trip around the north of Scotland was quite an experience with a completely new crew, most of whom had never been to sea before. In fact, there was a continuous queue outside the 'heads'! *[latrines]*

On arrival at Tobermoray we had our first experience of the notorious Vice Admiral Sir Gilbert Stephenson, who was well known throughout the navy for his tough training routine.

Immediately we anchored 'Monkey' as the admiral was known – mainly because he looked like one – sent for our Captain, so it was 'away, seaboats crew'. After quite an hilarious trip we arrived at the HQ ship, which was *HMS Western Isles*, a converted passenger steamer which used to ply between Liverpool and the Isle of Man.

We had several amusing episodes there, as 'Monkey' would suddenly arrive on board without any notice, to try and catch us all off-guard. On one occasion this was very effective. When he arrived on board in the middle of the night he found no one on watch at the gangway, the Quartermaster having to gone to make a cup of tea in the galley.

Vice Admiral Sir Gilbert Stephenson

Monkey, with the assistance of his boat's crew, then removed the safe containing the confidential documents and took it back on board the HQ ship. He then signalled the ship requesting details of the papers contained in the safe, much to the embarrassment of the Captain, who had to report the safe missing.

We carried two Newfoundland ratings on board who were a law unto themselves. *[When World War II broke out in 1939, Newfoundland was a Dominion administered directly from the UK, and was not yet a territorial part of Canada. Men from Newfoundland volunteered for the Royal Navy, many of them distinguishing themselves for their bravery. However, they were notoriously independent minded and often difficult to keep in order]* When 'Monkey' appeared in the early hours of the morning one of them was the Quartermaster on watch.

As soon as 'Monkey' arrived on board he took off his cap and promptly threw it into the sea, saying to the 'Newfy' "What are you going to do about that?", expecting the Quartermaster to call away the seaboat's crew. He was much surprised when he received the answer from the 'Newfy' "You slung it in...you get it out."

We were all surprised that he got away with it. Many years later, after the war, I was speaking to 'Monkey' when he was guest at a Mess Dinner of Croydon Flotilla of the RNR. I recounted the episode, which he remembered very well. He told me that it was the first time he had had that reaction, so he overlooked it!

Having completed our 'working up' procedure we were despatched to join the 2nd Escort Group lying in Londonderry in Northern Ireland.

The group consisted of *HMS Vidette* as escort leader, and the corvettes *Sunflower, Alisma, Dianella* and *Loosestrife.* In those early days the convoy assembled off Liverpool and the inshore escort took them up the Irish Sea and handed them over to us off Rathlin Island.

The convoy formation was of many columns numbered from the port hand column looking from inside the convoy and vessels were then numbered inside the column. So ship number 711 was the 11th ship in column seven.

The usual number of ships in the convoy was between 60 and 70. The largest number we had was with convoy HX300 when we had 169 ships made up from 19 columns with up to 11 ships per column.

With four cables *[approx 741 metres, or nearly half a mile]* between columns and two cables *[approx 370 metres, or just under a quarter of a mile]* between ships in column this took up quite a lot of ocean!

Having left Londonderry we went down the River Foyle and tied-up alongside the oiler, which was lying off Moville, which was in the Irish Republic.

We always had bum boats come alongside from the Republic selling butter, eggs, bacon etc, which of course were all on ration in the UK.

Having been issued with free cigarettes, called 'Nelson' – which were absolutely unsmokeable – we used to trade them for their farm produce. This went on for some time until the Paddys found that the cigarettes were so bad they could not sell them ashore. After that we had to pay cash in the normal way – but at least we supplemented our rations.

Having oiled we then proceeded to take over the convoy from the inshore escorts and proceeded up through The Minches, between the Hebrides and mainland Scotland. The convoy had to split into columns, as the local fishermen were out in force with their nets out across the fairway. We had several incidents with the fishermen claiming damage to their nets.

On arrival at Cape Wrath we reformed the convoy and the escorts took stations. The destroyer took the lead, sweeping ahead of the convoy. The corvettes were situated one on each corner of the convoy, with (eventually) one sweeping the stern of the convoy.

The speed of the convoy, of course, was the speed of the slowest ship and in those early days they used anything that floated, so it was quite normal to have one of the old coastal tramps trying to keep up with the convoy which was reduced to a speed of 2½ knots, which caused havoc as we and many of the ships in the convoy could not get down to that speed. Even then the old tramp was trying to keep up, belching out smoke and on one occasion we had to tell the offender to return to port.

Our route took us from Cape Wrath to 80 miles south of Iceland, where we handed the convoy over to the Yanks and accepted an incoming convoy from them. Although they were not in the war at that time they undertook the escort duties for us on the other side. This went on for a long time until, on one occasion, we had a Force 8 gale at the exchange point and we missed each other, so we carried on right across the Atlantic and the Yanks eventually ended up in Londonderry.

Ever after that we both went straight across the Atlantic. The only snag we had with this arrangement was that the destroyer did not have the range that the corvettes had and she had to go into Reykjavik to refuel.

Of course in the winter this northerly passage gave us extremely cold weather so we were all issued with Arctic clothing, including woollen long-johns which I could not wear...so I turned them into a hearth rug. Invariably we had an ice-chipping party as we had ice on the rigging and all over the upper deck. On the first occasion that we met pack ice, which was in the middle of the night, we all rushed up on deck wondering what the crashing and banging was, going down the ship's side. After this as soon as we experienced pack ice we tucked in behind one of the ships in the convoy and so had an easier passage.

On one trip we received a 'Mayday' from a Norwegian whaling factory of 14795 tonnes, the *Svend Foyne*, which had been torpedoed just to the north of us. So, being 'tail end charlie', which was our usual position, we were detailed-off to take her into Reykjavik. When we found her we found a hole in her side big enough for us to steam into. Apparently she was later converted into a tanker and when carrying 20,000 tonnes of High Flash Point fuel, was sunk by an iceberg. Anyway, we escorted her to Iceland and then proceeded up to Hvalfjiord, where we tied-up alongside the *Kent* to await the return convoy. We did not enjoy this one little bit, as she was too "pusser" for us *[ie, too correct or too 'regulation'. In this context he no doubt means they were not as swashbuckling as the Sunflower. HMS Kent was a heavy cruiser, built in the 1920's.]*

On another occasion we were 50 miles off *HMS Hood* when she was sunk by the *Bismark*. As she was heading straight for the convoy we were told to disperse the convoy and turn and engage the *Bismark* – with the biggest gun any of us possessed being a 4-incher. Luckily for us the *Bismark* turned south and we were told to rejoin the convoy, which by this time was scattered over half the North Atlantic.

The German battleship Bismark

With the speed of the convoy being so low it used to take us about 40 days to get across the "herring pond". We then had a glorious four days in which to re-provision, refuel and turn the ship around before we embarked on the return trip. The usual port of call on the other side was St John's, in Newfoundland, although on a couple of occasions we ended up in Halifax. St John's at this time looked more like a Wild West town, with timber buildings. In fact, the only brick-built place was the YMCA. The harbour, though, was fantastic. You went through an entrance through the cliffs, about two cables wide *[approx 370 metres, or just under a quarter of a mile]* and emerged into a lagoon with first-rate anchorages.

The accommodation on board was rather sparse. The messdecks were right forward in the bows, with the stokers' mess forward and the seamen's mess at the after end of the mess space, just under the 4-inch gun. We had to sleep in hammocks which were slung in the tween-deck spaces and in the messdecks. In rough weather we had water coming in through every available space, so when you got out of your hammock, invariably you ended-up in around six inches of water and then had to find your seaboots, which were floating about and usually full of water. When 'Action Stations' was sounded you had two minutes to get to your post, which in my case was manning the PAC rocket on the port side of 'Monkey's Island', which was above the Asdic Hut on the Bridge, where you were fully exposed to all the weather. This was so-named as it was one of the favourite places that 'Monkey' Stephenson used to go in order to oversee all that was going-on on board.

On one occasion my 'oppo' on the starboard rocket was on the sick list so the other CW candidate on board, Trevor Wing – who was a reporter on the Daily Telegraph in civilian life – took over his position on the rocket.

The PAC rocket *[it stands for Parachute And Cable, and was a means of laying a type of aerial minefield designed to bring down enemy aircraft]* was fired from a small mortar after having loaded a charge in the breech at the bottom. When the rocket was fired it went off in a shower of sparks and flame, so a lanyard was provided about one fathom *[six feet]* long so that you could get as far away as possible, the rocket then sending down a flare on a parachute at the top of its trajectory.

Of course, Trevor not knowing the procedure wound the lanyard around his hand and, being dark, I didn't see this. When he was told to "Fire PAC starboard!" he pulled his lanyard and the resultant sparks and flame set fire to his hair – so there we were with him running around Monkey's Island trying to put the flames out.

It was about this time that I had an episode with one of the Newfoundland ratings. Our watch consisted of four of us. When we were on watch we had two lookouts, one on each wing of the bridge, one quartermaster on the wheel and one boatswain's mate. When we changed watch the boatswain's mate went up and relieved one of the lookouts, who then took over the wheel and the previous quartermaster went up on the bridge to relieve the other lookout, who then became the boatswain's mate.

On this particular occasion, the Newfy who was on watch with me was on the wheel whilst I was the boatswain's mate. His steering was, to say the least, atrocious and as the First Lieutenant was on watch on the bridge he was constantly being given a 'blast' for being off-course and chasing the compass. After a while he said "Sod him!", left the wheel and walked out of the wheelhouse.

I immediately took over the wheel but when it came time to change the watch he was nowhere to be seen. After a while the First Lieutenant called down, asking what had happened to the change of watch, so I said that the Newfy had had a touch of the squitters and had gone down to the heads *[toilets].* Our WT *[Wireless Telegrapher's]* office was just at the back of the wheelhouse and I knew that the Coder, Peter Hammond, invariably slept there, so I left the wheel, went to the WT office and asked Peter Hammond to go below and find out what had happened to the Newfy.

He found that he had gone down and got his head down. He managed to get him up again and, fortunately, the First Lieutenant was none the wiser – but it was a bit of a close shave for a time.

It was only whilst reading the *Navy News* of June 1999 that I read that Canon Peter Hammond had died, aged 78, and that when he left the Royal Navy at the end of the war he had taken Holy Orders and became the Church of England's foremost authority on church architecture. He was appointed Canon and Prebendary of Lincoln Cathedral in 1987.

It was around this time in 1941 that we had to go to Cammel Laird's shipyard at Birkenhead to have a new device fitted. It was called RDF *[Radio Direction Finder]* and was the forerunner of Radar. We had a structure like a lighthouse tower built on the port side immediately abaft the bridge.

On one trip one of the RDF operators went sick and I was delegated to take over his watch. When you compare the set with Radar, it was very primitive indeed. It consisted of a screen similar to a PPI *[Pixels Per Inch – eg a Radar display]* screen but instead of a cursor sweeping around it had two lines across the screen and when you got an echo off an object it gave a 'blip' on the screen. You had to train the aerial round by means of a handle above you. When you obtained an echo that was suspicious you had to call up the bridge, give the relative bearing from the angle of the scanner above you and then read off the distance from the blip on the screen.

Having completed the refit we then returned to Londonderry to await the arrival of the rest of our Escort Group, who had all been away having their RDF sets fitted. However, we found that the number of our Escort Group had been changed to Bvii, that we had a new Escort Leader, the *Duncan*, a destroyer; another corvette was included, the *Poppy*, and that we were to be based in Argentia in Newfoundland, although we still returned to Londonderry. The reason for this was that we would provision and oil over the other side, thus saving the transport of our victuals and fuel over the Atlantic.

6 All at sea

Argentia was situated in Placentia Bay on the southern side and opposite the town of Placentia, which was about 20 miles away across the bay. This was one of the lease-lend bases that the Yanks had taken over.

When we first arrived there we found that all that was there was a T-shaped jetty, with the *USS Prairie*, a depot ship, tied-up at the outboard end. There was one small hut ashore and a railway line that ended in nothing – not even buffers, let alone a station!

We did have one bit of excitement there, however. On one occasion they had a fire on board the *USS Prairie*, and as we were all secured alongside we had to cast-off...the only snag being that the only one of us with steam up was the outboard ship, so you can imagine the fun we had being towed-off and going round and round in circles until we all managed to raise steam.

The other problem we faced was that although the *Prairie* had some wonderful PX shops on board and a very good cinema, we did not have any US dollars, so we had absolutely no chance of using their facilities.

When we arrived off the Grand Banks of Newfoundland the convoy was dispersed, with the individual ships going to their destination ports. Invariably we then searched around with the ASDIC and echo sounder to find a shoal of fish. When the fish had been located we used to get anything possible to get the fish out of the sea – including buckets on the end of a line – even down to the skipper's cane wastepaper basket on the end of a boathook. We then dropped a pattern of depth charges...and we had fish all over the place. However, we had to be quick in getting the fish aboard, as the depth charges had only stunned them and they soon revived and swam away.

After the Escort Group had been renumbered we abandoned the practice of going through The Minches and instead went straight out into the Atlantic from Malin Head towards Rockall. On one trip we were 300 miles out from Ireland when the Panamanian-registered ship *Chepow* was sunk at around midnight [*14 January 1942*]. Being 'Tail-end Charlie', as usual, we requested permission to pick up survivors. The request was refused as we were then under attack by a U-boat 'wolf pack'.

At about 0500 hrs we obtained permission from the Commodore to return and attempt to find survivors. Fortunately we had plotted the position of the *Chepow* when she sank and we immediately aimed for that point. It was very much like 'The Cruel Sea' [*a famous wartime novel by Nicholas Monsarrat – made into a successful black-and-white movie in 1953*], as we arrived on the site, going straight through the survivors.

We could not, of course, just put on the brakes but could only stop engines and sail through them. Fortunately nobody was injured in this manoeuvre and we turned and came back to them. To our horror they were shining their torches on our ship's side and shouting "Good old K41"! It took quite an effort to get them to turn out their lights.

We managed to rescue the entire ship's company with the exception of two of the engine room crew, although some of them were in a bad way and most were covered with fuel oil.

One of them said to me: "We have always looked at you bouncing up and down and thought how uncomfortable it must be – and now we are sharing it with you!"

The trouble was that we had picked up more survivors than ship's company. The weather worsened and before we got half way across we had run out of food and had to exist on the remains of the stores, which were all the items that the ship's company didn't like. And so we spent a fortnight living on ship's biscuits and tinned tomatoes, with the tomato juice being the only liquid that we had.

We had to wash in seawater and it was distinctly uncomfortable. I must say that ever after that I was unable to eat tomatoes.

Eventually, my time on the North Atlantic convoys came to an end when I had to return to the UK and report to *HMS King Alfred*, a shore establishment in Hove, East Sussex. I left a very happy ship's company and despite the continuous 'Action Stations!' and ships being blown up all around us – even, on one occasion, having a torpedo fired at us – I wouldn't have missed it for the world.

7 Going up in the world

From Londonderry I was sent to Portsmouth Barracks for a full medical and then on to Mowden school, which was part of *HMS King Alfred*, at the back of Hove. We were accommodated in private houses and had to go to the school during the day.

The Admiralty Board was at Mowden school and they called on each of us separately and questioned us on various types of Naval subjects. If you passed this exam you were then passed on to Lancing College, where the training-proper started.

While there my classmates discovered that I knew my signals. When we had to do our visual Morse we were paired-off in the quadrangle and one would read whilst the other took down the message. When it was my turn to read everyone got as near as possible to me and urged me to "speak up".

The difficulty came when I had to write down for my 'Oppo' when I had to have my back to the signal lamp. However, I soon found that by looking at the windows in front of me I could see the reflection of the light, so I did both the reading and the writing then!

Once the course was completed at Lancing you were then passed on to *HMS King Alfred* itself, which was a new baths complex that had been built in Hove and was alongside the RNVR *[Royal Navy Volunteer Reserve]* base. I was billeted in rooms above the Post Office nearby.

In all the time we were passing through the various phases we were being examined.

If you failed any of the tests you were sent back to general service as a Leading Seaman, so at least you got some promotion. Of course, with all the weeding-out that took place the numbers decreased rapidly. When we started at Mowden School we were more than 300 strong. When we eventually finished at *King Alfred* we numbered just 38.

Having taken the final exams we ordered our new uniforms and we were commissioned as Sub Lieutenants - as the photo shows!

8 Going Commando

Philip was now at a crossroads in his military career. He could more or less choose his own pathway and, with a boyish sense of adventure, opted for the Special Services Brigade. This had been formed in 1940, with the intention of carrying out raids on mainland Europe. After a number of reorganisations the Brigade would eventually fracture into the Commandos proper, the Parachute Regiment, the Special Air Service and the Special Boat Service. History books record that the Royal Navy established its own commando units in 1943. However, historians seem to have got it wrong, as Phil recounts. He takes up the story:

I had completed two years on North Atlantic Convoy escorts, serving in *HMS Sunflower.* Her commanding officer was Lieutenant Commander John Treasure Jones, who would later go on to end his career afloat as the last Captain of the *RMS Queen Mary.*

Conditions on board the *Sunflower* were rather bad as she was constantly rolling. We were wet-through most of the time and life was generally very uncomfortable, particularly as we spent part of our time operating in Arctic waters.

Having left the *Sunflower* I was one of 320 candidates for officer training at *HMS King Alfred,* from where 38 of us obtained commissions as Sub Lieutenants.

On completion of our training we could choose which appointment to take up. As I was then fed up with rolling around the ocean I saw an appointment for two officers for Special Service. I decided to apply, as it appeared to be something different, only to discover it was for the Royal Navy Commandos, who were then just forming.

Royal Navy Commandos badge

This was a new section of the Navy and at that time comprised Numbers 1 and 2 Commando, with two officers and 38 men per Commando, made up of a Leader, Deputy, two Petty Officers, two Telegraphists, two LTO's *[Leading Torpedoman]*, two Gunnery rates, one signalman and the remainder being Seamen. Most of the men they gave us came from Detention Centres. Obviously they thought that we were all expendable!

For our training we were sent to *HMS Armadillo*, a shore base at Loch Long in Scotland, which really was the back of beyond.

Location of the Commando training base

[Glenfinart House in Glenfinart Forest, Ardentinny, Argyle and Bute. This was requisitioned by the Royal Navy and from 1942 became the training centre for the RN Beach Commandos. It was their job to be first on the beach in any seaborne assault, to make the beach safe from underwater objects and mines, then to hold the beach while the main force arrived. Later just known as the Royal Navy Commandos, they had the dubious honour of always being the last troops to leave the beach when the assault concluded. Their motto was 'In Primo Exulto' – First in, last out. By the end of the war the Royal Navy Commando had expanded to become 22 units, each named alphabetically – A, B, C, D etc. Philip was in 'C' Commando by the time of the landings in Sicily and the Italian mainland.]

There we met up with our men and they were such a tough crowd that if they didn't like you, it was quite clear you were liable to get knifed.

Our initial training included unarmed combat – but not the usual type. We were taught to kill first and ask questions afterwards. For those we didn't kill we were taught how to take prisoners and tie them up so they couldn't escape.

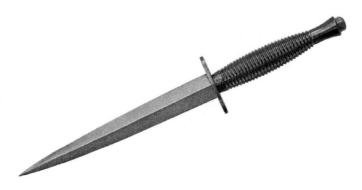

*The Fairbairn-Sykes fighting knife - the
famous Commando dagger*

We were taken over assault courses with increasing speed
and every morning we had to get up at 0400, go onto LCP(S)'s
[Landing Craft, Personnel] and were taken about ten miles
down the loch, the boat stopping about 20 yards off the beach,
when we had to go overboard in full equipment, including
a .303 SMLE *[Short, Magazine, Lee Enfield]* rifle, together with
ammunition, and swim for the beach.

On landing we then had to form up and routemarch back to
the camp, to be taken yet again over the assault course. When
we were dry and inspected we were then allowed to have our
breakfast.

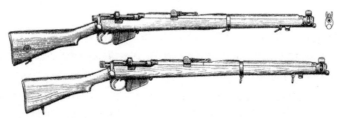

The SMLE .303 rifle - standard WW2 infantry issue

The landings we did from the boat were particularly
hazardous as we had been kitted out with 'Pongo' *[ie, army]*
battledress, full webbing equipment – including a back-pack

– plus a 'Mae West' lifejacket. On the first occasion that we carried out one of these landings one of the bright sparks decided that he did not require his Mae West inflated. On stepping off the boat he disappeared into about ten fathoms of water, losing most of his equipment on the way.

Originally we used the Naval-type battledress but found out it was too dark, which made us conspicuous, so we changed it for khaki, which then became standard wear.

We were taught to make a quiet landing on the beach despite being soaking wet and to carry out our allotted task.

Royal Navy Commandos being inspected
by Lord Louis Mountbatten

Other experimental landings were carried out using a Dory *[a small, shallow-draft boat with high sides and a flat bottom]* and rubber dinghys, the latter ending up as our method of making a landing from a submarine – our usual method of landing.

We were taught how to deal with the various types of beach defences, which were tripod, rail, scaffold pole and stake, and how to deal with booby traps and mines.

It was found that we had to work under water on some of these defences, so initially we tried just holding our breath but found that this was impractical. As scuba gear had not then been invented we devised our own diving gear, using a service respirator facepiece, attaching several extra hoses onto the existing one and then putting a large cork float with a hole in the middle over the end. We then filled our pockets with shingle to weigh us down and by this method found that we could work for up to 20 minutes under water.

Commandos on board a Landing Craft (Personnel)

Our objective was to clear passages through the beach defences. Having done this we then had to mark the channel, which we did by carrying a gross of condoms each, blowing them up, attaching a length of fishing line to them with a large stone on the other end, which made an ideal buoy. We often joked amongst ourselves that if Jerry captured us he would have thought we were a load of sex maniacs.

We also learned how to use plastic explosive underwater, to shear off the legs of some of the beach obstacles. Our tasks also included marking beach exits and, of course, we had to learn how to walk on shingle beaches without making a noise – no easy task in standard issue army boots.

HMS Armadillo jetty at Ardentinny

[It is worth observing here that the "Beach" commandos had to land on a hostile beach without being observed, locate and dismantle anti-tank obstacles, clear mines, mark-out safe routes across the beach for the main landing force following-on later and generally make the beach safe - all in silence, while soaking wet and in complete darkness, right under the very noses of German sentries. The stress and adrenalin levels of these young men must have been phenomenal!]

When we landed on beaches lookouts were posted and we had a warning 'alert', which was rather like the sound of the sea on shingle.

Once a beach was cleared we spread out along the back of the beach waiting for the assault to take place.

We were soon to put our training to the test.

9 DIEPPE

The Dieppe raid *[19 August 1942]* was the first major assault in which we were involved. No one on the Allied side at that stage had ever carried out large-scale landing operations so had no idea what they entailed. They could only make a guess at what was required although it was certain that to sustain a major landing a port must be captured.

At this time – 1942 – Stalin was pressing the Allies for a second front to be opened, to relieve the Nazi pressure on Russia.

The reasons for choosing Dieppe for this:
· Air cover had to be readily available
· A small port had to be captured
· The target area had to be close enough to reach under cover of darkness
· The radar station on the west headland adjacent to Dieppe was becoming a nuisance to the Allies.

Two alternative plans were produced. One was to make strong assaults on both flanks, with the centre kept under threat; the other was to make flank attacks and a strong attack on Dieppe itself. Plan 1 was discarded as the only suitable beach (apart from Dieppe itself) that tanks could land on and obtain access to the hinterland, was at Quiberville, which meant that the tanks would have to cross two rivers to get to the port.

It was decided that parachute troops would attack the flanks to destroy the coastal batteries and that landings would be made at Pourville and Puys to support the frontal attack on

Dieppe itself. This would be preceded by heavy air attack. Surprise was to be the main tactical achievement.

The original intention was to carry out the raid on 21 June. However, the final 'dress rehearsal' exercise was a complete fiasco, with troops being landed on the wrong beaches, some landing craft being up to an hour late, plus security was being breached by the Canadians.

Another rehearsal was held over 22/23 June which was better although there were still navigational difficulties, so that the correct beach was not always found, so it was decided to use infra-red beacons, which we had to set up as part of our beach clearance programme.

Three special Radar vessels were to be provided, equipped with infra-red directional finding apparatus.

One important change was made to the original plans: a heavy bombardment was discarded as it was thought that this would alert the enemy. It was agreed, however, that the destroyers and fighters would attack the beach defences just before touchdown.

The Naval flotilla was to consist of eight destroyers plus numerous ML's [motor launches] and gunboats, all to be under the command of Captain John Hughes-Hallet. As part of his preparation, it transpired, he had spent a month as Private Hallett with the Cameron Highlanders of Canada, to find out how this type of operation would seem from the army perspective. According to records he was remembered as being a good soldier and a bad card-player!

HMS Calpe [a Hunt-class destroyer Type II] was to be the HQ ship and was adapted to carry out this type of operation.

The attack itself was to be launched on a front extending for 11 miles, from Berneval in the east to Quiberville in the west. There were to be five main assaults which were divided into eight separate landings as follows:

Left flank	Berneval	Yellow 1
	Belleville	Yellow 2
Inner left:	Puys	Blue
Centre left:	Dieppe	Red
Centre right:	Dieppe	White
Inner right:	Pourville	Green
Right flank	Varengeville	Orange 1
	Quiberville	Orange 2

The difficulty was that the Royal Navy Commando could not cover the entire length of the landing beaches, especially as they were not continuous.

We carried out a night survey of the beaches over about five nights. It was decided that the flank beaches appeared to be fairly clear of obstacles but the main beach at Dieppe was heavily blocked. As this beach was divided by the harbour it was decided to use No. 1 Commando on Red and White beaches. This beach had to be used as it was the only one with any possibility of landing tanks and deploying them inland. The other beaches had steep ravine-type exits which were full of barbed wire going all the way up the cliffs.

Intelligence reports indicated there were two companies of infantry in the town of Dieppe and it was thought that it would take a good while for the enemy to reinforce the garrison.

The artillery seemed to be three coastal defence batteries – one at Berneval, one at Varengeville and one at Arques-la-Bataille.

In addition there were two four-gun batteries behind Dieppe and one four-gun battery on either side of the town. Also, the headlands flanking Dieppe beach were heavily fortified and the Casino at the western end of the beach had been turned into a strongpoint.

There were machine guns in concrete pillboxes all along the coast – even in the buildings on the clifftops. Altogether... a very tough nut to crack!

Time to go!

By the end of June all was ready and a date in early July was chosen. The troops embarked – but the weather changed and everyone was cooped-up for days on end, waiting for it to ease. It was decided that 8 July was the last possible date for a suitable combination of time and tide. By 7 July the weather was still bad and then another problem arose. Enemy planes had spotted the ships assembled in the Solent and attacked them with bombs and machine gun fire – so the landing [called Operation Rutter] was cancelled.

By mid-July it was once again approved and this time called Operation Jubilee. Changes were made to the plan, with the embarkation points dispersed. The date was set: 19 August.

The altered plan was that at 0445, Commando Group No 3 under Lt Col Durnford-Slater would land at Berneval and go for 'Goebbels' battery. At the same time, Group no 4, under Lt Col Lord Lovat, would go ashore at Quiberville and attack both the 'Hess' battery and radar station, then both groups would withdraw.

The main reason for attacking the radar station was that the Germans had perfected a piece of equipment for their radar which the Allies were very keen to obtain. So it was decided that as the troops had absolutely no idea what this item looked like, they would take along a civilian expert, kitted out in battledress, to obtain this item and then to evacuate him, which they eventually did very successfully.

At the same time as these assaults, the landings on the inner flank would go in: that on Blue Beach at Puys, who would attack the field battery behind the village, and that on Green Beach at Pourville to secure the village, attack the west headland and capture the fortified position known as Quatre Vents Farm, about one mile inland.

Half an hour later a landing would take place at Green Beach and assault the airfield at St Aubyn and the German HQ at Arques-la-Bataille, with this assault to be supported by tanks from Dieppe.

Finaly, at 0520 (ie, half an hour after the flank landings) the main assault would be made on the centre beaches under cover of a brief bombardment.

Once the beach was under control the Royal Marine Commando was to enter the harbour and seize or destroy any invasion barges that may be there.

The main thing was to obtain an element of surprise. Around 5000 Canadian troops and 1000 British Commandos of one sort or another took part.

What follows is what actually happened from my perspective:

At 2345 on 18 August we disembarked from a submarine one mile off the beach at Dieppe in four inflatable dinghies. The Royal Navy Commando was split into sections, with the Commanding Officer leading at Red Beach (centre left); myself at White Beach (centre right), one Petty Officer at Blue Beach (inner left); one Leading Seaman (the Petty Officer was sick) at Green Beach (inner right), with the remainder of the men being divided eight per beach.

On landing two lookouts were posted at the rear of the beach and the immediate surrounds were reconnoitred to find out the number and type of troops in the immediate vicinity.

We found two machine gun nests at the harbour entrance; two anti-tank guns were on the harbour wall and four batteries of 10cm field guns, as well as heavy coastal batteries, together with numerous pill-boxes containing machine guns. There were also machine guns in the hotels along the front.

In all this there were some lighter moments. On landing one of the seamen found that his battledress trousers had come out of his gaiters, so he sat on the beach to put matters right. The next thing we heard was our warning signal from him, so we went to investigate, only to find that he was sitting on a 'Teller' mine. These were a double-action mine designed to knock out tanks. If a tank went over the mine it triggered it but did not explode until the pressure was released, so that the rear of the tank – which was its weakest part, was destroyed. This meant that had the seaman attempted to stand up the mine would have exploded, so we had to defuse the mine underneath him. All he kept saying was "Mind my wedding tackle!"

As for the Dieppe defences there was no sign of an alert in operation. In fact only two sentries could be seen and they were lounging about and occasionally smoking.

There was a concrete sea wall, varying from six to ten feet in height, running right along the back of the beach. Access points were determined and the task of clearing beach obstacles began.

On investigation it was found that since our night survey, anti-personnel mines had been wired to the beach obstacles. These were removed. The obstacles were steel tripods with a curved front leg, which we later found out were old Czechoslovakian railway lines. These were held together by a single nut, which with typical German efficiency had been well-greased, so gave us no problems.

It didn't take long to dismantle the obstacles to make a clear water channel about one cables' length *[a cable is one tenth of a nautical mile – in other words, a cable's length is 100 fathoms, which translates to around 600 feet]* in each sector.

At the same time the anti-tank mines that were left on the beach were disposed of and piled up at the rear of the remaining obstacles. The landing channels were then marked by buoys and infra-red beacons were set up at the back of the beach, marking the channels.

We then cleared the remainder of the beach of mines and ran marking tape to show the exits from the beach. Having completed our main task we then dug slit trenches in the beach and positioned men armed with hand grenades at the back of the beach by the major gun emplacements.

By 0300 the beach was ready for landings, so we positioned ourselves at the back of the beach under the shelter of the sea wall.

At 0330 there was terrific gunfire out at sea which turned out to be a German inshore convoy of eight ships destined for Dieppe meeting one of the outlying ML's [motor launches] and a short engagement ensued, the Germans thinking that it was an odd ML on patrol. This, of course, aroused the Germans and they came down to the sea wall just above us, occasionally lobbing a cigarette butt over the top of us. Fortunately they did not look down or we would have been spotted.

With all the star shells being fired, the troops ashore immediately went to Action Stations. The engagement lasted about 20 minutes and at about 0400 the Dieppe outer harbour light started flashing and we then thought that they must discover us. We were completely illuminated every time the light came round. Once the convoy entered Dieppe harbour the troops stood down from their Action Stations.

Dieppe harbour and seafront, 1942

At Dieppe seafront, which is about one mile long, there was a promenade and then a boulevard named Boulevard Marechal Foch. Beyond the boulevard are lawns and gardens about 150 yards in depth and running the whole length of the front. There was then another boulevard, the Boulevard Verdun, which was lined with hotels and boarding houses on the landward side. To the left of the centre of the beach was the tobacco factory and on the extreme right, overlooking the beach and under the west headland, was the Casino.

There were many streets leading off the Boulevard Verdun to the centre of the town. The entrances to all of these streets had been blocked with concrete walls containing firing positions let into the wall. Heavy barbed wire defences stretched the full length of the beach. The west headland had many machine-gun positions covering the beach – and there were field guns in the castle on the west headland. Some obstacle!

At 0510 the Naval covering bombardment opened up and waves of bombers and fighters swept in to attack the hotels along the front. We were in our small slit trenches in the beach – fortunately for us. Immediately, the beach, gardens and hotels became an inferno, with exploding bombs and shells. We were fortunate that we only had one rating slightly hurt.

By this time the landing craft had been spotted and came under direct fire. The first landing craft hit the beach at 0523 and the troops landed to withering fire. The tanks which should have landed with the troops were nowhere to be seen. There had been an error in navigation and the LCT's [*Landing Craft, Tank*] with the tanks aboard had gone off course and arrived 15 minutes late, finally beaching at 0535. Fierce enemy fire and severe damage prevented many tanks from leaving the ships.

The tanks that did get off had difficulty in getting traction on the shingle and we cursed them for making the sides of our foxholes fall in. Timber ramps had been made for the tanks to get over the sea wall but these were so heavy that it took 20 men to lift them. As fast as they were lifted Jerry just picked the men off. Consequently, only one ramp managed to be positioned. Those tanks that managed to get into the gardens were unable to get into the town because of the concrete walls and tank traps. Some troops managed to enter the hotels from the rear and they accounted for many enemy snipers. In fact, six of our commandos were in this party.

At approximately 0900 there was a lull in the firing and one of our telegraphists, who was in the next trench to us, had a small Primus stove. He brewed-up, ran down the beach to us with two mugs of 'Char' – but Jerry opened up again, so he just dived into the trench. We got our tea alright – but we were covered in it!

By this time many of the Canadians had got into the town and were attacking machine gun positions and snipers. For a while the streets adjacent to the front were cleared of the enemy. The casino was taken and at 1030 we started to evacuate the beaches. This carried on until approximately 1300 in various phases, whenever a lull in fighting permitted.

The landing at Berneval on the flank was very successful. The landing at Quiberville was extremely successful, with the radar station being taken and the 'boffin' being taken off with his piece of equipment. In fact, Lord Lovat, with his commando, went inland, round the back of Dieppe and secured most of the back of the town.

The landing at Pourville (inner right) was successful, with penetration inland to Appeville at the back of Dieppe.

[What Philip has under-played is the fact that the men of C and D Commandos were involved in incredibly fierce combat, including hand-to-hand fighting with the German defenders. The casualty rate amongst the Commandos was high. In speaking about it during later years Philip was always very cagey about the extent of the fighting because it was at odds with his calm nature and his strict Methodist upbringing. He just said, "It was a question of kill or be killed."]

The lessons we learned:

1) New equipment was required, especially for navigation. Infra-red was to be used with leading lights and signals denoting the various beaches. There was a request for D/F *[direction finding]* to be produced, which eventually led to the invention of the directional-finding apparatus known as R/H.1

2) A more precise knowledge of booby traps was required, as many new types were appearing and many more were being used.

3) A bombardment was essential. All attempt at surprise landing was a failure.

4) Tanks must have direct exit from the beach, with the ability to overcome obstacles. Major General Percy Hobart was given the task of inventing these items.

5) A method of preventing loss of body heat by continuous immersion in water was needed. This led to development of the 'wet suit', although this had to be modified later.

6) A minimal amount of ammunition should be taken ashore by those undertaking beach clearance duties. This ammunition should not be carried about the person but taken in separate containers. The outcome of this was that during landings the ammunition pouches were used for all sorts of objects. In fact, on D-Day Roger McKinley, a Royal Naval Commando, joined one of

the groups attacking some pillboxes. His account went "unfortunately between us and the battle area were some of the enemy, so we decided to push our way through and do what we could to mop up the Germans on the way. We soon got bogged down by some 88's and machine gun nests. The Major called me up as the senior NCO and said 'Let's put some grenades in there and get rid of them.' He said 'Use your grenades' but although I had my pouches strapped on I was not carrying any grenades. I had only got shoe-cleaning gear and boot polish in one pouch and my soap and flannel in the other."

7) A Beachmaster was required to take control of the landings and to direct vehicles to beach exits.

8) It was not feasible to capture a port, so this ultimately led to the development of the Mulberry Harbour.

The following is a summary of the Dieppe raid compiled by the BBC for their web site, to commemorate the event:

The Dieppe raid, 1942

On 19 August 1942, a disastrous seaborne raid was launched by Allied forces on the German-occupied French port of Dieppe. Why was such a raid ever undertaken? Because, with Germany operating deep in the Soviet Union, the Russians were urging the Allies to relieve the pressure on them by opening a second front in north-west Europe.

At the same time the British Chief of Combined Operations, Rear Admiral Louis Mountbatten, was agitating for a practical trial beach landing, against real opposition, for his troops. In the face of this pressure, Churchill decided that Operation Rutter, a 'hit and run' raid on Dieppe, should go ahead.

The plan and the players

British Lieutenant General Bernard Montgomery's South-Eastern

Command provided the troops for the operation, and planned an unimaginative frontal assault, without heavy preliminary air bombardment. Montgomery was also being pressed by the Canadian government to ensure that Canadian troops saw some action, so the Canadian 2nd Division, under Major General Roberts, was selected for the main force.

These troops were to assault the town and port of Dieppe, while, as a distraction, British parachute units would attack German batteries on the headlands on either side of the Canadians.

The first rehearsal was a disaster, but a second try, ten days later, went better, and Montgomery was satisfied. On 1 July it was agreed that the raid would take place either on 4 July, or on the first day afterwards that promised favourable weather conditions.

The attack was to be mounted from five ports between Southampton and Newhaven, with forces made up of around 5,000 Canadians, 1,000 British troops, and 50 US Rangers. There were 237 ships and landing craft, and 74 squadrons of aircraft, of which 66 were fighter squadrons.

Changes and security

The weather was consistently bad, however, and on 7 July the operation was postponed. Montgomery wanted it cancelled altogether, as the troops had been briefed and he was afraid that word of the operation might leak out. Unusually for him, however, he did not persist with his demand, and preparations continued. He was not involved in the matter for long, in any case, as he was summoned to Egypt to command the Eighth Army.

Meanwhile, a number of changes to the plan were made. The codename was changed to Jubilee. The planned air bombardment on Dieppe was reduced, for fear of French casualties, and because of the continuing priority of the strategic bombing offensive on Germany. Eight destroyers were allocated to bombard the shore from seaward, as it was judged that battleships could not be used, being too vulnerable when they were close to the coast.

The parachute operation on the flanks, even more dependent on the weather than the seaborne assault, was cancelled. This task was instead given to Numbers 3 and 4 Army Commandos, to the relief of the Commanding Officer of 1st Parachute Battalion, who later commented that from the outset of the raid 'security was abysmal'.

It was decided that the Royal Marine Commando, which had been in the force from the outset, was to land in fast gunboats and motor boats after the main force had gone in. They were then to destroy the Dieppe dock installations, and capture documents in a safe in the port office. The break-in was to be the special responsibility of a marine who had been a burglar in civilian life.

Intelligence on the enemy was patchy. There were German gun positions dug into the sides of the headland cliffs, but these were not spotted by Allied air reconnaissance photographers. Planners assessed the beach gradient and its suitability for tanks only by scanning holiday snapshots. As a consequence, enemy strength and terrain were grossly underestimated.

In addition, the Germans were on high alert having been warned by French double agents that the British were showing interest in Dieppe. They had also detected increased radio traffic and the concentration of landing craft in Britain's south coast ports.

Initial assault

The raid began at 04.50 on 19 August, with attacks on the flanking coastal batteries, from west to east. These included Varengeville (Number 4 Commando), Pourville (the South Saskatchewan Regiment and the Queen's Own Cameron Highlanders of Canada), Puys (the Royal Regiment of Canada), and Berneval (Number 3 Commando).

By this time, however, the element of surprise that the planners had counted on was lost. Some of the landing craft escorts had already exchanged shots with a small German convoy off Puys and Berneval at 03.48.

Despite this, Number 4 Commando successfully stormed the Varengeville battery. This was the one unit that captured all of its objectives that day. Only 18 men from Number 3 Commando got ashore in the right place. Nevertheless, for a time they managed to distract the Berneval battery to such good effect that the gunners fired wildly all over the place, but the commandos were eventually forced to withdraw in the face of superior enemy forces.

At Puys, the Royal Regiment of Canada was annihilated. Just 60 men out of 543 were extracted from the beach. And only a handful of the men of the South Saskatchewan Regiment reached their objectives, with others from this regiment landing in the wrong place. The Queen's Own Cameron Highlanders of Canada, despite being landed late, did manage to penetrate further inland than any other troops that day, but they were soon forced back as German reinforcements rushed to the scene.

Main assault

Half an hour later the main frontal assault by the Essex Scottish Regiment and Royal Hamilton Light Infantry started, supported by 27 Churchill tanks of the 14th Canadian Army Tank Regiment.

The tracks of most of the tanks were stripped as they were driven on to the shingle beach, and the bogged-down vehicles became sitting ducks for German anti-tank guns. Those tanks that did cross the sea wall were stopped by concrete roadblocks. The infantry were slaughtered on the beach by vicious cross-fire from machine-guns hidden in the cliffs. Supporting fire by naval destroyers was far too light to have much effect.

To make things worse, Canadian Major General Roberts could not see the objective, because of a smoke screen laid by ships in support of the landings. As a result, acting on incorrect information and unaware of the mayhem on the beaches, he now made the mistake of reinforcing failure and sent in his two reserve units.

Les Fusiliers Mont-Royal, launched straight at the centre of the town, were pinned down under the cliffs, and Roberts ordered the Royal Marine Commando to land in order to support them. This was a completely new task, involving passing through the town and attacking batteries on the east headland. The last minute change of plan caused utter chaos. The commanding officer had to transfer all his men from gunboats and motor boats into landing craft used in the earlier waves, and brief them on the new mission in very short order.

Many of the RMC craft were hit and disabled on the run-in. Those men that did reach the shore were either killed or captured. The commanding officer, Lieutenant Colonel 'Tigger' Phillipps, seeing that the mission was suicidal, stood up on the stern of his craft and signalled to those following him that they should turn back. He was killed a few moments later.

At 11.00, under heavy fire, the withdrawal from the beaches began. It was completed by 14.00. Casualties from the raid included 3,367 Canadians killed, wounded or taken prisoner, and 275 British commandos. The Royal Navy lost one destroyer and 33 landing craft, suffering 550 dead and wounded. The RAF lost 106 aircraft to the Luftwaffe's 48. The German army casualties were 591.

Who to blame?

Churchill and the Chiefs of Staff - the heads of the Navy, Army and Air Force, who met daily to discuss strategy and advise Churchill - were responsible for this disastrous misjudgement. But, because no written record exists of the Chiefs of Staff approving the raid in its final form, it has sometimes been suggested that it was really Mountbatten who remounted it without authorisation. This is almost certainly nonsense.

The Chiefs of Staff disliked Mountbatten, regarding him as an upstart foisted on them by Churchill, so any unauthorised action on his part would have given them the ammunition to recommend his removal. Since Mountbatten was not removed, and the Chief of the Imperial General Staff, General Sir Alan Brooke, in his frank and detailed diary, makes no mention of his having exceeded his authority, it seems unlikely that Mountbatten can be accused of mounting the raid without authority.

General Brooke was in the Middle East from 1 August 1942, returning on the 24th, after the event. This was unfortunate, for, as the most forceful and intelligent of the Chiefs of Staff, had he been *in Britain in the days preceding the raid, he might have persuaded Churchill to call it off.*

Much has been said since about the fact that the Dieppe raid was a necessary precursor to the great amphibious operations that were to follow, in terms of the lessons learned and experience gained. Mountbatten pursued that line all his life. But as Chief of Combined Operations, he did bear some of the responsibility for mounting the operation, so one can only comment, 'he would say that, wouldn't he?'

The disaster did point up the need for much heavier firepower in future raids. It was recognised that this should include aerial bombardment, special arrangements to be made for land armour, and intimate fire support right up to the moment when troops crossed the waterline (the most dangerous place on the beach) and closed with their objectives.

However, it did not need a debacle like Dieppe to learn these lessons. As judged by General Sir Leslie Hollis - secretary to the Chiefs of Staff Committee and deputy head of the Military Wing of the War Cabinet with direct access to Churchill - the operation was a complete failure, and the many lives that were sacrificed in attempting it were lost with no tangible result.

10 Operation Torch

The North African landings
November 1942

The next landing that we took part in was that in North Africa, known as Operation Torch, which took place on 8 November 1942. As far as we were concerned this was a complete farce.

We were due to clear the beaches in preparation for the landing of American troops. When we landed we found that there were no defences, so we swept the beaches to make sure that they were clear of mines, marked all the beach exits and then sat back to await the Yanks. 'H' Hour came and went, with no sign of the landing force. When it reached H+2, or two hours after the time for the landing, we broke radio silence to find out what was happening – only to find that the American navigation was so bad that they had landed 25 miles down the coast. So we just packed up and returned to base.

[From studying official accounts of the landings, this would appear to be a beach to the east of Algiers. In the event, although some landings went to the wrong beaches, the outcome was acceptable. The area was held by troops from Vichy France, supported by Germans at various points, particularly the Luftwaffe. The Vichy French coastal batteries had been disabled by Free French resistance fighters, the Vichy French commander had defected to the Allies, so the landings were largely unopposed in that area. Other 'Torch' landings, which were opposed, were also taking place near Casablanca in Morocco and Oran in Algeria.]

11 Operation Husky - Sicily

The Sicilian landings came next and they were called 'Operation Husky'.

LST unloading in Sicily. The Commando 'Beachmaster' on the left is believed to be Sub Lt. Philip Humphries

The landing took place on 10 July 1943. We were allotted the beaches south of Syracuse *[on the south-east corner of Sicily. The commandos had the job of clearing the beaches in preparation for a landing by the British 8th Army]* and found that apart from barbed wire defences and some pole obstacles, mines were our biggest concern. These were all dealt with and we waited for the landings, which were fairly heavily opposed.

[The Husky landings were hampered by extremely strong winds, which led the defenders to believe that no one would be mad enough to contemplate an amphibious landing in such conditions. They were wrong. The Allies landed on 26 beaches along 105 miles of coast – the largest amphibious landing ever undertaken during World War II, in terms of the size of the landing area and the number of troops put ashore on the first day.]

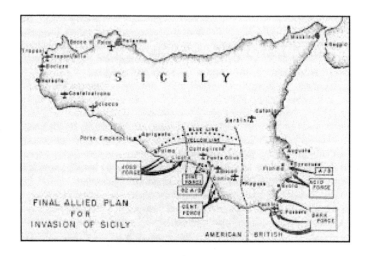

Operation Husky invasion plan

Tank Landing Ships, Operation Husky

12 Salerno

Our next objective was Salerno on the Italian mainland. This was known as 'Operation Avalanche' and took place on 9 September 1943. This was the first landing where we came under the jurisdiction of the American forces – and what a disaster that turned out to be!

We were told that we could not land as we had always done – by rubber dinghy from a submarine – as this method of landing would not work!

I personally told the American General Mark Clark that we had always landed in this way. But he was adamant that we would have to be taken in by LCA *[Landing Craft, Assault].* I pointed out to him the dangers of this method, especially as it meant going in at night, just under the Amalfi peninsular, where the phosphorescent wake of the LCA would be clearly seen. Unfortunately for us, General Clark was not going to be moved.

As we neared the beaches I was concerned that we might ground on a sandbank. So I went the wrong side of the armour-plated doors in the bow of the LCA, in order to hang over the bow to gauge the depth of the

An American assault landing craft at Salerno

water. What we had always feared then happened. The German defenders lobbed a "sobbing sister" 88mm mortar, which hit our landing craft on the stern and killed all my men. The only survivors were the coxswain steering our craft, who was in his armour-plated cockpit, and myself – because I happened to be on the wrong side of the armour plated doors.

Gen. Mark Clark, Operation Avalanche commander

I remember nothing of the incident. Apparently I was picked up out of the water later that morning. *[The operation was fairly disastrous for the Allied forces. The landings came at a heavy price of more than 7000 British troops either killed, wounded or missing in action. Additionally, the US losses amounted to more than 5000 men killed, wounded or missing. The Royal Navy losses – including the commandos involved in the incident described above – were 83 killed and 42 wounded, including the 25 men of Philip's unit who were lost.]*

I came round to find myself in the American hospital at Catania *[Sicily]*. Hearing movement I asked what time it was, to be told by a nurse that it was five o'clock. I then asked what time it would be daylight, to be met with a moment's silence, with the nurse saying that she would return shortly. She came back with a doctor, who said he was glad I was back with them again, as I had been unconscious for three days, but unfortunately it was five o'clock in the evening and it was broad daylight. I was totally blind. I had been hit by shrapnel in the right eye as, apparently, I must have been turning round to speak to the coxswain. This had affected the optic nerves to both eyes and I was to remain blind for around six months before my sight returned. At the hospital they taught me how to act and move like a blind man, which has been a useful skill ever since. But the outcome, of course, was that our Commando was completely wiped out.

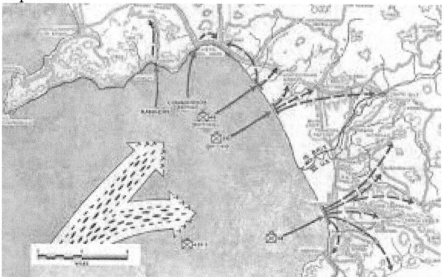

Salerno - Operation Avalanche attack plan

13 Take me back to dear old Blighty

When I regained my sight I was sent back to Scotland in a Flying Fortress, sitting the whole way on an ammunition box, which after a few hours became decidedly uncomfortable.

On arriving back I was sent to Port Glasgow to instruct on the fitting of the directional-finding apparatus RH1, as I was one of the few people who knew how it worked. Having trained quite a few ratings I then decided to take a course at Troon as Combined Operations Signal Officer, which I passed with flying colours. One part at the end of the course was to give a talk on any subject relating to signals.

I decided to talk about something that was probably little known to the Instructor. I went into town, bought a book... and swotted-up on the workings of radio.

We were supposed to talk for a quarter of an hour. When my time came I started speaking to them about everything I had gleaned from the book. In the end I was struggling quite a bit and realised I had been speaking for 25 minutes. The instructor said that he had let me carry on as he found it so interesting. If only he had known that I knew absolutely nothing about radio apart from the information I had read in the book!

I was then sent down to *HMS Lizard* at Brighton on the south coast to await onward appointment. This was where I met Wren Marie Presant, who was to become my wife.

The Wrens of HMS Lizard on parade on Hove seafront

14 HMS Glenroy and D-Day, 1944

HMS Glenroy was a cargo liner built for the Glen Line in 1938 of 9,182 tons and was taken over by the Admiralty as an LSI(L) *[Landing Ship Infantry(Large)]*. She carried 1,098 troops, the crew being Royal Navy personnel except for the engine room staff who were all T124x *[the agreement under which Merchant Navy seamen served on Royal Navy ships]*.

The cargo ship GLENROY was a most successful conversion and, in her final configuration, was armed with six 4-inch guns and had a carrying capacity of 27 landing craft and 1,098 troops.

HMS Glenroy

I joined the *Glenroy* on 1 April 1944 from *HMS Lizard*, as Force G.1. Signal Officer and the Aircraft Recognition Officer for the ship. Although I was a Combined Operations Signal Officer the captain insisted on making me take over Fleet Signal Officer's duties.

The Glenroy carried 21 LCA's *[Landing Craft, Assault]* operating as two Assault Flotillas. We carried out our main training for D-Day at Hayling Island, being based at Southampton. On one occasion we carried out a practice landing, using live ammunition, in Studland Bay when all the senior officers, including Winston Churchill, were present.

Wren Marie Presant and Sub Lt Philip Humphries

Of course, we had to have a break for lunch. As our captain was extremely nervous he insisted that I remain on the bridge for the whole period. During the lunchtime I spotted a German JU88 coming towards us from a low level and at high speed, so I immediately activated the Action Stations bell.

When the captain arrived on the bridge the plane had long gone and I received a 'blast' from the captain for activating the alarm. I assured him that it was a JU88 but he told me that I could not tell one plane from another. About an hour later we received a signal saying that the plane had been shot down and that it was on reconnaissance. The *Glenroy* was congratulated for being the only ship to be on full alert and in identifying the plane correctly. Needless to say, I never received an apology from the captain.

While we were at Southampton I used to catch a train every Wednesday to Hove, so that Marie and I could spend the evening together. I had all my secret orders and knew when D-Day was due, so on the Wednesday before, I told Marie that I could not see her the following week. She obviously wanted to know why but I could not tell her, which made her highly suspicious. When D-Day arrived she knew the reason why!

The *Glenroy* loaded troops on 30 May. They were The Hampshire Regiment. We also carried the BBC commentator Howard Marshall, who spent all his time in the captain's quarters, being eventually landed on the beaches with the troops.

HMS Glenroy off Utah Beach

Having loaded, we then proceeded to the Solent and anchored off Hampstead Ledge, along with *HMS's Bulolo, Nith, Empire Spearhead, Empire Arquebus* and *Empire Crossbow*. The Solent was becoming full of ships of various types and eventually was black with them.

As we were to be stuck out there for some time I thought of

trying to organise something like a 'Sod's Opera', so I put out feelers, trying to find some talent.

I found that with the army contingent we had bandleader Joe Loss's pianist, so we got together and presented a concert party on the After Well Deck, much to the disgust of the captain – especially as we lugged the Wardroom piano down there.

Life at this time was very boring, as we were a sealed ship, so we opened our orders and got everything organised for the 5th, only to have this postponed. We eventually sailed as a flotilla, the *Glenroy* being the Force G leader, on the late afternoon of 5 June, through the Hurst Point narrows, rounding The Needles and heading straight up the Channel. The idea was to try and fool any observers into believing that we were headed for the Pas de Calais area.

At dusk we were off Selsey Bill when we turned 90 degrees to starboard and headed for Area Z (popularly known as 'Piccadilly Circus'), which was the assembly area for taking our designated channel through the minefields.

Our captain was extremely scared and as we turned towards Area Z a strong force of Lancaster bombers came overhead and I had a furious argument with the captain, as he wanted to open fire on them. He insisted they were enemy planes, so I tried to explain that they were headed south and not north, so he said they must already have taken part in a raid. I produced the Aircraft Recognition handbook and finally convinced him when I told him that our orders were not to open fire until we were off the beaches. He was so scared of bombers that he had me on the bridge continuously for five days, even when we were in Southampton!

Having reached Area Z we took our appropriate channel and anchored five miles off the beaches on the starboard side of the channel, at 0545, there being nothing inshore of us except the battleships bombarding the beaches.

Being on the open bridge I had a wonderful view of all that was happening and I managed to get several photographs of the invasion fleet steaming past us. We had one scary moment when we heard a sound like an express train going over the top of us. This was something that we had never heard before and I think many people had to have an extensive 'dhobying' session afterwards! It turned out to be an LCT(R) *[Landing Craft Tank (Rockets)]* firing off its rockets right over the top of us.

They carried 1000 rockets and fired them off in banks of 100 as they were coming in, to clear a pathway up the beaches. It was both impressive and very noisy. It wasn't until afterwards that we found out that it was not unusual for some of the rockets to fall short.

After our first wave of LCAs went into the beaches we decided that as we had little opposition and no fire directed at us, that we would close the beaches to give the LCAs less distance to run, so we closed to two miles, which gave us a really excellent view of all the activity.

We saw many craft being hit and sinking but had very little activity directed towards us. The firing and shelling that we did witness was mainly towards the craft approaching the beaches and not those anchored off.

Having discharged all our troops, with the loss of only one LCA, we returned to Southampton and commenced a shuttle service to the beaches, only now we packed the troops in like sardines for the fairly short trip. In fact on D-Day itself we made three trips over to the beaches.

After a few days on one of our return trips we saw what appeared to be a very large cotton reel being towed towards the beaches. This rather mystified us as we could not imagine what this could be used for – but of course, it was PLUTO (Pipe Line Under The Ocean).

15 Out with a bang

These trips carried on day and night and on 17 June we had off-loaded 8000 Yanks onto Utah beach and were eastbound through the 'swept' channel when a mine went off underneath us at 1743. The force of the explosion was so great that the Bridge compass was thrown right out of the binnacle and landed on the deck. We were all thrown about two feet into the air. Then the forward boiler blew up, which added to the general confusion.

The engine-room was completely flooded, so we lost all power and lighting. Fortunately for us the American tug *Kiowa* was soon alongside and took us in tow. We managed to get the collision mat in place over the damaged section.

The ship's company were put ashore, leaving just a skeleton crew aboard and we were told to find our own way back. I managed to 'thumb a lift' in an American LST returning to Portland. They kindly gave me a cabin – so I promptly got my head down. Having been on watch for so long, however, they couldn't wake me up, so I did a further three trips to the beaches before I came-to.

They got the *Glenroy* into the King George V Graving Dock in Southampton at the top of the High Water springs, drawing 45 feet of water. There, the ship's company were paid off. The *Glenroy* was patched-up and towed to Barry Docks in Wales, where she was repaired.

USS Kiowa to the rescue!

D-Day itself was counted by virtually everyone as an adventure and there was a great deal of jollity on board. In fact, the engine-room staff asked if I could give them a running commentary on the Tannoy, as they were unable to see what was going on. This I did for about an hour. However, once we got into the shuttle routine and were working independently life became rather boring.

Viewing the landing of the troops, the destruction of the German defences and the general carnage from my position on the open Bridge, was almost as if I was looking at a TV show but with live action and sound. It was on one of these subsequent return trips that we saw PLUTO being towed across the Channel by two tugs and there was much discussion as to the purpose of these extremely large 'cotton reels'. The passage of the ships down the swept channels was almost like being on a motorway, being initially a continuous stream – although this did ease-off in the days after the landings.

When landing our final American troops at Utah beach I

obtained permission from the Captain to go ashore with one of the LCA's. It was quite an experience.

Viewing the beaches close-to, the one thing that stood out in my mind was the number of bodies floating around in the water. We passed close to one of the bodies – an American soldier. The Yanks in our boat asked the Coxswain to stop, so that they could pick him up and take him ashore. But on grasping his hand the whole arm came away and they immediately abandoned their attempt. I managed to get several photos of the beaches close inshore.

Being put onto the beaches after the *Glenroy* was mined, and walking amongst the debris of war left after the fighting, together with the sight of men clearing the bodies from the rear of the beach area, brought back vivid and sobering memories of my own previous wartime experiences on the beaches and of my comrades of those times. Particularly those who did not make it.

When the *Glenroy* was paid off I was told I would be sent back to my base, so I enquired where that was, only to be told '*HMS Mercury*'. I said that was not my base, so they asked where my base was. I said '*HMS Lizard*', as that was where my future wife was stationed, so I was sent there.

1944: On leave - windswept and interesting!

16 Back to Brighton

On arrival at Lizard I was greeted with open arms, as they did not have a Signal Officer, so I became part of the base staff. However, my stay at *Lizard* was brief as The Lords Commissioners soon found out what I had done, so they sent me back to Lancing College for re-training for General Service.

When my training was completed I was sent on leave and I married my fiancée, Marie, on 14 October 1944 at St Phillip's church, Norbury, south London, my Best Man being one of my fellow officers on my training course.

The newly-weds. Saturday, 14 October, 1944

17 Go East, young man!

December 1944

By December, Phil had been reassigned to his next ship, His Majesty's Landing Ship Tank 373. *It wasn't a particularly romantic or heroic name for a warship but it provided him with one of the most colourful periods of his naval career and left him with many happy memories of the last days of the war and the mopping-up operation. Not the least of the memories was the fact that during the course of this tour of duty he became, at the ripe old age of 23, one of the youngest ship's captains in the Royal Navy. Here, he sets the scene for the next adventure:*

LST 373 was built by Bethlehem Steel Co. Fore River for the United States Navy as *USLST 373*. Launched on 19 January 1943. The LSTs were 327ft 9 ins in length, 50ft ½ ins beam, displacement completely empty: 1435 tons. Laden with fuel ballast and fresh water 3800 tons with a laden draught of 7ft forward, 13ft 6ins aft. They had an endurance of 19,000 nautical miles at 10 knots or 21,000 nautical miles at nine knots, both fully laden.

The main engines were two General Motors type 12-567 V12 diesel 900 HP engines, driving twin screws with a diameter of seven ft. The tank deck was 231 ft long and 30 ft wide.

Loading: Since the combination of vehicles is almost infinite it is impossible to give exact figures – but to give you an idea: where the load is entirely of small vehicles, 120 could be carried. With assorted vehicles it was about 70. There was a heavyweight lift forward, which enabled lorries to be loaded on the upper deck.

The unromantically-named HMLST 373

LST 373 and I had followed similar paths in the war. She, like me, took part in Operation Husky – the invasion of Sicily. She also took part in Operation Avalanche (Salerno) and took part in the D-Day landings, being part of Force 'O', loading at Portland Harbour and arriving at Omaha Beach on 6 June.

The Royal Navy took-over *LST 373* on 9 December 1944 at Rhu Pier, Helensburgh, Scotland. Being the first British officer aboard, I was taken over the ship by one of the American officers. When we reached the after-flat I was confronted by two huge doors. On asking what lay behind the doors I was told that they were the freezers. This absolutely amazed me, as we did not even have a refrigerator on board my previous ships. I asked if I could look inside and on opening the first door all I could see were the ends of a lot of crates. On asking what they were I was told that they were chicken "...but don't worry, we'll get rid of them before we leave the ship." I told them to leave the chickens where they were and that we would take care of them. This was something we had not been able to get hold of throughout the war. He then opened the other freezer, which he said was the smaller of the two. I found myself going into a freezer about 20 feet square, with still more goodies inside.

We soon got our full complement of officers and ratings and we officially took over the ship from the Yanks. Our officers were: Lt Cdr F E Martin, RNR, in command; Lt J F Brigden, RNVR, as First Lieutenant; Lt E F Maxfield, RNVR, Engineer Officer; Sub Lt P H Humphries, RNVR as Navigating and Signal Officer; Sub Lt D McElwaine, RNVR and Sub Lt S P Merrifield, RNVR.

Having completed the handover we acquainted ourselves with the running of the ship. As it was taught to us previously that you had to keep a ship well off the 'putty' [Navy slang for 'aground'], now we had not only to put it up on the beach but to let it dry out when it was there! However, we soon got the hang of things and started to work together as a team.

We sailed from The Clyde and proceeded to Plymouth to have an LCT [Landing Craft, Tank] loaded on the upper deck – this being quite an event, as HMLST 373 was a fully welded ship and when we met some heavy seas, she would twist, with the bow going one way and the stern the other. Also, if we had a head sea we would have ripples going down the upper deck. When we first met this situation, going down the Irish Sea, we were worried that the ship was falling apart. We even thought about abandoning ship. But we soon got used to it and took it as an everyday happening.

We had to go to Plymouth as this was the only place that had a crane large enough to lift the LCT, which was placed on the upper deck, on prefabricated launchways, ready to be launched sideways on.

Eventually we sailed in convoy for Gibraltar en route for the Far East. We sailed independently through the Mediterranean, meeting one very severe storm on the way, when it was touch-and-go whether we would have to ditch the LCT, as we were rolling severely. When we were in the area of Tobruk we had VE Day [8 May, 1945] and eventually we arrived at Port Said, Egypt.

Our captain, being an ex- British India Line officer, told us to rig hoses on the stern, as the locals would try and secure themselves to the ship and get a tow through the Suez Canal. In this he was quite correct. When we sailed we had to 'repel boarders' with the hoses.

On our passage down the Red Sea, I was on the bridge with the captain when we saw what looked like a dark cloud to the west of us. On seeing this, the captain immediately ordered that all doors, scuttles and ventilators were to be closed and secured. We both left the bridge and retired to the wheelhouse just underneath the bridge. The reason for the panic was soon apparent.

The cloud we had seen was a massive swarm of locusts. Within a few minutes the whole of the ship was covered with them. They remained with us for several hours before they flew on. But even with all our precautions some managed to get below decks. We were then directed to go to Port Sudan, where we picked up some transport for Aden. We spent several days in Aden before sailing and then proceeded to Cochin, India, to offload the LCT and join the 6th LST flotilla, together with *LSTs 157, 164, 331, 371, 380, 413* and *427*.

On arriving off Cochin we had the radar pack up on us. As I was the only one on board who knew anything about radar, it was up to me to try and repair it.

The radar was rather essential as the entrance to the lagoon was only six feet above high-water level. I checked the set in the charthouse and could find no fault, so I put up a 'do not transmit' board and went up to the top of the mast to look at the scanner.

I had the back of the scanner off, fiddling about with the inside, when some clot switched the set on. I was hit with a 5000-volt surge which threw me straight off the top of the mast. Fortunately the awnings were rigged and I came down on them, bringing them down to the deck. Needless to say, the Rating involved was given the full benefit of my opinion.

We were moored fore and aft in the lagoon, opposite the village of Enakulam. When I looked out of my scuttle the next morning all I could see was a row of backsides, as the village had no sanitation and the lagoon was the only place they could use for a toilet. This was their daily routine – and they weren't about to change it for our benefit.

Out of uniform and enjoying the sunshine

We remained at Cochin for a while and then went up to Bombay and on to Karachi, where we had a mini-refit.

Whilst there we had an ENSA *[Entertainments National Service Association]* party come aboard to entertain us and we arranged with the party to go to Malibu beach the next day. This was the high-class beach area, with many beach huts along the back of the beach.

The only snag was that on going across the harbour we found that from the landing pier it was a mile to the beach, so we all hopped on camels for the trip. This is a means of travel not to be recommended. It was the most uncomfortable type of transport I have ever encountered.

Whilst we were in Karachi the General Election was held back in the UK. However, we were told that we would not be able to vote. We very nearly had a mutiny on board; apparently this feeling was general amongst the Forces in our area.

We then set sail around the southern tip of India and Ceylon *[modern day Sri Lanka]* and on up to Madras, where we stayed for some while.

Ticket to roam Bombay!

18 The war is over... almost

The Japanese surrendered on 15 August. We loaded with troops at Madras and on 1 September we sailed to join Operation Zipper – the planned liberation of Malaya and Singapore. *[Operation Zipper was originally planned as a wartime operation, with the intention of capturing Port Swettenham or Port Dickson in Malaya, as the bridgehead for landings to recapture Singapore. Following the Japanese surrender the original plan was scaled-down, although some of the landings went ahead on Penang to probe Japanese intentions. As history later recorded, although the Japanese Government may have surrendered, factions of the Imperial Japanese Army didn't all immediately receive the message, so were prepared to carry on fighting.]*

We arrived at Morib beaches, just south of Port Swettenham *[renamed in 1972 as Port Klang]* on 9 September at 0200 hrs. During the morning we beached and unloaded transport and troops.

Now, whoever chose that beach for the landing ought to have been shot. The sand on the beach was so soft that the vehicles immediately bogged-down on landing and we had to mount a rescue operation to free them.

Lord Louis Mountbatten accepts the Japanese surrender
in Singapore. On the left, obscured by the microphone,
is Lt Gen Bill Slim. On the right are Lt Gen Raymond
Wheeler and Air Chief Marshall Sir Keith Park

[Dad must have been on hand to witness the Japanese surrender
in Singapore. He took photos of the actual signing of the
surrender (below) and the photo of Lord Mountbatten giving his
speech on the steps of the Municipal Buildings. However, he gives
no eye-witness account of the historic event beyond writing on
the reverse of the main 'Mountbatten' photo reproduced here "I
will always remember this day."]

Dad continues: On 11 September we returned to Madras and loaded more troops and transport, then returned to the Morib beaches, where we unloaded. It was here that, tragically, Able Seaman Peter Ling broke his neck whilst diving off the stern of the ship. He was taken ashore to the Field Hospital but sadly died on 27 October. He is buried at Taiping War Cemetery, Malaysia, Plot 1, Row K, Grave 13.

There was one stroke of luck, however. While we were 'dried out' on Morib Beach we liberated a Jeep that had been abandoned up to its axles in sand. We recovered this and took it aboard, where the crew of REME *[Royal Electrical and Mechanical Engineers]* maintenance troops that we carried on board set-to and completely stripped-down the Jeep, as the whole of the inside of the engine and all other moving parts were completely covered in sand.

By the time we arrived back in Madras they had finished their task and we had a completely refurbished Jeep in good working order. I went ashore and got a permit from the authorities for our 'ship's Jeep'. It stayed with *HMLST 373* until after I had left the ship. The story goes that the captain took it ashore in Singapore Dockyard; an investigation was held and, unfortunately, they lost the Jeep.

After we had completed the takeover of Sumatra from the Japs we proceeded southwards, going through the Sunda Strait between Java and Sumatra.

19 Mopping up

Our next task was to ferry passengers under the RAPWI programme *[Recovery of Allied Prisoners of War and Internees].* In this case they were Dutch internees from Tanjong Priok, the port for Batavia - going to Singapore for onward routing to Holland in the liner *Nieuw Amsterdam.*

We had one trip up to Rangoon, returning with transport and where I got the chance to see Shwedagon Pagoda. It was a most impressive sight, its area covering a square mile. There were entrances on each of the four sides.

Shwedagon Pagoda

At the main entrance there was a flight of steps set into three stages, with landings in between. At the entrance of the bottom steps there was a small boy who took everyone's shoes, as shoes were not to be worn inside the pagoda.

The first flight of steps was lined each side with general shops; the second with religious shops but no shops at all on the third flight. On arriving at the top there was a vast platform with an enormous dome in the middle, covered with gold. All the way round the edge of the platform were various shrines and temples.

When we had finished sightseeing we returned, down the staircase. On reaching the bottom the small boy immediately went to my shoes, which were lined up on the steps with all the others. I thought this was quite remarkable as there were a large number of sailors there, all with identical shoes – but somehow he had managed to remember exactly which were mine!

Just to prove the point: the following photo shows British soldiers visiting the pagoda - and sorting out their own footwear - during World War II.

20 Japanese not quite surrendering

After completing Operation Zipper and the landings at Morib Beach, we returned to Madras to take on Indian troops and their transport, destined for Sumatra.

We were present at Padang in Sumatra for Operation Dulcis, when the handover was accepted from the Japs on 10 October. On entering Emmahaven Harbour, the port for Padang, we saw a Japanese officer, complete with sword, striding up and down the quayside. The regulations for the Japanese on surrender stated that they were all supposed to salute Allied officers. Our Captain, on seeing this, said "I bet that bugger wouldn't salute me if I went past!"

On securing the ship he went ashore and purposely walked past the Jap. Of course, there was no salute.

Our skipper asked the Jap why he did not salute and he replied, "I am in charge of the port and do not salute anybody."

Our Captain told him "You have surrendered and are not in charge of the port now," but the Jap still refused to salute, so our captain just booted him up the backside and sent him over the side of the quay and into the water. This soon changed his view and always after that, he saluted!

When we had been there a few days I decided to walk into the town, which was about two miles away from the port. After a while a Jeep driven by a Royal Marine captain drew up alongside me and he asked where I was going. I told him I was going to look around the town and he said he was planning to do the same thing, so he offered me a lift.

On arriving in the town we found there was an excellent market selling virtually everything. But when we attempted to buy various items we found that the market traders would not accept our new money but only the Japanese 'banana' money.

Japanese 'banana' money

The Marine captain said that he was returning to his ship - which was the HQ ship, *HMS Persimmon* – as the Japs had handed-in all their money just that morning. On arriving back alongside his ship the captain told me to wait in the Jeep. In a short while he came back with a mass of notes and split them with me. We returned to the town and went on a spending spree in the market – and it didn't cost us a cent!

[Now whether it was at this point during his tour of the Far East or at a separate time I am not sure, but in later life my father confided to one of his grown-up grandsons that life had been much more hedonistic than his sketchy memoirs suggest. Dad had vivid memories of what must have been some pretty wild and, we assume, alcohol-fuelled parties on palm-tree fringed beaches and driving around with giggling, naked girls lying prone across

the bonnet of the Jeep. He tempered his confession by saying to his grandson "...but don't tell your Gran." In his defence, I think he must have been seriously led astray by the anonymous Royal Marine captain. I hope so.]

21 The floating bomb

During our period in the East Indies we did a lot of work supporting our troops, who were in conflict with Indonesian freedom fighters. We also had to carry a consignment of petrol from Tanjong Priok to Surabaya and general cargo around the East Indies.

On the voyage to Surabaya on 4 November 1945 we were loaded at Tanjong Priok by the Japs, the whole of our tank deck being filled with five-gallon jerrycans of petrol, the remainder being placed on the upper deck in pyramid form right down the upper deck, and covered with tarpaulins.

We travelled overnight and were due to sight a single buoy which was anchored ten miles off the coast. This marked the entrance to the 'swept' channel through the minefield leading into the approach to the channel to Surabaya.

We couldn't locate the buoy and after a while I suggested that as the sun had risen virtually dead ahead we should take a sun sight using the position of the buoy as our estimated position.

This gave us the information that we had overshot the buoy, so we retraced our steps to that position but still could not find the buoy. We did, however, sight *HMS Sussex [heavy cruiser with eight no. 8" guns and other armament]* lying at the bar entrance, so we took a bearing of her and went down the bearing, which should have been the swept channel. It transpired that this was not the swept channel and that we had gone in over the minefield! On 5 November, after we arrived alongside the *Sussex*, a sister ship, *HMLST199*, went down the swept channel and unfortunately was mined.

From there we proceeded down the 22½ mile channel between the island and the mainland of Java, with the Indonesians firing at us from both sides. This, of course, punctured many of the jerrycans, so we had petrol pouring down our upper deck, out of the scuppers and down the side of the ship. It would only have taken one incendiary bullet and the whole lot – us included – would have gone up with one almighty bang!

While we were at Surabeya we were secured alongside Rotterdam Quay and we noticed some warehouses on the opposite side of a canal which ran to the east of our quay. We made enquiries and discovered that they had not been disturbed since the Japs surrendered, so we decided to investigate. The only trouble was that we had the canal between us and our destination.

We made some enquiries of the Army and they told us that there was a bridge a little way inland, the only snag being that it was in no-man's-land. But they said they had been able to get across previously by displaying a white flag. They agreed to lay-on transport for us if we wanted to try it again.

We were soon trundling down the road to the bridge, with the Indonesian troops on one side and our troops on the other. The warehouse was an Aladdin's Cave and we found plenty of useful equipment there. As a result we must have been the only LST with our own diving equipment on board.

One day, while at Rotterdam Quay, we spotted an LST which had been secured alongside Holland Pier in the inner harbour apparently with engine trouble, preparing to go to sea. We saw a small tug go alongside to assist her in negotiating the harbour entrance.

Once they got out into the main stream they appeared to increase speed without slipping the tug. For a few moments there was absolute panic on the tug, as the LST began to tow her sideways and backwards. As the tug began to list the crew began jumping overboard, with the engineer shooting out of the engine-room hatch like a cork out of a bottle.

The tug then capsized and sank, so a full scale rescue operation swung into action, with the crew being picked up and the line eventually being slipped from the sunken tug.

I never did hear the outcome of this incident. But I wouldn't mind betting that the captain of the LST was for the highjump!

22 Where the Royal Navy leads...

On one of our trips between Tanjong Priok and Singapore we were in the Bangka Strait between Borneo and Sumatra when we saw a ship coming towards us. She 'made her pennants' first and it turned out she was a United States Navy ship going from Manilla in the Phillipines to Singapore. This completely mystified us as she was still going south – and Singapore was to the north. We told them we had left Tanjong Priok en route for Singapore.

By this time she had passed us. After a few moments she called us up, saying "Which one of us is going the right way?" We immediately told them their position in the Bangka Strait, to which she replied "May we follow you, please?" – which she did.

When Singapore came over the horizon she went past us at a rate of knots, signalling "Thank you for your company". How she had managed to get so many hundreds of miles off-course we never did find out!

We changed our captain on 30 November, Lt Cdr Frank Martin going to Penang as Harbourmaster, our new Captain being Lt Cdr Simpson, RNR. However, I was only with him for a short while, as I received an appointment on 27 December 1945 as First Lieutenant on *HMLST 413*, then lying at Bombay. And so I left all my friends on board and hitched a lift on a Royal Fleet Auxiliary going to Bombay.

As a post-script, *HMLST 373* was handed back to the US Navy on 16 March at Subic Bay Naval Base in the Phillipines. In 1948 she was sold to Nationalist China and converted to a merchant ship, *Chung 118.* In 1949 she was taken over by the People's Republic of China and registered for Nationalist China. She was finally broken up in 1962.

23 Captain and Commander

HMLST 413 was built at Bethlehem-Fairfield Shipyard, Baltimore, USA, Maryland Yard Number 2185. She was launched on 10 November 1942 and handed-over to the Royal Navy, being commissioned on 6 January 1943.

HMLST 413 was 1625 tons, 327 feet long and with a beam of 50 feet. Her draught was three feet forward and 9½ feet aft. She had a complement of 86.

She sailed from New York for the Mediterranean, via Bermuda, in convoy UGS6A on 19 March 1943.

She was engaged in Operation Husky, the Sicilian invasion landing, near Noto, Sicily on 10 July 1943.

On 3 September 1943 she took part in Operations Baytown and Ferdy, the landings on the Toe of Italy. On 22 January 1944 she was part of Operation Single, the Anzio landings.

During the D-Day 'Operation Overlord' in June 1944 she was with Force J, in the 2nd LST Flotilla. On the build-up to D-Day she was anchored in The Solent in Area 22, which was just to the east of Cowes.

Out in the Far East she was with the 6th LST Flotilla (India). On 27 December 1945 I received an appointment as First Lieutenant of *LST 413*, being at that time the Navigating and Signal Officer of *LST 373*.

A Mk 2 LST, almost identical to LST 413

On arriving in Bombay I found that the Commanding Officer, Lt Cdr Phillips, was awaiting relief, as he was due for return to the UK for demobilisation. I then received a signal telling me that I was to take command. This had been approved with the proviso that I was promoted to Lieutenant Commander, as the ship was a Major War Vessel and a Lieutenant could not command a Major War Vessel.

I took over command on 20 February 1946. The officers were as follows:

Lt Cdr Philip Humphries RNVR in Command; Lt J W Cooper, RNR, First Lieutenant; Lt W W Owen, RNVR; Sub Lt J W Charlwood, RNVR; Sub Lt A Williams, RNVR and Sub Lt R D Allen, RNVR.

24 The red light district

When I took command of the ship she was in dry dock in Bombay. Even so, it was not without incident.

One evening we were in the Wardroom when the Quartermaster came rushing in to us, saying that there had been a terrible accident. One of the stokers, returning from shore leave, had fallen off the brow and into the bottom of the dry dock. We called for the Sick Berth attendant and rushed out on deck. We found the stoker wandering around the bottom of the dock, cursing and swearing because he could not find his way out. He was so pickled *[ie, drunk]* that, apart from a few cuts and bruises, he had not hurt himself.

On another occasion one of the ship's company asked for permission to have the afternoon off, as he had a "pusser" friend ashore *[Navy slang for anything that is military-like, or service issue: in the Royal Navy 'pusser' is the pronunciation of Purser, the ship's logistics officer. However, by extension it is also taken to mean anything connected with the official side of the Royal Navy, perhaps a minor officer, event or establishment.]* and they wished to go to an important cricket match that was being played that afternoon. Permission was granted.

A few days later I received a report from the Naval Provost Marshal, stating that he had been apprehended in a brothel in Forest Road and had assaulted an RAF Patrol.

I sent for him and asked what had happened, as he was supposed to be at a cricket match. He told me that he had met his friend, who was on the shore base, and that they had, indeed, gone to the match.

After it was over they had a meal in a restaurant and his friend said that he would show him the sights of Bombay, which of course included a trip down Grant and Forest Roads, the local 'Red Light' district.

He had ended up with a girl in the front, first floor room of a brothel when the RAF raided the place. The girl told him that there was a tree just outside the window and that if he went out on the balcony he could climb down the tree. This he did. But on arriving at the bottom he found the patrol waiting for him.

He admitted that he did not like the RAF at the best of times, so he proceeded to "fill them in". I could well believe this, as he was an extremely big chap, so I asked how they knew his identity. He said that he waited for them to come round and then showed them his papers.

25 Mutiny!

We were in Bombay undergoing a refit when the Royal Indian Navy mutiny took place.

[Explanatory note needed! The Royal Indian Navy Mutiny of 1946 was one of the most significant incidents in the run-up to Indian independence - and far more dangerous than Dad's narrative would suggest. It ran for just over a week, from 18 - 25 February 1946 and involved more than 20,000 sailors in 78 ships and shore establishments.

The mutiny began in Bombay with a strike by Naval ratings in protest at their poor living conditions and food. This was at a time of widespread civil unrest, as the population of India sensed that independence was now within their grasp and took the opportunity to vent their feelings on the British Raj.

The mutineers gained encouragement from a little-publicised mutiny in January 1946 by British airmen of the RAF stationed in India, who were protesting about the slow speed of their demobilisation. In effect, the RAF mutineers pretty much got away with it, without significant punishment. Taking their lead from that incident, small mutinies broke out in eastern India amongst the Indian army, followed by strikes and acts of vandalism throughout the Indian forces.

Royal Indian Navy sailors, whose senior officers were largely British, had inclined to insubordination throughout the 1940s. On 8 February 1946, a number of ratings were court martialed for being insubordinate; dissent spread through the ranks and on 18 February, all seamen below the rank of Petty Officer at HMIS Talwar, the main navy shore establishment in Bombay, began refusing to take orders from their commanding officer.

The ratings seized control of the shore establishment, expelled the officers and within a day the mutiny had spread to 22 ships in the harbour and 12 other shore establishments. By then the mutiny was beyond the control of navy commanders and on 19 February the mutineers invaded the city, armed with weapons. By the next day they had seized 45 warships in the harbour, plus the Fort and Castle barracks. They swarmed through the city, causing widespread disruption, skirmished with Royal Marines and Indian army troops sent to quell them and commandeered shore batteries and anti-aircraft guns.

At such times as this you do begin to question the sanity of the British Admiralty and the British establishment in general. It was common practice, when ships were being re-fitted, to remove all ammunition for safety's sake - as in the case of Dad's ship. When the mutiny posed a serious danger to the life and limb of all British service personnel, officers going ashore were instructed to be armed with revolvers for their own safety. I don't suppose it ever occurred to the Admiralty that these revolvers might prove useless without ammunition.

Eventually, the mutiny was put down by a combination of threats from the British High Command to disband the Royal Indian Navy and a good talking-too by Indian political leaders who did not want the mutiny to disrupt negotiations over independence.

As a post-script, following the mutiny there were arrests and courts martial, and 476 sailors from the Royal Indian Navy were dismissed. None were ever reinstated in either the Indian or Pakistani navies after independence.]

I was summoned by the Staff Officer Operations, who turned out to be Captain Hordern, who was the captain of *HMS Lizard*, the shore-based training establishment in Hove, whilst I was there. He recognised me immediately as the officer who had "pinched one of my Wrens". Marie, my wife, was at that time one of the WRNS detail at *HMS Lizard* and we were married from there in October 1944.

His reason for sending for me was to order me to cease the refit and take some of the mutineers to an island off the coast. I had to refuse, informing him that we were de-ammunitioned for the refit and that the mutineers would have been able to take over the ship. He accepted this.

While on the way to his office I had come across a gang of the mutineers stripping a Eurasian [mixed race] Wren in the street. As we had been instructed to carry sidearms I immediately produced my pistol and they quickly dispersed. I then took the Wren to the office with me. If only the mutineers had known that I did not have any ammunition for my pistol the result might have been different!

On completing the refit we were ordered to anchor in the harbour. On going through the lock gates we had the Royal Indian Navy Shore Base directly ahead. The mutineers sent a signal to us stating that we must hand over our ship or they would open fire. We trained all of our guns on them, small though they were. We sent back the signal "Bollocks" – a rather unorthodox signal but very effective, as they took no further action. If only they had known that we had still not re-ammunitioned!

Royal Indian Navy mutineer 'assisting with enquiries'

26 Singapore… and trouble ahead

Soon after, we were ordered to sail for Singapore, calling at Trincomalee *[a port on the north-east coast of what is now Sri Lanka – then called Ceylon]* on the way. When we entered Trinco harbour I received an RPC *[naval abbreviation for 'request the pleasure of your company']* from the Staff Officer Operations, which I accepted. On going ashore I found out it was Lt Cdr John Battersby, who was with me at *HMS King Alfred [the Royal Navy basic training base at what in pre-war days was Butlins holiday camp at Skegness, Lincs. There is a memorial at Butlins to this day to the men who passed through during the war, on their way to career advancement and greater glory].*

We had a very good evening together reminiscing and as I was about to catch my boat back to the ship he told me that I had a passenger for the trip to Singapore. I said that this was no trouble as we had plenty of accommodation on board. He then told me the passenger's name, which meant nothing to me, apart from the fact that he was a Royal Navy captain. He warned me to "watch things", as this captain was renowned for causing trouble.

The very next morning our passenger arrived on board and immediately told me that I must vacate my cabin, as he was going to take it over. Of course, I refused.

I told him that my cabin was in direct communication with

the Bridge and that there was absolutely no way he could occupy it. A cabin had already been allocated to him.

This displeased him no end. Then when we started our five day trip across the Bay of Bengal he, of course, wanted to come up on the Bridge. After a while he asked if he could use the sextant and take some sun sights. He was soon telling me that we were off course. The next day I made sure that I obtained some very good sights, which put us right on course. But he was still telling me that we were even further off course.

On the fourth day he said that if I did not alter course he would report me to the C-in-C *[Commander-in-Chief]* East Indies as soon as we arrived in Singapore. As we were still on our course line I of course refused, and he stormed off the Bridge.

We were due to go between Pulo Wey, the island off the north tip of Sumatra, and the mainland at 0630 the next morning. So on going down to my cabin I ordered the Officer of the Watch to arrange for me to have a call at 0500 the next morning – but if anything was sighted during the night I was to be called immediately. If we had been off course we would have ended up amongst the islands off the west coast of Sumatra in the early hours of the morning.

I received my call at 0500 and on going up to the Bridge I found that our passenger had been there all night! I looked around and said to him "There's nothing in sight yet," to which he did not answer.

After a short while Pulo Wey came up on the port bow, with the mainland on the starboard bow. We went between the island and the mainland ten minutes late, without altering course at all. I said to him "We seem to have made it alright." He was absolutely furious and stormed off the Bridge.

We arrived in Singapore Harbour at 0230 next day and dropped anchor. As soon as I got down to my cabin I received a signal from the C-in-C, ordering me to report to his office at 0900. I feared the worst. I sent for the Signalman and asked if the captain had made a signal ashore and I was informed that he had not. I then sent for the Telegraphist and asked him the same thing but no signal had been sent, which rather mystified me.

27 Lord Louis Mountbatten

On arriving at the C-in-C's office later that morning I was told that he had not yet arrived and that I should wait for him. About ten minutes later Lord Louis Mountbatten arrived and asked me to come into his office.

Not knowing what to expect, I was agreeably surprised when he asked me if I had had a good trip. He asked if I had experienced any trouble.

I replied that we had had an uneventful trip and that any trouble had been dealt with. He then told me that he had been very worried, as he knew the reputation of our passenger captain and was concerned in case he had tried to carry out what was apparently his usual ploy of getting his own way with everything, right or wrong. I told him that he had tried but had been unsuccessful.

Lord Louis then said that he had wanted to meet me, as I was the youngest officer that he had ever known in command of a Major War Vessel. I was 23 at the time. My thoughts were what a marvellous man to have taken such an interest in an officer that he had never met before!

The days passed and we were working as a Flotilla with SOLST *[meaning unclear]* afloat in one of the LST's *[Landing Ship Tank]*. One day, having been ashore on duty, I was waiting at Clifford Pier for my boat, to return to the ship, when I saw a CPO *[Chief Petty Officer]* walking up and down. I seemed to recognise his face. Eventually I said to him "I have met you somewhere before." He said he was thinking the same about me, so we started going back over the various ships. It turned out he was the Leading Steward on *HMS Sunflower* when I was aboard. By this time my boat had arrived, so I asked him if he could come over to my ship in the morning at about 1100hrs, when we could have a "wet" together and go over old times. He told me that he was SOLST's steward and he could arrange a boat to bring him over.

My day cabin was just abreast the accommodation ladder and the next morning, when his boat came alongside, I heard him ask the Quartermaster for me.

"Oh, you mean the Skipper?" was the response. This absolutely took him aback, as when we were on the *Sunflower* he was the one who always had me scrubbing out the Wardroom flat!

Eventually the time came for us to hand the ship back to the US Navy. We had a meeting of all the Commanding Officers and we were told to return all our 'Confidential' books whilst we were at Singapore and to ditch everything else on board, so that we just handed back the hull to the Yanks.

I enquired if everything was to be ditched, only to be told that if I wanted to take anything I was quite at liberty to do so. When I returned to the ship I sent for the 'Chippy' *[the ship's carpenter]* and asked him to make some crates for me, which he did, so I managed to get quite a few 'rabbits' *[Navy slang for things taken ashore improperly]*.

We then set sail for the Phillipines as a flotilla. We arrived at Subic Bay on 2 April 1946 and I returned the ship to the Americans on 14 April. I returned to the UK on 16 April aboard *HMS Rocksand [an infantry landing ship on lease-lend from the United States. She, too, was returned to the US Navy, later in 1946]*.

One thing I will never forget is that on the day of the handover to the Yanks I cleared the Lower Deck and gave a talk to the ship's company. In return I received three cheers – a most unexpected response (and one gladly accepted).

Crew of HMLST 413

On return to the UK I found that my wife had arranged for us to go to Jersey with all the rest of the extended family. I had arrived with only two days to spare before we left for the holiday. I was eventually demobilised at Wembley in August 1946 – the end of my big adventure and world travels and marking a return to the normality of civilian life.

[In fact, by his own admission, Dad would never comfortably settle back into civilian life. In later years he was to admit to a consuming love for the sea. He became an active member of the Royal Naval Association in retirement at Bexhill, where he was made Honorary Life President.]

28 Korean war

- and recall into the Royal Navy

When the Korean War (1950 - 1953) began I was approached by Commander W Crocker of the London Flotilla RNVSR, telling me that the Admiralty wished to recall me for the emergency. However, as there were surplus numbers of Lieutenant Commanders they would like to recall me as a Senior Lieutenant, providing that I agreed and that I would be re-instated as Lieutenant Commander on cessation of my recall.

I agreed to this and received my recall papers telling me to report to *HMS Pembroke [The Royal Navy barracks at Chatham dockyard. HMS Pembroke closed in 1961]* for a medical on 17 May 1951. Provided my medical was satisfactory I would be sent to *RMAS Minerva,* with the Reserve Fleet at Sheerness as Boats Officer. *[RMAS stands for Royal Maritime Auxiliary Service. The vessel was a former World War 1 monitor, later coastal minesweeper and then, basically, a floating workshop and office. She was eventually sold by the Government in the 1980's to Hampshire County Council, having been kept in good condition throughout. She was handed over to the National Museum of the Royal Navy in 2014. Now restored and renamed as HMS M33, she is located at Portsmouth Historic Dockyard. She is one of only three ships surviving from World War I and the only surviving ship from the Gallipoli campaign of 1915.]*

RMAS Minerva - now restored and at Portsmouth

My medical proving satisfactory, I then caught the picket boat and reported on board *HMS Duncansby Head [a repair workshop ship]* to the First Lieutenant, Lt Cdr Len S Brady, RN, and commenced my time aboard doing Watchkeeping duties. This was quite a boring time as there was very little happening. After some time I relieved Lt Robertson, RN, as Captain's Secretary, which proved more of an interesting occupation.

The First Lieutenant found out that I was growing mushrooms indoors at home and asked me if it would be possible to grow them on board. I assured him that it was. He said we could use the workshops, as they were not in use at the time.

We obtained some long ammunition boxes and asked the Dockyard Transport Department if we could have some horse manure. The controller said that until then he always had trouble trying to get rid of it – and here we were asking to have some delivered!

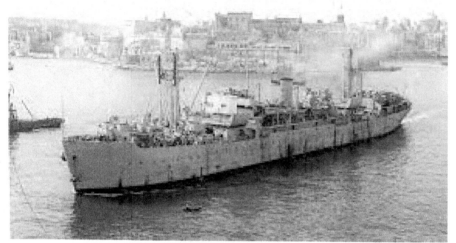

HMS Duncansby Head

This proved to be quite a successful venture and as we were now having fresh mushrooms with our breakfast, the First Lieutenant suggested that we try and keep chickens.

Again, we went to the Dockyard and managed to get hold of an old meat screen. As it was completely open, with a mesh top and sides, it was ideal. So now we had fresh eggs as well!

About the time that we were up and running and had all this going at full pelt, the Senior Officer Reserve Fleet decided to have an inspection. So Len Brady, the First Lieutenant, got hold of a large tarpaulin. When we covered over the chickens they thought it was night and all went to roost, so we locked up the workshop.

When the inspection was over, we were all having a drink in the Wardroom, when the Senior Officer Reserve Fleet, Captain Leonard Sinker, RN, said, "Well, I have been all over the ship and I know that you have chickens and mushrooms on board – but I can't find them. Where are they?" We had no option but to show them to him. We expected to get a 'blast'. Instead, he congratulated us on our initiative.

29 Court martial

The captain of *HMS Duncansby Head* was Lt Cdr Alistair Mars, RN, a former submarine ace who was due to be relieved and who kept getting offered appointments to different posts, all of which he refused. Eventually he was relieved of his duties and sent to Haslar, the Royal Navy hospital at Portsmouth, as a psychiatric case. In time he was summoned to appear before a Court Martial at Portsmouth.

As Captain's Secretary I was ordered to attend the court to verify the handwriting on several letters that Lt Cdr Mars had written. When the court was due to convene I was on pre-planned leave with the family at Pevensey Bay, in East Sussex. To be fully prepared I had taken my full uniform plus a borrowed dress sword with me when we went on holiday.

On the day of the Court Martial I tried to obtain a taxi to take me to Eastbourne Station but nothing was available. As it was imperative that I caught the train my brother-in-law, Cyril, said that he would run me into Eastbourne on the back of his tandem. So there I was in full Royal Navy officer's uniform, complete with sword, pedalling off along the coast to Eastbourne on the back of a bicycle-made-for-two.

The Court Martial was held in the Great Cabin of *HMS Victory*, probably the most impressive naval setting imaginable – where once Nelson had paced the deck.

I was called to give my evidence. The outcome was that Lt Cdr Mars was found guilty and dismissed the Service.

Lt Cdr Alistair Mars, DSO DSC and Bar - war hero

[As an aside, I have to say that Dad was a little economical with the information regarding this Court Martial and the part it played in Royal Navy history. It was probably the most notorious Court Martial of the 20th Century, mostly for the fact that it illustrated the horrifyingly shabby treatment the Admiralty can hand out to its war heroes if their faces do not fit.

As with all other branches of civil and public service, it was always known and understood that to achieve advancement up through the ranks, you had to be well-in with those at the top, in this case Their Lordships of the Admiralty. It was a prime example of the Old Boys network. If you were the product of the Public School system, particularly if you had friends or relatives already in high places, you were half way there.

Unfortunately for Lt Cdr Alastair Campbell Gillespie Mars, DSO, DSC and Bar, he was neither Public School by background, nor was he even British.

He was born in St John's, Newfoundland, in 1915 and joined the Royal Navy in 1932 as a cadet. He was a career sailor, and rose through the ranks by dint of his own hard work and competence, to become one of Britain's most decorated submarine commanders and war heroes. He achieved prominence as the Commander of the submarine HMS Unbroken *during a distinguished and heroic campaign around the Mediterranean during World War II. It is worth remembering that his principal awards for gallantry, the Distinguished Service Order and the Distinguished Service Cross, rate not far behind the Victoria Cross. The DSO is awarded for "Distinguished services during active operations against the enemy." It is rated at one below the Victoria Cross. The DSC is awarded "in recognition of an act or acts of exemplary gallantry during active operations against the enemy at sea." In military terms, it is rated as just behind the DSO and just above the Military Cross. In other words, Lt Cdr Mars was a very brave man indeed. An exemplary naval officer.*

These days we might take a more considered view and recognise that Lt Cdr Mars's war service may have led to Post Traumatic Stress Disorder or some similar condition. In those days mental ill health was not so widely recognised or understood. What we do know is that after completing his war service Lt Cdr Mars spent some time as a psychiatric patient at Haslar, the Royal Navy hospital at Gosport.

His court martial, which took place on 24 June 1952, was the culmination of several years of disputes with the Admiralty in the post war years. You can only conclude that Their Lordships of the Admiralty became thoroughly disenchanted with the war hero, leading to charges that he was insubordinate and had been absent without leave.

He wrote about the case in what was a best-seller of the 1950's, an autobiographical account entitled 'Court Martial'. What happened was that after the war he was appointed to a navy post in New Zealand, where he found his weekly pay of $39 was totally inadequate to support him, his wife and two children. He argued the case with the Admiralty for four years before they finally paid him an extra living allowance.

He was then assigned to a post in Hong Kong where, with a sick wife, he found he was unable to afford even the single hotel room assigned to them. He returned to the UK, sick himself and heavily in debt, which is when he was admitted to hospital. Upon his discharge he asked the Admiralty for a period of leave to put his affairs in order but this was refused. He, in turn, refused to accept subsequent naval postings and instead requested that he could take retirement. Instead, he was court martialed for insubordination and for taking absence without leave. He was dismissed from the Navy.

At the time the case caused a great deal of controversy, that a war hero could be treated in such a shabby way, and even led to questions being raised in the House of Commons.

Part of Lt Cdr Mars's defence was that he was accused of insubordination for failing to take up an appointment. He maintained that insubordination could only be claimed if the appointment had been made by a senior officer. Instead, his appointment seems to have been in the form of a note written by a secretary at The Admiralty. As such, in his view, it did not constitute a valid order or instruction.

Subsequently Lt Cdr Mars became a successful author of around a dozen novels and factual books about the navy. He died at Ipswich, Suffolk, in 1985.

I don't recall my father passing any sort of moral judgement on his former captain but the general tone of the time would have been very unsympathetic towards anyone with a psychiatric illness, hero or not.]

Dad continues the story:

30 Whisky galore!

The *Duncansby Head* had to go to Chatham for a refit. Whilst there she went into Dry Dock, where 140 tons of mussels were scraped off her bottom. Before we went into Chatham we were advised that the Chief Customs Officer would come on board when we arrived and that it was advisable to offer him a whisky. This we did and we were granted the privilege of keeping our Duty Free open.

Shortly after we arrived, HMS Glasgow *[a light cruiser of 9,100 tons with armament of 12 six-inch guns]* followed on. Unfortunately for them, they had not been primed about the whisky 'tradition' and, as a result, they lost their Duty Free privilege. *[HMS Glasgow had a noteworthy war record, of sorts. She took part in the famous 1940 raid on Taranto, in southern Italy, when the Fleet Air Arm, flying 'Swordfish' bi-planes armed with torpedoes crippled the Italian fleet in harbour. However, the* Glasgow *ended-up being better known for her 'unfortunate experience' of having sunk two allied ships during the war – one through accidental collision – coincidentally just off the coast of Duncansby Head, in thick fog - the other an Indian Navy patrol vessel by gunfire as a result of mistaken identity. They thought the Indian ship was a Japanese submarine! After the Chatham refit* HMS Glasgow *became the flagship of the Mediterranean Fleet, based at Malta under Admiral the Earl Mountbatten of Burma.]*

HMS Glasgow

When the refit was completed the *Duncansby Head* was then towed to Plymouth and I was returned to Sheerness, where I was transferred to *HMS Berry Head* and where I was put in charge of all the boats.

31 The cold war

My next move was an appointment as First Lieutenant of *HMS Tiree*, Pennant Number P41, as from 18 July 1953 and I reported on board at Portland, Dorset.

The Commanding Officer was Lt Cdr Timothy J C Williams, who was relieved by Lt Cdr F L Stickland on 16 September 1953. The other officer on board was Warrant Officer Harry Porter, who was subsequently succeeded by Warrant Officer John Kennedy – and what a character he turned out to be!

Without his glasses, John was virtually blind. When we had to have our annual medical he always got me to go first. When I came out he would ask me what the first letter on the Ophthalmic board was, as he knew all the boards off by heart. He could not even see the first letter on the board!

When I received the appointment I enquired what type of ship *HMS Tiree* was – and I was told that she was an Isles Class Trawler. Not only that, she was a coal-burner. I thought they had gone out with The Ark. But apart from the period when we were coaling, when coal dust got everywhere, life was not at all bad.

HMS Tiree

One amusing incident that I had whilst stationed at Portland was that I became friendly with the Commanding Officer of the fast patrol boat, *HMS Gay Crusader*. Whilst having a drink on board his boat on one occasion he asked me if I was going on weekend leave the following weekend. I said I was and he invited me to go with him to Portsmouth instead of going by train from Weymouth. I asked him if it would be quicker and he said 'why not try it?' – so I did.

I reported on board and after having a drink in the Wardroom, went up on the Bridge for the trip. Imagine my surprise (to say the least) when we accelerated up to a speed of 62 knots! This was the first time that I had done anything like this sort of speed at sea. Apart from the bumping and crashing as we hit the waves and the very bumpy journey, it was one of my greatest experiences.

HMS Gay Archer, sister ship to Gay Crusader

[The 'Gay' class of fast patrol boat were the last petrol-fuelled ships ordered by the Royal Navy and were used to patrol UK coastal waters during the 1950's. There were around 14 boats in the Class, all named 'Gay' and then some military-type suffix, such as 'Archer', 'Bombardier' and so on. As befits such a swashbuckling craft, many of them had interesting careers. One appeared in the film 'The Ship that Died of Shame' *[a 1955 Ealing Studios black and white film starring Richard Attenborough], another blew up – volatile petrol fumes below decks were always a problem – and another, once its Navy days had come to an end, was impounded by Spanish authorities, suspected of being involved in smuggling. It later saw service with the Spanish navy. There is a semi-official list of 'Gay' class boats, which amounts to 12 in number. I could not find Gay Crusader named on the list, although there are references to it, plus another 'Gay' fast patrol boat, elsewhere in other naval records. Dad had an excellent memory for everything naval, so he must have the correct name for the vessel, bearing in mind that he knew its*

'skipper' well.]

32 Shh! Top Secret

We were working for the Admiralty Scientific and Research Establishment on Top Secret work. As this was a new project we had a big meeting with all the Boffins at Portland. This work related to detection of submarines under water and with the equipment used they could detect a submarine up to 1000 miles from the British Isles.

In fact later in the programme we went to one of their shore stations at Perranporth in Cornwall, where one of their projects was picking up a single wave off the coast of Brazil and tracking it day and night, giving its course, height and speed continuously, until it broke eventually on the Portuguese coast.

I don't think it wise to dwell on the exact details of the operation, as the Russians were trying to establish what we were up to – and I am sure they would still like to know.

However, at the meeting with the Boffins one thing they impressed on us was that they wanted precise navigation. As it had been established that I would be doing the navigating while on operations I enquired exactly what they meant by "precise navigation"? I was told that it had to be between Plus and Minus 50 yards. This, of course, was in the days before satellite navigation. I asked them how far out from land this would be and they replied "up to 300 miles". I told them that this sort of accuracy was impossible at those distances and they replied that it was possible... and that we were going to achieve it. Thankfully, we did eventually achieve this level of accuracy, with the assistance of Two Way Decca, the system used by the Survey Ships and Loran [short for Long Range Navigation – a system developed in the United States during World War II].

To show the accuracy of their system, on one of the later exercises where we were working 250 miles north of The Shetlands, we had been steaming out from Muckle Flugga, the northernmost point of The Shetlands, for some time.

The bleak landscape of Skaw, near Muckle Flugga

It was always our method of working that on reaching ten miles from our designated position we always closed up to 'Action Stations'. On this occasion, with me on the Chartdesk, the captain said "How far have we got to go, Number One?" to which I replied "A quarter of a mile, sir." The captain replied "I am telling them that we are in position", to which the reply came back "You have a quarter of a mile to go yet."

On another occasion, again whilst working north of the Shetlands, we received a message from the Boffins that we had an intruder in our area.

We immediately went out onto the open bridge and

on sweeping round found nothing in sight anywhere. We therefore informed the Boffins that they must be mistaken. They then sent back details of the bearing, distance, speed, course and depth of the intruder, which was obviously a submarine. The ASDIC set was activated and picked up the intruder, so we sent a message to the Admiralty requesting details of all NATO submarines in the area. The answer came back "None". This meant it must be a Russian submarine, so we immediately packed up and returned to base.

We had an immense amount of trouble with the so-called Russian 'fishing fleet', which operated with a mother ship and around a dozen trawlers – all bristling with radio aerials. They would assemble on the western side of the Shetlands whilst we were in Lerwick.

As soon as we sailed they also sailed and would try to follow us in an attempt to glean details of the work we were carrying out. This resulted in a cat-and-mouse operation, trying to shake them off. If we could not succeed we always returned to Muckle Flugga until they disappeared.

On one occasion whilst this was going on we had a Force 12 gale and for two or three days all we could do was to steam slow ahead, directly into it. This was quite uncomfortable as some of the waves were around 90 feet high!

When it was all over we assessed our damage. We had the mainmast sheared off at deck level; the seaboats were smashed to smithereens and the steel bulkhead on the fore side of the Bridge was concertina-ed inwards. We heard later that the Russians had lost two of their trawlers without trace. It was quite an experience all-round.

While we were operating off the Shetland Isles, from our base in Plymouth, our method of operating was to go up there 'east about' and return 'west about', thereby circumnavigating the British Isles. One thing the Boffins had always impressed on us was that we were never to appear in pristine Naval condition but were to appear as scruffy as possible, so that we did not attract attention but looked like any other trawler, complete with rust streaks down the sides. As far as I was concerned this did wonders for my paint allowance. Of course, the C-in-C Plymouth was privy to what we had to achieve.

On one occasion, when we were going 'east about', along the English Channel, what should we encounter but the Royal Yacht. Of course, we 'piped the side' *[a naval salute of respect, involving mustering a 'side party' to greet a senior officer or dignitary with a particular piping 'call' made on Bo'sun's Calls, the naval pipe used to communicate signals at sea]* as she went past and we received a signal from her, requesting the name and rank of our Commanding Officer. On return to Plymouth we heard that the Royal Yacht had complained about the disgraceful condition of our ship. By all accounts the C-in-C Plymouth told them in no uncertain terms to mind their own business.

Since we were operating as an independent command, when we had time to spare we would obtain permission to visit various ports on our return trips. By this means we visited Stornaway and Londonderry, where we had been based for a while.

33 Collision course!

It was while we were based at Londonderry that we had a particularly bizarre incident. While at sea on one occasion we met with one of the Mac Brayn line ships heading straight towards us. Following the 'rules of the road' at sea, we kept to the starboard side of the channel, as close as possible to the buoys marking the shallows on that side of the River Foyle. However, the Mac Brayn ship carried on towards us on our side of the river, making a head-on collision almost inevitable.

To avoid the collision we went just inside the line of the buoys, giving sound signals, but still she headed straight for us – and eventually hit us.

At the subsequent inquiry the Captain of the Mac Brayn ship said that they took the action they did because their ship always came into port in that manner! Needless to say, we were completely vindicated.

Perhaps the most memorable event while at Londonderry occurred one Christmas. It was the custom for the choirs of all the denominational churches to get together during the Festive Season to present Handel's 'Messiah' at The Guildhall.

On this particular occasion I was invited to one of their rehearsals, which took place in a church hall. Suddenly, all the lights went out. A main fuse had blown. We were left in complete darkness when somebody started singing the 23rd Psalm. Everyone joined in, all singing their different parts and all taking place in complete darkness. It was one of the most moving things that I had ever experienced.

Another time we were operating off the north coast of Cornwall and had gone into St Ives Bay to anchor for the night. We were in the Wardroom when the Quartermaster came down and told us that there was a fishing boat coming into the bay. Thinking that we could get come fish to supplement our diet, we went up on deck and called the fishing boat alongside. She turned out to be a French crabber – and the crew agreed to let us have some crabs.

Accordingly they gave us two big sacks of crabs in exchange for some corned beef. Taking the sacks into the galley, we soon had crabs running all over the deck, with the cook chasing them to put them in the pot. I must say, however, that they were absolutely delicious.

Still on the food theme: when we were anchored in Muckle Flugga fjord on another occasion we had a radio message from the Boffins ashore in their portacabin, asking if we liked mushrooms. When we replied that we would, indeed, like some, they told us that there were plenty in the field they were in and that they would send down transport to pick us up.

We armed ourselves with a bucket, caught the Land Rover and went up to the Boffins, only to find that their field was absolutely white with mushrooms. We had to send back to the ship for some sacks and spent several hours picking mushrooms, which were very much appreciated on board!

Whilst ashore we met some of the locals and during the course of our conversation we asked them what they did with themselves in winter. They replied that their main occupations were farming, fishing and fornicating – but in the winter the land was too wet and cold for farming, the seas too rough for fishing, so there was only one thing left for them to do!

On one trip up to the Shetlands we received a message from The Admiralty that we were to call-in to Newcastle-upon-Tyne and escort an RNR training ship up the coast to Dundee.

Although this was a most welcome break, along with a visit to two new ports, we never did find out why we had to escort her. I shouldn't think that she would have lost her way just going up the coast. Just one more example of the mystery and intrigue of the time!

34 Ghost ship?

Another occasion saw us coming down the Irish Sea. We were just around the same latitude as Liverpool when we saw a ship coming across our bows from the Port side.

The Rule of the Road at sea states that a ship having the Port light of a ship on her starboard side has to give way to the other ship. This one did not give way to us, so we altered course to go around her stern, at the same time hailing her by way of the Aldis Lamp. She did not respond to our signal lamp.

We called her up with the 10" SP. Again, she did not respond, so we altered course parallel to hers and used the Loud Hailer. This still had no effect, so we went alongside and boarded her.

Eerily, there was no one on watch. We investigated and discovered that all the crew had turned-in for the night and were fast asleep. It appears that this was their usual practice. She regularly sailed the route between Liverpool and Dublin. On leaving Liverpool they would set their course for Dublin, lash the wheel in position, then make for their bunks and a good night's sleep. When they awoke in the morning they would very conveniently find themselves off the coast of Ireland, approaching Dublin. Who would have believed it? Sometimes the truth is far stranger than fiction.

Still in the Irish Sea but on another voyage, we were proceeding northbound for Londonderry. Our Steward, Jimmy Green, had just made some 'Kye' [Naval slang for cocoa], when he slipped while coming down the Wardroom ladder, upsetting the Kye all over his legs and scalding them severely.

We had to administer First Aid and quickly got him ashore and off to hospital in Londonderry for treatment. Poor Jimmy apparently carried the scars on his legs for ever more.

As I have mentioned previously, we were a coal-powered ship. When we requested coal while at Lerwick in the Shetlands, imagine our surprise to find it arrive alongside in baskets on a horse-drawn cart – surely one of the more unusual methods of coaling that we ever experienced!

After a while the Boffins decided that we should have underwater television fitted to our ship, so we had a hut constructed on the upper deck, just abaft the funnel, to house all the equipment, with a generator being sited on the Fore Well deck. We also carried one of the Boffins as a supernumerary. He was John McCloy, a most pleasant Ulsterman who sadly came to an untimely end after I had left the ship, when he was electrocuted and lost his life.

On one of our trips we had to call at the port of Leith in the Firth of Forth. When we left we ran smack into a gale howling up the Forth. After a while, with the ship pitching violently, the generator on the Fore Well Deck started to come adrift.

I called out the Duty Watch and went down with them to secure the generator. When we had finished I returned to the Bridge to find our Boffin up there. He told me it was the first time that he had actually seen people working under water!

35 Land's End ahoy!

Returning home on one trip, down the western side of the British Isles, I had gone up to take over the forenoon watch on the Bridge. At the time we were in St George's Channel, just north of Land's End. The normal route to take was round the Longships Lighthouse, which marked the western end of the rocks that jutted out from Land's End, and then proceed up the channel.

I had heard from one of the previous officers on board that there was a channel through the rocks under Land's End and that on one occasion he had taken the ship through there by following a fishing boat.

As this route would save us a great deal of time and distance I sent for the large-scale chart of the area. Sure enough, there was quite a large channel straight through the rocks, with a huge rock at the southern end called the Black Knight. Showing this to the Coxswain I told him that I was going through the channel and asked him to take the wheel.

It was when we were part-way through that the Captain came tearing up onto the Bridge. He gasped that he had been looking out of the scuttle [porthole] in his cabin when he saw rocks sliding past the ship's side. To say that this alarmed him was an understatement.

I told him what I was doing and to his credit he had enough faith in me to be able to tell me to carry on and get the ship through. In the event it was a worthwhile experience, with Lands End looming right up above us. It shaved about 18 miles off our journey.

That was not the only close shave we had with a rocky coastline.

36 Mind that island!

Once, when going south through The Minches – the strait in north west Scotland separating the Inner Hebrides from Lewis and Harris in the Outer Hebrides – I went up on the Bridge to relieve the captain and take over the forenoon watch.

I discovered that our radar had broken down at about 2300 the previous night. Unfortunately we were in a pea-souper fog throughout the night, so no fixes had been obtained to establish our exact position. We had been proceeding on 'dead reckoning' and our exact position was uncertain. As luck would have it (or otherwise), the island of Tiree, after which our ship had been named, lay right across the channel somewhere ahead of us. To avoid it, our course should have taken us around its westernmost point. Naturally I was a little uncertain about our future.

I told the lookout I was going into the Asdic hut, to try and work out our exact position. I told him to keep his eyes peeled and to report anything unusual to me immediately. I went back to our last confirmed fix and plotted-in tidal streams and wind speed to give me an estimated position. The calculation gave our position as being right on top of the centre of the island of Tiree.

I rushed out onto the Bridge to see rocks about a cable ahead of us [approximately 600 feet]. I immediately gave the order "Hard a-starboard; full ahead" to the Quartermaster and said to the lookout "Didn't you see those rocks?" He replied "I wasn't looking."

This, I think, was probably the closest that an Isles Class Trawler came to being wrecked on her namesake island!

HMS Warrior, now fully restored and at Portsmouth

But it wasn't all work and no play. On one of our exercises we had to call in to Milford Haven in south-west Wales. We were ordered to secure our ship at the end of one of the jetties. When we arrived we found that the hulk we were expected to secure-to was the famous old Victorian battleship *HMS Warrior* – at that stage abandoned and neglected, despite its importance in Royal Navy history.

To get ashore we had to pass through the old ships 'Tween Decks', which were extremely low and gave us a good indication of some of the hardships that those Victorian seamen had to endure. Since those days, fortunately, *HMS Warrior* has been rescued and restored to its original glory and now lies at Portsmouth, where it is open to the public.

37 Goodbye to all that

My time on *HMS Tiree* came to an end in November 1955. I was very sorry to leave her, as she had been a very happy ship. I had spent some of the best times of my Naval career while on board. But that was not entirely the end of my connection with that happy ship.

One rather remarkable coincidence came many years later. For some 28 years I was a school governor at Norbury Manor schools in Croydon. On one occasion I went into the Headmaster's study and on the wall behind his desk I spotted a photograph of an Isles Class Trawler. As I could not get close to it, I asked the Headmaster the name of the ship. He replied that it was *HMS Tiree.* It turned out that he had been in command of her during the war, when they used to ply between Scotland and Iceland. He was Lt Cdr Frederick Hayes, RNVR, who commanded the ship from October 1942 until July 1943.

After that we had many naval occasions, when he used to accompany me to meetings of the Croydon Flotilla, RNVSR.

Yet another incident occurred about six months after I had left the *Tiree*. I was sitting in my car at the traffic lights at Streatham Station in south London, when a motorbike drew up alongside me. The pillion passenger said "Good morning, sir!" It was one of our National Service seamen.

A few months later, while walking down the slip road from London Bridge to Upper Thames Street in The City, a Whitbread brewery lorry stopped alongside me and the driver said "I thought it was you!" – another of our National

Service seamen. Quite a coincidence.

The Royal Navy had not quite finished with me. When the Suez crisis began in October 1956 I received a letter from The Admiralty enclosing my recall orders and a travel warrant, with details of my next appointment. I was told that on receipt of a coded signal by telegram I was to catch the next train and make my way to Londonderry in Northern Ireland, to join my ship as First Lieutenant.

Fortunately the crisis fizzled out before I was needed. I received a letter stating that I was to return all my papers to Their Lordships at The Admiralty.

Footnote: *Dad remained constantly on-call and available for the remainder of his life, in the event that the Admiralty might require his services once more. He confessed on more than one occasion that he had had a lifelong love of the sea.*

After leaving the Navy he worked in a variety of jobs, in sales and marketing. He worked for the South London Brewery at Waterloo (where one of his work colleagues was the father of the actress Joanna Lumley); he worked for a wine merchant in Westminster Bridge Road; he worked for a family friend in the mosaic and terrazzo trade; he worked for another family friend at a wholesale butchers in Smithfield.

In retirement Mum and Dad moved to Bexhill, on the Sussex coast, where they were within constant range of the sea air and never more than a few minutes walk from the beach.

My father was an active member (later President) of the local branch of the Royal Naval Association and he was a member of the Landing Craft Association. He remained in contact with his old scout group, returning to Acton in West London every Remembrance Sunday for the church service and parade, for as long as he could manage it and until he realised that all his old chums had faded away. One of his Scout group contemporaries, Len Probert, had been my metalwork master at Grammar School in the early 1960's.

Mum died of cancer in October 2008. Dad followed her the

following August after falling victim to cancer of the bowel and liver. He spent his final few days at St Michael's Hospice in St Leonard's, in a room with a view of the sea.

On his last morning I received a call from the hospice that he was fading fast. Sadly he faded a little too fast. I arrived there mid-morning just a few minutes after he died. I kissed his forehead and sat with him for half an hour or so, to say my goodbyes.

His bed was next to open French windows, from where a terrace scattered with pink rose petals gave a clear view of the English Channel and the beach. I noticed that, as with all true sailors, his spirit had simply gone out with the tide that morning.

Both Mum and Dad had loved the sea. It seemed fitting, when it came to scattering their ashes some weeks after Dad's funeral, that they should be together. I took both their urns of ashes down onto the beach in Bexhill near to where they had previously lived, at the Cooden end. At low tide late on a warm, sunny afternoon I mingled their ashes and scattered them on the sand, where the ripples of the incoming tide washed them away together. Amongst Dad's ashes I had noticed small traces of green – the copper content of the metal from the golden buttons on the Royal Navy uniform in which he had been cremated. He had Been Prepared for duty right to the very end.

The End

Dad's war medals in order (left to right): The 1939-45 Star; the Atlantic Star (with France and Germany clasp); the Burma Star; the Defence Medal; the War Medal 1939-1945; the Naval General Service Medal (with SE Asia 1945-46 clasp).

Lt Cdr Philip Humphries RNVR (1922-2009)

Photo sources:

Humphries family archive;

Pinkerton's Photo Sourcing;

Archivepix

LT CDR PHILIP HUMPHRIES

Printed in Great Britain
by Amazon

83669508R00098